The Kabbalistic Bible

Deuteronomy

Technology for the Soul™

Edited by
RAV YEHUDA BERG

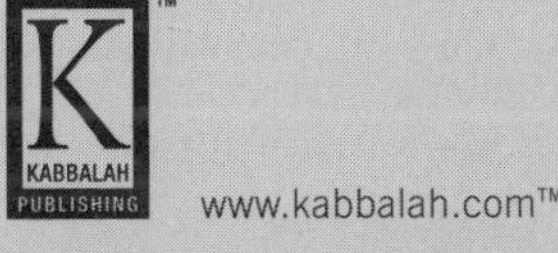

www.kabbalah.com™

Published by
The Kabbalah Centre International Inc.
1.800.KABBALAH www.kabbalah.com

155 E. 48th St., New York, NY 10017
1062 S. Robertson Blvd., Los Angeles, CA 90035

Director Rav Berg

First Printing 2004

ISBN: 1-57189-321-0

Printed in USA

To

Rav and **Karen Berg**

Yehuda, **Michael** and their families

And all the Chevre

May all prayers be answered.

To my children

Bert and **Terry**

My grandchildren

Jessica and **Michael**

May you experience

long and lasting love.

Sharon

Table of Contents

Introduction

We often hear people say, "If only I knew then what I know now!"

In Devarim, the Bible offers us a second chance because everything that came before is presented here again: Devarim repeats the story of the exodus from Egypt, which in essence is the story of our own lives. But Devarim is more than just repletion in a conventional sense. It's a chance for us to relive past events with a new consciousness. How do we do this is by living now differently. If we're honest with ourselves, we know we're making the same mistakes today as we did in the past.

What does Devarim's "second chance" really mean for us? According to Kabbalah, if we don't change our consciousness or the way we view life, then our lives don't change. Devarim gives us the energy to change our experience of life by changing our consciousness. Specifically, we can receive three distinct and seemingly different forms of energy to help us make that very difficult change: the energy to work on ourselves, the energy of excitement, and the energy of perseverance. The purpose and power of Devarim is to infuse our lives with those three wavelengths of the Creator's Light to give us the wisdom and power to change the movie.

Kabbalah teaches that spiritual work is not called work for nothing. It isn't easy, and it isn't meant to be easy. Spiritual work is a process of growth, of getting beyond the boundaries and the comfort zones. It's going against our inborn reactive tendencies and consciously choosing the proactive alternative. It's refusing the temptations of the victim's role and taking full responsibility for what goes on in our lives.

The power of excitement we receive from the Book of Devarim is something different from what we find at the movies or a sports event. This kind of excitement isn't like the light of a flash bulb that illuminates everything for a split second, and then leaves us in darkness all over again. It's not like a TV show whose end brings up that uncomfortable question, "What else is on?" Spiritual excitement is closer to what psychologists call a flow state—an experience in which time seems to speed up, fatigue is not a factor, and the process becomes worthwhile not only because of what it leads to, but for its own sake as well. It's the excitement generated from within, not from without, from a sense of purpose, from seeing a much bigger picture, from taking responsibility for a change and acting on it with excitement, knowing it will bring us to a better place.

In the same way, the energy of perseverance that we gain from Devarim is not like the perseverance required to do a large load of laundry or to change the oil in a car. It's simply a form of energy characterized by its inexhaustible quality—inexhaustible because it powers us toward the Light. If a person living in poverty suddenly got word that a million dollars awaited him in a bank across town, he'd find a way to get there and persevere even if there was an earthquake. A hungry person would persevere to obtain a meal, and if he were hungry enough he might persevere through just about anything. Yet this perseverance is only a tiny fraction of the energy we gain when the goal is connection with the Light. However, as with spiritual work, there's a paradoxical quality to the perseverance we acquire from Devarim. Effort is definitely expended, but it's free of the negative aspects that effort usually entails in the everyday world. Once again, the fact that we gain this power from the Book of Devarim is as much a miracle of Kabbalah as the teachings and events we find in its pages.

Many of the events of Devarim take place in the same desert locations as in previous biblical books, just as many of the events of our lives involve the same actions and responsibilities from one year to the next. But remember: With the new consciousness that Devarim brings us—and with the infusion of Light that accompanies that consciousness—we can change everything. We can revolutionize our lives, not just by changing our jobs, our income, or anything else in the physical realm, but by remaking ourselves at the deepest level of our being. That's what transformation really means—and the power to make it happen awaits you in these pages.

May the Book of Devarim bring you all the Light that is your most authentic desire and your truest destiny.

Lesson of Devarim

Regarding Shabbat Chazon

The portion of Devarim is read every year on the Shabbat before the 9th day of Av. This Shabbat is called *Shabbat Chazon*, "the Shabbat of the Vision," because its haftarah concerns the vision of Isaiah Ben Amotz. In his vision, Isaiah saw the destruction of the Temple on the 9th of Av, which began the worst era in history of mankind. More recently, the 9th of Av was the date that the Nazis began their reign of terror during World War II.

Yet, according to the teachings of the great Kabbalist Rav Isaac Luria, the 9th of Av is also the day on which the Messiah will be born!

So the question for us is this: How can we prevent any more of the pain and suffering that takes place on the 9th of Av while at the same time connecting to the positive energy of that date?

There is a story that reveals the antidote to any chaos or darkness.

Rav Elimelech and Rav Zusha, brothers and great kabbalists, had another brother named Rav Mordechai, whose views were strongly opposed to those of his brothers. He disagreed with them at every turn.

Rav Mordechai became ill. His doctors concluded that he had a very serious, contagious disease. He was told that his days were numbered and that he had to be quarantined.

There was an old man who loved Rav Mordechai and who wanted to be there for him. The old man locked himself in a room with the teacher, with the intention of doing whatever he could to help. But soon it became clear that Rav Mordechai was dying. The old man lit candles, took the teacher off the bed, and gently placed him on the floor.

Then all of a sudden, the old man noticed that a new soul was beating inside Rav Mordechai. With every passing moment, the teacher's face seemed to become more radiant with life, and opening his eyes, he asked for something to eat. By morning, Rav Mordechai was well again.

This was a wondrous thing for the old man to behold, and he asked Rav Mordechai to describe everything the teacher had gone through during his miraculous recovery. Rav Mordechai said the following:

"When my soul left my body, I was brought in front of the court in the Upper World. There I found my brother Rav Elimelech, who asked, 'What are you doing here?' I told him that I had been sentenced to die and that my soul had been taken. My brother became very upset and shouted, 'Is it right to chop down a tree while it is still growing or to kill a young man who has a wife and children?' He ordered the Divine Court to overturn the judgment against me, but to no avail.

"Then my other brother, Rav Zusha, arrived, holding a book under his arm. He took my hand and said, 'Come with me!'

"At this, the judges of the heavenly tribunal were shocked. They demanded, 'Who is this person with such nerve who takes the one who needs to be judged?'

"Rav Zusha identified himself and said that the book under his arm was the *Holy Zohar*, which gave him power over death itself. It was then that my soul came back to me."

As this story shows, nothing can stand against the power of the Zohar, not even the judgments of the Upper World. Even if we don't merit this power, it will come to us if we are truly connected to the Zohar. Through this connection, we can reverse any decree—even a decree of death.

Regarding "These are the things"

In the portion of Devarim, Moses speaks to the people about the errors they've made and about what can be done to correct them. This seems reasonable, but why did Moses wait 40 years to speak about the people's mistakes and shortcomings?

To understand this, we must remember that everything Moses did had a positive intention. Here, Moses' desire to help teaches us a great lesson. When someone does something to upset or hurt us, how do we react? Usually, we want to express our anger to the person who has caused us pain—and we want to do this immediately. We do this not because we are concerned about him or his soul but simply because we felt hurt by him. We just want to "get back at him."

When we are on a spiritual path, however, we must learn to reveal the mistakes of others, not through anger about what has been done to us but through a sincere desire to help them. For this reason, Kabbalah teaches that we should wait three days before we respond to a perceived misdeed. Until then, any reaction would be coming from the Negative Side. Some of our sages assert that we should wait until at least one Shabbat has passed. But no matter how long we wait, the negative energy in our anger and pain may always be present.

This is the lesson of Moses' 40-year delay in speaking to the people about their wrongdoings. The lesson contains an important principle of spiritual work: If an action doesn't help, it hurts.

Consider this story: Once a poor man came to his teacher's house and said that he needed a certain amount of money for his daughter's wedding. He had promised a dowry that he could not provide.

The teacher listened, then turned to one of his students and said, "Let's go see Josef about this." The student was shocked. Josef was a rich miser who never shared his wealth with anyone.

Still, they went to see Josef. The miser was very surprised to see the teacher since he himself never came to the synagogue. He asked if his guests wanted anything to eat or drink, but the teacher declined and just sat there in silence for 20 minutes. Then saying good-bye, he left with his student. The student didn't understand, and of course, Josef didn't understand either.

The next morning, the miser came to the teacher and asked about what had happened. Why did the teacher come to his house and why didn't he say a word? The teacher said nothing, and the next day, Josef came again. This time, the teacher said he would answer under one condition: that the miser agree to do whatever was asked of him. Josef agreed, and the teacher told him about the poor man who needed money for the wedding. Then the teacher asked the miser to give the poor man the whole amount.

Josef protested that he couldn't do so, but the teacher reminded him of his promise, so the miser was forced to agree. But he asked, "Why did you come to my house and remain silent? If you wanted money, you could have just asked." The teacher answered, "I wanted to ask you, but I remembered the teaching that we should not speak to a person who will not listen." This event changed the miser completely, not because of anything the teacher had said but because the teacher knew when to say nothing.

The lesson is very clear. It's important to say things with a positive consciousness. It's also important to say nothing when people are not ready to hear.

Synopsis of Devarim

In English, this book is called Deuteronomy. In Hebrew, its name is *Devarim*, which means "words." Devarim connects us to the world of action and physicality. The idea is that spirituality is not about pondering life, meditating, and isolating oneself on a mountaintop; It is about who we are and how we live our daily lives in the physical world. If we don't share and deal proactively with people, then all we have is knowledge, which is worthless without action. We need to use what we have learned because if we don't, then the wisdom is essentially wasted.

First Reading - Abraham - Chesed

1 אֵלֶּה הַדְּבָרִים אֲשֶׁר דִּבֶּר ראה מֹשֶׁה מהש אֶל־כָּל ילי ־יִשְׂרָאֵל
בְּעֵבֶר הַיַּרְדֵּן בַּמִּדְבָּר בָּעֲרָבָה זרע מוֹל סוּף בֵּין־פָּארָן
וּבֵין־תֹּפֶל וְלָבָן וַחֲצֵרֹת וְדִי זָהָב׃ 2 אַחַד אהבה, דאגה עָשָׂר
יוֹם נגד, מזבח, זן מֵחֹרֵב דֶּרֶךְ הַר־שֵׂעִיר עַד קָדֵשׁ בַּרְנֵעַ׃ 3 וַיְהִי
בְּאַרְבָּעִים שָׁנָה בְּעַשְׁתֵּי־עָשָׂר חֹדֶשׁ י"ב הויות בְּאֶחָד אהבה,
דאגה לַחֹדֶשׁ י"ב הויות דִּבֶּר ראה מֹשֶׁה מהש אֶל־בְּנֵי יִשְׂרָאֵל כְּכֹל ילי
אֲשֶׁר צִוָּה יְהוָֹהאדניאהדונהי אֹתוֹ אֲלֵהֶם׃ 4 אַחֲרֵי הַכֹּתוֹ אֵת
סִיחֹן מֶלֶךְ הָאֱמֹרִי אֲשֶׁר יוֹשֵׁב בְּחֶשְׁבּוֹן וְאֵת עוֹג מֶלֶךְ
הַבָּשָׁן אֲשֶׁר־יוֹשֵׁב בְּעַשְׁתָּרֹת בְּאֶדְרֶעִי׃ 5 בְּעֵבֶר הַיַּרְדֵּן
בְּאֶרֶץ מוֹאָב הוֹאִיל מֹשֶׁה מהש בֵּאֵר קנ"א-ב"ן אֶת־הַתּוֹרָה
הַזֹּאת לֵאמֹר׃ 6 יְהוָֹהאדניאהדונהי אֱלֹהֵינוּ ילה דִּבֶּר ראה אֵלֵינוּ
בְּחֹרֵב לֵאמֹר רַב־לָכֶם שֶׁבֶת בָּהָר הַזֶּה והו׃ 7 פְּנוּ | וּסְעוּ
לָכֶם וּבֹאוּ הַר הָאֱמֹרִי וְאֶל־כָּל ילי ־שְׁכֵנָיו בָּעֲרָבָה זרע
בָּהָר וּבַשְּׁפֵלָה וּבַנֶּגֶב וּבְחוֹף הַיָּם ילי אֶרֶץ הַכְּנַעֲנִי וְהַלְּבָנוֹן

בְּאַרְבָּעִים - At this point in the Torah, Moses, after 40 years of leading the Israelites, finally speaks about his feelings. He tells the people about all the mistakes they've made since the beginning of time. Moses was always the protector, but only now is he letting go and speaking his mind. If we wait a while before telling people things, we can avoid reactive emotions. So if someone hurts us or if something goes wrong, we should wait until we can speak about the incident objectively, not emotionally.

עַד־הַנָּהָר הַגָּדֹל להוו נְהַר־פְּרָת׃ 8 רְאֵה ראה נָתַתִּי לִפְנֵיכֶם
אֶת־הָאָרֶץ אלף למד הה יוד מם בֹּאוּ וּרְשׁוּ אֶת־הָאָרֶץ אלף למד הה יוד
מם אֲשֶׁר נִשְׁבַּע יְהֹוָאדהאהדונהי לַאֲבֹתֵיכֶם לְאַבְרָהָם לְיִצְחָק
וּלְיַעֲקֹב יאהדונהי, אידהנויה לָתֵת לָהֶם וּלְזַרְעָם אַחֲרֵיהֶם׃ 9 וָאֹמַר
אֲלֵכֶם בָּעֵת הַהִוא לֵאמֹר לֹא־אוּכַל לְבַדִּי שְׂאֵת אֶתְכֶם׃
10 יְהֹוָאדהאהדונהי אֱלֹהֵיכֶם ילה הִרְבָּה אֶתְכֶם וְהִנְּכֶם הַיּוֹם נגד,
מזבח, זן כְּכוֹכְבֵי הַשָּׁמַיִם כוזו, י״פ טל לָרֹב׃ 11 יְהֹוָאדהאהדונהי אֱלֹהֵי דמב,
ילה אֲבוֹתֵכֶם יֹסֵף עֲלֵיכֶם כָּכֶם אֶלֶף פְּעָמִים וִיבָרֵךְ אֶתְכֶם
כַּאֲשֶׁר דִּבֶּר ראה לָכֶם׃

Second Reading - Isaac - Gvurah

12 אֵיכָה אֶשָּׂא לְבַדִּי טָרְחֲכֶם וּמַשַּׂאֲכֶם וְרִיבְכֶם׃ 13 הָבוּ
לָכֶם אֲנָשִׁים חֲכָמִים וּנְבֹנִים וִידֻעִים לְשִׁבְטֵיכֶם וַאֲשִׂימֵם
בְּרָאשֵׁיכֶם׃ 14 וַתַּעֲנוּ אֹתִי וַתֹּאמְרוּ טוֹב והו ־הַדָּבָר ראה
אֲשֶׁר־דִּבַּרְתָּ לַעֲשׂוֹת׃ 15 וָאֶקַּח אֶת־רָאשֵׁי שִׁבְטֵיכֶם
אֲנָשִׁים חֲכָמִים וִידֻעִים וָאֶתֵּן אֹתָם רָאשִׁים עֲלֵיכֶם שָׂרֵי
אֲלָפִים וְשָׂרֵי מֵאוֹת וְשָׂרֵי חֲמִשִּׁים וְשָׂרֵי עֲשָׂרֹת וְשֹׁטְרִים

בְּרָאשֵׁיכֶם - Moses appointed as judges people he prepared to lead the nation when he would no longer be there. He taught them to look at problems clearly and without a personal agenda, which always obscures the real situation. This section helps us remove the obstructions that keep us from judging fairly.

לְשִׁבְטֵיכֶם׃ 16 וָאֲצַוֶּה אֶת־שֹׁפְטֵיכֶם בָּעֵת הַהִוא לֵאמֹר
שָׁמֹעַ בֵּין־אֲחֵיכֶם וּשְׁפַטְתֶּם צֶדֶק בֵּין־אִישׁ וּבֵין־אָחִיו וּבֵין
גֵּרוֹ׃ 17 לֹא־תַכִּירוּ פָנִים בַּמִּשְׁפָּט כַּקָּטֹן כַּגָּדֹל תִּשְׁמָעוּן
לֹא תָגוּרוּ מִפְּנֵי חכמה, בינה ־אִישׁ כִּי הַמִּשְׁפָּט לֵאלֹהִים מום, ילה
הוּא וְהַדָּבָר ראה אֲשֶׁר יִקְשֶׁה מִכֶּם תַּקְרִבוּן אֵלַי וּשְׁמַעְתִּיו׃
18 וָאֲצַוֶּה אֶתְכֶם בָּעֵת הַהִוא אֵת כָּל ילי ־הַדְּבָרִים אֲשֶׁר
תַּעֲשׂוּן׃ 19 וַנִּסַּע מֵחֹרֵב וַנֵּלֶךְ אֵת כָּל ילי ־הַמִּדְבָּר הַגָּדוֹל להח,
מבה וְהַנּוֹרָא הַהוּא אֲשֶׁר רְאִיתֶם דֶּרֶךְ הַר הָאֱמֹרִי כַּאֲשֶׁר
צִוָּה יְהֹוָהאדניאהדונהי אֱלֹהֵינוּ ילה אֹתָנוּ וַנָּבֹא עַד קָדֵשׁ בַּרְנֵעַ׃
20 וָאֹמַר אֲלֵכֶם בָּאתֶם עַד־הַר הָאֱמֹרִי אֲשֶׁר־יְהֹוָהאדניאהדונהי
אֱלֹהֵינוּ ילה נֹתֵן ושר, אבג יתץ, אהבת חינם לָנוּ׃ 21 רְאֵה ראה נָתַן ושר, אבג יתץ,
אהבת חינם יְהֹוָהאדניאהדונהי אֱלֹהֶיךָ לְפָנֶיךָ אֶת־הָאָרֶץ אלף למד הה יוד מם
עֲלֵה רֵשׁ כַּאֲשֶׁר דִּבֶּר ראה יְהֹוָהאדניאהדונהי אֱלֹהֵי דמב, ילה אֲבֹתֶיךָ
לָךְ אַל־תִּירָא וְאַל־תֵּחָת׃

Third Reading - Jacob - Tiferet

22 וַתִּקְרְבוּן אֵלַי כֻּלְּכֶם וַתֹּאמְרוּ נִשְׁלְחָה אֲנָשִׁים לְפָנֵינוּ

נִשְׁלְחָה - Moses recounts the story of the spies to show how, in an instant, an agenda can bring about the destruction of even the most elevated of people. The spies who were sent to Israel came back with a report based on a personal agenda, and they were killed. As a result of their selfish thinking, an entire generation had to die before the people were allowed to enter Israel.

וְיַחְפְּרוּ־לָנוּ אֶת־הָאָרֶץ אלף למד הה יוד מם וְיָשִׁבוּ אֹתָנוּ דָּבָר ראה
אֶת־הַדֶּרֶךְ ב״פ יב״ק אֲשֶׁר נַעֲלֶה־בָּהּ וְאֵת הֶעָרִים אֲשֶׁר נָבֹא
אֲלֵיהֶן׃ 23 וַיִּיטַב בְּעֵינַי הַדָּבָר ראה וָאֶקַּח מִכֶּם שְׁנֵים עָשָׂר
אֲנָשִׁים אִישׁ אֶחָד אהבה, דאגה לַשָּׁבֶט׃ 24 וַיִּפְנוּ וַיַּעֲלוּ הָהָרָה
וַיָּבֹאוּ עַד־נַחַל אֶשְׁכֹּל וַיְרַגְּלוּ אֹתָהּ׃ 25 וַיִּקְחוּ בְיָדָם מִפְּרִי
הָאָרֶץ אלף למד הה יוד מם וַיּוֹרִדוּ אֵלֵינוּ וַיָּשִׁבוּ אֹתָנוּ דָבָר ראה
וַיֹּאמְרוּ טוֹבָה אכא הָאָרֶץ אלף למד הה יוד מם אֲשֶׁר־יְהוָהאדני יאהדונהי
אֱלֹהֵינוּ ילה נֹתֵן ושר, אבג יתץ, אהבת חנם לָנוּ׃ 26 וְלֹא אֲבִיתֶם
לַעֲלֹת וַתַּמְרוּ אֶת־פִּי יְהוָהאדני יאהדונהי אֱלֹהֵיכֶם ילה׃ 27 וַתֵּרָגְנוּ
בְאָהֳלֵיכֶם וַתֹּאמְרוּ בְּשִׂנְאַת יְהוָהאדני יאהדונהי אֹתָנוּ הוֹצִיאָנוּ
מֵאֶרֶץ מִצְרָיִם מצר לָתֵת אֹתָנוּ בְּיַד הָאֱמֹרִי לְהַשְׁמִידֵנוּ׃
28 אָנָה ׀ אֲנַחְנוּ עֹלִים אַחֵינוּ הֵמַסּוּ אֶת־לְבָבֵנוּ לֵאמֹר עַם
גָּדוֹל להח, מבה וָרָם מִמֶּנּוּ עָרִים גְּדֹלֹת וּבְצוּרֹת בַּשָּׁמָיִם כוזו, י״פ
טל וְגַם־בְּנֵי עֲנָקִים רָאִינוּ שָׁם׃ 29 וָאֹמַר אֲלֵכֶם לֹא־תַעַרְצוּן
וְלֹא־תִירְאוּן מֵהֶם׃ 30 יְהוָהאדני יאהדונהי אֱלֹהֵיכֶם ילה הַהֹלֵךְ
לִפְנֵיכֶם הוּא יִלָּחֵם לָכֶם כְּכֹל ילי אֲשֶׁר עָשָׂה אִתְּכֶם
בְּמִצְרַיִם מצר לְעֵינֵיכֶם׃ 31 וּבַמִּדְבָּר אֲשֶׁר רָאִיתָ אֲשֶׁר נְשָׂאֲךָ
יְהוָהאדני יאהדונהי אֱלֹהֶיךָ כַּאֲשֶׁר יִשָּׂא־אִישׁ אֶת־בְּנוֹ בְּכָל לכב
־הַדֶּרֶךְ ב״פ יב״ק אֲשֶׁר הֲלַכְתֶּם עַד־בֹּאֲכֶם עַד־הַמָּקוֹם

הַזֶּה (והו): 32 וּבַדָּבָר (ראה) הַזֶּה (והו) אֵינְכֶם מַאֲמִינִם בַּיהֹוָ(אדני)אהדונהי
אֱלֹהֵיכֶם (ילה): 33 הַהֹלֵךְ לִפְנֵיכֶם בַּדֶּרֶךְ לָתוּר לָכֶם מָקוֹם
לַחֲנֹתְכֶם בָּאֵשׁ | לַיְלָה (מלה) לַרְאֹתְכֶם בַּדֶּרֶךְ (ב״פ יב״ק) אֲשֶׁר
תֵּלְכוּ־בָהּ וּבֶעָנָן יוֹמָם: 34 וַיִּשְׁמַע יְהֹוָ(אדני)אהדונהי אֶת־קוֹל
דִּבְרֵיכֶם וַיִּקְצֹף וַיִּשָּׁבַע לֵאמֹר: 35 אִם (יוהך) ־יִרְאֶה (רי״ו, גבורה)
אִישׁ בָּאֲנָשִׁים הָאֵלֶּה הַדּוֹר הָרָע הַזֶּה (והו) אֵת הָאָרֶץ (אלף למד)
הַטּוֹבָה (אכא) אֲשֶׁר נִשְׁבַּעְתִּי לָתֵת לַאֲבֹתֵיכֶם: 36 זוּלָתִי
כָּלֵב בֶּן־יְפֻנֶּה הוּא יִרְאֶנָּה וְלוֹ־אֶתֵּן אֶת־הָאָרֶץ (אלף למד הה יוד מם)
אֲשֶׁר דָּרַךְ־בָּהּ וּלְבָנָיו יַעַן אֲשֶׁר מִלֵּא אַחֲרֵי יְהֹוָ(אדני)אהדונהי:
37 גַּם־בִּי הִתְאַנַּף יְהֹוָ(אדני)אהדונהי בִּגְלַלְכֶם לֵאמֹר גַּם־אַתָּה
לֹא־תָבֹא שָׁם: 38 יְהוֹשֻׁעַ בִּן־נוּן הָעֹמֵד לְפָנֶיךָ הוּא יָבֹא
שָׁמָּה (יוד הא ואו הא) אֹתוֹ חַזֵּק (פהל) כִּי־הוּא יַנְחִלֶנָּה אֶת־יִשְׂרָאֵל:

Fourth Reading - Moses - Netzach

39 **וְטַפְּכֶם** אֲשֶׁר אֲמַרְתֶּם לָבַז יִהְיֶה (ייי) וּבְנֵיכֶם אֲשֶׁר
לֹא־יָדְעוּ הַיּוֹם (נגד, מזבח, זן) טוֹב (והו) וָרָע הֵמָּה (יוד הא ואו הא) יָבֹאוּ
שָׁמָּה (יוד הא ואו הא) וְלָהֶם אֶתְּנֶנָּה וְהֵם יִירָשׁוּהָ: 40 וְאַתֶּם פְּנוּ

וְטַפְּכֶם - The Israelites complained that their children would be destroyed. However, for all of the energy they put into complaining, they did not really care about their children. For a parent, caring means putting the needs of the child ahead of everything else.

לָכֶם וּסְעוּ הַמִּדְבָּרָה דֶּרֶךְ יַם יְלֹי ־סוּף: 41 וַתַּעֲנוּ | וַתֹּאמְרוּ

אֵלַי חָטָאנוּ לַיהֹוָ֨אֲדֹנָי֙יאהדונהי אֲנַחְנוּ נַעֲלֶה וְנִלְחַמְנוּ כְּכֹל יְלֹי

אֲשֶׁר־צִוָּנוּ יְהֹוָ֨אֲדֹנָי֙יאהדונהי אֱלֹהֵינוּ יְלֹה וַתַּחְגְּרוּ אִישׁ אֶת־כְּלֵי

מִלְחַמְתּוֹ וַתָּהִינוּ לַעֲלֹת הָהָרָה: 42 וַיֹּאמֶר יְהֹוָ֨אֲדֹנָי֙יאהדונהי אֵלַי

אֱמֹר לָהֶם לֹא תַעֲלוּ וְלֹא־תִלָּחֲמוּ כִּי אֵינֶנִּי בְּקִרְבְּכֶם

וְלֹא תִּנָּגְפוּ לִפְנֵי חכמה, בינה אֹיְבֵיכֶם: 43 וָאֲדַבֵּר אֲלֵיכֶם וְלֹא

שְׁמַעְתֶּם וַתַּמְרוּ אֶת־פִּי יְהֹוָ֨אֲדֹנָי֙יאהדונהי וַתָּזִדוּ וַתַּעֲלוּ הָהָרָה:

44 וַיֵּצֵא הָאֱמֹרִי הַיֹּשֵׁב בָּהָר הַהוּא לִקְרַאתְכֶם וַיִּרְדְּפוּ

אֶתְכֶם כַּאֲשֶׁר תַּעֲשֶׂינָה הַדְּבֹרִים וַיַּכְּתוּ אֶתְכֶם בְּשֵׂעִיר

עַד־חָרְמָה: 45 וַתָּשֻׁבוּ וַתִּבְכּוּ לִפְנֵי חכמה, בינה יְהֹוָ֨אֲדֹנָי֙יאהדונהי

וְלֹא־שָׁמַע יְהֹוָ֨אֲדֹנָי֙יאהדונהי בְּקֹלְכֶם וְלֹא הֶאֱזִין אֲלֵיכֶם:

46 וַתֵּשְׁבוּ בְקָדֵשׁ יָמִים גלך רַבִּים כַּיָּמִים גלך אֲשֶׁר יְשַׁבְתֶּם:

2 1 וַנֵּפֶן וַנִּסַּע הַמִּדְבָּרָה דֶּרֶךְ יַם יְלֹי ־סוּף כַּאֲשֶׁר דִּבֶּר ראה

יְהֹוָ֨אֲדֹנָי֙יאהדונהי אֵלָי וַנָּסָב אֶת־הַר־שֵׂעִיר יָמִים גלך רַבִּים:

Fifth Reading - Aaron - Hod

2 וַיֹּאמֶר יְהֹוָ֨אֲדֹנָי֙יאהדונהי אֵלַי לֵאמֹר: 3 רַב־לָכֶם סֹב אֶת־

הָהָר הַזֶּה והו פְּנוּ לָכֶם צָפֹנָה: 4 וְאֶת־הָעָם צַו פוי לֵאמֹר אַתֶּם

וַיֹּאמֶר - In one verse of this portion, the time frame jumps ahead 38 years. Time is the process between cause and effect. It can either be long or short, depending on the path one takes. We can look back and ask where ten

עֹבְרִים בִּגְבוּל אֲחֵיכֶם בְּנֵי־עֵשָׂו הַיֹּשְׁבִים בְּשֵׂעִיר וְיִירְאוּ
מִכֶּם וְנִשְׁמַרְתֶּם מְאֹד׃ 5 אַל־תִּתְגָּרוּ בָם מכ כִּי לֹא־אֶתֵּן
לָכֶם מֵאַרְצָם עַד מִדְרַךְ כַּף־רָגֶל כִּי־יְרֻשָּׁה לְעֵשָׂו נָתַתִּי
אֶת־הַר שֵׂעִיר׃ 6 אֹכֶל תִּשְׁבְּרוּ מֵאִתָּם בַּכֶּסֶף וַאֲכַלְתֶּם
וְגַם־מַיִם ילי תִּכְרוּ מֵאִתָּם בַּכֶּסֶף וּשְׁתִיתֶם׃ 7 כִּי יְהוָה אדני יאהדונהי
אֱלֹהֶיךָ בֵּרַכְךָ בְּכֹל לכב מַעֲשֵׂה יָדֶךָ יָדַע לֶכְתְּךָ אֶת־
הַמִּדְבָּר הַגָּדֹל הַזֶּה והו זֶה ׀ אַרְבָּעִים שָׁנָה יְהוָה אדני יאהדונהי
אֱלֹהֶיךָ ילה עִמָּךְ לֹא חָסַרְתָּ דָּבָר ראה׃ 8 וַנַּעֲבֹר מֵאֵת אַחֵינוּ
בְנֵי־עֵשָׂו הַיֹּשְׁבִים בְּשֵׂעִיר מִדֶּרֶךְ ב"פ יב"ק הָעֲרָבָה זרע מֵאֵילַת
וּמֵעֶצְיֹן גָּבֶר ☐ וַנֵּפֶן וַנַּעֲבֹר דֶּרֶךְ מִדְבַּר ראה מוֹאָב׃
9 וַיֹּאמֶר יְהוָה אדני יאהדונהי אֵלַי אַל־תָּצַר אֶת־מוֹאָב וְאַל־תִּתְגָּר
בָּם מכ מִלְחָמָה כִּי לֹא־אֶתֵּן לְךָ מֵאַרְצוֹ יְרֻשָּׁה כִּי לִבְנֵי־
לוֹט נָתַתִּי אֶת־עָר יְרֻשָּׁה׃ 10 הָאֵמִים לְפָנִים יָשְׁבוּ בָהּ עַם
גָּדוֹל להח, מבה וְרַב וָרָם כָּעֲנָקִים׃ 11 רְפָאִים יֵחָשְׁבוּ אַף־הֵם

years of our lives went, or we can live each day fully and with conscious awareness.

☐ - A break in the middle of one of the verses means that we can travel in time: We can go backward to correct things we need to fix or we can leap forward. According to Kabbalah, we are not limited by time or space.

כָּעֲנָקִים וְהַמֹּאָבִים יִקְרְאוּ לָהֶם אֵמִים׃ 12 וּבְשֵׂעִיר יָשְׁבוּ
הַחֹרִים לְפָנִים וּבְנֵי עֵשָׂו יִירָשׁוּם וַיַּשְׁמִידוּם מִפְּנֵיהֶם
וַיֵּשְׁבוּ תַּחְתָּם כַּאֲשֶׁר עָשָׂה יִשְׂרָאֵל לְאֶרֶץ יְרֻשָּׁתוֹ אֲשֶׁר־
נָתַן יְהֹוָהאדנייאהדונהי לָהֶם׃ 13 עַתָּה קֻמוּ וְעִבְרוּ לָכֶם אֶת־נַחַל
זָרֶד וַנַּעֲבֹר אֶת־נַחַל זָרֶד׃ 14 וְהַיָּמִים נלך אֲשֶׁר־הָלַכְנוּ ׀
מִקָּדֵשׁ בַּרְנֵעַ עַד אֲשֶׁר־עָבַרְנוּ אֶת־נַחַל זֶרֶד שְׁלֹשִׁים
וּשְׁמֹנֶה פוי פוי פוי שָׁנָה עַד־תֹּם כָּל ילי ־הַדּוֹר אַנְשֵׁי הַמִּלְחָמָה
מִקֶּרֶב הַמַּחֲנֶה כַּאֲשֶׁר נִשְׁבַּע יְהֹוָהאדנייאהדונהי לָהֶם׃ 15 וְגַם
יַד־יְהֹוָהאדנייאהדונהי הָיְתָה בָּם מב לְהֻמָּם מִקֶּרֶב הַמַּחֲנֶה עַד
תֻּמָּם׃ 16 וַיְהִי כַאֲשֶׁר־תַּמּוּ כָּל ילי ־אַנְשֵׁי הַמִּלְחָמָה לָמוּת
מִקֶּרֶב הָעָם׃ 17 וַיְדַבֵּר יְהֹוָהאדנייאהדונהי אֵלַי לֵאמֹר׃ 18 אַתָּה
עֹבֵר הַיּוֹם נגד, מזבח, זן אֶת־גְּבוּל מוֹאָב אֶת־עָר׃ 19 וְקָרַבְתָּ
מוּל בְּנֵי עַמּוֹן אַל־תְּצֻרֵם וְאַל־תִּתְגָּר בָּם מב כִּי לֹא־אֶתֵּן
מֵאֶרֶץ בְּנֵי־עַמּוֹן לְךָ יְרֻשָּׁה כִּי לִבְנֵי־לוֹט נְתַתִּיהָ יְרֻשָּׁה׃
20 אֶרֶץ־רְפָאִים תֵּחָשֵׁב אַף־הִוא רְפָאִים יָשְׁבוּ־בָהּ לְפָנִים

מוֹאָב - Although Balak, the king of Amon and Moab, was a very wicked man, the Israelites were not supposed to hurt the Moabites because Ruth, the great-grandmother of King David, would come from the nation of Moab. She was so pure that due to her merit, the whole nation was spared. This reveals the power of a single person's positive energy. Even if a whole family is negative, one person can be a beacon of Light to provide protection and energy, just as Ruth was chosen to be the one to save the people of Moab.

וְהָעַמֹּנִים יִקְרְאוּ לָהֶם זַמְזֻמִּים: 21 עַם גָּדוֹל להחו, מבה וְרַב
וָרָם כָּעֲנָקִים וַיַּשְׁמִידֵם יְהֹוָאדנהי אהדונהי מִפְּנֵיהֶם וַיִּירָשֻׁם
וַיֵּשְׁבוּ תַחְתָּם: 22 כַּאֲשֶׁר עָשָׂה לִבְנֵי עֵשָׂו הַיֹּשְׁבִים בְּשֵׂעִיר
אֲשֶׁר הִשְׁמִיד אֶת־הַחֹרִי מִפְּנֵיהֶם וַיִּירָשֻׁם וַיֵּשְׁבוּ תַחְתָּם
עַד הַיּוֹם נגד, מזבח, זן הַזֶּה והו: 23 וְהָעַוִּים הַיֹּשְׁבִים בַּחֲצֵרִים
עַד־עַזָּה כַּפְתֹּרִים הַיֹּצְאִים מִכַּפְתֹּר הִשְׁמִידֻם וַיֵּשְׁבוּ
תַחְתָּם: 24 קוּמוּ סְּעוּ וְעִבְרוּ אֶת־נַחַל אַרְנֹן רְאֵה ראה נָתַתִּי
בְיָדְךָ אֶת־סִיחֹן מֶלֶךְ־חֶשְׁבּוֹן הָאֱמֹרִי וְאֶת־אַרְצוֹ הָחֵל
רָשׁ וְהִתְגָּר בּוֹ מִלְחָמָה: 25 הַיּוֹם נגד, מזבח, זן הַזֶּה והו אָחֵל תֵּת פַּחְדְּךָ
וְיִרְאָתְךָ עַל־פְּנֵי חכמה, בינה הָעַמִּים תַּחַת כָּל ילי ־הַשָּׁמָיִם כוזו,
י״פ טל אֲשֶׁר יִשְׁמְעוּן שִׁמְעֲךָ וְרָגְזוּ וְחָלוּ מִפָּנֶיךָ: 26 וָאֶשְׁלַח
מַלְאָכִים מִמִּדְבַּר קְדֵמוֹת אֶל־סִיחוֹן מֶלֶךְ חֶשְׁבּוֹן דִּבְרֵי
שָׁלוֹם לֵאמֹר: 27 אֶעְבְּרָה בְאַרְצֶךָ בַּדֶּרֶךְ בַּדֶּרֶךְ אֵלֵךְ
לֹא אָסוּר יָמִין וּשְׂמֹאול: 28 אֹכֶל בַּכֶּסֶף תַּשְׁבִּרֵנִי וְאָכַלְתִּי
וּמַיִם ילי בַּכֶּסֶף תִּתֶּן ב״פ כהת ־לִי וְשָׁתִיתִי רַק אֶעְבְּרָה בְרַגְלָי:
29 כַּאֲשֶׁר עָשׂוּ־לִי בְּנֵי עֵשָׂו הַיֹּשְׁבִים בְּשֵׂעִיר וְהַמּוֹאָבִים

פַּחְדְּךָ - In this section, the Israelites are supposed to let go of their fears and begin their march towards Israel. Fear is so powerful that it can prevent us from getting what we deserve in life. If we look back at things we were afraid of, we will realize how baseless our fears were. By hearing this portion, we get assistance to move forward when we are afraid.

הַיֹּשְׁבִים בְּעָר עַד אֲשֶׁר־אֶעֱבֹר אֶת־הַיַּרְדֵּן אֶל־הָאָרֶץ אלף
למד הה יוד מם אֲשֶׁר־יְהֹוָהאדניאהדונהי אֱלֹהֵינוּ ילה נֹתֵן ושר, אבג יתץ, אהבת חנם
לָנוּ׃ 30 וְלֹא אָבָה סִיחֹן מֶלֶךְ חֶשְׁבּוֹן הַעֲבִרֵנוּ בּוֹ כִּי־הִקְשָׁה
יְהֹוָהאדניאהדונהי אֱלֹהֶיךָ אֶת־רוּחוֹ וְאִמֵּץ אֶת־לְבָבוֹ לְמַעַן תִּתּוֹ
בְיָדְךָ כַּיּוֹם נגד, מזבח, זן הַזֶּה והו׃

Sixth Reading - Joseph - Yesod

31 וַיֹּאמֶר יְהֹוָהאדניאהדונהי אֵלַי רְאֵה ראה הַחִלֹּתִי תֵּת לְפָנֶיךָ
אֶת־סִיחֹן וְאֶת־אַרְצוֹ הָחֵל רָשׁ לָרֶשֶׁת אֶת־אַרְצוֹ׃ 32 וַיֵּצֵא
סִיחֹן לִקְרָאתֵנוּ הוּא וְכָל ילי ־עַמּוֹ לַמִּלְחָמָה יָהְצָה׃
33 וַיִּתְּנֵהוּ יְהֹוָהאדניאהדונהי אֱלֹהֵינוּ ילה לְפָנֵינוּ וַנַּךְ אֹתוֹ וְאֶת־
בָּנָיו (כתיב: בנו) וְאֶת־כָּל ילי ־עַמּוֹ׃ 34 וַנִּלְכֹּד אֶת־כָּל ילי ־עָרָיו
בָּעֵת הַהִוא וַנַּחֲרֵם אֶת־כָּל ילי ־עִיר ערי, בוזזוף, סנדלפון מְתִם
וְהַנָּשִׁים וְהַטָּף לֹא הִשְׁאַרְנוּ שָׂרִיד׃ 35 רַק הַבְּהֵמָה לכב
בָּזַזְנוּ לָנוּ וּשְׁלַל הֶעָרִים אֲשֶׁר לָכָדְנוּ׃ 36 מֵעֲרֹעֵר אֲשֶׁר
עַל־שְׂפַת־נַחַל אַרְנֹן וְהָעִיר ערי, בוזזוף, סנדלפון אֲשֶׁר בַּנַּחַל וְעַד־
הַגִּלְעָד לֹא הָיְתָה קִרְיָה אֲשֶׁר שָׂגְבָה מִמֶּנּוּ אֶת־הַכֹּל ילי

הַחִלֹּתִי - On the way toward Israel, Moses and the Israelites defeat two kings. This was the turning point in their consciousness. There had been so much negativity among the Israelites, but now, 40 years after the incident of the Golden Calf, there is salvation. Once we make a decision to have a positive life, real progress becomes possible.

נָתַן יְהֹוָהאדניאהדונהי אֱלֹהֵינוּ ילה לְפָנֵינוּ׃ 37 רַק אֶל־אֶרֶץ בְּנֵי־
עַמּוֹן לֹא קָרָבְתָּ כָּל ילי ־יַד נַחַל יַבֹּק אלהים ‑ יהוה, אהיה ‑ אדני
‑ יהוה וְעָרֵי הָהָר וְכֹל ילי אֲשֶׁר־צִוָּה יְהֹוָהאדניאהדונהי אֱלֹהֵינוּ ילה׃
3 1 וַנֵּפֶן וַנַּעַל דֶּרֶךְ הַבָּשָׁן וַיֵּצֵא עוֹג מֶלֶךְ־הַבָּשָׁן לִקְרָאתֵנוּ
הוּא וְכָל ילי ־עַמּוֹ לַמִּלְחָמָה אֶדְרֶעִי׃ 2 וַיֹּאמֶר יְהֹוָהאדניאהדונהי
אֵלַי אַל־תִּירָא אֹתוֹ כִּי בְיָדְךָ נָתַתִּי אֹתוֹ וְאֶת־כָּל ילי ־עַמּוֹ
וְאֶת־אַרְצוֹ וְעָשִׂיתָ לּוֹ כַּאֲשֶׁר עָשִׂיתָ לְסִיחֹן מֶלֶךְ הָאֱמֹרִי
אֲשֶׁר יוֹשֵׁב בְּחֶשְׁבּוֹן׃ 3 וַיִּתֵּן יְהֹוָהאדניאהדונהי אֱלֹהֵינוּ ילה בְּיָדֵנוּ
גַּם אֶת־עוֹג מֶלֶךְ־הַבָּשָׁן וְאֶת־כָּל ילי ־עַמּוֹ וַנַּכֵּהוּ עַד־בִּלְתִּי
הִשְׁאִיר־לוֹ שָׂרִיד׃ 4 וַנִּלְכֹּד אֶת־כָּל ילי ־עָרָיו בָּעֵת הַהִוא
לֹא הָיְתָה קִרְיָה אֲשֶׁר לֹא־לָקַחְנוּ מֵאִתָּם שִׁשִּׁים עִיר ערי,
םןץףך, סנדלפון כָּל ילי ־חֶבֶל אַרְגֹּב מַמְלֶכֶת עוֹג בַּבָּשָׁן׃ 5 כָּל ילי
־אֵלֶּה עָרִים בְּצֻרֹת חוֹמָה גְבֹהָה דְּלָתַיִם וּבְרִיחַ לְבַד
מֵעָרֵי הַפְּרָזִי הַרְבֵּה מְאֹד׃ 6 וַנַּחֲרֵם אוֹתָם כַּאֲשֶׁר עָשִׂינוּ
לְסִיחֹן מֶלֶךְ חֶשְׁבּוֹן הַחֲרֵם כָּל ילי ־עִיר ערי, םןץףך, סנדלפון מְתִם
הַנָּשִׁים וְהַטָּף׃ 7 וְכָל ילי ־הַבְּהֵמָה לכב וּשְׁלַל הֶעָרִים בַּזּוֹנוּ
לָנוּ׃ 8 וַנִּקַּח בָּעֵת הַהִוא אֶת־הָאָרֶץ אלף למד הה יוד מם מִיַּד שְׁנֵי
מַלְכֵי נלך הָאֱמֹרִי אֲשֶׁר בְּעֵבֶר הַיַּרְדֵּן מִנַּחַל אַרְנֹן עַד־הַר
חֶרְמוֹן׃ 9 צִידֹנִים יִקְרְאוּ לְחֶרְמוֹן שִׂרְיֹן וְהָאֱמֹרִי יִקְרְאוּ־

לוֹ שְׂנִיר׃ 10 כֹּל ילי | עָרֵי הַמִּישֹׁר וְכָל ילי ־הַגִּלְעָד וְכָל ילי
־הַבָּשָׁן עַד־סַלְכָה וְאֶדְרֶעִי עָרֵי מַמְלֶכֶת עוֹג בַּבָּשָׁן׃
11 כִּי רַק־עוֹג מֶלֶךְ הַבָּשָׁן נִשְׁאַר מִיֶּתֶר הָרְפָאִים הִנֵּה
עַרְשׂוֹ עֶרֶשׂ בַּרְזֶל ר״ת - בלהה רחל זילפה לאה הֲלֹה הִוא בְּרַבַּת בְּנֵי
עַמּוֹן תֵּשַׁע אַמּוֹת אָרְכָּהּ וְאַרְבַּע אַמּוֹת רָחְבָּהּ בְּאַמַּת ז״פ ס״ג
־אִישׁ׃ 12 וְאֶת־הָאָרֶץ אלף למד הה יוד מם הַזֹּאת יָרַשְׁנוּ בָּעֵת הַהִוא
מֵעֲרֹעֵר אֲשֶׁר־עַל־נַחַל אַרְנֹן וַחֲצִי הַר־הַגִּלְעָד וְעָרָיו נָתַתִּי
לָראוּבֵנִי וְלַגָּדִי והו׃ 13 וְיֶתֶר הַגִּלְעָד וְכָל ילי ־הַבָּשָׁן מַמְלֶכֶת
עוֹג נָתַתִּי לַחֲצִי שֵׁבֶט הַמְנַשֶּׁה כֹּל ילי חֶבֶל הָאַרְגֹּב לְכָל יה
אדני ילי ־הַבָּשָׁן הַהוּא יִקָּרֵא אֶרֶץ רְפָאִים׃ 14 יָאִיר בֶּן־מְנַשֶּׁה
לָקַח אֶת־כָּל ילי ־חֶבֶל אַרְגֹּב עַד־גְּבוּל הַגְּשׁוּרִי וְהַמַּעֲכָתִי
וַיִּקְרָא אֹתָם עַל־שְׁמוֹ אֶת־הַבָּשָׁן חַוֺּת יָאִיר עַד הַיּוֹם נגד,
מזבח, זן הַזֶּה והו׃

Seventh Reading - David - Malchut

15 וּלְמָכִיר נָתַתִּי אֶת־הַגִּלְעָד׃ 16 וְלָראוּבֵנִי וְלַגָּדִי והו נָתַתִּי
מִן־הַגִּלְעָד וְעַד־נַחַל אַרְנֹן תּוֹךְ הַנַּחַל וּגְבֻל וְעַד יַבֹּק אלהים ־

נָתַתִּי - There is an inheritance given to the tribes of Reuben, Gad, and Menasheh. Despite the fact that they knew that it was coming to them, they did not give up their fight for it. Even when we really want and deserve something, we often give it up as soon as obstacles appear. We must always persevere and move forward.

יהוה, אהיה ‑ אדני ‑ יהוה הַנַּחַל גְּבוּל בְּנֵי עַמּוֹן׃ 17 וְהָעֲרָבָה זרע וְהַיַּרְדֵּן
וּגְבֻל מִכִּנֶּרֶת וְעַד יָם ילי הָעֲרָבָה זרע יָם ילי הַמֶּלַח ג״פ יהו״ה תַּחַת
אַשְׁדֹּת הַפִּסְגָּה מִזְרָחָה׃ 18 וָאֲצַו אֶתְכֶם בָּעֵת הַהִוא לֵאמֹר
יְהֹוָהאדניאהדונהי אֱלֹהֵיכֶם ילה נָתַן לָכֶם אֶת־הָאָרֶץ אלף למד הה יוד מם
הַזֹּאת לְרִשְׁתָּהּ חֲלוּצִים תַּעַבְרוּ לִפְנֵי חכמה, בינה אֲחֵיכֶם בְּנֵי־
יִשְׂרָאֵל כָּל ילי ־בְּנֵי־חָיִל ומב׃ 19 רַק נְשֵׁיכֶם וְטַפְּכֶם וּמִקְנֵכֶם
יָדַעְתִּי כִּי־מִקְנֶה רַב לָכֶם יֵשְׁבוּ בְּעָרֵיכֶם אֲשֶׁר נָתַתִּי
לָכֶם׃

Maftir

20 עַד אֲשֶׁר־יָנִיחַ יְהֹוָהאדניאהדונהי | לַאֲחֵיכֶם כָּכֶם וְיָרְשׁוּ גַם־
הֵם אֶת־הָאָרֶץ אלף למד הה יוד מם אֲשֶׁר יְהֹוָהאדניאהדונהי אֱלֹהֵיכֶם ילה
נֹתֵן ושר, אבג יתץ, אהבת חנם לָהֶם בְּעֵבֶר הַיַּרְדֵּן וְשַׁבְתֶּם אִישׁ
לִירֻשָּׁתוֹ אֲשֶׁר נָתַתִּי לָכֶם׃ 21 וְאֶת־יְהוֹשׁוּעַ צִוֵּיתִי בָּעֵת
הַהִוא לֵאמֹר עֵינֶיךָ הָרֹאֹת אֵת כָּל ילי ־אֲשֶׁר עָשָׂה
יְהֹוָהאדניאהדונהי אֱלֹהֵיכֶם ילה לִשְׁנֵי הַמְּלָכִים הָאֵלֶּה כֵּן־יַעֲשֶׂה
יְהֹוָהאדניאהדונהי לְכָל יה אדני ילי ־הַמַּמְלָכוֹת אֲשֶׁר אַתָּה עֹבֵר
שָׁמָּה יוד הא ואו הא׃ 22 לֹא תִּירָאוּם כִּי יְהֹוָהאדניאהדונהי אֱלֹהֵיכֶם ילה
הוּא הַנִּלְחָם לָכֶם׃

Haftarah of Devarim

This haftarah is always read the week before the 9th of Av. It deals with the destruction of the Temple, which took place because hatred for no reason existed among the people. In each generation that the Temple is not rebuilt, it's as if it is being destroyed all over again. We have to meditate on loving for no reason. If there's anyone we hate, we should send them love to rebuild our personal temple, if not the Temple for the whole world.

Isaiah 1 — ישעיהו פרק 1

1 וַחֲזוֹן יְשַׁעְיָהוּ בֶן־אָמוֹץ אֲשֶׁר חָזָה עַל־יְהוּדָה וִירוּשָׁלָםִ
בִּימֵי עֻזִּיָּהוּ יוֹתָם אָחָז יְחִזְקִיָּהוּ מַלְכֵי נלך יְהוּדָה׃ 2 שִׁמְעוּ
שָׁמַיִם כוזו, י״פ טל וְהַאֲזִינִי אֶרֶץ כִּי יְהֹוָהאדניאהדונהי דִּבֵּר ראה בָּנִים
גִּדַּלְתִּי וְרוֹמַמְתִּי וְהֵם פָּשְׁעוּ בִי׃ 3 יָדַע שׁוֹר ושר, אבג יתץ, אהבת
חנם קֹנֵהוּ וַחֲמוֹר אֵבוּס בְּעָלָיו יִשְׂרָאֵל לֹא יָדַע עַמִּי לֹא
הִתְבּוֹנָן׃ 4 הוֹי | גּוֹי חֹטֵא עַם כֶּבֶד עָוֺן זֶרַע מְרֵעִים בָּנִים
מַשְׁחִיתִים עָזְבוּ אֶת־יְהֹוָהאדניאהדונהי נִאֲצוּ אֶת־קְדוֹשׁ יִשְׂרָאֵל
נָזֹרוּ אָחוֹר׃ 5 עַל מֶה הקס יוד הא ואו הא תֻכּוּ עוֹד תּוֹסִיפוּ סָרָה
כָּל ילי ־רֹאשׁ לָחֳלִי וְכָל ילי ־לֵבָב בוכו דַּוָּי׃ 6 מִכַּף־רֶגֶל וְעַד־
רֹאשׁ אֵין־בּוֹ מְתֹם פֶּצַע וְחַבּוּרָה וּמַכָּה היי טְרִיָּה לֹא־זֹרוּ
וְלֹא חֻבָּשׁוּ וְלֹא רֻכְּכָה בַּשָּׁמֶן׃ 7 אַרְצְכֶם שְׁמָמָה יוד הא ואו
הא עָרֵיכֶם שְׂרֻפוֹת אֵשׁ אַדְמַתְכֶם לְנֶגְדְּכֶם זָרִים אֹכְלִים
אֹתָהּ וּשְׁמָמָה כְּמַהְפֵּכַת זָרִים׃ 8 וְנוֹתְרָה בַת־צִיּוֹן יוסף כְּסֻכָּה
בְכָרֶם כִּמְלוּנָה בְמִקְשָׁה כְּעִיר ערי, סוזפר, סנדלפון נְצוּרָה׃ 9 לוּלֵי

יְהֹוָאדניאהדונהי צְבָאוֹת הוֹתִיר לָנוּ שָׂרִיד כִּמְעָט כִּסְדֹם הָיִינוּ
לַעֲמֹרָה דָּמִינוּ׃ 10 שִׁמְעוּ דְבַר ראה ־יְהֹוָאדניאהדונהי קְצִינֵי סְדֹם
הַאֲזִינוּ תּוֹרַת אֱלֹהֵינוּ ילה עַם עֲמֹרָה׃ 11 לָמָּה יוד הא ואו הא ־לִּי
רֹב־זִבְחֵיכֶם יֹאמַר יְהֹוָאדניאהדונהי שָׂבַעְתִּי עֹלוֹת אֵילִים
וְחֵלֶב מְרִיאִים וְדַם פָּרִים וּכְבָשִׂים וְעַתּוּדִים לֹא חָפָצְתִּי׃
12 כִּי תָבֹאוּ לֵרָאוֹת פָּנָי וחכמה, בינה מִי ילי ־בִקֵּשׁ זֹאת מִיֶּדְכֶם
רְמֹס חֲצֵרָי׃ 13 לֹא תוֹסִיפוּ הָבִיא מִנְחַת־שָׁוְא קְטֹרֶת
תּוֹעֵבָה הִיא לִי חֹדֶשׁ י״ב הויות וְשַׁבָּת קְרֹא מִקְרָא לֹא־אוּכַל
אָוֶן וַעֲצָרָה׃ 14 חָדְשֵׁיכֶם י״ב הויות וּמוֹעֲדֵיכֶם שָׂנְאָה נַפְשִׁי הָיוּ
עָלַי לָטֹרַח נִלְאֵיתִי נְשֹׂא׃ 15 וּבְפָרִשְׂכֶם כַּפֵּיכֶם אַעְלִים
עֵינַי מִכֶּם גַּם כִּי־תַרְבּוּ תְפִלָּה אֵינֶנִּי שֹׁמֵעַ יְדֵיכֶם דָּמִים
מָלֵאוּ׃ 16 רַחֲצוּ הִזַּכּוּ הָסִירוּ רֹעַ מַעַלְלֵיכֶם מִנֶּגֶד זן, מזבח עֵינָי
חִדְלוּ הָרֵעַ׃ 17 לִמְדוּ הֵיטֵב דִּרְשׁוּ מִשְׁפָּט אַשְּׁרוּ חָמוֹץ
שִׁפְטוּ יָתוֹם רִיבוּ אַלְמָנָה׃ 18 לְכוּ־נָא וְנִוָּכְחָה יֹאמַר
יְהֹוָאדניאהדונהי אִם יוהך ־יִהְיוּ חֲטָאֵיכֶם כַּשָּׁנִים כַּשֶּׁלֶג יַלְבִּינוּ
אִם יוהך ־יַאְדִּימוּ כַתּוֹלָע כַּצֶּמֶר מצר יִהְיוּ׃ 19 אִם יוהך ־תֹּאבוּ
וּשְׁמַעְתֶּם טוּב והו הָאָרֶץ אלף למד הה יוד מם תֹּאכֵלוּ׃ 20 וְאִם יוהך
־תְּמָאֲנוּ וּמְרִיתֶם חֶרֶב תְּאֻכְּלוּ כִּי פִּי יְהֹוָאדניאהדונהי דִּבֵּר ראה׃
21 אֵיכָה הָיְתָה לְזוֹנָה קִרְיָה נֶאֱמָנָה מְלֵאֲתִי מִשְׁפָּט צֶדֶק

יָלִין בָּהּ וְעַתָּה מְרַצְּחִים׃ 22 כַּסְפֵּךְ הָיָה יהה לְסִיגִים סָבְאֵךְ
מָהוּל בַּמָּיִם׃ 23 שָׂרַיִךְ סוֹרְרִים וְחַבְרֵי גַּנָּבִים כֻּלּוֹ אֹהֵב
שֹׁחַד וְרֹדֵף שַׁלְמֹנִים יָתוֹם לֹא יִשְׁפֹּטוּ וְרִיב אַלְמָנָה
לֹא־יָבוֹא אֲלֵיהֶם׃ 24 לָכֵן נְאֻם הָאָדוֹן אני יְהוָה אדני יאהדונהי
צְבָאוֹת אֲבִיר הרוז יִשְׂרָאֵל הוֹי אֶנָּחֵם מִצָּרַי מצפצ, אלף למד הי יוד מם
וְאִנָּקְמָה מֵאוֹיְבָי׃ 25 וְאָשִׁיבָה יָדִי עָלַיִךְ וְאֶצְרֹף כַּבֹּר סִיגָיִךְ
וְאָסִירָה כָּל יכ׳ ־בְּדִילָיִךְ׃ 26 וְאָשִׁיבָה שֹׁפְטַיִךְ כְּבָרִאשֹׁנָה
וְיֹעֲצַיִךְ כְּבַתְּחִלָּה אַחֲרֵי־כֵן יִקָּרֵא לָךְ עִיר ערי, סוזהר, סנדלפון
הַצֶּדֶק קִרְיָה נֶאֱמָנָה׃ 27 צִיּוֹן יוסף בְּמִשְׁפָּט תִּפָּדֶה וְשָׁבֶיהָ
בִּצְדָקָה א אל אלה אלהי אלהים׃

Lesson of Va'etchanan

The Secret of Shabbat Nachamu

The portion of Va'etchanan, which is also called *Shabbat Nachamu*, is always read in the week after the 9th day of Av. The Shabbat following the 9th of Av is known as the Shabbat of Consolation —as if it were possible to forget the pain just because Shabbat arrives! The energy of Shabbat is very powerful, but can one Shabbat give us the power to forget all the troubles we have endured?

To answer this, we must understand that the power of the Negative Side lies not only in causing us to doubt but also in keeping us in doubt and fear for a day, a week, a year, or even many years. Often, when we do something that we regret, we ask ourselves, "Why did I do that? How could I have done it?" This feeling can stay with us throughout our lives—and that is the Negative Side at work!

The Shabbat of Consolation does not teach us to ignore negative events. Yes, the Temple was burned, and there was so much pain. But should we cry that we don't have a Temple or should we work to create a new one? It is written that hatred for no reason caused the destruction of the Temple. Only love for no reason can restore it, so we need to we must ensure that love for no reason is our spiritual work.

Every time a disaster strikes us, we ask, "Why?" Every time we do something wrong, we ask, "How could I have done such a thing?" But the key to our fulfillment is asking the question: "When will I start working to make things better?" Remember, the power of the Negative Side is not only to bring us down but also to keep us without hope of positive change. This Shabbat, the Shabbat of Consolation, gives us the power to rise after we fall.

Anyone can connect to the Tree of Life

Toward the end of the World War I, there lived in Russia a great sage known as the Chafetz Chaim. This was the time of the Russian Revolution, and the revolutionaries had entered the town where the Chafetz Chaim lived. They immediately created turmoil by releasing all the criminals from jail, including a notorious thief and murderer named Moshe. Using threats and intimidation, Moshe soon became a powerful person in the town.

One day when the Chafetz Chaim was out walking with two of his students, Moshe came walking towards them. The Chafetz Chaim looked straight at him and said, "Shabbat Shalom, Moshe," to which Moshe answered, "Shabbat Shalom, my Master." The Chafetz Chaim then said, "Perhaps you'll join us for the third meal of Shabbat?" Moshe replied, "I've already had the third meal," but the Chafetz Chaim asked him again, saying, "Well, maybe you'll come with us anyway."

Then Moshe understood that the Chafetz Chaim had something important to reveal, so he agreed to go.

When they arrived at the house, the Chafetz Chaim directed his students to leave so that he could be alone with Moshe. But the students left the door open just a crack, so they could hear what was about to transpire.

The Chafetz Chaim spoke to the criminal, saying, "Moshe, I want to teach you a word of Torah." Moshe answered, "What do I care about the Torah?" But the Chafetz Chaim continued, "Moshe, please listen. It is written in the beginning of the Torah: 'And God planted a garden in Eden.' Why did God have to put the Tree of Life purposefully in the middle of the Garden? Because if the Tree of Life was at a corner of the Garden, the distance to the Tree from one side would be farther than from the other. Therefore, God put it in the middle so that the distance to the Tree would be even from all sides."

He continued, "After Shabbat, I am leaving. You and the revolutionaries have promised to give food and shelter to everyone in this town. But so far, you've done nothing but cause trouble. I myself provide food for 42 families. When I'm gone, who will feed them? That is why I told you about the Tree of Life in the Garden, which is accessible from all sides in the World to Come. If you promise me you'll give food to all the families, I promise you that you will reach the Tree of Life."

Moshe answered, "I agree, my Master. I promise. We have a deal!" Then Moshe went out and saw that the students had overheard what he said. He said to the eavesdroppers, "If there were more masters like him in the world, we wouldn't need a revolution!"

This teaches us that literally anyone can reach the Tree of Life, which is in the middle of the Garden of Eden; it is a merit that we have. The Rav, like the Chafetz Chaim, cares nothing about what a person may have done in the past. The important thing is how each and every one of us can reach the Tree of Life.

Another important matter

The great sage Yosef Bluch once wrote a beautiful allegory: A man was getting ready to go to America from the Middle East. In those days, the journey took several months by sea, and the ship was scheduled to stop in France for two weeks to load food that would last for the rest of the journey.

Since the man knew he would be stopping in France, he decided to learn French before departing on the trip. By the time the ship sailed, he had indeed managed to learn French, but he didn't have time to learn English, the language of his final destination. When the ship reached France, the man disembarked and enjoyed every minute of his stay, and knowing the French language helped him immensely. Then after two weeks, he returned to the ship to continue his trip to America.

When he arrived in America, he again tried to speak French, but no one could understand him. The Americans told him, "You're a fool! You were in France for only two weeks, but for the rest of your life you're going to be in America. You went and learned French instead of learning English, which is the language you'll need for your whole life."

This is an allegory that we can apply to our lives as a whole. Our existence here in this physical world is analogous to the man's visit to France. We stay here only a little while, and yet we work hard to learn the language. But the "language" that we really need to know is the desire to receive for the sake of sharing. By learning *this* language, we will merit to see the face of Messiah—and to see the building of the Temple in our own days.

Synopsis of Va'etchanan

This portion opens with Moses pleading to God. We must understand that we're not alone in this world and that we must ask God for help. If we have a great gift coming to us, we might not get it if we don't ask for it. Asking God is not something to do only in time of need; it's a tool we should use all the time to connect to the Light.

First Reading - Abraham - Chesed

23 וָאֶתְחַנַּן אֶל־יְהֹוָה יאהדונהי בָּעֵת הַהִוא לֵאמֹר׃ 24 אֲדֹנָי
יְהֹוִה יאהדונהי אַתָּה הַחִלּוֹתָ לְהַרְאוֹת אֶת־עַבְדְּךָ פוי אֶת־גָּדְלְךָ
וְאֶת־יָדְךָ הַחֲזָקָה אֲשֶׁר מִי ילי ־אֵל בַּשָּׁמַיִם כוזו, י״פ טל וּבָאָרֶץ
אֲשֶׁר־יַעֲשֶׂה כְמַעֲשֶׂיךָ וְכִגְבוּרֹתֶךָ׃ 25 אֶעְבְּרָה־נָּא וְאֶרְאֶה
אֶת־הָאָרֶץ אלף למד הה יוד מם הַטּוֹבָה אכא אֲשֶׁר בְּעֵבֶר הַיַּרְדֵּן
הָהָר הַטּוֹב והו הַזֶּה והו וְהַלְּבָנֹן׃ 26 וַיִּתְעַבֵּר יְהֹוָה יאהדונהי בִּי
לְמַעַנְכֶם וְלֹא שָׁמַע אֵלָי וַיֹּאמֶר יְהֹוָה יאהדונהי אֵלַי רַב־לָךְ
אַל־תּוֹסֶף דַּבֵּר ראה אֵלַי עוֹד בַּדָּבָר ראה הַזֶּה והו׃ 27 עֲלֵה |
רֹאשׁ הַפִּסְגָּה וְשָׂא עֵינֶיךָ יָמָּה וְצָפֹנָה וְתֵימָנָה וּמִזְרָחָה
וּרְאֵה ראה בְעֵינֶיךָ כִּי־לֹא תַעֲבֹר אֶת־הַיַּרְדֵּן הַזֶּה והו׃ 28 וְצַו פוי
אֶת־יְהוֹשֻׁעַ וְחַזְּקֵהוּ וְאַמְּצֵהוּ כִּי־הוּא יַעֲבֹר לִפְנֵי חכמה,
בינה הָעָם הַזֶּה והו וְהוּא יַנְחִיל אוֹתָם אֶת־הָאָרֶץ אלף למד הה
יוד מם אֲשֶׁר תִּרְאֶה׃ 29 וַנֵּשֶׁב בַּגָּיְא מוּל בֵּית ב״פ ראה פְּעוֹר׃
4 1 וְעַתָּה יִשְׂרָאֵל שְׁמַע אֶל־הַחֻקִּים וְאֶל־הַמִּשְׁפָּטִים

וָאֶתְחַנַּן - Moses pleads with God to allow him to enter the land of Israel. There are many lessons here, but one of the biggest is to never give up. God had already told Moses he couldn't enter, but Moses kept trying. We never know how many curtains there are that separate us from the Light. Every effort we make removes a curtain, and if we keep trying, that final try might take us to the Light.

אֲשֶׁר אָנֹכִי איע מְלַמֵּד אֶתְכֶם לַעֲשׂוֹת לְמַעַן תִּחְיוּ וּבָאתֶם
וִירִשְׁתֶּם אֶת־הָאָרֶץ אלף למד הה יוד מם אֲשֶׁר יְהֹוָהאדניאהדונהי
אֱלֹהֵי דמב, ילה אֲבֹתֵיכֶם נֹתֵן ושר, אבג יתץ, אהבת חנם לָכֶם: 2 לֹא
תֹסִפוּ עַל־הַדָּבָר ראה אֲשֶׁר אָנֹכִי איע מְצַוֶּה אֶתְכֶם וְלֹא
תִגְרְעוּ מִמֶּנּוּ לִשְׁמֹר אֶת־מִצְוֹת יְהֹוָהאדניאהדונהי אֱלֹהֵיכֶם ילה
אֲשֶׁר אָנֹכִי איע מְצַוֶּה אֶתְכֶם: 3 עֵינֵיכֶם הָרֹאוֹת אֵת אֲשֶׁר־
עָשָׂה יְהֹוָהאדניאהדונהי בְּבַעַל פְּעוֹר כִּי כָל ילי ־הָאִישׁ אֲשֶׁר
הָלַךְ מיה אַחֲרֵי בַעַל־פְּעוֹר הִשְׁמִידוֹ יְהֹוָהאדניאהדונהי אֱלֹהֶיךָ
מִקִּרְבֶּךָ: 4 וְאַתֶּם הַדְּבֵקִים בַּיהֹוָהאדניאהדונהי אֱלֹהֵיכֶם ילה
חַיִּים בינה כֻּלְּכֶם הַיּוֹם נגד, מזבח, זן:

Second Reading - Isaac - Gvurah

5 רְאֵה ראה | לִמַּדְתִּי אֶתְכֶם חֻקִּים וּמִשְׁפָּטִים כַּאֲשֶׁר צִוַּנִי
יְהֹוָהאדניאהדונהי אֱלֹהָי דמב, ילה לַעֲשׂוֹת כֵּן בְּקֶרֶב הָאָרֶץ אלף למד הה
יוד מם אֲשֶׁר אַתֶּם בָּאִים שָׁמָּה יוד הא ואו הא לְרִשְׁתָּהּ: 6 וּשְׁמַרְתֶּם

הַדְּבֵקִים - The Ten Utterances are revealed in this section. If we live in Israel, we can follow them all. When we're not in Israel, our first step is to connect to being there. We do that through prayers and meditations. When we connect to the Creator during prayer and meditation, we take ourselves to Israel. If we don't have the consciousness of being in Israel when we pray, it's as though we didn't pray at all.

וַעֲשִׂיתֶם כִּי הִוא חָכְמַתְכֶם וּבִינַתְכֶם לְעֵינֵי הָעַמִּים אֲשֶׁר
יִשְׁמְעוּן אֵת כָּל ילי ־הַחֻקִּים הָאֵלֶּה וְאָמְרוּ רַק עַם־חָכָם
וְנָבוֹן הַגּוֹי הַגָּדוֹל להח, מבה הַזֶּה והו׃ 7 כִּי מִי ילי ־גוֹי גָּדוֹל להח,
מבה אֲשֶׁר־לוֹ אֱלֹהִים מום, ילה קְרֹבִים אֵלָיו כַּיהוָהאדניאהדונהי
אֱלֹהֵינוּ ילה בְּכָל לכב ־קָרְאֵנוּ אֵלָיו׃ 8 וּמִי ילי גּוֹי גָּדוֹל להח, מבה
אֲשֶׁר־לוֹ חֻקִּים וּמִשְׁפָּטִים צַדִּיקִם כְּכֹל ילי הַתּוֹרָה הַזֹּאת
אֲשֶׁר אָנֹכִי איע נֹתֵן ושר, אבג יתץ, אהבת חינם לִפְנֵיכֶם הַיּוֹם נגד, מזבח,
זן׃ 9 רַק הִשָּׁמֶר לְךָ וּשְׁמֹר נַפְשְׁךָ מְאֹד פֶּן־תִּשְׁכַּח אֶת־
הַדְּבָרִים אֲשֶׁר־רָאוּ עֵינֶיךָ וּפֶן־יָסוּרוּ מִלְּבָבְךָ כֹּל ילי יְמֵי
חַיֶּיךָ וְהוֹדַעְתָּם לְבָנֶיךָ וְלִבְנֵי בָנֶיךָ׃ 10 יוֹם נגד, מזבח, זן אֲשֶׁר
עָמַדְתָּ לִפְנֵי וחכמה, בינה יְהוָהאדניאהדונהי אֱלֹהֶיךָ ילה בְּחֹרֵב בֶּאֱמֹר

וַעֲשִׂיתֶם - The section discusses the difference between the people who listen to the Torah and those who do not. This does not mean Israelites versus non-Israelites. The real difference is between people who want to connect to the Light through spiritual work and transformation and those who don't. Anyone who connects to the Torah through the Zohar can transform. God is close to us, but we can only reach Him if we come to know the true meaning of God through the Zohar.

פֶּן־תִּשְׁכַּח - The Torah tells us that we have to remember what happened on Mount Sinai. The most important things to remember are not the Ten Utterances themselves, but the fact that we reached immortality and 40 days later, we lost it. We have the power to create or destroy our own transformation. It's all up to us.

יְהֹוָהאדני יאהדונהי אֵלַי הַקְהֶל־לִי אֶת־הָעָם וְאַשְׁמִעֵם אֶת־
דְּבָרָי אֲשֶׁר יִלְמְדוּן לְיִרְאָה רי״ו, גבורה אֹתִי כָּל ילי ־הַיָּמִים נלך
אֲשֶׁר הֵם חַיִּים בינה עַל־הָאֲדָמָה וְאֶת־בְּנֵיהֶם יְלַמֵּדוּן׃
11 וַתִּקְרְבוּן וַתַּעַמְדוּן תַּחַת הָהָר וְהָהָר בֹּעֵר בָּאֵשׁ עַד־
לֵב הַשָּׁמַיִם כוזו, י״פ טל חֹשֶׁךְ עָנָן וַעֲרָפֶל׃ 12 וַיְדַבֵּר יְהֹוָהאדני יאהדונהי
אֲלֵיכֶם מִתּוֹךְ הָאֵשׁ קוֹל דְּבָרִים אַתֶּם שֹׁמְעִים וּתְמוּנָה
אֵינְכֶם רֹאִים זוּלָתִי קוֹל׃ 13 וַיַּגֵּד לָכֶם אֶת־בְּרִיתוֹ אֲשֶׁר
צִוָּה אֶתְכֶם לַעֲשׂוֹת עֲשֶׂרֶת הַדְּבָרִים וַיִּכְתְּבֵם עַל־שְׁנֵי
לֻחוֹת אֲבָנִים׃ 14 וְאֹתִי צִוָּה יְהֹוָהאדני יאהדונהי בָּעֵת הַהִוא לְלַמֵּד
אֶתְכֶם חֻקִּים וּמִשְׁפָּטִים לַעֲשֹׂתְכֶם אֹתָם בָּאָרֶץ אֲשֶׁר
אַתֶּם עֹבְרִים שָׁמָּה יוד הא ואו הא לְרִשְׁתָּהּ׃ 15 וְנִשְׁמַרְתֶּם מְאֹד
לְנַפְשֹׁתֵיכֶם כִּי לֹא רְאִיתֶם כָּל ילי ־תְּמוּנָה בְּיוֹם נגד, מזבח, זן
דִּבֶּר ראה יְהֹוָהאדני יאהדונהי אֲלֵיכֶם בְּחֹרֵב מִתּוֹךְ הָאֵשׁ׃ 16 פֶּן־
תַּשְׁחִתוּן וַעֲשִׂיתֶם לָכֶם פֶּסֶל תְּמוּנַת כָּל ילי ־סָמֶל תַּבְנִית
זָכָר אוֹ נְקֵבָה׃ 17 תַּבְנִית כָּל ילי ־בְּהֵמָה לכב אֲשֶׁר בָּאָרֶץ
תַּבְנִית כָּל ילי ־צִפּוֹר כָּנָף אלף הה יוד הה, אדני ־ אלהים אֲשֶׁר תָּעוּף

פֶּסֶל - In this passage, there's a long discussion of idols. Idols really symbolize the temptation to place trust in anything other than the Light. If we worship idols, we can receive only the energy of the idol we worship, which is not much! Where do we believe our Light comes from? Our answer determines how much Light we will receive.

בַּשָּׁמָיִם כוזו, י״פ טל: 18 תַּבְנִית כָּל ילי ־רֹמֵשׂ בָּאֲדָמָה תַּבְנִית
כָּל ילי ־דָּגָה אֲשֶׁר־בַּמַּיִם מִתַּחַת לָאָרֶץ: 19 וּפֶן־תִּשָּׂא עֵינֶיךָ
הַשָּׁמַיְמָה וְרָאִיתָ אֶת־הַשֶּׁמֶשׁ וְאֶת־הַיָּרֵחַ וְאֶת־הַכּוֹכָבִים
כֹּל ילי צְבָא הַשָּׁמַיִם כוזו, י״פ טל וְנִדַּחְתָּ וְהִשְׁתַּחֲוִיתָ לָהֶם
וַעֲבַדְתָּם אֲשֶׁר חָלַק יְהֹוָאדהנָי איאהדונהי אֱלֹהֶיךָ ילה אֹתָם לְכֹל יה
אדני ילי הָעַמִּים תַּחַת כָּל ילי ־הַשָּׁמָיִם כוזו, י״פ טל: 20 וְאֶתְכֶם לָקַח
יְהֹוָאדהנָי איאהדונהי וַיּוֹצִא אֶתְכֶם מִכּוּר הַבַּרְזֶל ר״ת - בלהה רחל זילפה
לאה מִמִּצְרָיִם מצר לִהְיוֹת לוֹ לְעַם עלם נַחֲלָה כַּיּוֹם נגד, מזבח, זן
הַזֶּה והו: 21 וַיהֹוָאדהנָי איאהדונהי הִתְאַנַּף־בִּי עַל־דִּבְרֵיכֶם וַיִּשָּׁבַע
לְבִלְתִּי עָבְרִי אֶת־הַיַּרְדֵּן וּלְבִלְתִּי־בֹא אֶל־הָאָרֶץ אלף למד
הה יוד מם הַטּוֹבָה אכא אֲשֶׁר יְהֹוָאדהנָי איאהדונהי אֱלֹהֶיךָ נֹתֵן ושר, אבג יתץ,
אהבת חנם לְךָ נַחֲלָה: 22 כִּי אָנֹכִי איע מֵת בָּאָרֶץ הַזֹּאת אֵינֶנִּי
עֹבֵר אֶת־הַיַּרְדֵּן וְאַתֶּם עֹבְרִים וִירִשְׁתֶּם אֶת־הָאָרֶץ אלף למד
הה יוד מם הַטּוֹבָה אכא הַזֹּאת: 23 הִשָּׁמְרוּ לָכֶם פֶּן־תִּשְׁכְּחוּ אֶת־

מֵת - Connecting to our personal Moses: Moses tells the people he is not going with them into Israel. This was because the people weren't ready for him: He was too elevated for their consciousness. Moses was ahead of his time. The people didn't connect to him in the right way, and this is also true for the Moses present in every generation. We never listen to what's good for us. We think our teacher doesn't understand our question when we don't get the right answer. We have to connect to our teachers and to the Light so that we can be guided the right direction. We have to connect to our own personal Moses.

בְּרִית יְהוָהאדני יאהדונהי אֱלֹהֵיכֶם ילה אֲשֶׁר כָּרַת עִמָּכֶם וַעֲשִׂיתֶם
לָכֶם פֶּסֶל תְּמוּנַת כֹּל ילי אֲשֶׁר צִוְּךָ יְהוָהאדני יאהדונהי אֱלֹהֶיךָ׃
24 כִּי יְהוָהאדני יאהדונהי אֱלֹהֶיךָ אֵשׁ אֹכְלָה הוּא אֵל קַנָּא׃
25 כִּי־תוֹלִיד בָּנִים וּבְנֵי בָנִים וְנוֹשַׁנְתֶּם בָּאָרֶץ וְהִשְׁחַתֶּם
וַעֲשִׂיתֶם פֶּסֶל תְּמוּנַת כֹּל ילי וַעֲשִׂיתֶם הָרַע בְּעֵינֵי יְהוָהאדני־
אֱלֹהֶיךָ יאהדונהי לְהַכְעִיסוֹ׃ 26 הַעִידֹתִי בָכֶם הַיּוֹם נגד, מזבח, זן אֶת־
הַשָּׁמַיִם כוזו, י"פ טל וְאֶת־הָאָרֶץ אלף למד הה יוד מם כִּי־אָבֹד תֹּאבֵדוּן
מַהֵר מֵעַל עלם הָאָרֶץ אלף למד הה יוד מם אֲשֶׁר אַתֶּם עֹבְרִים אֶת־
הַיַּרְדֵּן שָׁמָּה יוד הא ואו הא לְרִשְׁתָּהּ לֹא־תַאֲרִיכֻן יָמִים נלך עָלֶיהָ
כִּי הִשָּׁמֵד תִּשָּׁמֵדוּן׃ 27 וְהֵפִיץ יְהוָהאדני יאהדונהי אֶתְכֶם בָּעַמִּים
וְנִשְׁאַרְתֶּם מְתֵי מִסְפָּר בַּגּוֹיִם אֲשֶׁר יְנַהֵג יְהוָהאדני יאהדונהי
אֶתְכֶם שָׁמָּה יוד הא ואו הא׃ 28 וַעֲבַדְתֶּם־שָׁם אֱלֹהִים מום, ילה
מַעֲשֵׂה יְדֵי אָדָם מ"ה, יוד הא ואו הא עֵץ וָאֶבֶן אֲשֶׁר לֹא־יִרְאוּן וְלֹא
יִשְׁמְעוּן וְלֹא יֹאכְלוּן וְלֹא יְרִיחֻן׃ 29 וּבִקַּשְׁתֶּם מִשָּׁם אֶת־
יְהוָהאדני יאהדונהי אֱלֹהֶיךָ וּמָצָאתָ כִּי תִדְרְשֶׁנּוּ בְּכָל לכב ־לְבָבְךָ

כִּי - We read this portion on *Tisha B'av* (the 9th of Av) and it concerns exile and return. If the people had instantly corrected themselves, the Temple would have returned, but they did not. Whenever we fall, it's like another exile and destruction of the Temple. The Temple is destroyed once again in every generation that fails to rebuild it. We have to take personal responsibility to rebuild the Temple by coming back to the Light.

וּבְכָל לכב ־נַפְשֶׁךָ׃ 30 בַּצַּר לְךָ וּמְצָאוּךָ כֹּל ילי הַדְּבָרִים
הָאֵלֶּה בְּאַחֲרִית הַיָּמִים נלך וְשַׁבְתָּ עַד־יְהֹוָאדני יאהדונהי אֱלֹהֶיךָ
וְשָׁמַעְתָּ בְּקֹלוֹ׃ 31 כִּי אֵל רַחוּם יְהֹוָאדני יאהדונהי אֱלֹהֶיךָ
לֹא יַרְפְּךָ וְלֹא יַשְׁחִיתֶךָ וְלֹא יִשְׁכַּח אֶת־בְּרִית אֲבֹתֶיךָ
אֲשֶׁר נִשְׁבַּע לָהֶם׃ 32 כִּי שְׁאַל־נָא לְיָמִים נלך רִאשֹׁנִים אֲשֶׁר־
הָיוּ לְפָנֶיךָ לְמִן־הַיּוֹם נגד, מזבח, זן אֲשֶׁר בָּרָא קנ"א-ב"ן אֱלֹהִים מום,
ילה | אָדָם מ"ה, יוד הא ואו הא עַל־הָאָרֶץ אלף למד הה יוד מם וּלְמִקְצֵה
הַשָּׁמַיִם כוזו, י"פ טל וְעַד־קְצֵה הַשָּׁמָיִם כוזו, י"פ טל הֲנִהְיָה כַּדָּבָר ראה
הַגָּדוֹל להח, מבה הַזֶּה והו אוֹ הֲנִשְׁמַע כָּמֹהוּ׃ 33 הֲשָׁמַע עָם
קוֹל אֱלֹהִים מום, ילה מְדַבֵּר ראה מִתּוֹךְ־הָאֵשׁ כַּאֲשֶׁר־שָׁמַעְתָּ
אַתָּה וַיֶּחִי׃ 34 אוֹ | הֲנִסָּה אֱלֹהִים מום, ילה לָבוֹא לָקַחַת לוֹ
גוֹי מִקֶּרֶב גּוֹי בְּמַסֹּת בְּאֹתֹת וּבְמוֹפְתִים וּבְמִלְחָמָה וּבְיָד
חֲזָקָה וּבִזְרוֹעַ נְטוּיָה וּבְמוֹרָאִים גְּדֹלִים כְּכֹל ילי אֲשֶׁר־עָשָׂה
לָכֶם יְהֹוָאדני יאהדונהי אֱלֹהֵיכֶם ילה בְּמִצְרַיִם מצר לְעֵינֶיךָ׃ 35 אַתָּה

לֹא יַרְפְּךָ - God never abandons us, even when we feel totally alone. He just puts us in that situation so that we can learn from it. We should know that God is always with us. If we think He's not there, that's when He's there the most.

הֲשָׁמַע - God always sends His voice for us to hear, but we don't usually listen because Satan's voice is louder. The more closely we listen to the still, quiet voice, the more we have a chance to connect to the Creator.

הָרְאֵתָ לָדַעַת כִּי יְהֹוָהאדניאהדונהי הוּא הָאֱלֹהִים מום, ילה אֵין עוֹד
מִלְבַדּוֹ: 36 מִן־הַשָּׁמַיִם כוזו, י״פ טל הִשְׁמִיעֲךָ אֶת־קֹלוֹ לְיַסְּרֶךָּ
וְעַל־הָאָרֶץ אלף למד הה יוד מם הֶרְאֲךָ אֶת־אִשּׁוֹ הַגְּדוֹלָה וּדְבָרָיו
שָׁמַעְתָּ מִתּוֹךְ הָאֵשׁ: 37 וְתַחַת כִּי אָהַב אֶת־אֲבֹתֶיךָ וַיִּבְחַר
בְּזַרְעוֹ אַחֲרָיו וַיּוֹצִאֲךָ בְּפָנָיו בְּכֹחוֹ הַגָּדֹל להח מִמִּצְרָיִם מצר:
38 לְהוֹרִישׁ גּוֹיִם גְּדֹלִים וַעֲצֻמִים מִמְּךָ מִפָּנֶיךָ לַהֲבִיאֲךָ
לָתֶת־לְךָ אֶת־אַרְצָם נַחֲלָה כַּיּוֹם נגד, מזבח, זן הַזֶּה והו: 39 וְיָדַעְתָּ
הַיּוֹם נגד, מזבח, זן וַהֲשֵׁבֹתָ אֶל־לְבָבֶךָ כִּי יְהֹוָהאדניאהדונהי הוּא
הָאֱלֹהִים מום, ילה בַּשָּׁמַיִם כוזו, י״פ טל מִמַּעַל עלם וְעַל־הָאָרֶץ אלף
למד הה יוד מם מִתָּחַת אֵין עוֹד: 40 וְשָׁמַרְתָּ אֶת־חֻקָּיו וְאֶת־
מִצְוֺתָיו אֲשֶׁר אָנֹכִי איע מְצַוְּךָ הַיּוֹם נגד, מזבח, זן אֲשֶׁר יִיטַב
לְךָ וּלְבָנֶיךָ אַחֲרֶיךָ וּלְמַעַן תַּאֲרִיךְ יָמִים נלך עַל־הָאֲדָמָה
אֲשֶׁר יְהֹוָהאדניאהדונהי אֱלֹהֶיךָ נֹתֵן ושר, אבג יתץ, אהבת חנם לְךָ כָּל ילי
־הַיָּמִים נלך:

Third Reading - Jacob - Tiferet

41 אָז יַבְדִּיל מֹשֶׁה מהש שָׁלֹשׁ עָרִים בְּעֵבֶר הַיַּרְדֵּן מִזְרְחָה
שָׁמֶשׁ: 42 לָנֻס יוד הא ואו הא - אדני שָׁמָּה יוד הא ואו הא רוֹצֵחַ אֲשֶׁר יִרְצַח

אָז - Moses knows that he won't enter the land of Israel, but he continues to support the Israelites who *will* go there. Moses never gave up but always did the most he could. He connected to whatever Light was present. He could

אֶת־רֵעֵהוּ בִּבְלִי־דַעַת וְהוּא לֹא־שֹׂנֵא לוֹ מִתְּמֹל שִׁלְשֹׁם
וְנָס יוד הא ואו הא - אדני אֶל־אַחַת מִן־הֶעָרִים הָאֵל לאה וָחָי׃ 43 אֶת־
בֶּצֶר בַּמִּדְבָּר בְּאֶרֶץ הַמִּישֹׁר לָראוּבֵנִי וְאֶת־רָאמֹת
בַּגִּלְעָד לַגָּדִי והו וְאֶת־גּוֹלָן בַּבָּשָׁן לַמְנַשִּׁי׃ 44 וְזֹאת הַתּוֹרָה
אֲשֶׁר־שָׂם מֹשֶׁה מהש לִפְנֵי חוכמה, בינה בְּנֵי יִשְׂרָאֵל׃ 45 אֵלֶּה
הָעֵדֹת וְהַחֻקִּים וְהַמִּשְׁפָּטִים אֲשֶׁר דִּבֶּר ראה מֹשֶׁה מהש
אֶל־בְּנֵי יִשְׂרָאֵל בְּצֵאתָם מִמִּצְרָיִם מצר׃ 46 בְּעֵבֶר הַיַּרְדֵּן
בַּגַּיְא מוּל בֵּית ב״פ ראה פְּעוֹר בְּאֶרֶץ סִיחֹן מֶלֶךְ הָאֱמֹרִי
אֲשֶׁר יוֹשֵׁב בְּחֶשְׁבּוֹן אֲשֶׁר הִכָּה הי״ מֹשֶׁה מהש וּבְנֵי יִשְׂרָאֵל
בְּצֵאתָם מִמִּצְרָיִם מצר׃ 47 וַיִּירְשׁוּ אֶת־אַרְצוֹ וְאֶת־אֶרֶץ | עוֹג
מֶלֶךְ־הַבָּשָׁן שְׁנֵי מַלְכֵי נלך הָאֱמֹרִי אֲשֶׁר בְּעֵבֶר הַיַּרְדֵּן
מִזְרַח שָׁמֶשׁ׃ 48 מֵעֲרֹעֵר אֲשֶׁר עַל־שְׂפַת־נַחַל אַרְנֹן וְעַד־
הַר שִׂיאֹן הוּא חֶרְמוֹן׃ 49 וְכָל ילי ־הָעֲרָבָה זרע עֵבֶר הַיַּרְדֵּן
מִזְרָחָה וְעַד יָם ילי הָעֲרָבָה זרע תַּחַת אַשְׁדֹּת הַפִּסְגָּה׃

Fourth Reading - Moses - Netzach

5 1 וַיִּקְרָא מֹשֶׁה מהש אֶל־כָּל ילי ־יִשְׂרָאֵל וַיֹּאמֶר אֲלֵהֶם
שְׁמַע יִשְׂרָאֵל אֶת־הַחֻקִּים וְאֶת־הַמִּשְׁפָּטִים אֲשֶׁר אָנֹכִי איע

have given up and stopped being a leader, but he still cared about everyone and did the work even if he wouldn't benefit from it himself. Even when we know that we won't personally benefit from our actions, we should still put in our best effort.

דִּבֵּר ראה בְּאָזְנֵיכֶם הַיּוֹם נגד, מזבח, זן וּלְמַדְתֶּם אֹתָם וּשְׁמַרְתֶּם
לַעֲשֹׂתָם: 2 יְהֹוָהאדניאהדונהי אֱלֹהֵינוּ ילה כָּרַת עִמָּנוּ בְּרִית בְּחֹרֵב:
3 לֹא אֶת־אֲבֹתֵינוּ כָּרַת יְהֹוָהאדניאהדונהי אֶת־הַבְּרִית הַזֹּאת כִּי
אִתָּנוּ אֲנַחְנוּ אֵלֶּה פֹה מילה הַיּוֹם נגד, מזבח, זן כֻּלָּנוּ חַיִּים בינה:
4 פָּנִים | בְּפָנִים דִּבֶּר ראה יְהֹוָהאדניאהדונהי עִמָּכֶם בָּהָר מִתּוֹךְ
הָאֵשׁ: 5 אָנֹכִי איע עֹמֵד בֵּין־יְהֹוָהאדניאהדונהי וּבֵינֵיכֶם בָּעֵת הַהִוא
לְהַגִּיד לָכֶם אֶת־דְּבַר ראה יְהֹוָהאדניאהדונהי כִּי יְרֵאתֶם מִפְּנֵי חכמה,
בינה הָאֵשׁ וְלֹא־עֲלִיתֶם בָּהָר לֵאמֹר: 6 אָנֹכִי איע יְהֹוָהאדניאהדונהי
אֱלֹהֶיךָ אֲשֶׁר הוֹצֵאתִיךָ מֵאֶרֶץ מִצְרַיִם מצר מִבֵּית ב״פ ראה

בְּאָזְנֵיכֶם - This section teaches us to understand the Torah as if it had been given to us personally. Every single part is about us; we're the ones who made the wrong decisions and the right ones. It's not about what happened 3300 years ago but about what is happening to us today. When we read about the Golden Calf in the Torah, we realize that it's *our* Golden Calf. If there's a story about someone with ego, it's about *our* ego. It's all about us, and we should take the messages the Torah gives as if they were there just for us.

The Ten Utterances are our connection to immortality:

First Utterance: *Keter*

אָנֹכִי יְהֹוָהאדניאהדונהי - Believe in the existence of the Creator. If we fail to have a connection to the Creator, then we fall to the level of the world's mixed multitudes. The only way to avoid life's ups and downs is to always bring the Creator into our consciousness. If we experience mood swings and fluctuations of fortune, we must realize that we are not yet connecting to the Light of the Creator at the optimal level. True belief in the existence of the Creator means bringing the Light into every moment of every day.

עֲבָדִים: 7 לֹא־יִהְיֶה ייי לְךָ אֱלֹהִים מום, ילה אֲחֵרִים עַל־
פָּנָי חכמה, בינה: 8 לֹא־תַעֲשֶׂה לְךָ פֶסֶל | כָּל ילי ־תְּמוּנָה אֲשֶׁר
בַּשָּׁמַיִם כוזו, י״פ טל | מִמַּעַל עלם וַאֲשֶׁר בָּאָרֶץ מִתָּחַת וַאֲשֶׁר
בַּמַּיִם | מִתַּחַת לָאָרֶץ: 9 לֹא־תִשְׁתַּחֲוֶה לָהֶם וְלֹא תָעָבְדֵם
כִּי אָנֹכִי איע יְהֹוָהאדניאהדונהי אֱלֹהֶיךָ ילה אֵל קַנָּא פֹּקֵד עֲוֺן אָבוֹת
עַל־בָּנִים וְעַל־שִׁלֵּשִׁים וְעַל־רִבֵּעִים לְשֹׂנְאָי: 10 וְעֹשֶׂה
חֶסֶד יוד הי ויו הי, י יה יהו יהוה לַאֲלָפִים לְאֹהֲבַי וּלְשֹׁמְרֵי מִצְוֺתָי (כתיב:
מצותו): 11 לֹא תִשָּׂא אֶת־שֵׁם־יְהֹוָהאדניאהדונהי אֱלֹהֶיךָ לַשָּׁוְא כִּי
לֹא יְנַקֶּה יְהֹוָהאדניאהדונהי אֵת אֲשֶׁר־יִשָּׂא אֶת־שְׁמוֹ לַשָּׁוְא:
12 שָׁמוֹר אֶת־יוֹם נגד, מזבח, זן הַשַּׁבָּת לְקַדְּשׁוֹ כַּאֲשֶׁר צִוְּךָ |

Second Utterance: *Chochmah*

לֹא־יִהְיֶה - Do not believe in any gods other than the Creator. In our day, we must understand that our idols are often money, power, fame, security, ego, and a thousand other false energy sources. Looking for the Light in these areas is an obvious and foolish mistake. Why do we continue to make that mistake?

Third Utterance: *Binah*

לֹא תִשָּׂא - Do not use the Name of God in vain. If we use a Name, we call to us the powers associated with that Name. By calling upon the Name of God for minor and unimportant reasons, we are debasing the power of that Name. We deprive ourselves of the true power of the Name for when we really need it.

יְהֹוָה יאהדונהי אֱלֹהֶיךָ׃ 13 שֵׁשֶׁת יָמִים נלך תַּעֲבֹד וְעָשִׂיתָ כָּל ילי
־מְלַאכְתֶּךָ׃ 14 וְיוֹם נגד, מזבח, זן הַשְּׁבִיעִי שַׁבָּת ׀ לַיהֹוָה יאהדונהי
אֱלֹהֶיךָ לֹא תַעֲשֶׂה כָל ילי ־מְלָאכָה אַתָּה וּבִנְךָ־וּבִתֶּךָ
וְעַבְדְּךָ־וַאֲמָתֶךָ וְשׁוֹרְךָ וַחֲמֹרְךָ וְכָל ילי ־בְּהֶמְתֶּךָ וְגֵרְךָ אֲשֶׁר
בִּשְׁעָרֶיךָ לְמַעַן יָנוּחַ עַבְדְּךָ פוי וַאֲמָתְךָ כָּמוֹךָ׃ 15 וְזָכַרְתָּ כִּי
עֶבֶד הָיִיתָ ׀ בְּאֶרֶץ מִצְרַיִם מצר וַיֹּצִאֲךָ יְהֹוָה יאהדונהי
אֱלֹהֶיךָ ילה מִשָּׁם בְּיָד חֲזָקָה וּבִזְרֹעַ נְטוּיָה עַל־כֵּן צִוְּךָ
יְהֹוָה יאהדונהי אֱלֹהֶיךָ לַעֲשׂוֹת אֶת־יוֹם נגד, מזבח, זן הַשַּׁבָּת׃
16 כַּבֵּד אֶת־אָבִיךָ וְאֶת־אִמֶּךָ כַּאֲשֶׁר צִוְּךָ יְהֹוָה יאהדונהי
אֱלֹהֶיךָ לְמַעַן ׀ יַאֲרִיכֻן יָמֶיךָ וּלְמַעַן יִיטַב לָךְ עַל הָאֲדָמָה
אֲשֶׁר־יְהֹוָה יאהדונהי אֱלֹהֶיךָ נֹתֵן ושר, אבג יתץ, אהבת חנם לָךְ׃

Fourth Utterance: *Chesed*

הַשַּׁבָּת - Honor the Shabbat day. Shabbat includes not only our actions on the seventh day but also the consciousness we have on that day. At a minimum, we should take five minutes to think about our lives, where we are spiritually, and what we need to work on. Or we may choose the full 25 hours of honoring every precept of Shabbat. We all need to connect with the energy of Shabbat somewhere within this spectrum.

Fifth Utterance: *Gevurah*

כַּבֵּד - Honor your father and mother. There are certain people whose gifts we can never repay. The act of bringing us into this world—there is nothing we can ever hope to do to repay that. Although this is true, we should not simply give up trying to repay. The solution is to have true appreciation. More important than anything we could do for our parents, we must have appreciation for the gift they have given us - our life.

17 לֹא תִרְצָח וְלֹא תִנְאָף וְלֹא תִגְנֹב וְלֹא־תַעֲנֶה בְרֵעֲךָ
עֵד שָׁוְא׃ 18 וְלֹא תַחְמֹד אֵשֶׁת רֵעֶךָ וְלֹא תִתְאַוֶּה בֵּית ב"פ

Sixth Utterance: *Tiferet*

לֹא תִרְצָח - Do not commit murder. Murder is not limited to physical slaying: It can include destroying others through our words, our business dealings, or any form of negative action.

Seventh Utterance: *Netzach*

וְלֹא תִנְאָף - Do not commit adultery. This utterance is very important because it concerns trust, not just between a married couple but also between friends, business associates, and between us and God.

Eighth Utterance: *Hod*

וְלֹא תִגְנֹב - Do not steal. We commit theft whenever we behave as if we deserve something that we do not in fact deserve. Stealing has two ramifications: First, we may take a physical object from someone, but the Light of that object remains with the original owner. All we have is the physical aspect—not the energy—of the object. Second, the person who steals pays a tremendous price. Every year, the sustenance that comes to us is determined Above. When we steal, we are taking in a negative way something that might have come to us anyway. We are also forfeiting any further sustenance that could have come to us as well as spiritual Light that would have been ours.

Ninth Utterance: *Yesod*

וְלֹא־תַעֲנֶה - Do not bear false witness. This includes *lashon hara* (gossip, slander). The Zohar says that it is almost impossible to repent for evil speech. Once something is said, it can never be taken back.

Tenth Utterance: *Malchut*

וְלֹא תַחְמֹד - Do not covet. When we want what someone else has, we are in essence saying that God is wrong, that He isn't giving us what we need. When we have this consciousness, we are ignoring the fact that each person has a particular spiritual path with its own unique twists and turns. Someone

ראה רֵעֶךָ שָׂדֵהוּ וְעַבְדּוֹ וַאֲמָתוֹ שׁוֹרוֹ וַחֲמֹרוֹ וְכֹל ילי אֲשֶׁר
לְרֵעֶךָ׃

Fifth Reading - Aaron - Hod

19 אֶת־הַדְּבָרִים הָאֵלֶּה **דִּבֶּר** ראה יְהֹוָהאדני יאהדונהי אֶל־כָּל ילי ־
קְהַלְכֶם בָּהָר מִתּוֹךְ הָאֵשׁ שאה הֶעָנָן וְהָעֲרָפֶל קוֹל גָּדוֹל להח,
מבה וְלֹא יָסָף וַיִּכְתְּבֵם עַל־שְׁנֵי לֻחֹת אֲבָנִים וַיִּתְּנֵם אֵלָי׃
20 וַיְהִי כְּשָׁמְעֲכֶם אֶת־הַקּוֹל מִתּוֹךְ הַחֹשֶׁךְ וְהָהָר בֹּעֵר
בָּאֵשׁ וַתִּקְרְבוּן אֵלַי כָּל ילי ־רָאשֵׁי שִׁבְטֵיכֶם וְזִקְנֵיכֶם׃
21 וַתֹּאמְרוּ הֵן הֶרְאָנוּ יְהֹוָהאדני יאהדונהי אֱלֹהֵינוּ ילה אֶת־כְּבֹדוֹ
וְאֶת־גָּדְלוֹ וְאֶת־קֹלוֹ שָׁמַעְנוּ מִתּוֹךְ הָאֵשׁ הַיּוֹם נגד, מזבח, זן
הַזֶּה והו רָאִינוּ כִּי־יְדַבֵּר אֱלֹהִים מום, ילה אֶת־הָאָדָם מ"ה, יוד הא
ואו הא וָחָי׃ 22 וְעַתָּה לָמָּה יוד הא ואו הא נָמוּת כִּי תֹאכְלֵנוּ הָאֵשׁ

with a perfect house may have health problems or trouble with relationships. We each have our own particular spiritual path that is meant for us to do our *tikkune*, or correction process. When we try to pick and choose according to our own inclinations, we are not allowing the Creator's Light into our lives.

דִּבֶּר - The first two commandments were actually delivered to the Israelites by the voice of God. Then Moses delivered the rest because the people were afraid to listen anymore. This section helps us overcome our fears. The great sage Rav Nachman says the whole world is like a narrow bridge and the key to crossing it is to be unafraid. Fear is one of Satan's most powerful weapons. We must realize that the greater the fear we have, the more Light there is to be revealed by overcoming it.

הַגְּדֹלָה הַזֹּאת אִם יוהך ־יֹסְפִים | אֲנַחְנוּ לִשְׁמֹעַ אֶת־קוֹל
יְהֹוָהאדנייאהדונהי אֱלֹהֵינוּ ילה עוֹד וָמָתְנוּ: 23 כִּי מִי ילי כָל ילי ־בָּשָׂר
אֲשֶׁר שָׁמַע קוֹל אֱלֹהִים מום, ילה חַיִּים בינה מְדַבֵּר ראה מִתּוֹךְ־
הָאֵשׁ כָּמֹנוּ וַיֶּחִי: 23 קְרַב אַתָּה וּשְׁמָע אֵת כָּל ילי ־אֲשֶׁר
יֹאמַר יְהֹוָהאדנייאהדונהי אֱלֹהֵינוּ ילה וְאַתְּ | תְּדַבֵּר אֵלֵינוּ אֵת כָּל ילי
־אֲשֶׁר יְדַבֵּר יְהֹוָהאדנייאהדונהי אֱלֹהֵינוּ ילה אֵלֶיךָ וְשָׁמַעְנוּ וְעָשִׂינוּ:
25 וַיִּשְׁמַע יְהֹוָהאדנייאהדונהי אֶת־קוֹל דִּבְרֵיכֶם בְּדַבֶּרְכֶם אֵלָי
וַיֹּאמֶר יְהֹוָהאדנייאהדונהי אֵלַי שָׁמַעְתִּי אֶת־קוֹל דִּבְרֵי הָעָם
הַזֶּה והו אֲשֶׁר דִּבְּרוּ אֵלֶיךָ הֵיטִיבוּ כָּל ילי ־אֲשֶׁר דִּבֵּרוּ:
26 מִי ילי ־יִתֵּן וְהָיָה יהוה, יהה לְבָבָם זֶה לָהֶם **לְיִרְאָה** רי"ו, גבורה
אֹתִי וְלִשְׁמֹר אֶת־כָּל ילי ־מִצְוֹתַי כָּל ילי ־הַיָּמִים נלך לְמַעַן
יִיטַב לָהֶם וְלִבְנֵיהֶם לְעֹלָם: 27 לֵךְ אֱמֹר לָהֶם שׁוּבוּ לָכֶם
לְאָהֳלֵיכֶם: 28 וְאַתָּה פֹּה מילה עֲמֹד עִמָּדִי וַאֲדַבְּרָה אֵלֶיךָ
אֵת כָּל ילי ־הַמִּצְוָה וְהַחֻקִּים וְהַמִּשְׁפָּטִים אֲשֶׁר תְּלַמְּדֵם
וְעָשׂוּ בָאָרֶץ אֲשֶׁר אָנֹכִי איע נֹתֵן ושר, אבג יתץ, אהבת חינם לָהֶם

לְיִרְאָה - God said that the people were afraid, so Moses intended to get all the Light for them by being a channel. At this moment, he was elevated to being half-human, half-angel. Moses is our bridge to the Light. But Moses never forgot he was half-human even when he became half-angel. He retained all he was before, but he became greater. Today, when people achieve power, they often change for the worse. Moses remained all that he was as a human being, but more elevated spiritually.

לְרִשְׁתָּהּ׃ 29 וּשְׁמַרְתֶּם לַעֲשׂוֹת כַּאֲשֶׁר צִוָּה יְהֹוָהאדני יאהדונהי
אֱלֹהֵיכֶם ילה אֶתְכֶם לֹא תָסֻרוּ יָמִין וּשְׂמֹאל׃ 30 בְּכָל לכב
־הַדֶּרֶךְ אֲשֶׁר צִוָּה יְהֹוָהאדני יאהדונהי אֱלֹהֵיכֶם ילה אֶתְכֶם תֵּלֵכוּ
לְמַעַן תִּחְיוּן וְטוֹב והו לָכֶם וְהַאֲרַכְתֶּם יָמִים נלך בָּאָרֶץ אֲשֶׁר
תִּירָשׁוּן׃ 6 1 וְזֹאת הַמִּצְוָה הַחֻקִּים וְהַמִּשְׁפָּטִים אֲשֶׁר צִוָּה
יְהֹוָהאדני יאהדונהי אֱלֹהֵיכֶם ילה לְלַמֵּד אֶתְכֶם לַעֲשׂוֹת בָּאָרֶץ
אֲשֶׁר אַתֶּם עֹבְרִים שָׁמָּה יוד הא ואו הא לְרִשְׁתָּהּ׃ 2 לְמַעַן
תִּירָא אֶת־יְהֹוָהאדני יאהדונהי אֱלֹהֶיךָ לִשְׁמֹר אֶת־כָּל ילי ־חֻקֹּתָיו
וּמִצְוֹתָיו אֲשֶׁר אָנֹכִי איע מְצַוֶּךָ אַתָּה וּבִנְךָ וּבֶן־בִּנְךָ כֹּל ילי
יְמֵי חַיֶּיךָ וּלְמַעַן יַאֲרִכֻן יָמֶיךָ׃ 3 וְשָׁמַעְתָּ יִשְׂרָאֵל וְשָׁמַרְתָּ
לַעֲשׂוֹת אֲשֶׁר יִיטַב לְךָ וַאֲשֶׁר תִּרְבּוּן מְאֹד כַּאֲשֶׁר
דִּבֶּר ראה יְהֹוָהאדני יאהדונהי אֱלֹהֵי דמב, ילה אֲבֹתֶיךָ לָךְ אֶרֶץ זָבַת
חָלָב וּדְבָשׁ׃

Sixth Reading - Joseph - Yesod

4 שְׁמַע יִשְׂרָאֵל יְהֹוָהאדני יאהדונהי אֱלֹהֵינוּ ילה יְהֹוָהאדני יאהדונהי |
אֶחָד׃ 5 וְאָהַבְתָּ ב״פ - אור, רז אֵת יְהֹוָהאדני יאהדונהי אֱלֹהֶיךָ

שְׁמַע - The prayer and meditation of the *Shema* is in this portion, with a

בְּכָל לכב ־לְבָבְךָ וּבְכָל לכב ־נַפְשְׁךָ וּבְכָל לכב ־מְאֹדֶךָ׃
6 וְהָיוּ הַדְּבָרִים הָאֵלֶּה אֲשֶׁר אָנֹכִי איע מְצַוְּךָ הַיּוֹם נגד, מזבח,
זן עַל־לְבָבֶךָ׃ 7 וְשִׁנַּנְתָּם לְבָנֶיךָ וְדִבַּרְתָּ בָּם מב בְּשִׁבְתְּךָ
בְּבֵיתֶךָ וּבְלֶכְתְּךָ בַדֶּרֶךְ וּבְשָׁכְבְּךָ וּבְקוּמֶךָ׃ 8 וּקְשַׁרְתָּם
לְאוֹת עַל־יָדֶךָ וְהָיוּ לְטֹטָפֹת בֵּין עֵינֶיךָ׃ 9 וּכְתַבְתָּם
עַל־מְזֻזוֹת נית בֵּיתֶךָ וּבִשְׁעָרֶיךָ׃ 10 וְהָיָה יהוה, יהה כִּי יְבִיאֲךָ |
יְהֹוָהאדני יאהדונהי אֱלֹהֶיךָ אֶל־הָאָרֶץ אלף למד הה יוד מם אֲשֶׁר נִשְׁבַּע
לַאֲבֹתֶיךָ לְאַבְרָהָם לְיִצְחָק וּלְיַעֲקֹב יאהדונהי, אידהנויה לָתֶת לָךְ׃

large *ayin* and *dalet* in it. Large letters always connect us to *Binah*. Together, these letters make up the word "witness." If we perform a negative action, there are many witnesses to it, not just people but even the room we're in. Wherever we are or whatever we do, even the inanimate objects around us are aware of it.

וְאָהַבְתָּ - The "Ve'ahavta" section of the *Shema* has 42 words, connecting us to the power of the *Ana Beko'ach*. This is one of the most important prayers and meditations, because the 42 letters control the spiritual world above. So the *Shema* is our bridge to the Upper Realm, the world of miracles. For this reason, we do the *Shema* and the *Ana Beko'ach* every day.

מְזֻזוֹת - One of the last words in the *Shema* is *mezuzot*, which has the same numerical value as *nun yud tav* ("The Death to Death," one of The 72 Names of God). Rearranging the letters of *Mezuzot* creates *Zaz Mavet*, or the ability to overcome death in our lives.

וְהָיָה - If we are connected to the Light of the Creator, our work is done. When we complete our work in the spiritual realm, we get everything in the physical realm as well. The physical catches up to the metaphysical. When we focus on the 99 percent, we become complete throughout.

עָרִים גְּדֹלֹת וְטֹבֹת אֲשֶׁר לֹא־בָנִיתָ׃ 11 וּבָתִּים מְלֵאִים
כָּל ילי ־טוּב והו אֲשֶׁר לֹא־מִלֵּאתָ וּבֹרֹת חֲצוּבִים אֲשֶׁר
לֹא־חָצַבְתָּ כְּרָמִים וְזֵיתִים אֲשֶׁר לֹא־נָטָעְתָּ וְאָכַלְתָּ
וְשָׂבָעְתָּ׃ 12 הִשָּׁמֶר לְךָ פֶּן־תִּשְׁכַּח אֶת־יְהֹוָהאדניאהדונהי אֲשֶׁר
הוֹצִיאֲךָ מֵאֶרֶץ מִצְרַיִם מצר מִבֵּית ב״פ ראה עֲבָדִים׃ 13 אֶת־
יְהֹוָהאדניאהדונהי אֱלֹהֶיךָ **תִּירָא** וְאֹתוֹ תַעֲבֹד וּבִשְׁמוֹ תִּשָּׁבֵעַ׃
14 לֹא תֵלְכוּן אַחֲרֵי אֱלֹהִים מום, ילה אֲחֵרִים מֵאֱלֹהֵי דמב, ילה
הָעַמִּים אֲשֶׁר סְבִיבוֹתֵיכֶם׃ 15 כִּי אֵל קַנָּא יְהֹוָהאדניאהדונהי
אֱלֹהֶיךָ ילה בְּקִרְבֶּךָ פֶּן־יֶחֱרֶה אַף־יְהֹוָהאדניאהדונהי אֱלֹהֶיךָ ילה בָּךְ
וְהִשְׁמִידְךָ מֵעַל עלם פְּנֵי חכמה, בינה הָאֲדָמָה׃ 16 לֹא תְנַסּוּ אֶת־
יְהֹוָהאדניאהדונהי אֱלֹהֵיכֶם ילה כַּאֲשֶׁר נִסִּיתֶם בַּמַּסָּה׃ 17 שָׁמוֹר
תִּשְׁמְרוּן אֶת־מִצְוֹת יְהֹוָהאדניאהדונהי אֱלֹהֵיכֶם ילה וְעֵדֹתָיו וְחֻקָּיו
אֲשֶׁר צִוָּךְ׃ 18 וְעָשִׂיתָ הַיָּשָׁר וְהַטּוֹב והו בְּעֵינֵי יְהֹוָהאדניאהדונהי
לְמַעַן יִיטַב לָךְ וּבָאתָ וְיָרַשְׁתָּ אֶת־הָאָרֶץ אלף למד הה יוד מם
הַטֹּבָה אֲשֶׁר־נִשְׁבַּע יְהֹוָהאדניאהדונהי לַאֲבֹתֶיךָ׃ 19 לַהֲדֹף

תִּירָא - We need to have trust in the Creator beyond the realm of just believing. It has to be about knowing *without a doubt* that the Creator is there for us. The more difficult the situations we face, the more He's there. Don't ever question that. Have complete certainty and know that what we have is what we need to have.

אֶת־כָּל ילי -אֹיְבֶיךָ מִפָּנֶיךָ כַּאֲשֶׁר דִּבֶּר ראה יְהֹוָהאדניאהדונהי׃
20 כִּי־יִשְׁאָלְךָ בִנְךָ מָחָר לֵאמֹר מָה יוד הא ואו הא הָעֵדֹת וְהַחֻקִּים
וְהַמִּשְׁפָּטִים אֲשֶׁר צִוָּה יְהֹוָהאדניאהדונהי אֱלֹהֵינוּ ילה אֶתְכֶם׃
21 וְאָמַרְתָּ לְבִנְךָ עֲבָדִים הָיִינוּ לְפַרְעֹה בְּמִצְרָיִם מצר וַיֹּצִיאֵנוּ
יְהֹוָהאדניאהדונהי מִמִּצְרַיִם מצר בְּיָד חֲזָקָה׃ 22 וַיִּתֵּן יְהֹוָהאדניאהדונהי
אוֹתֹת וּמֹפְתִים גְּדֹלִים וְרָעִים | בְּמִצְרַיִם מצר בְּפַרְעֹה
וּבְכָל לכב -בֵּיתוֹ לְעֵינֵינוּ׃ 23 וְאוֹתָנוּ הוֹצִיא מִשָּׁם לְמַעַן
הָבִיא אֹתָנוּ לָתֶת לָנוּ מום, אלהים, אהיה - אדני אֶת־הָאָרֶץ אלף למד הה
יוד מם אֲשֶׁר נִשְׁבַּע לַאֲבֹתֵינוּ׃ 24 וַיְצַוֵּנוּ יְהֹוָהאדניאהדונהי לַעֲשׂוֹת
אֶת־כָּל ילי -הַחֻקִּים הָאֵלֶּה לְיִרְאָה רי״ו, גבורה אֶת־יְהֹוָהאדניאהדונהי
אֱלֹהֵינוּ ילה לְטוֹב והו לָנוּ מום, אלהים, אהיה - אדני כָּל ילי -הַיָּמִים נלך
לְחַיֹּתֵנוּ כְּהַיּוֹם הַזֶּה והו׃ 25 וּצְדָקָה א אל אלה אלהי אלהים תִּהְיֶה־לָּנוּ
כִּי־נִשְׁמֹר לַעֲשׂוֹת אֶת־כָּל ילי -הַמִּצְוָה הַזֹּאת לִפְנֵי חכמה, בינה
יְהֹוָהאדניאהדונהי אֱלֹהֵינוּ ילה כַּאֲשֶׁר צִוָּנוּ׃

בִּנְךָ - It is the responsibility of parents to teach their children everything on the physical and the spiritual levels. Children must be taught the meaning of "Egypt" on a spiritual level. Through Kabbalah, they can get out of their personal Egypt. Egypt represents all forms of slavery: slavery to our jobs, society, our families - even addictions are a form of slavery.

Seventh Reading - David - Malchut

7 1 כִּי יְבִיאֲךָ יְהֹוָאדִנָּהֵי אהדונהי אֱלֹהֶיךָ אֶל־הָאָרֶץ אלף למד הה
יוד מם אֲשֶׁר־אַתָּה בָא־שָׁמָּה יוד הא ואו הא לְרִשְׁתָּהּ וְנָשַׁל גּוֹיִם־
רַבִּים ׀ מִפָּנֶיךָ הַחִתִּי וְהַגִּרְגָּשִׁי וְהָאֱמֹרִי וְהַכְּנַעֲנִי וְהַפְּרִזִּי
וְהַחִוִּי וְהַיְבוּסִי שִׁבְעָה גּוֹיִם רַבִּים וַעֲצוּמִים מִמֶּךָּ׃ 2 וּנְתָנָם
יְהֹוָאדִנָּהֵי אהדונהי אֱלֹהֶיךָ לְפָנֶיךָ וְהִכִּיתָם הַחֲרֵם תַּחֲרִים
אֹתָם לֹא־תִכְרֹת לָהֶם בְּרִית וְלֹא תְחָנֵּם׃ 3 וְלֹא תִתְחַתֵּן
בָּם מב בִּתְּךָ לֹא־תִתֵּן ב״פ כהת לִבְנוֹ וּבִתּוֹ לֹא־תִקַּח לִבְנֶךָ׃
4 כִּי־יָסִיר אֶת־בִּנְךָ מֵאַחֲרַי וְעָבְדוּ אֱלֹהִים מום, ילה אֲחֵרִים
וְחָרָה אַף־יְהֹוָאדִנָּהֵי אהדונהי בָּכֶם וְהִשְׁמִידְךָ מַהֵר׃ 5 כִּי־אִם יוהך
־כֹּה היי תַעֲשׂוּ לָהֶם מִזְבְּחוֹתֵיהֶם תִּתֹּצוּ וּמַצֵּבֹתָם תְּשַׁבֵּרוּ
וַאֲשֵׁירֵהֶם תְּגַדֵּעוּן וּפְסִילֵיהֶם תִּשְׂרְפוּן בָּאֵשׁ׃ 6 כִּי עַם
קָדוֹשׁ אַתָּה לַיהֹוָאדִנָּהֵי אהדונהי אֱלֹהֶיךָ בְּךָ בָּחַר ׀ יְהֹוָאדִנָּהֵי אהדונהי
אֱלֹהֶיךָ לִהְיוֹת לוֹ לְעַם עלם סְגֻלָּה מִכֹּל ילי הָעַמִּים אֲשֶׁר עַל־
פְּנֵי חכמה, בינה הָאֲדָמָה׃ 7 לֹא מֵרֻבְּכֶם מִכָּל ילי ־הָעַמִּים חָשַׁק

יְבִיאֲךָ - When the Israelites reached the land of Israel, they were very negative. We have to make sure that whatever we do is what we're supposed to be doing. In a relationship, for example, we have to be certain it's the relationship we're supposed to be in. If it's not, we've erred twice: once because we're not where we're supposed to be, and second because we're taking another person's place. We always have to make sure we're in the right place in all we do.

יְהֹוָהאדני יאהדונהי בָּכֶם וַיִּבְחַר בָּכֶם כִּי־אַתֶּם הַמְעַט מִכָּל ילי
־הָעַמִּים: 8 כִּי מֵאַהֲבַת יְהֹוָהאדני יאהדונהי אֶתְכֶם וּמִשָּׁמְרוֹ
אֶת־הַשְּׁבֻעָה אֲשֶׁר נִשְׁבַּע לַאֲבֹתֵיכֶם הוֹצִיא יְהֹוָהאדני יאהדונהי
אֶתְכֶם בְּיָד חֲזָקָה וַיִּפְדְּךָ מִבֵּית ב"פ ראה עֲבָדִים מִיַּד פַּרְעֹה
מֶלֶךְ־מִצְרָיִם מצר:

Maftir

9 וְיָדַעְתָּ כִּי־יְהֹוָהאדני יאהדונהי אֱלֹהֶיךָ הוּא הָאֱלֹהִים מום, ילה
הָאֵל לאה הַנֶּאֱמָן שֹׁמֵר הַבְּרִית וְהַחֶסֶד יוד הי ויו הי, י יה יהו יהוה
לְאֹהֲבָיו וּלְשֹׁמְרֵי מִצְוֹתָיו (כתיב: מצותו) לְאֶלֶף דּוֹר: 10 וּמְשַׁלֵּם
לְשֹׂנְאָיו אֶל־פָּנָיו לְהַאֲבִידוֹ לֹא יְאַחֵר לְשֹׂנְאוֹ אֶל־פָּנָיו
יְשַׁלֶּם־לוֹ: 11 וְשָׁמַרְתָּ אֶת־הַמִּצְוָה וְאֶת־הַחֻקִּים וְאֶת־
הַמִּשְׁפָּטִים אֲשֶׁר אָנֹכִי איע מְצַוְּךָ הַיּוֹם נגד, מזבח, זן לַעֲשׂוֹתָם:

וְיָדַעְתָּ - With God, it's never "personal." It's all about cause and effect. If we love and open the channel for love, love flows between us and God. If we open the channel for hate, hate flows through us, and forms the basis for our relationship with God.

Haftarah of Va'etchanan

This haftarah starts the process of the seven consecutive haftarahs that console us and give us energy to rebuild the Temple. They all follow *Tisha b'Av* (the 9th of Av). We learn that the Temple can be rebuilt. When it was there, no one appreciated it. Now that it's gone, people need to come together to rebuild it.

Isaiah 40 | ישעיהו פרק 40

1 נַחֲמוּ נַחֲמוּ עַמִּי יֹאמַר אֱלֹהֵיכֶם ילה: 2 דַּבְּרוּ עַל־לֵב
יְרוּשָׁלַםִ וְקִרְאוּ אֵלֶיהָ כִּי מָלְאָה צְבָאָהּ כִּי נִרְצָה עֲוֺנָהּ כִּי
לָקְחָה מִיַּד יְהוָהאדני יאהדונהי כִּפְלַיִם בְּכָל לכב ־חַטֹּאתֶיהָ: 3 קוֹל
קוֹרֵא בַּמִּדְבָּר פַּנּוּ דֶּרֶךְ יְהוָהאדני יאהדונהי יַשְּׁרוּ בָּעֲרָבָה זרע
מְסִלָּה לֵאלֹהֵינוּ ילה: 4 כָּל ילי ־גֶּיא יִנָּשֵׂא וְכָל ילי ־הַר וְגִבְעָה
יִשְׁפָּלוּ וְהָיָה יהוה, יהה הֶעָקֹב מום-מום לְמִישׁוֹר וְהָרְכָסִים לְבִקְעָה:
5 וְנִגְלָה כְּבוֹד יְהוָהאדני יאהדונהי וְרָאוּ כָל ילי ־בָּשָׂר יַחְדָּו כִּי פִּי
יְהוָהאדני יאהדונהי דִּבֵּר ראה: 6 קוֹל אֹמֵר קְרָא וְאָמַר מָה יוד הא
ואו הא אֶקְרָא כָּל ילי ־הַבָּשָׂר חָצִיר וְכָל ילי ־חַסְדּוֹ כְּצִיץ מנק
הַשָּׂדֶה: 7 יָבֵשׁ חָצִיר נָבֵל צִיץ מנק כִּי רוּחַ יְהוָהאדני יאהדונהי
נָשְׁבָה בּוֹ אָכֵן חָצִיר הָעָם: 8 יָבֵשׁ חָצִיר נָבֵל צִיץ מנק
וּדְבַר ראה ־אֱלֹהֵינוּ ילה יָקוּם לְעוֹלָם: 9 עַל הַר־גָּבֹהַּ עֲלִי־
לָךְ מְבַשֶּׂרֶת צִיּוֹן יוסף הָרִימִי בַכֹּחַ קוֹלֵךְ מְבַשֶּׂרֶת יְרוּשָׁלָםִ
הָרִימִי אַל־תִּירָאִי אִמְרִי לְעָרֵי יְהוּדָה הִנֵּה אֱלֹהֵיכֶם ילה:
10 הִנֵּה אֲדֹנָי יְהוָהאדני יאהדונהי בְּחָזָק פהל יָבוֹא וּזְרֹעוֹ מֹשְׁלָה לוֹ

הִנֵּה שְׂכָרוֹ אִתּוֹ וּפְעֻלָּתוֹ לְפָנָיו׃ 11 כְּרֹעֶה רהע עֶדְרוֹ יִרְעֶה
בִּזְרֹעוֹ יְקַבֵּץ טְלָאִים וּבְחֵיקוֹ יִשָּׂא עָלוֹת יְנַהֵל׃ 12 מִי ילי
־מָדַד בְּשָׁעֳלוֹ מַיִם ילי וְשָׁמַיִם כוזו, י״פ טל בַּזֶּרֶת תִּכֵּן וְכָל ילי
בַּשָּׁלִשׁ עֲפַר הָאָרֶץ אלף למד הה יוד מם וְשָׁקַל נמם בַּפֶּלֶס הָרִים
וּגְבָעוֹת בְּמֹאזְנָיִם׃ 13 מִי ילי ־תִכֵּן אֶת־רוּחַ יְהֹוָה אדני יאהדונהי וְאִישׁ
עֲצָתוֹ יוֹדִיעֶנּוּ׃ 14 אֶת־מִי ילי נוֹעָץ וַיְבִינֵהוּ וַיְלַמְּדֵהוּ בְּאֹרַח
מִשְׁפָּט וַיְלַמְּדֵהוּ דַעַת וְדֶרֶךְ תְּבוּנוֹת יוֹדִיעֶנּוּ׃ 15 הֵן גּוֹיִם
כְּמַר מִדְּלִי וּכְשַׁחַק מֹאזְנַיִם נֶחְשָׁבוּ הֵן אִיִּים כַּדַּק יִטּוֹל׃
16 וּלְבָנוֹן אֵין דֵּי בָּעֵר וְחַיָּתוֹ אֵין דֵּי עוֹלָה׃ 17 כָּל ילי ־הַגּוֹיִם
כְּאַיִן נֶגְדּוֹ מֵאֶפֶס וָתֹהוּ נֶחְשְׁבוּ־לוֹ׃ 18 וְאֶל־מִי ילי תְּדַמְּיוּן אֵל
וּמַה יוד הא ואו הא ־דְּמוּת תַּעַרְכוּ לוֹ׃ 19 הַפֶּסֶל נָסַךְ חָרָשׁ וְצֹרֵף
בַּזָּהָב יְרַקְּעֶנּוּ וּרְתֻקוֹת כֶּסֶף צוֹרֵף׃ 20 הַמְסֻכָּן תְּרוּמָה עֵץ
לֹא־יִרְקַב יִבְחָר חָרָשׁ חָכָם יְבַקֶּשׁ־לוֹ לְהָכִין פֶּסֶל לֹא
יִמּוֹט׃ 21 הֲלוֹא תֵדְעוּ הֲלוֹא תִשְׁמָעוּ הֲלוֹא הֻגַּד מֵרֹאשׁ
לָכֶם הֲלוֹא הֲבִינֹתֶם מוֹסְדוֹת הָאָרֶץ אלף למד הה יוד מם׃ 22 הַיֹּשֵׁב
עַל־חוּג הָאָרֶץ אלף למד הה יוד מם וְיֹשְׁבֶיהָ כַּחֲגָבִים הַנּוֹטֶה כַדֹּק
שָׁמַיִם כוזו, י״פ טל וַיִּמְתָּחֵם כָּאֹהֶל לָשָׁבֶת׃ 23 הַנּוֹתֵן ושר, אבג יתץ, אהבת
חנם רוֹזְנִים לְאָיִן שֹׁפְטֵי אֶרֶץ כַּתֹּהוּ עָשָׂה׃ 24 אַף בַּל־נִטָּעוּ
אַף בַּל־זֹרָעוּ אַף בַּל־שֹׁרֵשׁ בָּאָרֶץ גִּזְעָם וְגַם־נָשַׁף בָּהֶם

וַיִּבָשׁוּ וּסְעָרָה כַּקַּשׁ תִּשָּׂאֵם׃ 25 וְאֶל־מִי ילי תְדַמְּיוּנִי וְאֶשְׁוֶה
יֹאמַר קָדוֹשׁ׃ 26 שְׂאוּ־מָרוֹם עֵינֵיכֶם וּרְאוּ מִי ילי ־בָרָא קנ״א־ב״ן
אֵלֶּה הַמּוֹצִיא בְמִסְפָּר צְבָאָם לְכֻלָּם בְּשֵׁם יִקְרָא מֵרֹב
אוֹנִים וְאַמִּיץ כֹּחַ אִישׁ לֹא נֶעְדָּר׃

Lesson of Ekev

"And if you will listen..."

The portion begins by considering what happens when we are on course in our spiritual work— or, God forbid, when we're not. But before we discuss what we should do to be on course, there is a great lesson we must learn.

Consider this story: Long ago, in a small town in Europe, there lived a butcher. One night, his deceased father came to him in a dream. The father said, "A woman will come to you on a Friday before Shabbat. She'll ask that you slaughter a chicken for her. Don't refuse her. You must slaughter the chicken for her."

But Friday came and went, and there was no woman.

Seventy years passed. Then, one Friday before Shabbat, the butcher was on his way to the synagogue when a woman approached him and said, 'Please, I know it's late, but if you don't slaughter this chicken, I won't have anything to eat on Shabbat!'

The butcher looked at his watch, then shook his head. "I'm very sorry I'd like to help you, but I just don't have time." And he departed.

But later that night in the middle of Kiddush, he suddenly remembered the dream he had had many years earlier and wondered how he could slaughter the chicken for the woman he had met. How would he find her? He sprang into action. He told his wife about the woman, instructing her to give the woman food if she ever saw her because he knew that he himself had missed his chance. Indeed, that night the butcher left this world. But he had the merit of completing his task through the actions of his family.

Most of us are not righteous. It's much more likely that we are here to perform a single action that we missed in our past life. Sometimes, it's more than one action, but it's always connected to the same principle: that there are those who come to give charity, and those who come because they need to help one particular person. But, nevertheless it's always one action or another that needs to be completed or corrected.

Of course, we don't know what that particular action is! Thus it is written: "Be as careful with a small action of sharing as with a large one." In the story, the butcher had a dream that told him clearly what he had to do. But he forgot. In the end, however, he was able to make a correction through his family. Each of us has "dreams" or experiences that give us important messages. We should be open not just to receive them but also to act upon them.

In our hearts, we all know where we're going wrong. We all know how we're departing from our spiritual path. The problem is that we're either afraid of this knowledge or we don't want to do the work of correction that it requires. If only we would open ourselves and listen and not be afraid! Then, as Rav Nachman of Breslov says: "The whole world is a thin bridge, and the most important thing is not to be afraid to cross it." We must not be afraid of knowing what we have to do because if we don't do it, we will have to come back to this world again and again.

"*Not on bread alone...*"

"Not on bread alone will a man live, because on whatever comes from Lightforch's mouth will man live." When a person takes a piece of bread and says, "Blessed are You, Creator," then the inner spiritual energy of the bread is awakened. Just as bread is food for the body, this energy is food for the soul.

On this subject, there is a story about a student of Rav Aharon of Carlin. Once when the student was at Rav Aharon's house, the teacher took an apple, blessed it, and ate it. The student looked at the teacher eating the apple, and a thought crossed his mind: "Even the great sage is simply eating an apple."

Rav Aharon felt the students thoughts, then turned to him and said, "You know, I was thinking to myself, what is the difference between us? I eat an apple and you eat an apple, I bless and you bless, so what is the big difference?" "The difference is that I get up in the morning, look out the window, and see an apple tree. I get excited and say, How plentiful are Your actions, Creator of the universe! The earth is full of Your creations! And I dont leave this thought: I go deeper and think, What does the Torah mean when it says: like an apple in the trees of the forest? And I get so excited that I have a passion to bless and thank the Creator, for the tree and for the apples, and I say, Blessed are You, Creator of the world, Who created the fruit of the tree. And since we are not allowed to bless without a purpose or to say the Creator's name in vain, I take an apple."

"But you," the teacher went on, "you do this a little differently. You go out to the street, see the apple tree, and think to yourself: Oh, what a beautiful tree! And what beautiful apples! And then, you have a great desire to eat one.

"But since you are not a thief, you go to the store, buy yourself an apple, go home, and are ready to eat the apple. Still, you have awe for the Creator, and therefore you think to yourself: Can anything be eaten without a blessing? If I eat something today without a blessing, tomorrow my teeth will be taken away from me, and I won't be able to eat apples anymore. Therefore, you say the blessing and then you eat the apple.

"What is the conclusion of all this? It is true that I bless and eat the apple and you also bless and eat the apple. But I eat the apple so that I can say a blessing, and you say a blessing so that you'll be able to eat the apple."

More regarding this week's portion

This week's portion starts with the verse: "And if you will listen." We all have disagreements with people, and that's perfectly all right. The problem is that most of the time, we don't hear each other's points of view. We don't want to listen because we "know everything." We think to ourselves: "If I listen to what he has to say, maybe he'll be right. Then I, God forbid, will have to say that I made a mistake, and there's nothing worse than that!"

This not only hurts us in our personal relationships but ultimately blocks our connection to the Light. When we cut ourselves off from others, the Creator cuts Himself off from us. It is written: "God is your shadow." If we move, our shadow moves also, and not one iota differently. As we act with others, so the Creator acts with us. The Creator cannot give us more than we give others. This is not to say that the Creator is angry with us. But our actions in this world are like a boomerang: If we do good, then good comes back to us, but if we cause pain, then pain comes back to us.

Rav Brandwein, tells this story of Rav Elimelech in one of his letters to my father, Rav Berg: One of his students came to Rav Elimelech and said, "I've been praying for 15 years, and the Creator hasn't answered my prayers and meditations. I pray three times a day. I say the prayer and meditation at midnight. I say the *Shema* every night before I go to sleep. I do everything I possibly can. But the Creator does not do His part. He has not answered my prayers yet. What do I need to do?"

Rav Elimelech looked at him and answered, "The Creator did answer your prayers—and the answer was 'No.'"

Often, we deny many different things to many different people. Therefore, the Creator denies us also. But if we say yes to others, then the Creator will say yes to us.

Synopsis of Ekev

Ekev means "heel." The kabbalists tell us that in our generation today, all the souls that are reincarnated come from the body of Adam. What's left of Adam now—the souls that are here today—are from the heels and the feet of Adam. The heels and feet were the parts of Adam most connected to *Malchut*, the physical world that Satan inhabits. Since we're all from the feet of Adam, we always have this contact with Satan. But Satan also knows that when we elevate above the feet, we're out of his reach, so he's fighting for his life. He knows that if he loses this fight, he's done for.

First Reading - Abraham - Chesed

12 וְהָיָה יהוה, יהה | עֵקֶב מום+מום תִּשְׁמְעוּן אֵת הַמִּשְׁפָּטִים הָאֵלֶּה
וּשְׁמַרְתֶּם וַעֲשִׂיתֶם אֹתָם וְשָׁמַר יְהֹוָאדני יאהדונהי אֱלֹהֶיךָ לְךָ
אֶת־הַבְּרִית וְאֶת־הַחֶסֶד יוד הי ויו הי, י יה יהו יהוה אֲשֶׁר נִשְׁבַּע
לַאֲבֹתֶיךָ׃ 13 וַאֲהֵבְךָ וּבֵרַכְךָ וְהִרְבֶּךָ וּבֵרַךְ פְּרִי־בִטְנְךָ
וּפְרִי־אַדְמָתֶךָ דְּגָנְךָ וְתִירֹשְׁךָ וְיִצְהָרֶךָ שְׁגַר־אֲלָפֶיךָ
וְעַשְׁתְּרֹת צֹאנֶךָ עַל הָאֲדָמָה אֲשֶׁר־נִשְׁבַּע לַאֲבֹתֶיךָ לָתֶת
לָךְ׃ 14 בָּרוּךְ תִּהְיֶה מִכָּל ילי ־הָעַמִּים לֹא־יִהְיֶה ייי בְךָ עָקָר
וַעֲקָרָה וּבִבְהֶמְתֶּךָ׃ 15 וְהֵסִיר יְהֹוָאדני יאהדונהי מִמְּךָ כָּל ילי
־חֹלִי וְכָל ילי ־מַדְוֵי מִצְרַיִם מצר הָרָעִים אֲשֶׁר יָדַעְתָּ לֹא
יְשִׂימָם בָּךְ וּנְתָנָם בְּכָל לכב ־שֹׂנְאֶיךָ׃ 16 וְאָכַלְתָּ אֶת־כָּל ילי
־הָעַמִּים אֲשֶׁר יְהֹוָאדני יאהדונהי אֱלֹהֶיךָ ילה נֹתֵן ושר, אבג יתץ, אהבת חנם
לָךְ לֹא־תָחוֹס עֵינְךָ עֲלֵיהֶם וְלֹא תַעֲבֹד אֶת־אֱלֹהֵיהֶם ילה
כִּי־מוֹקֵשׁ הוּא לָךְ׃ 17 כִּי תֹאמַר בִּלְבָבְךָ רַבִּים הַגּוֹיִם
הָאֵלֶּה מִמֶּנִּי אֵיכָה אוּכַל לְהוֹרִישָׁם׃ 18 לֹא תִירָא מֵהֶם
זָכֹר תִּזְכֹּר אֵת אֲשֶׁר־עָשָׂה יְהֹוָאדני יאהדונהי אֱלֹהֶיךָ לְפַרְעֹה

וַאֲהֵבְךָ - This section discusses the reward of being with the Light. The reward for caring is that you are cared for. Here's an analogy: The brain is the nerve center for the rest of the body but has no nerves itself. It feels nothing, but all the things we feel come from there. We have to be like the brain—feeling for everyone else but feeling no pain of our own.

וּלְכָל יה אדני ילי ־מִצְרָיִם מצר: 19 הַמַּסֹּת הַגְּדֹלֹת אֲשֶׁר־רָאוּ
עֵינֶיךָ וְהָאֹתֹת וְהַמֹּפְתִים וְהַיָּד וזהו הַחֲזָקָה וְהַזְּרֹעַ הַנְּטוּיָה
אֲשֶׁר הוֹצִאֲךָ יְהֹוָאדהנהיאהדונהי אֱלֹהֶיךָ כֵּן־יַעֲשֶׂה יְהֹוָאדהנהיאהדונהי
אֱלֹהֶיךָ ילה לְכָל יה אדני ילי ־הָעַמִּים אֲשֶׁר־אַתָּה יָרֵא מִפְּנֵיהֶם:
20 וְגַם אֶת־הַצִּרְעָה יְשַׁלַּח יְהֹוָאדהנהיאהדונהי אֱלֹהֶיךָ בָּם מב עַד־
אֲבֹד הַנִּשְׁאָרִים וְהַנִּסְתָּרִים מִפָּנֶיךָ: 21 לֹא תַעֲרֹץ מִפְּנֵיהֶם
כִּי־יְהֹוָאדהנהיאהדונהי אֱלֹהֶיךָ ילה בְּקִרְבֶּךָ אֵל גָּדוֹל להח, מבה וְנוֹרָא:
22 וְנָשַׁל יְהֹוָאדהנהיאהדונהי אֱלֹהֶיךָ אֶת־הַגּוֹיִם הָאֵל לאה מִפָּנֶיךָ
מְעַט מְעָט לֹא תוּכַל כַּלֹּתָם מַהֵר פֶּן־תִּרְבֶּה עָלֶיךָ חַיַּת
הַשָּׂדֶה: 23 וּנְתָנָם יְהֹוָאדהנהיאהדונהי אֱלֹהֶיךָ לְפָנֶיךָ וְהָמָם מְהוּמָה
גְדֹלָה עַד הִשָּׁמְדָם: 24 וְנָתַן אבג יתץ, ושר, אהבת חנם מַלְכֵיהֶם בְּיָדֶךָ
וְהַאֲבַדְתָּ אֶת־שְׁמָם מִתַּחַת הַשָּׁמָיִם כוזו, י״פ טל לֹא־יִתְיַצֵּב אִישׁ
בְּפָנֶיךָ עַד הִשְׁמִדְךָ אֹתָם: 25 פְּסִילֵי אֱלֹהֵיהֶם ילה תִּשְׂרְפוּן
בָּאֵשׁ לֹא־תַחְמֹד כֶּסֶף וְזָהָב עֲלֵיהֶם וְלָקַחְתָּ לָךְ פֶּן תִּוָּקֵשׁ
בּוֹ כִּי תוֹעֲבַת יְהֹוָאדהנהיאהדונהי אֱלֹהֶיךָ הוּא: 26 וְלֹא־תָבִיא
תוֹעֵבָה אֶל־בֵּיתֶךָ וְהָיִיתָ חֵרֶם כָּמֹהוּ שַׁקֵּץ מנק | תְּשַׁקְּצֶנּוּ

וְנָשַׁל - The Creator tells the Israelites He'll be with them in Israel and will destroy anything in their path. This shows us that there's nothing we can't change or overcome when we have certainty. The Light doesn't recognize the concept of impossibility.

וְתַעֵב | תְּתַעֲבֶנּוּ כִּי־חֵרֶם הוּא: 8 1 כָּל ילי ־הַמִּצְוָה אֲשֶׁר
אָנֹכִי איע מְצַוְּךָ הַיּוֹם נגד, מזבח, זן תִּשְׁמְרוּן לַעֲשׂוֹת לְמַעַן תִּחְיוּן
וּרְבִיתֶם וּבָאתֶם וִירִשְׁתֶּם אֶת־הָאָרֶץ אלף למד הה יוד מם אֲשֶׁר־
נִשְׁבַּע יְהֹוָאדהנויאהדונהי לַאֲבֹתֵיכֶם: 2 וְזָכַרְתָּ אֶת־כָּל ילי ־הַדֶּרֶךְ
אֲשֶׁר הוֹלִיכֲךָ יְהֹוָאדהנויאהדונהי אֱלֹהֶיךָ זֶה אַרְבָּעִים שָׁנָה
בַּמִּדְבָּר לְמַעַן עַנֹּתְךָ לְנַסֹּתְךָ לָדַעַת אֶת־אֲשֶׁר בִּלְבָבְךָ
הֲתִשְׁמֹר מִצְוֹתָו אִם יוהך ־לֹא: 3 וַיְעַנְּךָ וַיַּרְעִבֶךָ וַיַּאֲכִלְךָ אֶת־
הַמָּן אֲשֶׁר לֹא־יָדַעְתָּ וְלֹא יָדְעוּן אֲבֹתֶיךָ לְמַעַן הוֹדִיעֲךָ
כִּי לֹא עַל־הַלֶּחֶם ג״פ יהו״ה לְבַדּוֹ מ״ב יִחְיֶה הָאָדָם מ״ה, יוד הא ואו הא
כִּי עַל־כָּל ילי ־מוֹצָא פִי־יְהֹוָאדהנויאהדונהי יִחְיֶה הָאָדָם מ״ה, יוד הא
ואו הא: 4 שִׂמְלָתְךָ לֹא בָלְתָה מֵעָלֶיךָ וְרַגְלְךָ לֹא בָצֵקָה
זֶה אַרְבָּעִים שָׁנָה: 5 וְיָדַעְתָּ עִם־לְבָבֶךָ כִּי כַּאֲשֶׁר יְיַסֵּר
אִישׁ אֶת־בְּנוֹ יְהֹוָאדהנויאהדונהי אֱלֹהֶיךָ מְיַסְּרֶךָּ: 6 וְשָׁמַרְתָּ אֶת־
מִצְוֺת יְהֹוָאדהנויאהדונהי אֱלֹהֶיךָ לָלֶכֶת בִּדְרָכָיו וּלְיִרְאָה רי״ו, גבורה
אֹתוֹ: 7 כִּי יְהֹוָאדהנויאהדונהי אֱלֹהֶיךָ מְבִיאֲךָ אֶל־אֶרֶץ טוֹבָה אכא
אֶרֶץ נַחֲלֵי מָיִם ילי עֲיָנֹת וּתְהֹמֹת יֹצְאִים בַּבִּקְעָה וּבָהָר:

לֹא בָלְתָה - In the desert, the people's clothes didn't wear out; they lasted forever. In fact, the DNA of physical things, even our bodies, is structured to last forever. When our bodies don't last, it's because we have let in the consciousness of Satan. We need to be aware of this fact—the world wasn't meant to die. Then all we have to do is think and act accordingly.

8 אֶרֶץ חִטָּה אכא וּשְׂעֹרָה וְגֶפֶן וּתְאֵנָה וְרִמּוֹן אֶרֶץ־זֵית שֶׁמֶן
וּדְבָשׁ׃ 9 אֶרֶץ אֲשֶׁר לֹא בְמִסְכֵּנֻת תֹּאכַל־בָּהּ לֶחֶם ג"פ יהו"ה
לֹא־תֶחְסַר כֹּל ילי בָּהּ אֶרֶץ אֲשֶׁר אֲבָנֶיהָ בַרְזֶל ר"ת - בלהה רחל
זילפה לאה וּמֵהֲרָרֶיהָ תַּחְצֹב נְחֹשֶׁת׃ 10 וְאָכַלְתָּ וְשָׂבָעְתָּ וּבֵרַכְתָּ
אֶת־יְהֹוָ‍ה‍ אדני אהדונהי אֱלֹהֶיךָ עַל־הָאָרֶץ אלף למד הה יוד מם הַטֹּבָה
אֲשֶׁר נָתַן־לָךְ׃

Second Reading - Isaac - Gvurah

11 הִשָּׁמֶר לְךָ פֶּן־תִּשְׁכַּח אֶת־יְהֹוָ‍ה‍ אדני אהדונהי אֱלֹהֶיךָ לְבִלְתִּי
שְׁמֹר מִצְוֺתָיו וּמִשְׁפָּטָיו וְחֻקֹּתָיו אֲשֶׁר אָנֹכִי איע מְצַוְּךָ
הַיּוֹם נגד, מזבח, זן׃ 12 פֶּן־תֹּאכַל וְשָׂבָעְתָּ וּבָתִּים טֹבִים תִּבְנֶה
וְיָשָׁבְתָּ׃ 13 וּבְקָרְךָ וְצֹאנְךָ יִרְבְּיֻן וְכֶסֶף וְזָהָב יִרְבֶּה־לָּךְ
וְכֹל ילי אֲשֶׁר־לְךָ יִרְבֶּה׃ 14 וְרָם לְבָבֶךָ וְשָׁכַחְתָּ אֶת־

אֶרֶץ - Food is discussed here. Food is supposed to have all the nutrients we need. But food that's contaminated (e.g., with pesticides and pollutants) isn't nutritious anymore. We have to gain protection from negative food. Furthermore, if we're living to eat instead of eating to live, we're guaranteed to experience negative effects from our food. Our consciousness when we eat is what determines the nutritional value we get from food. If we have the right consciousness, the Light comes in and protects us.

פֶּן־תִּשְׁכַּח - We have to connect to the Creator when things are good for us so that we can stay with Him when things are difficult. We can't forget about the Light when we don't feel we need it. We should never reach the point of thinking there is a force supporting us other than the Creator. The worst mistake is replacing the Creator with something or someone else.

יְהֹוָהאדנייאהדונהי אֱלֹהֶיךָ הַמּוֹצִיאֲךָ מֵאֶרֶץ מִצְרַיִם מצר מִבֵּית ב״פ
ראה עֲבָדִים: 15 הַמּוֹלִיכְךָ בַּמִּדְבָּר | הַגָּדֹל להח וְהַנּוֹרָא נָחָשׁ |
שָׂרָף וְעַקְרָב וְצִמָּאוֹן אֲשֶׁר אֵין־מָיִם ילי הַמּוֹצִיא לְךָ מַיִם ילי
מִצּוּר אלף למד הה יוד מם הַחַלָּמִישׁ: 16 הַמַּאֲכִלְךָ מָן בַּמִּדְבָּר
אֲשֶׁר לֹא־יָדְעוּן אֲבֹתֶיךָ לְמַעַן עַנֹּתְךָ וּלְמַעַן נַסֹּתֶךָ
לְהֵיטִבְךָ בְּאַחֲרִיתֶךָ: 17 וְאָמַרְתָּ בִּלְבָבֶךָ כֹּחִי וְעֹצֶם יָדִי
עָשָׂה לִי אֶת־הַחַיִל ומב הַזֶּה והו: 18 וְזָכַרְתָּ אֶת־יְהֹוָהאדנייאהדונהי
אֱלֹהֶיךָ כִּי הוּא הַנֹּתֵן ושר, אבג יתץ, אהבת חנם לְךָ כֹּחַ לַעֲשׂוֹת
חָיִל ומב לְמַעַן הָקִים אֶת־בְּרִיתוֹ אֲשֶׁר־נִשְׁבַּע לַאֲבֹתֶיךָ
כַּיּוֹם נגד, מזבח, זן הַזֶּה והו: 19 וְהָיָה יהוה, יהה אִם יוהך ־שָׁכֹחַ תִּשְׁכַּח
אֶת־יְהֹוָהאדנייאהדונהי אֱלֹהֶיךָ וְהָלַכְתָּ אַחֲרֵי אֱלֹהִים מום, ילה
אֲחֵרִים וַעֲבַדְתָּם וְהִשְׁתַּחֲוִיתָ לָהֶם הַעִדֹתִי בָכֶם הַיּוֹם נגד,
מזבח, זן כִּי אָבֹד תֹּאבֵדוּן: 20 כַּגּוֹיִם אֲשֶׁר יְהֹוָהאדנייאהדונהי מַאֲבִיד
מִפְּנֵיכֶם כֵּן תֹּאבֵדוּן עֵקֶב מום־מום לֹא תִשְׁמְעוּן בְּקוֹל
יְהֹוָהאדנייאהדונהי אֱלֹהֵיכֶם ילה: 9 1 שְׁמַע יִשְׂרָאֵל אַתָּה עֹבֵר
הַיּוֹם נגד, מזבח, זן אֶת־הַיַּרְדֵּן לָבֹא לָרֶשֶׁת גּוֹיִם גְּדֹלִים וַעֲצֻמִים
מִמֶּךָּ עָרִים גְּדֹלֹת וּבְצֻרֹת בַּשָּׁמָיִם כוזו, י״פ טל: 2 עַם־גָּדוֹל להח,
מבה וָרָם בְּנֵי עֲנָקִים אֲשֶׁר אַתָּה יָדַעְתָּ וְאַתָּה שָׁמַעְתָּ מִי ילי
יִתְיַצֵּב לִפְנֵי חכמה, בינה בְּנֵי עֲנָק: 3 וְיָדַעְתָּ הַיּוֹם נגד, מזבח, זן כִּי

יְהֹוָה יאהדונהי אֱלֹהֶיךָ הוּא־הָעֹבֵר לְפָנֶיךָ אֵשׁ אֹכְלָה הוּא
יַשְׁמִידֵם וְהוּא יַכְנִיעֵם לְפָנֶיךָ וְהוֹרַשְׁתָּם וְהַאֲבַדְתָּם מַהֵר
כַּאֲשֶׁר דִּבֶּר ראה יְהֹוָה יאהדונהי לָךְ׃

Third Reading - Jacob - Tiferet

4 אַל־תֹּאמַר בִּלְבָבְךָ בַּהֲדֹף יְהֹוָה יאהדונהי אֱלֹהֶיךָ אֹתָם ׀
מִלְּפָנֶיךָ לֵאמֹר בְּצִדְקָתִי הֱבִיאַנִי יְהֹוָה יאהדונהי לָרֶשֶׁת
אֶת־הָאָרֶץ אלף למד הה יוד מם הַזֹּאת וּבְרִשְׁעַת הַגּוֹיִם הָאֵלֶּה
יְהֹוָה יאהדונהי מוֹרִישָׁם מִפָּנֶיךָ׃ 5 לֹא בְצִדְקָתְךָ וּבְיֹשֶׁר
לְבָבְךָ אַתָּה בָא לָרֶשֶׁת אֶת־אַרְצָם כִּי בְּרִשְׁעַת ׀
הַגּוֹיִם הָאֵלֶּה יְהֹוָה יאהדונהי אֱלֹהֶיךָ ילה מוֹרִישָׁם מִפָּנֶיךָ
וּלְמַעַן הָקִים אֶת־הַדָּבָר ראה אֲשֶׁר נִשְׁבַּע יְהֹוָה יאהדונהי
לַאֲבֹתֶיךָ לְאַבְרָהָם לְיִצְחָק וּלְיַעֲקֹב יאהדונהי, אידהנויה׃ 6 וְיָדַעְתָּ
כִּי לֹא בְצִדְקָתְךָ יְהֹוָה יאהדונהי אֱלֹהֶיךָ נֹתֵן ושר, אבג יתץ, אהבת חנם
לְךָ אֶת־הָאָרֶץ אלף למד הה יוד מם הַטּוֹבָה אכא הַזֹּאת לְרִשְׁתָּהּ
כִּי עַם־קְשֵׁה־עֹרֶף אָתָּה׃ 7 זְכֹר אַל־תִּשְׁכַּח אֵת אֲשֶׁר־
הִקְצַפְתָּ אֶת־יְהֹוָה יאהדונהי אֱלֹהֶיךָ בַּמִּדְבָּר לְמִן־הַיּוֹם נגד,

לַאֲבֹתֶיךָ - Whenever we read about Abraham, Isaac, and Jacob, we should be reminded of the three-column system. This system is what gives us power in our lives—knowing when to take, when to share, and when to restrict.

מזבח, זן אֲשֶׁר־יָצָאתָ | מֵאֶרֶץ מִצְרַיִם מצר עַד־בֹּאֲכֶם עַד־
הַמָּקוֹם הַזֶּה והו מַמְרִים הֱיִיתֶם עִם־יְהֹוָאדני אהדונהי: 8 וּבְחֹרֵב
הִקְצַפְתֶּם אֶת־יְהֹוָאדני אהדונהי וַיִּתְאַנַּף יְהֹוָאדני אהדונהי בָּכֶם
לְהַשְׁמִיד אֶתְכֶם: 9 בַּעֲלֹתִי הָהָרָה לָקַחַת לוּחֹת הָאֲבָנִים
לוּחֹת הַבְּרִית אֲשֶׁר־כָּרַת יְהֹוָאדני אהדונהי עִמָּכֶם וָאֵשֵׁב בָּהָר
אַרְבָּעִים יוֹם נגד, מזבח, זן וְאַרְבָּעִים לַיְלָה מלה לֶחֶם ג"פ יהו"ה לֹא
אָכַלְתִּי וּמַיִם ילי לֹא שָׁתִיתִי: 10 וַיִּתֵּן יְהֹוָאדני אהדונהי אֵלַי אֶת־
שְׁנֵי לוּחֹת הָאֲבָנִים כְּתֻבִים בְּאֶצְבַּע אֱלֹהִים מום, ילה וַעֲלֵיהֶם
כְּכָל ילי ־הַדְּבָרִים אֲשֶׁר דִּבֶּר ראה יְהֹוָאדני אהדונהי עִמָּכֶם בָּהָר
מִתּוֹךְ הָאֵשׁ בְּיוֹם נגד, מזבח, זן הַקָּהָל: 11 וַיְהִי מִקֵּץ מנק אַרְבָּעִים
יוֹם נגד, מזבח, זן וְאַרְבָּעִים לַיְלָה מלה נָתַן יְהֹוָאדני אהדונהי אֵלַי אֶת־
שְׁנֵי לֻחֹת הָאֲבָנִים לֻחוֹת הַבְּרִית: 12 וַיֹּאמֶר יְהֹוָאדני אהדונהי
אֵלַי קוּם רֵד מַהֵר מִזֶּה כִּי שִׁחֵת עַמְּךָ אֲשֶׁר הוֹצֵאתָ
מִמִּצְרָיִם מצר סָרוּ מַהֵר מִן־הַדֶּרֶךְ ב"פ יב"ק אֲשֶׁר צִוִּיתִם
עָשׂוּ לָהֶם **מַסֵּכָה**: 13 וַיֹּאמֶר יְהֹוָאדני אהדונהי אֵלַי לֵאמֹר
רָאִיתִי אֶת־הָעָם הַזֶּה והו וְהִנֵּה עַם־קְשֵׁה־עֹרֶף הוּא: 14 הֶרֶף
מִמֶּנִּי וְאַשְׁמִידֵם וְאֶמְחֶה אֶת־שְׁמָם מִתַּחַת הַשָּׁמָיִם כוזו, י"פ

מַסֵּכָה - Moses tells the people about the Golden Calf. The Golden Calf was more than a statue; it walked, talked, and was alive. Satan creates entities that seem completely real—for example, drugs that alter consciousness. Never forget Satan's power. If we know his strength, we can defeat him.

טל וְאֶעֱשֶׂה אוֹתְךָ לְגוֹי־עָצוּם וָרָב מִמֶּנּוּ׃ 15 וָאֵפֶן וָאֵרֵד מִן־
הָהָר וְהָהָר בֹּעֵר בָּאֵשׁ וּשְׁנֵי לוּחֹת הַבְּרִית עַל שְׁתֵּי יָדָי׃
16 וָאֵרֶא וְהִנֵּה חֲטָאתֶם לַיהֹוָהאדני יאהדונהי אֱלֹהֵיכֶם ילה עֲשִׂיתֶם
לָכֶם עֵגֶל מַסֵּכָה סַרְתֶּם מַהֵר מִן־הַדֶּרֶךְ אֲשֶׁר־צִוָּה
יְהֹוָהאדני יאהדונהי אֶתְכֶם׃ 17 וָאֶתְפֹּשׂ בִּשְׁנֵי הַלֻּחֹת וָאַשְׁלִכֵם
מֵעַל עלם שְׁתֵּי יָדָי וָאֲשַׁבְּרֵם לְעֵינֵיכֶם׃ 18 וָאֶתְנַפַּל לִפְנֵי חכמה,
בינה יְהֹוָהאדני יאהדונהי כָּרִאשֹׁנָה אַרְבָּעִים יוֹם נגד, מזבח, זן וְאַרְבָּעִים
לַיְלָה מלה לֶחֶם ג״פ יהו״ה לֹא אָכַלְתִּי וּמַיִם ילי לֹא שָׁתִיתִי עַל
כָּל עמם, ילי ־חַטַּאתְכֶם אֲשֶׁר חֲטָאתֶם לַעֲשׂוֹת הָרַע בְּעֵינֵי
יְהֹוָהאדני יאהדונהי לְהַכְעִיסוֹ׃ 19 כִּי יָגֹרְתִּי מִפְּנֵי חכמה, בינה הָאַף
וְהַחֵמָה אֲשֶׁר קָצַף יְהֹוָהאדני יאהדונהי עֲלֵיכֶם לְהַשְׁמִיד אֶתְכֶם
וַיִּשְׁמַע יְהֹוָהאדני יאהדונהי אֵלַי גַּם בַּפַּעַם מנק הַהִוא׃ 20 וּבְאַהֲרֹן
הִתְאַנַּף יְהֹוָהאדני יאהדונהי מְאֹד לְהַשְׁמִידוֹ וָאֶתְפַּלֵּל גַּם־בְּעַד
אַהֲרֹן בָּעֵת הַהִוא׃ 21 וְאֶת־חַטַּאתְכֶם אֲשֶׁר־עֲשִׂיתֶם אֶת־
הָעֵגֶל לָקַחְתִּי וָאֶשְׂרֹף אֹתוֹ | בָּאֵשׁ וָאֶכֹּת אֹתוֹ טָחוֹן הֵיטֵב
עַד אֲשֶׁר־דַּק לְעָפָר וָאַשְׁלִךְ אֶת־עֲפָרוֹ אֶל־הַנַּחַל הַיֹּרֵד
מִן־הָהָר׃ 22 וּבְתַבְעֵרָה וּבְמַסָּה וּבְקִבְרֹת הַתַּאֲוָה מַקְצִפִים
הֱיִיתֶם אֶת־יְהֹוָהאדני יאהדונהי׃ 23 וּבִשְׁלֹחַ יְהֹוָהאדני יאהדונהי אֶתְכֶם
מִקָּדֵשׁ בַּרְנֵעַ לֵאמֹר עֲלוּ וּרְשׁוּ אֶת־הָאָרֶץ אלף למד הה יוד מם

אֲשֶׁר נָתַתִּי לָכֶם וַתַּמְרוּ אֶת־פִּי יְהוָה יאהדונהי אֱלֹהֵיכֶם ילה
וְלֹא הֶאֱמַנְתֶּם לוֹ וְלֹא שְׁמַעְתֶּם בְּקֹלוֹ׃ 24 **מַמְרִים** הֱיִיתֶם
עִם־יְהוָה יאהדונהי מִיּוֹם נגד, מזבח, זן דַּעְתִּי אֶתְכֶם׃ 25 וָאֶתְנַפַּל
לִפְנֵי חכמה, בינה יְהוָה יאהדונהי אֵת אַרְבָּעִים הַיּוֹם נגד, מזבח, זן וְאֶת־
אַרְבָּעִים הַלַּיְלָה מלה אֲשֶׁר הִתְנַפָּלְתִּי כִּי־אָמַר יְהוָה יאהדונהי
לְהַשְׁמִיד אֶתְכֶם׃ 26 וָאֶתְפַּלֵּל אֶל־יְהוָה יאהדונהי וָאֹמַר
אֲדֹנָי יְהוִה יאהדונהי אַל־תַּשְׁחֵת עַמְּךָ וְנַחֲלָתְךָ אֲשֶׁר פָּדִיתָ
בְּגָדְלֶךָ אֲשֶׁר־הוֹצֵאתָ מִמִּצְרַיִם מצר בְּיָד חֲזָקָה׃ 27 זְכֹר
לַעֲבָדֶיךָ לְאַבְרָהָם לְיִצְחָק וּלְיַעֲקֹב יאהדונהי, אידהנויה אַל־תֵּפֶן
אֶל־קְשִׁי הָעָם הַזֶּה והו וְאֶל־רִשְׁעוֹ וְאֶל־חַטָּאתוֹ׃ 28 פֶּן־
יֹאמְרוּ הָאָרֶץ אלף למד הה יוד מם אֲשֶׁר הוֹצֵאתָנוּ מִשָּׁם מִבְּלִי
יְכֹלֶת יְהוָה יאהדונהי לַהֲבִיאָם אֶל־הָאָרֶץ אלף למד הה יוד מם
אֲשֶׁר־דִּבֶּר ראה לָהֶם וּמִשִּׂנְאָתוֹ אוֹתָם הוֹצִיאָם לַהֲמִתָם
בַּמִּדְבָּר׃ 29 וְהֵם עַמְּךָ וְנַחֲלָתְךָ אֲשֶׁר הוֹצֵאתָ בְּכֹחֲךָ
הַגָּדֹל להח וּבִזְרֹעֲךָ הַנְּטוּיָה׃

מַמְרִים - One of the reasons we're stubborn is that part of each one of us is connected to Aries. We make the same mistakes over and over, yet when we make a mistake once and learn from it, it's as though we never made a mistake at all. We're built to make mistakes. It only becomes a problem when we repeat the same mistakes. What we need to fix in life are the things we consistently fail at, and these are usually obvious. They're the things Satan will try to use on us again and again.

Fourth Reading - Moses - Netzach

10 1 בָּעֵ֨ת הַהִ֜וא אָמַ֧ר יְהֹוָ֣אדהויאהדונהי אֵלַ֗י פְּסָל־לְךָ֞ שְׁנֵֽי־
לוּחֹ֤ת אֲבָנִים֙ כָּרִ֣אשֹׁנִ֔ים וַעֲלֵ֥ה אֵלַ֖י הָהָ֑רָה וְעָשִׂ֥יתָ לְּךָ֖
אֲר֥וֹן עֵֽץ׃ 2 וְאֶכְתֹּב֙ עַל־הַלֻּחֹ֔ת אֶת־הַ֨דְּבָרִ֔ים אֲשֶׁ֥ר הָי֛וּ עַל־
הַלֻּחֹ֥ת הָרִאשֹׁנִ֖ים אֲשֶׁ֣ר שִׁבַּ֑רְתָּ וְשַׂמְתָּ֖ם בָּאָרֽוֹן׃ 3 וָאַ֤עַשׂ
אֲרוֹן֙ עֲצֵ֣י שִׁטִּ֔ים וָאֶפְסֹ֛ל שְׁנֵֽי־לֻחֹ֥ת אֲבָנִ֖ים כָּרִאשֹׁנִ֑ים וָאַ֣עַל
הָהָ֔רָה וּשְׁנֵ֥י הַלֻּחֹ֖ת בְּיָדִֽי׃ 4 וַיִּכְתֹּ֨ב עַל־הַלֻּחֹ֜ת כַּמִּכְתָּ֣ב
הָרִאשׁ֗וֹן אֵ֚ת עֲשֶׂ֣רֶת הַדְּבָרִ֔ים אֲשֶׁר֩ דִּבֶּ֨ר ראה יְהֹוָ֧אדהויאהדונהי
אֲלֵיכֶ֛ם בָּהָ֖ר מִתּ֣וֹךְ הָאֵ֑שׁ בְּי֣וֹם נגד, מזבח, זן הַקָּהָ֑ל וַיִּתְּנֵ֥ם
יְהֹוָ֖אדהויאהדונהי אֵלָֽי׃ 5 וָאֵ֗פֶן וָֽאֵרֵד֙ מִן־הָהָ֔ר וָֽאָשִׂם֙ אֶת־הַלֻּחֹ֔ת
בָּאָר֖וֹן אֲשֶׁ֣ר עָשִׂ֑יתִי וַיִּ֣הְיוּ שָׁ֔ם כַּאֲשֶׁ֥ר צִוַּ֖נִי יְהֹוָֽאדהויאהדונהי׃
6 וּבְנֵ֣י יִשְׂרָאֵ֗ל נָֽסְעוּ֙ מִבְּאֵרֹ֣ת בְּנֵי־יַעֲקָ֖ן מוֹסֵרָ֑ה שָׁ֣ם מֵ֤ת
אַהֲרֹן֙ וַיִּקָּ֣בֵר שָׁ֔ם וַיְכַהֵ֛ן אֶלְעָזָ֥ר בְּנ֖וֹ תַּחְתָּֽיו׃ 7 מִשָּׁ֥ם נָסְע֖וּ
הַגֻּדְגֹּ֑דָה וּמִן־הַגֻּדְגֹּ֣דָה יָטְבָ֔תָה אֶ֖רֶץ נַ֥חֲלֵי מָֽיִם יל׳׃ 8 בָּעֵ֣ת

כָּרִ֣אשֹׁנִ֔ים - Moses breaks the tablets of the Ten Utterances. But The Creator gives him a second set of tablets, which represents our being given a second chance. It's when we learn from our past that we become stronger: We're supposed to fail, learn, and then become strong. When a person is a *tzaddik,* a righteous person, his entire life, he's not as high as a person who's failed and then transformed. Kabbalah was revealed in the tablets. The second set was for us to discover it and to bring it to the entire world to create the Ultimate Redemption. Our purpose, yours and mine, is to spread Kabbalah and bring about the redemption in a merciful manner.

הַהִוא הִבְדִּיל יְהֹוָאדנָיאהדונהי אֶת־שֵׁבֶט הַלֵּוִי לָשֵׂאת אֶת־
אֲרוֹן בְּרִית־יְהֹוָאדנָיאהדונהי לַעֲמֹד לִפְנֵי חכמה, בינה יְהֹוָאדנָיאהדונהי
לְשָׁרְתוֹ וּלְבָרֵךְ בִּשְׁמוֹ עַד הַיּוֹם נגד, מזבח, זן הַזֶּה והו׃ 9 עַל־כֵּן
לֹא־הָיָה ההה יהה לְלֵוִי חֵלֶק וְנַחֲלָה עִם־אֶחָיו יְהֹוָאדנָיאהדונהי
הוּא נַחֲלָתוֹ כַּאֲשֶׁר דִּבֶּר ראה יְהֹוָאדנָיאהדונהי אֱלֹהֶיךָ לוֹ׃
10 וְאָנֹכִי איע עָמַדְתִּי בָהָר כַּיָּמִים נלך הָרִאשֹׁנִים אַרְבָּעִים
יוֹם נגד, מזבח, זן וְאַרְבָּעִים לַיְלָה מלה וַיִּשְׁמַע יְהֹוָאדנָיאהדונהי אֵלַי גַּם
בַּפַּעַם מנק הַהִוא לֹא־אָבָה יְהֹוָאדנָיאהדונהי הַשְׁחִיתֶךָ׃ 11 וַיֹּאמֶר
יְהֹוָאדנָיאהדונהי אֵלַי קוּם לֵךְ לְמַסַּע לִפְנֵי חכמה, בינה הָעָם וְיָבֹאוּ
וְיִירְשׁוּ אֶת־הָאָרֶץ אלף למד הה יוד מם אֲשֶׁר־נִשְׁבַּעְתִּי לַאֲבֹתָם
לָתֵת לָהֶם׃

Fifth Reading - Aaron - Hod

12 וְעַתָּה יִשְׂרָאֵל מָה יוד הא ואו הא יְהֹוָאדנָיאהדונהי אֱלֹהֶיךָ שֹׁאֵל
מֵעִמָּךְ כִּי אִם יוהך -לְיִרְאָה ר״ו, גבורה אֶת־יְהֹוָאדנָיאהדונהי
אֱלֹהֶיךָ לָלֶכֶת בְּכָל לכב -דְּרָכָיו וּלְאַהֲבָה אחד, דאגה אֹתוֹ
וְלַעֲבֹד אֶת־יְהֹוָאדנָיאהדונהי אֱלֹהֶיךָ בְּכָל לכב -לְבָבְךָ

לְיִרְאָה - We read that all the Creator asks from us is for us to fear Him. This means fearing the element of the Creator that's in everyone because we must remember that the Creator is in everyone. If we saw the Creator in others, we'd never treat anyone badly. We should always act with the awareness that the Creator is present and talk to each other as if we were talking to Him.

וּבְכָל לכב ־נַפְשֶׁךָ׃ 13 לִשְׁמֹר אֶת־מִצְוֺת יְהֹוָהאדניאהדונהי וְאֶת־

חֻקֹּתָיו אֲשֶׁר אָנֹכִי איע מְצַוְּךָ הַיּוֹם נגד, מזבח, זן לְטוֹב והו לָךְ׃

14 הֵן לַיהֹוָהאדניאהדונהי אֱלֹהֶיךָ הַשָּׁמַיִם כוזו, י"פ טל וּשְׁמֵי ילי ילי ילי

הַשָּׁמָיִם כוזו, י"פ טל הָאָרֶץ אלף למד הה יוד מם וְכָל ילי ־אֲשֶׁר־בָּהּ׃

15 רַק בַּאֲבֹתֶיךָ חָשַׁק יְהֹוָהאדניאהדונהי לְאַהֲבָה אחד, דאגה אוֹתָם

וַיִּבְחַר בְּזַרְעָם אַחֲרֵיהֶם בָּכֶם מִכָּל ילי ־הָעַמִּים כַּיּוֹם נגד,

מזבח, זן הַזֶּה והו׃ 16 וּמַלְתֶּם אֵת עָרְלַת לְבַבְכֶם וְעָרְפְּכֶם לֹא

תַקְשׁוּ עוֹד׃ 17 כִּי יְהֹוָהאדניאהדונהי אֱלֹהֵיכֶם ילה הוּא אֱלֹהֵי דמב,

ילה הָאֱלֹהִים מום, ילה וַאֲדֹנֵי הָאֲדֹנִים הָאֵל לאה הַגָּדֹל להח הַגִּבֹּר

וְהַנּוֹרָא אֲשֶׁר לֹא־יִשָּׂא פָנִים וְלֹא יִקַּח וזעם שֹׁחַד׃ 18 עֹשֶׂה

מִשְׁפַּט יָתוֹם וְאַלְמָנָה וְאֹהֵב גֵּר לָתֶת לוֹ לֶחֶם ג"פ יהו"ה

וְשִׂמְלָה׃ 19 וַאֲהַבְתֶּם אֶת־הַגֵּר כִּי־גֵרִים הֱיִיתֶם בְּאֶרֶץ

מִצְרָיִם מצר׃ 20 אֶת־יְהֹוָהאדניאהדונהי אֱלֹהֶיךָ תִּירָא אֹתוֹ תַעֲבֹד

וּבוֹ תִדְבָּק וּבִשְׁמוֹ תִּשָּׁבֵעַ׃ 21 הוּא תְהִלָּתְךָ וְהוּא אֱלֹהֶיךָ

אֲשֶׁר־עָשָׂה אִתְּךָ אֶת־הַגְּדֹלֹת וְאֶת־הַנּוֹרָאֹת הָאֵלֶּה אֲשֶׁר

רָאוּ עֵינֶיךָ׃ 22 בְּשִׁבְעִים נֶפֶשׁ יָרְדוּ אֲבֹתֶיךָ מִצְרָיְמָה וְעַתָּה

שֹׁחַד - God doesn't take bribes. Bribing God means making deals: "If I pray three times a day, will You take care of me?" But our work in this world is not about bribing through a few good actions. It's about doing what we came here to do, which is to elevate and transform.

שָׂמְךָ יְהֹוָה יאהדונהי אֱלֹהֶיךָ כְּכוֹכְבֵי הַשָּׁמַיִם כוזו, י"פ טל לָרֹב׃
11 1 וְאָהַבְתָּ ב"פ - אור, רז אֵת יְהֹוָה יאהדונהי אֱלֹהֶיךָ וְשָׁמַרְתָּ
מִשְׁמַרְתּוֹ וְחֻקֹּתָיו וּמִשְׁפָּטָיו וּמִצְוֺתָיו כָּל ילי ־הַיָּמִים נלך׃
2 וִידַעְתֶּם הַיּוֹם נגד, מזבח, זן כִּי | לֹא אֶת־בְּנֵיכֶם אֲשֶׁר לֹא־
יָדְעוּ וַאֲשֶׁר לֹא־רָאוּ אֶת־מוּסַר יְהֹוָה יאהדונהי אֱלֹהֵיכֶם ילה
אֶת־גָּדְלוֹ אֶת־יָדוֹ הַחֲזָקָה וּזְרֹעוֹ הַנְּטוּיָה׃ 3 וְאֶת־אֹתֹתָיו
וְאֶת־מַעֲשָׂיו אֲשֶׁר עָשָׂה בְּתוֹךְ מִצְרָיִם מצר לְפַרְעֹה מֶלֶךְ־
מִצְרַיִם מצר וּלְכָל יה אדני ילי ־אַרְצוֹ׃ 4 וַאֲשֶׁר עָשָׂה לְחֵיל ומב
מִצְרַיִם מצר לְסוּסָיו וּלְרִכְבּוֹ אֲשֶׁר הֵצִיף אֶת־מֵי ילי יַם ילי
־סוּף עַל־פְּנֵיהֶם בְּרָדְפָם אַחֲרֵיכֶם וַיְאַבְּדֵם יְהֹוָה יאהדונהי
עַד הַיּוֹם נגד, מזבח, זן הַזֶּה והו׃ 5 וַאֲשֶׁר עָשָׂה לָכֶם בַּמִּדְבָּר עַד־
בֹּאֲכֶם עַד־הַמָּקוֹם הַזֶּה והו׃ 6 וַאֲשֶׁר עָשָׂה לְדָתָן וְלַאֲבִירָם
בְּנֵי אֱלִיאָב בֶּן־רְאוּבֵן אֲשֶׁר פָּצְתָה הָאָרֶץ אלף למד הה יוד מם
אֶת־פִּיהָ וַתִּבְלָעֵם וְאֶת־בָּתֵּיהֶם וְאֶת־אָהֳלֵיהֶם וְאֵת כָּל ילי
־הַיְקוּם אֲשֶׁר בְּרַגְלֵיהֶם בְּקֶרֶב כָּל ילי ־יִשְׂרָאֵל׃ 7 כִּי

וִידַעְתֶּם - The Creator speaks about the people who saw all the miracles in the desert yet still didn't learn. If we saw the splitting of the sea, would we question the Creator? It's not about seeing; it's about making a decision. If we're in a questioning mode, if we're looking for faults, we'll always find what's wrong. So what are we looking for? If we're looking for what's right, that's what we'll find.

עֵינֵיכֶם הָרֹאֹת אֶת־כָּל ילי ־מַעֲשֵׂה יְהֹוָהאדניאהדונהי הַגָּדֹל להח
אֲשֶׁר עָשָׂה: 8 וּשְׁמַרְתֶּם אֶת־כָּל ילי ־הַמִּצְוָה אֲשֶׁר אָנֹכִי איע
מְצַוְּךָ הַיּוֹם נגד, מזבח, זן לְמַעַן תֶּחֶזְקוּ וּבָאתֶם וִירִשְׁתֶּם אֶת־
הָאָרֶץ אלף למד הה יוד מם אֲשֶׁר אַתֶּם עֹבְרִים שָׁמָּה יוד הא ואו הא
לְרִשְׁתָּהּ: 9 וּלְמַעַן תַּאֲרִיכוּ יָמִים נלך עַל־הָאֲדָמָה אֲשֶׁר
נִשְׁבַּע יְהֹוָהאדניאהדונהי לַאֲבֹתֵיכֶם לָתֵת לָהֶם וּלְזַרְעָם אֶרֶץ
זָבַת חָלָב וּדְבָשׁ:

Sixth Reading - Joseph - Yesod

10 כִּי הָאָרֶץ אלף למד הה יוד מם אֲשֶׁר אַתָּה בָא־שָׁמָּה יוד הא ואו הא
לְרִשְׁתָּהּ לֹא כְאֶרֶץ מִצְרַיִם מצר הִוא אֲשֶׁר יְצָאתֶם מִשָּׁם
אֲשֶׁר תִּזְרַע אֶת־זַרְעֲךָ וְהִשְׁקִיתָ בְרַגְלְךָ כְּגַן הַיָּרָק:
11 וְהָאָרֶץ אלף למד הה יוד מם אֲשֶׁר אַתֶּם עֹבְרִים שָׁמָּה יוד הא ואו
הא לְרִשְׁתָּהּ אֶרֶץ הָרִים וּבְקָעֹת לִמְטַר הַשָּׁמַיִם כוזו, י"פ טל

הָאָרֶץ - The Torah often refers to the greatness of Israel, yet throughout history, this land was a hotbed of negativity. Why? It's because the people weren't handling the energy correctly. It was too immense for them; they couldn't deal with it. If a person is in Israel, his energy has to be expressed. So if he's not spiritual, negativity will come out. It's similar to the person who's supposed to be an achiever but never makes anything of himself: The potential is there, and it has to come out somehow. And it might come out badly. We have to make sure we use our potential in a positive way. If we feel a burning inside, it's because we have something in us—a surrounding Light, *or mekif* – that has to be expressed.

תִּשְׁתֶּה־מָּיִם יל״י: 12 אֶרֶץ אֲשֶׁר־יְהֹוָהאדניאהדונהי אֱלֹהֶיךָ דֹּרֵשׁ
אֹתָהּ תָּמִיד נתה, קס״א - קנ״א - קמ״ג עֵינֵי יְהֹוָהאדניאהדונהי אֱלֹהֶיךָ ילה בָּהּ
מֵרֵשִׁית הַשָּׁנָה וְעַד אַחֲרִית שָׁנָה: 13 **וְהָיָה** יהוה, יהה אִם יוהך
־שָׁמֹעַ תִּשְׁמְעוּ אֶל־מִצְוֹתַי אֲשֶׁר אָנֹכִי איע מְצַוֶּה אֶתְכֶם
הַיּוֹם נגד, מזבח, זן לְאַהֲבָה אחד, דאגה אֶת־יְהֹוָהאדניאהדונהי אֱלֹהֵיכֶם ילה
וּלְעָבְדוֹ בְּכָל לכב ־לְבַבְכֶם וּבְכָל לכב ־נַפְשְׁכֶם: 14 וְנָתַתִּי
מְטַר־אַרְצְכֶם בְּעִתּוֹ יוֹרֶה וּמַלְקוֹשׁ וְאָסַפְתָּ דְגָנֶךָ וְתִירֹשְׁךָ
וְיִצְהָרֶךָ: 15 וְנָתַתִּי עֵשֶׂב בְּשָׂדְךָ לִבְהֶמְתֶּךָ וְאָכַלְתָּ וְשָׂבָעְתָּ:
16 הִשָּׁמְרוּ לָכֶם פֶּן יִפְתֶּה לְבַבְכֶם וְסַרְתֶּם וַעֲבַדְתֶּם
אֱלֹהִים מום, ילה אֲחֵרִים וְהִשְׁתַּחֲוִיתֶם לָהֶם: 17 וְחָרָה אַף־
יְהֹוָהאדניאהדונהי בָּכֶם וְעָצַר אֶת־הַשָּׁמַיִם כוזו, י״פ טל וְלֹא־יִהְיֶה ייי
מָטָר וְהָאֲדָמָה לֹא תִתֵּן ב״פ כהת אֶת־יְבוּלָהּ וַאֲבַדְתֶּם מְהֵרָה
מֵעַל עלם הָאָרֶץ אלף למד הה יוד מם הַטֹּבָה אֲשֶׁר יְהֹוָהאדניאהדונהי
נֹתֵן ושר, אבג יתץ, אהבת חנם לָכֶם: 18 **וְשַׂמְתֶּם** אֶת־דְּבָרַי אֵלֶּה

וְהָיָה - The second part of the *Shema* is in this portion. It has 72 words, corresponding to The 72 Names of God. Through these Names, we can achieve the power of mind over matter and thus control anything that comes to us in our lives.

וְשַׂמְתֶּם - The third part of the *Shema* has 50 words, connecting us to 50 gates of *Binah*. These words also correspond to the 50 gates of negativity, which we climb to enter the gates of *Binah*.

עַל־לְבַבְכֶם וְעַל־נַפְשְׁכֶם וּקְשַׁרְתֶּם אֹתָם לְאוֹת עַל־
יֶדְכֶם וְהָיוּ לְטוֹטָפֹת בֵּין עֵינֵיכֶם׃ 19 וְלִמַּדְתֶּם אֹתָם
אֶת־בְּנֵיכֶם לְדַבֵּר ראה בָּם מב בְּשִׁבְתְּךָ בְּבֵיתֶךָ וּבְלֶכְתְּךָ
בַדֶּרֶךְ וּבְשָׁכְבְּךָ וּבְקוּמֶךָ׃ 20 וּכְתַבְתָּם עַל־מְזוּזוֹת בֵּיתֶךָ
וּבִשְׁעָרֶיךָ׃ 21 לְמַעַן יִרְבּוּ יְמֵיכֶם וִימֵי בְנֵיכֶם עַל הָאֲדָמָה
אֲשֶׁר נִשְׁבַּע יְהֹוָאדנָי אהדונהי לַאֲבֹתֵיכֶם לָתֵת לָהֶם כִּימֵי
הַשָּׁמַיִם כוזו, י"פ טל עַל־הָאָרֶץ אלף למד הה יוד מם׃

Seventh Reading - David - Malchut
Maftir

22 כִּי אִם יוהך ־שָׁמֹר תִּשְׁמְרוּן אֶת־כָּל ילי ־הַמִּצְוָה הַזֹּאת
אֲשֶׁר אָנֹכִי איע מְצַוֶּה אֶתְכֶם לַעֲשֹׂתָהּ לְאַהֲבָה אחד, דאגה
אֶת־יְהֹוָאדנָי אהדונהי אֱלֹהֵיכֶם ילה לָלֶכֶת בְּכָל לכב ־דְּרָכָיו
וּלְדָבְקָה־בוֹ׃ 23 וְהוֹרִישׁ יְהֹוָאדנָי אהדונהי אֶת־כָּל ילי ־הַגּוֹיִם
הָאֵלֶּה מִלִּפְנֵיכֶם וִירִשְׁתֶּם גּוֹיִם גְּדֹלִים וַעֲצֻמִים מִכֶּם׃
24 כָּל ילי ־הַמָּקוֹם אֲשֶׁר תִּדְרֹךְ כַּף־רַגְלְכֶם בּוֹ לָכֶם יִהְיֶה ייי
מִן־הַמִּדְבָּר וְהַלְּבָנוֹן מִן־הַנָּהָר נְהַר־פְּרָת וְעַד הַיָּם ילי
הָאַחֲרוֹן יִהְיֶה ייי גְּבֻלְכֶם׃ 25 לֹא־יִתְיַצֵּב אִישׁ בִּפְנֵיכֶם

שָׁמֹר - The word *shamor* is used, meaning "keep in a safe place." Each and every lesson we have, we must try to keep with us. The easiest way to keep something is to share it with others. If we learn something today and share it, we will remember it and be able to access it later.

פַּחְדְּכֶם וּמוֹרַאֲכֶם יִתֵּן | יְהֹוָהאדנייאהדונהי אֱלֹהֵיכֶם ילה עַל־
פְּנֵי חכמה, בינה כָל ילי ־הָאָרֶץ אלף למד הה יוד מם אֲשֶׁר תִּדְרְכוּ־בָהּ
כַּאֲשֶׁר דִּבֶּר ראה לָכֶם׃

Haftarah of Ekev

The Creator will change the desert from a wasteland into the Garden of Eden. By opening our hearts, we can create something from nothing. We have the power to turn the worst into the best. Our best times can be challenging moments when we become strong.

Isaiah 49 — ישעיהו פרק 49

14 וַתֹּאמֶר צִיּוֹן יוסף עֲזָבַנִי יְהֹוָאדנהי אהדונהי וַאדֹנָי שְׁכֵחָנִי׃
15 הֲתִשְׁכַּח אִשָּׁה עוּלָהּ מֵרַחֵם אברהם, רמ״ח בֶּן־בִּטְנָהּ גַּם־
אֵלֶּה תִשְׁכַּחְנָה וְאָנֹכִי איע לֹא אֶשְׁכָּחֵךְ׃ 16 הֵן עַל־כַּפַּיִם אלף
הה יוד הה, אדני + אלהים חַקֹּתִיךְ חוֹמֹתַיִךְ נֶגְדִּי תָּמִיד נתה, קס״א + קנ״א +
קמ״ג׃ 17 מִהֲרוּ בָּנָיִךְ מְהָרְסַיִךְ וּמַחֲרִבַיִךְ מִמֵּךְ יֵצֵאוּ׃ 18 שְׂאִי־
סָבִיב עֵינַיִךְ קס״א, אלף הי יוד הי וּרְאִי כֻּלָּם נִקְבְּצוּ בָאוּ־לָךְ חַי־
אָנִי אני נְאֻם־יְהֹוָאדנהי אהדונהי כִּי כֻלָּם כַּעֲדִי תִלְבָּשִׁי וּתְקַשְּׁרִים
כַּכַּלָּה מלה׃ 19 כִּי חָרְבֹתַיִךְ וְשֹׁמְמֹתַיִךְ וְאֶרֶץ הֲרִסֻתֵךְ כִּי
עַתָּה תֵּצְרִי מִיּוֹשֵׁב וְרָחֲקוּ מְבַלְּעָיִךְ׃ 20 עוֹד יֹאמְרוּ בְאָזְנַיִךְ
בְּנֵי שִׁכֻּלָיִךְ צַר־לִי הַמָּקוֹם גְּשָׁה־לִּי וְאֵשֵׁבָה׃ 21 וְאָמַרְתְּ
בִּלְבָבֵךְ מִי ילי יָלַד־לִי אֶת־אֵלֶּה וַאֲנִי אני שְׁכוּלָה וְגַלְמוּדָה
גֹּלָה | וְסוּרָה וְאֵלֶּה מִי ילי גִדֵּל הֵן אֲנִי אני נִשְׁאַרְתִּי לְבַדִּי
אֵלֶּה אֵיפֹה הֵם׃ 22 כֹּה היי ־אָמַר אֲדֹנָי יְהֹוָאדנהי אהדונהי הִנֵּה
אֶשָּׂא אֶל־גּוֹיִם יָדִי וְאֶל־עַמִּים אָרִים נִסִּי וְהֵבִיאוּ בָנַיִךְ
בְּחֹצֶן וּבְנֹתַיִךְ עַל־כָּתֵף תִּנָּשֶׂאנָה׃ 23 וְהָיוּ מְלָכִים אֹמְנַיִךְ

וְשָׂרוֹתֵיהֶם מֵינִיקֹתַיִךְ אַפַּיִם אֶרֶץ יִשְׁתַּחֲווּ לָךְ וַעֲפַר
רַגְלַיִךְ יְלַחֵכוּ וְיָדַעַתְּ כִּי־אֲנִי אני יְהֹוָהאדני יאהדונהי אֲשֶׁר לֹא־
יֵבֹשׁוּ קֹוָי׃ 24 הֲיֻקַּח וזעם מִגִּבּוֹר מַלְקוֹחַ וְאִם יוהך ־שְׁבִי צַדִּיק
יִמָּלֵט׃ 25 כִּי־כֹה היי | אָמַר יְהֹוָהאדני יאהדונהי גַּם־שְׁבִי גִבּוֹר
יֻקָּח וזעם וּמַלְקוֹחַ עָרִיץ יִמָּלֵט וְאֶת־יְרִיבֵךְ אָנֹכִי איע אָרִיב
וְאֶת־בָּנַיִךְ אָנֹכִי איע אוֹשִׁיעַ׃ 26 וְהַאֲכַלְתִּי אֶת־מוֹנַיִךְ אֶת־
בְּשָׂרָם וְכֶעָסִיס דָּמָם יִשְׁכָּרוּן וְיָדְעוּ כָל ילי ־בָּשָׂר כִּי אֲנִי אני
יְהֹוָהאדני יאהדונהי מוֹשִׁיעֵךְ וְגֹאֲלֵךְ אֲבִיר הרוז יַעֲקֹב יאהדונהי, אידהנויה׃
50 1 כֹּה היי | אָמַר יְהֹוָהאדני יאהדונהי אֵי זֶה סֵפֶר כְּרִיתוּת אִמְּכֶם
אֲשֶׁר שִׁלַּחְתִּיהָ אוֹ מִי ילי מִנּוֹשַׁי אֲשֶׁר־מָכַרְתִּי אֶתְכֶם לוֹ הֵן
בַּעֲוֹנֹתֵיכֶם נִמְכַּרְתֶּם וּבְפִשְׁעֵיכֶם שֻׁלְּחָה אִמְּכֶם׃ 2 מַדּוּעַ
בָּאתִי וְאֵין אִישׁ קָרָאתִי וְאֵין עוֹנֶה הֲקָצוֹר קָצְרָה יָדִי
מִפְּדוּת וְאִם יוהך ־אֵין־בִּי כֹחַ לְהַצִּיל הֵן בְּגַעֲרָתִי אַחֲרִיב
יָם ילי אָשִׂים נְהָרוֹת מִדְבָּר ראה תִּבְאַשׁ דְּגָתָם מֵאֵין מַיִם ילי
וְתָמֹת בַּצָּמָא׃ 3 אַלְבִּישׁ שָׁמַיִם כוזו, י״פ טל קַדְרוּת וְשַׂק אָשִׂים
כְּסוּתָם׃ 4 אֲדֹנָי יְהֹוִהאדני יאהדונהי נָתַן לִי לְשׁוֹן לִמּוּדִים מאה
לָדַעַת לָעוּת אֶת־יָעֵף דָּבָר ראה יָעִיר | בַּבֹּקֶר בַּבֹּקֶר יָעִיר
לִי אֹזֶן לִשְׁמֹעַ כַּלִּמּוּדִים מאה׃ 5 אֲדֹנָי יְהֹוִהאדני יאהדונהי פָּתַח־
לִי אֹזֶן וְאָנֹכִי איע לֹא מָרִיתִי אָחוֹר לֹא נְסוּגֹתִי׃ 6 גֵּוִי נָתַתִּי

לְמַכִּים וּלְחָיַי לְמֹרְטִים פָּנַי חכמה, בינה לֹא הִסְתַּרְתִּי מִכְּלִמּוֹת
וָרֹק׃ 7 וַאדֹנָי יֱהֹוִהאדני יאהדונהי יַעֲזָר־לִי עַל־כֵּן לֹא נִכְלָמְתִּי
עַל־כֵּן שַׂמְתִּי פָנַי חכמה, בינה כַּחַלָּמִישׁ וָאֵדַע כִּי־לֹא אֵבוֹשׁ׃
8 קָרוֹב מַצְדִּיקִי מִי ילי־יָרִיב אִתִּי נַעַמְדָה יָּחַד מִי ילי־בַעַל
מִשְׁפָּטִי יִגַּשׁ אֵלָי׃ 9 הֵן אֲדֹנָי יֱהֹוִהאדני יאהדונהי יַעֲזָר־לִי מִי ילי
־הוּא יַרְשִׁיעֵנִי הֵן כֻּלָּם כַּבֶּגֶד יִבְלוּ עָשׁ יֹאכְלֵם׃ 10 מִי ילי
בָכֶם יְרֵא יְהֹוָהאדני יאהדונהי שֹׁמֵעַ בְּקוֹל עַבְדּוֹ אֲשֶׁר | הָלַךְ
חֲשֵׁכִים וְאֵין נֹגַהּ מוזי לוֹ יִבְטַח בְּשֵׁם יְהֹוָהאדני יאהדונהי וְיִשָּׁעֵן
בֵּאלֹהָיו ילה׃ 11 הֵן כֻּלְּכֶם קֹדְחֵי אֵשׁ מְאַזְּרֵי זִיקוֹת לְכוּ |
בְּאוּר רז, אין סוף אֶשְׁכֶם וּבְזִיקוֹת בִּעַרְתֶּם מִיָּדִי הָיְתָה־זֹּאת
לָכֶם לְמַעֲצֵבָה תִּשְׁכָּבוּן׃ 51 1 שִׁמְעוּ אֵלַי רֹדְפֵי צֶדֶק
מְבַקְשֵׁי יְהֹוָהאדני יאהדונהי הַבִּיטוּ אֶל־צוּר אלף למד הה יוד מם חֻצַּבְתֶּם
וְאֶל־מַקֶּבֶת בּוֹר נֻקַּרְתֶּם׃ 2 הַבִּיטוּ אֶל־אַבְרָהָם אֲבִיכֶם
וְאֶל־שָׂרָה תְּחוֹלֶלְכֶם כִּי־אֶחָד אהבה, דאגה קְרָאתִיו וַאֲבָרְכֵהוּ
וְאַרְבֵּהוּ׃ 3 כִּי־נִחַם יְהֹוָהאדני יאהדונהי צִיּוֹן יוסף נִחַם כָּל ילי
־חָרְבֹתֶיהָ וַיָּשֶׂם מִדְבָּרָהּ כְּעֵדֶן וְעַרְבָתָהּ כְּגַן־יְהֹוָהאדני יאהדונהי
שָׂשׂוֹן וְשִׂמְחָה יִמָּצֵא בָהּ תּוֹדָה וְקוֹל זִמְרָה׃

Lesson of Re'eh

Seeing the Truth

This portion begins: "See, what I am giving before you today...." We might ask why the Creator has to tell us to see? Yet the real question is not *why* the Creator tells us to see, but *what* He tells us to see. At every moment, our eyes take in the physical world around us, yet we don't see the deeper truth.

Of course, we don't even really see the physical world as it is. For example, our eyes invert an image, which our brains have to reverse again. This is the reality of vision although it takes place without our conscious awareness. Why did the Creator make eyes that do not see things as they really are? It's to teach us that what we think we're seeing in other people is really a mirror of ourselves. Only the righteous see without being fooled; they see the truth because they don't see themselves in others.

In what way are the righteous different from the rest of us? Especially this week, when it's the Rav's birthday, we need to consider the qualities of a righteous person. Recognizing a true prophet and the topic of sight are both closely connected to this portion

At the outset, it is important for us to know that we have the merit of having a truly righteous person amongst us and that when we have a problem, it can be solved by asking the Rav. Furthermore, by truly understanding what we are capable of doing, we can certainly be more spiritual and reveal more Light—and perhaps become truly righteous people ourselves.

Rav Ashlag said that anyone can be Rav Shimon Bar Yochai and that anyone can be Moses. But this transformation must begin with a real desire to be like these righteous individuals. Then, the key spiritual tools need to be available. Desire, without the tools of how or what to do, is not enough.

Prayer is one of these key tools. Why is it that when a righteous person prays, he is answered from above? To understand this, we must first remember that prayers are carried into the Upper Worlds by angels. Most people don't realize that angels have free will. But there are even angels that sinned—Azza and Azazel, for example, and the snake that ate from the Tree of Knowledge before Adam did: If they didn't have free will and a desire to receive for the self alone, how could they have sinned?

Angels don't sin as often as the rest of us only because they are so close to the Creator and they see what the Light really is. If we were that close to the Light, we wouldn't want to sin either. We wouldn't want to lose the Light just for the physical enjoyments of this world. But we are so far from the Light that we can't recognize our own best interests. To us, it seems as if the desire to receive for the self alone is good because that's what we're connected to.

This brings us back to the nature of a righteous person. Because of his closeness to the Light, he is like an angel. He has freedom of choice, but he always chooses the good because, like an angel, he understands what the true good is. Because of this, a righteous person doesn't need an angel to elevate his prayers: His prayers go "straight up." He has a negative side but never acts on it. For this reason, righteous people's prayers are always answered, while ours are answered only sometimes.

Many of us believe that the most important person in the world is, without question, "me." So when we pray, the Creator tells us, "If you're so important, why are you praying to Me? What do you need Me for? If you are so powerful, then you can answer your prayers yourself."

It is written in the *Midrash* of the portion of Toldot that the Creator listened when Isaac prayed for his wife. Isaac prayed because he felt Rebecca's pain at being unable to bear a child. A righteous person truly feels another's pain. So the Creator says, "If he feels the pain, then I, too, must feel the pain."

Last week, we read a story about Rav Elimelech and the student who told him that his prayers were not being answered. Rav Elimelech replied that the prayers were indeed being answered but that the answer was no. The important thing, however, is to keep asking. For a righteous person, there is no such thing as "no."

There is a story that will help us to better understand the nature of truly righteous people. One Friday, the Seer of Lublin went to the synagogue. Meanwhile at his home, his wife was looking all over the house for money to buy Shabbat candles, but there was none to be found. So she went outside and waited for someone who might give her a couple of coins to buy candles. And then (as occurs in every kabbalistic story), one of the rich people of the town happened to pass by on his way to his weekly meeting with his mistress.

He recognized the wife of the holy Seer of Lublin and saw that she was crying. When he got off his horse and asked what the matter was, she told him that she didn't have any money to buy candles for Shabbat. So he gave her money, and she blessed him with the Light of Shabbat. Then off he went to meet his girlfriend.

While all this was happening, the holy Seer was praying. He prayed for three hours, and his students couldn't understand what was taking him so long. When he finished, his students asked him what had happened. He told them that his soul had elevated, and he saw that the forces of good and evil were at war. He was told, "We are using you to win the battle with darkness! But your wife blessed that wicked man with the Light of Shabbat! How could she do such a thing?" Then the Seer told his students that he had replied to the angels, "That man is wicked only because he never tasted the Light of Shabbat. Give him a chance! Let him taste the Light of Shabbat."

When the Seer left the synagogue, he encountered the rich man who had given the money to his wife for candles. The rich man said, "Please, I would like to spend one Shabbat with you because for the first time in my life, I would like to feel what Shabbat really is. Just now, I'm feeling such a presence of Light and I don't know where it's coming from. The only explanation I can think of is that it's Shabbat and I need to be next to my Shabbat candles." The Seer replied, "Please join us then." And the rich man became the most devoted student of the Seer of Lublin and later became the Seer's successor.

What does this tale teach us? It teaches us that if we can just once give a person the opportunity to touch the Light—even a little bit—he will want more. How many people do we have in the Centre who only a few years ago were considered "wicked" in the eyes of others? Yet the Centre and the Rav brought them to where they are today. Now they come to listen to the Torah reading and to connect to the Light. This transformation can happen only when we bring the Light of the Creator to those who have never known it.

Synopsis of Re'eh

This is the only portion where one of The 72 Names is the title of the portion. This gives us an extra connection to the power of miracles and wonders. In addition, the number of verses in this portion is 126, which is the numerical value of *pliyah*, or "wonderment," another indication that this week is all about the power of going beyond physical reality.

First Reading - Abraham - Chesed

26 רְאֵה ראה אָנֹכִי איע נֹתֵן ושר, אבג יתץ, אהבת חינם לִפְנֵיכֶם הַיּוֹם נגד,
מזבח, זן בְּרָכָה וּקְלָלָה: 27 אֶת־הַבְּרָכָה אֲשֶׁר תִּשְׁמְעוּ אֶל־
מִצְוֹת יְהֹוָאֲדֹנָיאהדונהי אֱלֹהֵיכֶם ילה אֲשֶׁר אָנֹכִי איע מְצַוֶּה אֶתְכֶם
הַיּוֹם נגד, מזבח, זן: 28 וְהַקְּלָלָה אִם יוהך ־לֹא תִשְׁמְעוּ אֶל־מִצְוֹת
יְהֹוָאֲדֹנָיאהדונהי אֱלֹהֵיכֶם ילה וְסַרְתֶּם מִן־הַדֶּרֶךְ אֲשֶׁר אָנֹכִי איע
מְצַוֶּה אֶתְכֶם הַיּוֹם נגד, מזבח, זן לָלֶכֶת אַחֲרֵי אֱלֹהִים מום, ילה
אֲחֵרִים אֲשֶׁר לֹא־יְדַעְתֶּם: 29 וְהָיָה יהוה, יהה כִּי יְבִיאֲךָ
יְהֹוָאֲדֹנָיאהדונהי אֱלֹהֶיךָ אֶל־הָאָרֶץ אלף למד הה יוד מם אֲשֶׁר־אַתָּה
בָא־שָׁמָּה יוד הא ואו הא לְרִשְׁתָּהּ וְנָתַתָּה אֶת־הַבְּרָכָה עַל־הַר
גְּרִזִים וְאֶת־הַקְּלָלָה עַל־הַר עֵיבָל: 30 הֲלֹא־הֵמָּה יוד הא ואו הא
בְּעֵבֶר הַיַּרְדֵּן אַחֲרֵי דֶּרֶךְ מְבוֹא הַשֶּׁמֶשׁ בְּאֶרֶץ הַכְּנַעֲנִי
הַיֹּשֵׁב בָּעֲרָבָה זרע מוּל הַגִּלְגָּל אֵצֶל אֵלוֹנֵי מֹרֶה: 31 כִּי אַתֶּם

אָנֹכִי - The word *anochi* gives us the power to see the difference between the good and the bad in our lives…and to make the correct choice.

וְהָיָה - There were two mountains—one for curses and one for blessings—but both were next to the city of Shechem. We know that Joseph is buried in Shechem, so therein lies a tremendous amount of Light. But from the moment that Jacob's sons killed everyone in town, it has been the center of negativity in the Middle East—the epitome of conflict throughout history. In all areas of life, we see the struggle between good and evil. To win, we must be able to recognize which is which and to acknowledge that there is a constant war between the two.

עֹבְרִים אֶת־הַיַּרְדֵּן לָבֹא לָרֶשֶׁת אֶת־הָאָרֶץ אלף למד הה יוד מם
אֲשֶׁר־יְהֹוָהאדניאהדונהי אֱלֹהֵיכֶם ילה נֹתֵן ושר, אבג יתץ, אהבת חיים לָכֶם
וִירִשְׁתֶּם אֹתָהּ וִישַׁבְתֶּם־בָּהּ׃ 32 וּשְׁמַרְתֶּם לַעֲשׂוֹת אֵת כָּל ילי
־הַחֻקִּים וְאֶת־הַמִּשְׁפָּטִים אֲשֶׁר אָנֹכִי איע נֹתֵן ושר, אבג יתץ, אהבת
חיים לִפְנֵיכֶם הַיּוֹם נגד, מזבח, זן׃ 12 1 אֵלֶּה הַחֻקִּים וְהַמִּשְׁפָּטִים
אֲשֶׁר תִּשְׁמְרוּן לַעֲשׂוֹת בָּאָרֶץ אֲשֶׁר נָתַן יְהֹוָהאדניאהדונהי
אֱלֹהֵי דמב, ילה אֲבֹתֶיךָ לְךָ לְרִשְׁתָּהּ כָּל ילי ־הַיָּמִים נלך אֲשֶׁר־
אַתֶּם חַיִּים בינה עַל־הָאֲדָמָה׃ 2 אַבֵּד תְּאַבְּדוּן אֶת־כָּל ילי
־הַמְּקֹמוֹת אֲשֶׁר עָבְדוּ־שָׁם הַגּוֹיִם אֲשֶׁר אַתֶּם יֹרְשִׁים
אֹתָם אֶת־אֱלֹהֵיהֶם ילה עַל־הֶהָרִים הָרָמִים וְעַל־הַגְּבָעוֹת
וְתַחַת כָּל ילי ־עֵץ רַעֲנָן׃ 3 וְנִתַּצְתֶּם אֶת־מִזְבְּחֹתָם וְשִׁבַּרְתֶּם
אֶת־מַצֵּבֹתָם וַאֲשֵׁרֵיהֶם תִּשְׂרְפוּן בָּאֵשׁ וּפְסִילֵי אֱלֹהֵיהֶם ילה
תְּגַדֵּעוּן וְאִבַּדְתֶּם אֶת־שְׁמָם מִן־הַמָּקוֹם הַהוּא׃ 4 לֹא־

הָאָרֶץ - This verse discusses the land of Israel and the sanctity of the land—the power that resides in the land. There has always been conflict in the land of Israel, whether with the Greeks, the Romans, the Turks, or the British. The source of this conflict is the fact that religiosity has essentially succeeded in eliminating spirituality. When spirituality returns to religion, we will find it so much easier to treat others with kindness. Then lasting peace will come. Israel is a mirror for what is happening in the world. Throughout the world and on a daily basis, we are lacking in human dignity. To remedy this situation, we must focus on spreading Kabbalah.

תַעֲשׂוּן כֵּן לַיהֹוָאדני יאהדונהי אֱלֹהֵיכֶם ילה: 5 כִּי אִם יוהך אֶל־
הַמָּקוֹם אֲשֶׁר־יִבְחַר יְהֹוָאדני יאהדונהי אֱלֹהֵיכֶם ילה מִכָּל ילי
־שִׁבְטֵיכֶם לָשׂוּם אֶת־שְׁמוֹ שָׁם לְשִׁכְנוֹ תִדְרְשׁוּ וּבָאתָ
שָׁמָּה יוד הא ואו הא: 6 וַהֲבֵאתֶם שָׁמָּה יוד הא ואו הא עֹלֹתֵיכֶם
וְזִבְחֵיכֶם וְאֵת מַעְשְׂרֹתֵיכֶם וְאֵת תְּרוּמַת יֶדְכֶם וְנִדְרֵיכֶם
וְנִדְבֹתֵיכֶם וּבְכֹרֹת בְּקַרְכֶם וְצֹאנְכֶם: 7 וַאֲכַלְתֶּם־שָׁם
לִפְנֵי חכמה, בינה יְהֹוָאדני יאהדונהי אֱלֹהֵיכֶם ילה וּשְׂמַחְתֶּם בְּכֹל לכב
מִשְׁלַח יֶדְכֶם אַתֶּם וּבָתֵּיכֶם אֲשֶׁר בֵּרַכְךָ יְהֹוָאדני יאהדונהי
אֱלֹהֶיךָ: 8 לֹא תַעֲשׂוּן כְּכֹל ילי אֲשֶׁר אֲנַחְנוּ עֹשִׂים פֹּה מילה
הַיּוֹם נגד, מזבח, זן אִישׁ כָּל ילי ־הַיָּשָׁר בְּעֵינָיו: 9 כִּי לֹא־בָאתֶם
עַד־עָתָּה אֶל־הַמְּנוּחָה וְאֶל־הַנַּחֲלָה אֲשֶׁר־יְהֹוָאדני יאהדונהי
אֱלֹהֶיךָ נֹתֵן ושר, אבג יתץ, אהבת חינם לָךְ: 10 וַעֲבַרְתֶּם אֶת־הַיַּרְדֵּן
וִישַׁבְתֶּם בָּאָרֶץ אֲשֶׁר־יְהֹוָאדני יאהדונהי אֱלֹהֵיכֶם ילה מַנְחִיל
אֶתְכֶם וְהֵנִיחַ לָכֶם מִכָּל ילי ־אֹיְבֵיכֶם מִסָּבִיב וִישַׁבְתֶּם־
בֶּטַח:

הַמָּקוֹם - This describes the place in which the Temple would stand and the connections we are supposed to make there. Different places in this world were chosen as sources of spiritual energy. Our job is not to travel to these places and be spiritual there, but to be spiritual at all times, drawing energy from those places when we need it. The real spiritual fight is not at the sources of energy but wherever we are on a daily basis as we wage war with Satan.

Second Reading - Isaac - Gvurah

11 וְהָיָה יהוה, יהה הַמָּקוֹם אֲשֶׁר־יִבְחַר יְהֹוָאדניאהדונהי
אֱלֹהֵיכֶם ילה בּוֹ לְשַׁכֵּן שְׁמוֹ מהש שָׁם שָׁמָּה יוד הא ואו הא תָבִיאוּ
אֵת כָּל ילי ־אֲשֶׁר אָנֹכִי איע מְצַוֶּה אֶתְכֶם עוֹלֹתֵיכֶם וְזִבְחֵיכֶם
מַעְשְׂרֹתֵיכֶם וּתְרֻמַת יֶדְכֶם וְכֹל ילי מִבְחַר נִדְרֵיכֶם אֲשֶׁר
תִּדְּרוּ לַיהֹוָאדניאהדונהי: 12 וּשְׂמַחְתֶּם לִפְנֵי חכמה, בינה יְהֹוָאדניאהדונהי
אֱלֹהֵיכֶם ילה אַתֶּם וּבְנֵיכֶם וּבְנֹתֵיכֶם וְעַבְדֵיכֶם וְאַמְהֹתֵיכֶם
וְהַלֵּוִי אֲשֶׁר בְּשַׁעֲרֵיכֶם כִּי אֵין לוֹ חֵלֶק וְנַחֲלָה אִתְּכֶם:
13 הִשָּׁמֶר לְךָ פֶּן־תַּעֲלֶה עֹלֹתֶיךָ בְּכָל לכב ־מָקוֹם אֲשֶׁר
תִּרְאֶה: 14 כִּי אִם יוהך ־בַּמָּקוֹם אֲשֶׁר־יִבְחַר יְהֹוָאדניאהדונהי
בְּאַחַד אהבה, דאגה שְׁבָטֶיךָ שָׁם תַּעֲלֶה עֹלֹתֶיךָ וְשָׁם תַּעֲשֶׂה
כֹּל ילי אֲשֶׁר אָנֹכִי איע מְצַוֶּךָּ: 15 רַק בְּכָל לכב ־אַוַּת נַפְשְׁךָ
תִּזְבַּח | וְאָכַלְתָּ בָשָׂר כְּבִרְכַּת יְהֹוָאדניאהדונהי אֱלֹהֶיךָ אֲשֶׁר
נָתַן־לְךָ בְּכָל לכב ־שְׁעָרֶיךָ הַטָּמֵא וְהַטָּהוֹר י״פ אכא יֹאכְלֶנּוּ
כַּצְּבִי וְכָאַיָּל: 16 רַק הַדָּם לֹא תֹאכֵלוּ עַל־הָאָרֶץ אלף

הַדָּם - The Torah speaks of not consuming the blood of animals because the soul of the animal resides primarily in the blood. If we drink the blood, we connect only to the physical part of the animal. We should never perform actions merely of a physical nature. Our deeper purpose is to gain spiritual nutrition. With animals, we don't want to lower ourselves to their level. The irony is that we act like animals all too often. In fact, we do to other human beings what animals would not even do to one another. By not drinking

למד הה יוד מם תִּשְׁפְּכֶנּוּ כַּמָּיִם: 17 לֹא־תוּכַל לֶאֱכֹל בִּשְׁעָרֶיךָ
מַעְשַׂר דְּגָנְךָ וְתִירֹשְׁךָ וְיִצְהָרֶךָ וּבְכֹרֹת בְּקָרְךָ וְצֹאנֶךָ
וְכָל ילי ־נְדָרֶיךָ אֲשֶׁר תִּדֹּר וְנִדְבֹתֶיךָ וּתְרוּמַת יָדֶךָ: 18 כִּי
אִם יוהך ־לִפְנֵי וחכמה, בינה יְהֹוָאדנָיאהדונהי אֱלֹהֶיךָ תֹּאכְלֶנּוּ בַּמָּקוֹם
אֲשֶׁר יִבְחַר יְהֹוָאדנָיאהדונהי אֱלֹהֶיךָ ילה בּוֹ אַתָּה וּבִנְךָ וּבִתֶּךָ
וְעַבְדְּךָ פוי וַאֲמָתֶךָ וְהַלֵּוִי אֲשֶׁר בִּשְׁעָרֶיךָ וְשָׂמַחְתָּ לִפְנֵי וחכמה,
בינה יְהֹוָאדנָיאהדונהי אֱלֹהֶיךָ בְּכֹל לכב מִשְׁלַח יָדֶךָ: 19 הִשָּׁמֶר
לְךָ פֶּן־תַּעֲזֹב אֶת־הַלֵּוִי כָּל ילי ־יָמֶיךָ עַל־אַדְמָתֶךָ: 20 כִּי־
יַרְחִיב יְהֹוָאדנָיאהדונהי אֱלֹהֶיךָ אֶת־גְּבֻלְךָ כַּאֲשֶׁר דִּבֶּר ראה
־לָךְ וְאָמַרְתָּ אֹכְלָה בָשָׂר כִּי־תְאַוֶּה נַפְשְׁךָ לֶאֱכֹל בָּשָׂר
בְּכָל לכב ־אַוַּת נַפְשְׁךָ תֹּאכַל בָּשָׂר: 21 כִּי־יִרְחַק מִמְּךָ
הַמָּקוֹם אֲשֶׁר יִבְחַר יְהֹוָאדנָיאהדונהי אֱלֹהֶיךָ ילה לָשׂוּם שְׁמוֹ
שָׁם וְזָבַחְתָּ מִבְּקָרְךָ וּמִצֹּאנְךָ אֲשֶׁר נָתַן יְהֹוָאדנָיאהדונהי לְךָ
כַּאֲשֶׁר צִוִּיתִךָ וְאָכַלְתָּ בִּשְׁעָרֶיךָ בְּכֹל לכב אַוַּת נַפְשֶׁךָ:
22 אַךְ כַּאֲשֶׁר יֵאָכֵל אֶת־הַצְּבִי וְאֶת־הָאַיָּל כֵּן תֹּאכְלֶנּוּ

animal blood, we can keep ourselves from connecting to any animalistic tendencies.

יַרְחִיב - When the Creator will expand…: The Ari, Rav Isaac Luria, says that the land will eventually expand to accommodate all the souls who will come down at the time of Messiah, in order to accept all of us.

הַטָּמֵא וְהַטָּהוֹר ייפ אכא יַחְדָּו יֹאכְלֶנּוּ: 23 רַק חֲזַק פהל לְבִלְתִּי
אֲכֹל הַדָּם כִּי הַדָּם הוּא הַנָּפֶשׁ וְלֹא־תֹאכַל הַנֶּפֶשׁ עִם־
הַבָּשָׂר: 24 לֹא תֹּאכְלֶנּוּ עַל־הָאָרֶץ אלף למד הה יוד מם תִּשְׁפְּכֶנּוּ
כַּמָּיִם: 25 לֹא תֹּאכְלֶנּוּ לְמַעַן יִיטַב לְךָ וּלְבָנֶיךָ אַחֲרֶיךָ
כִּי־תַעֲשֶׂה הַיָּשָׁר בְּעֵינֵי יְהֹוָה אהדונהי: 26 רַק קָדָשֶׁיךָ אֲשֶׁר־
יִהְיוּ לְךָ וּנְדָרֶיךָ תִּשָּׂא וּבָאתָ אֶל־הַמָּקוֹם אֲשֶׁר־יִבְחַר
יְהֹוָה אהדונהי: 27 וְעָשִׂיתָ עֹלֹתֶיךָ הַבָּשָׂר וְהַדָּם עַל־מִזְבַּח זן,
נגד יְהֹוָה אהדונהי אֱלֹהֶיךָ וְדַם־זְבָחֶיךָ יִשָּׁפֵךְ עַל־מִזְבַּח זן, נגד
יְהֹוָה אהדונהי אֱלֹהֶיךָ וְהַבָּשָׂר תֹּאכֵל: 28 שְׁמֹר וְשָׁמַעְתָּ אֵת
כָּל ילי ־הַדְּבָרִים הָאֵלֶּה אֲשֶׁר אָנֹכִי איע מְצַוֶּךָּ לְמַעַן יִיטַב
לְךָ וּלְבָנֶיךָ אַחֲרֶיךָ עַד־עוֹלָם כִּי תַעֲשֶׂה הַטּוֹב והו וְהַיָּשָׁר
בְּעֵינֵי יְהֹוָה אהדונהי אֱלֹהֶיךָ:

Third Reading - Jacob - Tiferet

29 כִּי־יַכְרִית יְהֹוָה אהדונהי אֱלֹהֶיךָ אֶת־הַגּוֹיִם אֲשֶׁר אַתָּה
בָא־שָׁמָּה יוד הא ואו הא לָרֶשֶׁת אוֹתָם מִפָּנֶיךָ וְיָרַשְׁתָּ אֹתָם
וַיָּשַׁבְתָּ בְּאַרְצָם: 30 הִשָּׁמֶר לְךָ פֶּן־תִּנָּקֵשׁ אַחֲרֵיהֶם אַחֲרֵי

הִשָּׁמֶר - When the Israelites entered the Promised Land, the people who lived there before had already departed because they were too negative and thus did not merit living in the land of Israel. The Torah warns us: "Don't become like them because you'll have to leave just like them." That is why the Temple was eventually destroyed. When we don't transform ourselves

הַשָּׁמְדָם מִפָּנֶיךָ וּפֶן־תִּדְרֹשׁ לֵאלֹהֵיהֶם ילה לֵאמֹר אֵיכָה
יַעַבְדוּ הַגּוֹיִם הָאֵלֶּה אֶת־אֱלֹהֵיהֶם ילה וְאֶעֱשֶׂה־כֵּן גַּם־
אָנִי אני׃ 31 לֹא־תַעֲשֶׂה כֵן לַיהוָה יאהדונהי אֱלֹהֶיךָ כִּי כָל ילי
־תּוֹעֲבַת יְהוָה יאהדונהי אֲשֶׁר שָׂנֵא עָשׂוּ לֵאלֹהֵיהֶם ילה כִּי
גַּם אֶת־בְּנֵיהֶם וְאֶת־בְּנֹתֵיהֶם יִשְׂרְפוּ בָאֵשׁ לֵאלֹהֵיהֶם ילה׃
13 1 אֵת כָּל ילי ־הַדָּבָר ראה אֲשֶׁר אָנֹכִי איע מְצַוֶּה אֶתְכֶם
אֹתוֹ תִשְׁמְרוּ לַעֲשׂוֹת לֹא־תֹסֵף עָלָיו וְלֹא תִגְרַע מִמֶּנּוּ׃
2 כִּי־יָקוּם בְּקִרְבְּךָ נָבִיא אוֹ חֹלֵם חֲלוֹם וְנָתַן אבג יתץ, ושר,
אהבת חנם אֵלֶיךָ אוֹת אוֹ מוֹפֵת׃ 3 וּבָא הָאוֹת וְהַמּוֹפֵת אֲשֶׁר־
דִּבֶּר ראה אֵלֶיךָ לֵאמֹר נֵלְכָה אַחֲרֵי אֱלֹהִים מום, ילה אֲחֵרִים

or appreciate what we have, we lose the tremendous blessings in our lives. For example, when we finally merit marrying our soulmate, we cannot continue on the same spiritual level as we did before the marriage. We must move forward constantly, to acknowledge and show appreciation for this tremendous gift. We have to be better people after good things happen, or these things will be taken away from us.

יָקוּם - False prophets: The idea of false prophets is important, especially for people on a spiritual path. It is almost better not to study at all than to study and teach others without having the proper training, without being strong enough, and without being spiritual enough. It's not a problem to share wisdom with others, but when we become another person's spiritual teacher, we must be 100 percent ready. When or where we achieve this state of readiness is usually not for us to decide. That is why Rav Berg works for a certain amount of time with the teachers and why our teachers must study in the Centre for a minimum amount of time.

אֲשֶׁר לֹא־יְדַעְתָּם וְנָעָבְדֵם׃ 4 לֹא תִשְׁמַע אֶל־דִּבְרֵי
הַנָּבִיא הַהוּא אוֹ אֶל־חוֹלֵם הַחֲלוֹם הַהוּא כִּי מְנַסֶּה
יְהֹוָהאדניאהדונהי אֱלֹהֵיכֶם ילה אֶתְכֶם לָדַעַת הֲיִשְׁכֶם אֹהֲבִים
אֶת־יְהֹוָהאדניאהדונהי אֱלֹהֵיכֶם ילה בְּכָל לכב ־לְבַבְכֶם וּבְכָל לכב
־נַפְשְׁכֶם׃ 5 אַחֲרֵי יְהֹוָהאדניאהדונהי אֱלֹהֵיכֶם ילה תֵּלֵכוּ וְאֹתוֹ
תִירָאוּ וְאֶת־מִצְוֹתָיו תִּשְׁמֹרוּ וּבְקֹלוֹ תִשְׁמָעוּ וְאֹתוֹ תַעֲבֹדוּ
וּבוֹ תִדְבָּקוּן׃ 6 וְהַנָּבִיא הַהוּא אוֹ חֹלֵם הַחֲלוֹם הַהוּא יוּמָת
כִּי דִבֶּר ראה ־סָרָה עַל־יְהֹוָהאדניאהדונהי אֱלֹהֵיכֶם ילה הַמּוֹצִיא
אֶתְכֶם | מֵאֶרֶץ מִצְרַיִם מצר וְהַפֹּדְךָ מִבֵּית ב״פ ראה עֲבָדִים
לְהַדִּיחֲךָ מִן־הַדֶּרֶךְ אֲשֶׁר צִוְּךָ יְהֹוָהאדניאהדונהי אֱלֹהֶיךָ לָלֶכֶת
בָּהּ וּבִעַרְתָּ הָרָע מִקִּרְבֶּךָ׃ 7 כִּי יְסִיתְךָ אָחִיךָ בֶן־אִמֶּךָ
אוֹ־בִנְךָ אוֹ־בִתְּךָ אוֹ | אֵשֶׁת חֵיקֶךָ אוֹ רֵעֲךָ אֲשֶׁר כְּנַפְשְׁךָ
בַּסֵּתֶר ב״פ מצר לֵאמֹר נֵלְכָה וְנַעַבְדָה אֱלֹהִים מום, ילה אֲחֵרִים
אֲשֶׁר לֹא יָדַעְתָּ אַתָּה וַאֲבֹתֶיךָ׃ 8 מֵאֱלֹהֵי דמב, ילה הָעַמִּים
אֲשֶׁר סְבִיבֹתֵיכֶם הַקְּרֹבִים אֵלֶיךָ אוֹ הָרְחֹקִים מִמֶּךָּ
מִקְצֵה הָאָרֶץ אלף למד הה יוד מם וְעַד־קְצֵה הָאָרֶץ אלף למד הה יוד מם׃

יְסִיתְךָ - “Your brother, your sister takes you away, even your wife…”: Anyone can be a messenger of Satan. Anyone—even the person closest to us—can become negative. Even a great person can be consumed by hate at any moment, and bring Satan into the lives of others.

9 לֹא־תֹאבֶה לוֹ וְלֹא תִשְׁמַע אֵלָיו וְלֹא־תָחוֹס עֵינְךָ עָלָיו
וְלֹא־תַחְמֹל וְלֹא־תְכַסֶּה עָלָיו׃ 10 כִּי הָרֹג תַּהַרְגֶנּוּ יָדְךָ
תִּהְיֶה־בּוֹ בָרִאשׁוֹנָה לַהֲמִיתוֹ וְיַד כָּל ילי ־הָעָם בָּאַחֲרֹנָה׃
11 וּסְקַלְתּוֹ בָאֲבָנִים וָמֵת כִּי בִקֵּשׁ לְהַדִּיחֲךָ מֵעַל ע״לם
יְהוָֹהאדניאהדונהי אֱלֹהֶיךָ הַמּוֹצִיאֲךָ מֵאֶרֶץ מִצְרַיִם מצר מִבֵּית ב״פ
ראה עֲבָדִים׃ 12 וְכָל ילי ־יִשְׂרָאֵל יִשְׁמְעוּ וְיִרָאוּן וְלֹא־יוֹסִפוּ
לַעֲשׂוֹת כַּדָּבָר ראה הָרָע הַזֶּה והו בְּקִרְבֶּךָ׃ 13 כִּי־תִשְׁמַע
בְּאַחַת עָרֶיךָ אֲשֶׁר יְהוָֹהאדניאהדונהי אֱלֹהֶיךָ נֹתֵן ושר, אבג יתץ,
אהבת חנם לְךָ לָשֶׁבֶת שָׁם לֵאמֹר׃ 14 יָצְאוּ אֲנָשִׁים בְּנֵי־בְלִיַּעַל
מִקִּרְבֶּךָ וַיַּדִּיחוּ אֶת־יֹשְׁבֵי עִירָם לֵאמֹר נֵלְכָה וְנַעַבְדָה
אֱלֹהִים מום, ילה אֲחֵרִים אֲשֶׁר לֹא־יְדַעְתֶּם׃ 15 וְדָרַשְׁתָּ וְחָקַרְתָּ
וְשָׁאַלְתָּ הֵיטֵב וְהִנֵּה אֱמֶת ז״פ ס״ג נָכוֹן הַדָּבָר ראה נֶעֶשְׂתָה
הַתּוֹעֵבָה הַזֹּאת בְּקִרְבֶּךָ׃ 16 הַכֵּה היי תַכֶּה כהת, משיח בן דוד
אֶת־יֹשְׁבֵי הָעִיר ערי, בוזפך, סנדלפון הַהִוא לְפִי־חָרֶב הַחֲרֵם אֹתָהּ
וְאֶת־כָּל ילי ־אֲשֶׁר־בָּהּ וְאֶת־בְּהֶמְתָּהּ לְפִי־חָרֶב׃ 17 וְאֶת־

עָרֶיךָ - The Torah describes a whole city that was overtaken by Satan—a spiritual black hole. We know this actually can't be because there is always some Light in every situation. The Torah is not actually talking about a situation created by humans, but rather about the negative entities that the Zohar describes as totally black. When we feel depressed for no reason, these entities are the source of our misery.

כָּל ילי -שְׁלָלָהּ תִּקְבֹּץ אֶל־תּוֹךְ רְחֹבָהּ וְשָׂרַפְתָּ בָאֵשׁ אֶת־
הָעִיר ערי, בוזך, סנדלפון וְאֶת־כָּל ילי -שְׁלָלָהּ כָּלִיל לַיהֹוָהאדניאהדונהי
אֱלֹהֶיךָ וְהָיְתָה תֵּל עוֹלָם לֹא תִבָּנֶה עוֹד: 18 וְלֹא־יִדְבַּק
בְּיָדְךָ מְאוּמָה מִן־הַחֵרֶם לְמַעַן יָשׁוּב יְהֹוָהאדניאהדונהי מֵחֲרוֹן
אַפּוֹ וְנָתַן אבג יתץ, ושר, אהבת חנם -לְךָ רַחֲמִים וְרִחַמְךָ וְהִרְבֶּךָ
כַּאֲשֶׁר נִשְׁבַּע לַאֲבֹתֶיךָ: 19 כִּי תִשְׁמַע בְּקוֹל יְהֹוָהאדניאהדונהי
אֱלֹהֶיךָ לִשְׁמֹר אֶת־כָּל ילי -מִצְוֹתָיו אֲשֶׁר אָנֹכִי איע מְצַוְּךָ
הַיּוֹם נגד, מזבח, זן לַעֲשׂוֹת הַיָּשָׁר בְּעֵינֵי יְהֹוָהאדניאהדונהי אֱלֹהֶיךָ:

Fourth Reading - Moses - Netzach

14 1 בָּנִים אַתֶּם לַיהֹוָהאדניאהדונהי אֱלֹהֵיכֶם ילה לֹא תִתְגֹּדְדוּ
וְלֹא־תָשִׂימוּ קָרְחָה בֵּין עֵינֵיכֶם לָמֵת: 2 כִּי עַם קָדוֹשׁ
אַתָּה לַיהֹוָהאדניאהדונהי אֱלֹהֶיךָ וּבְךָ בָּחַר יְהֹוָהאדניאהדונהי לִהְיוֹת
לוֹ לְעָם עלם סְגֻלָּה מִכֹּל ילי הָעַמִּים אֲשֶׁר עַל־פְּנֵי חכמה, בינה
הָאֲדָמָה: 3 לֹא תֹאכַל כָּל ילי -תּוֹעֵבָה: 4 זֹאת הַבְּהֵמָה לכב

בָּנִים - We are supposed to feel that we are children of Light, and the way to do this is three-fold: through reading Zohar each day, through prayer, and through true sharing. We must reach a spiritual level in which we feel so close to the Lightforce that we are His children.

לֹא תֹאכַל - Non-kosher foods: We must try as much as possible to elevate sparks of Light when we perform physical actions, including eating. Simply put, there are more sparks of Light in kosher food than in non-kosher food. The Torah is like a map, guiding us on how to get more Light. The

אֲשֶׁר תֹּאכֵלוּ שׁוֹר ושׁר, אבג יתץ, אהבת חנם שֵׂה כְשָׂבִים וְשֵׂה
עִזִּים: 5 אַיָּל וּצְבִי וְיַחְמוּר וְאַקּוֹ וְדִישֹׁן וּתְאוֹ וָזָמֶר: 6 וְכָל ילי
-בְּהֵמָה לכב מַפְרֶסֶת פַּרְסָה וְשֹׁסַעַת שֶׁסַע שְׁתֵּי פְרָסוֹת
מַעֲלַת גֵּרָה בַּבְּהֵמָה לכב אֹתָהּ תֹּאכֵלוּ: 7 אַךְ אֶת-זֶה לֹא
תֹאכְלוּ מִמַּעֲלֵי הַגֵּרָה וּמִמַּפְרִיסֵי הַפַּרְסָה הַשְּׁסוּעָה
אֶת-הַגָּמָל וְאֶת-הָאַרְנֶבֶת וְאֶת-הַשָּׁפָן כִּי-מַעֲלֵה גֵרָה
הֵמָּה יוד הא ואו הא וּפַרְסָה לֹא הִפְרִיסוּ טְמֵאִים הֵם לָכֶם:
8 וְאֶת-הַחֲזִיר כִּי-מַפְרִיס פַּרְסָה הוּא וְלֹא גֵרָה טָמֵא הוּא
לָכֶם מִבְּשָׂרָם לֹא תֹאכֵלוּ וּבְנִבְלָתָם לֹא תִגָּעוּ: 9 אֶת-
זֶה תֹּאכְלוּ מִכֹּל ילי אֲשֶׁר בַּמָּיִם כֹּל ילי אֲשֶׁר-לוֹ סְנַפִּיר
וְקַשְׂקֶשֶׂת תֹּאכֵלוּ: 10 וְכֹל ילי אֲשֶׁר אֵין-לוֹ סְנַפִּיר וְקַשְׂקֶשֶׂת
לֹא תֹאכֵלוּ טָמֵא הוּא לָכֶם: 11 כָּל ילי -צִפּוֹר טְהֹרָה

more closely we follow this path, the more Light we receive. Eating kosher food elevates sparks of Light that come to help us and give us support. Conversely, if a negative person eats kosher food, it does not help in the same way it helps a positive person. It's all about following the cosmic blueprint.

בַּמָּיִם - Fish: We know that until a few years ago, nuclear testing took place in our oceans. This section helps us gain protection from the contamination that resulted from this kind of testing.

צִפּוֹר - Birds: Birds are not affected by gravity the way human beings are. We want to eventually get to the point where we are not constrained by the force that keeps us down, which is our desire to receive for the self alone.

תֹּאכֵלוּ׃ 12 וְזֶה אֲשֶׁר לֹא־תֹאכְלוּ מֵהֶם הַנֶּשֶׁר וְהַפֶּרֶס
וְהָעָזְנִיָּה׃ 13 וְהָרָאָה ראה וְאֶת־הָאַיָּה וְהַדַּיָּה לְמִינָהּ׃ 14 וְאֵת
כָּל ילי ־עֹרֵב לְמִינוֹ׃ 15 וְאֵת בַּת הַיַּעֲנָה וְאֶת־הַתַּחְמָס וְאֶת־
הַשָּׁחַף וְאֶת־הַנֵּץ לְמִינֵהוּ׃ 16 אֶת־הַכּוֹס מום, אלהים, אהיה ־ אדני
וְאֶת־הַיַּנְשׁוּף וְהַתִּנְשָׁמֶת׃ 17 וְהַקָּאָת וְאֶת־הָרָחָמָה וְאֶת־
הַשָּׁלָךְ׃ 18 וְהַחֲסִידָה וְהָאֲנָפָה לְמִינָהּ וְהַדּוּכִיפַת וְהָעֲטַלֵּף׃
19 וְכֹל ילי שֶׁרֶץ הָעוֹף טָמֵא הוּא לָכֶם לֹא יֵאָכֵלוּ׃ 20 כָּל ילי
־עוֹף טָהוֹר י"פ אכא תֹּאכֵלוּ׃ 21 לֹא תֹאכְלוּ כָל ילי ־נְבֵלָה לַגֵּר
אֲשֶׁר־בִּשְׁעָרֶיךָ תִּתְּנֶנָּה וַאֲכָלָהּ אוֹ מָכֹר לְנָכְרִי כִּי עַם
קָדוֹשׁ אַתָּה לַיהוָהאדניאהדונהי אֱלֹהֶיךָ לֹא־תְבַשֵּׁל גְּדִי והו
בַּחֲלֵב אִמּוֹ׃

Fifth Reading - Aaron - Hod

22 עַשֵּׂר תְּעַשֵּׂר אֵת כָּל ילי ־תְּבוּאַת זַרְעֶךָ הַיֹּצֵא הַשָּׂדֶה
שָׁנָה שָׁנָה׃ 23 וְאָכַלְתָּ לִפְנֵי חכמה, בינה | יְהוָהאדניאהדונהי אֱלֹהֶיךָ

If we could resist our evil inclination the way birds do, we too would be capable of flying. We know that the *tzaddikim* (righteous people) were able to use The 72 Names to move from place to place because they did not allow their desires to hold them back.

עַשֵּׂר - Giving a tenth of the produce of the land, or tithing, is good business. If we don't give the ten percent to what the *Malchut,* the 1%, deserves, we lose what we have.

בַּמָּקוֹם אֲשֶׁר־יִבְחַר לְשַׁכֵּן שְׁמוֹ שָׁם מַעְשַׂר דְּגָנְךָ תִּירֹשְׁךָ
וְיִצְהָרֶךָ וּבְכֹרֹת בְּקָרְךָ וְצֹאנֶךָ לְמַעַן תִּלְמַד לְיִרְאָה רי״ו,
גבורה אֶת־יְהֹוָהאדניאהדונהי אֱלֹהֶיךָ כָּל ילי ־הַיָּמִים נלך׃ 24 וְכִי־יִרְבֶּה
מִמְּךָ הַדֶּרֶךְ כִּי לֹא תוּכַל שְׂאֵתוֹ כִּי־יִרְחַק מִמְּךָ הַמָּקוֹם
אֲשֶׁר יִבְחַר יְהֹוָהאדניאהדונהי אֱלֹהֶיךָ לָשׂוּם שְׁמוֹ שָׁם כִּי יְבָרֶכְךָ
יְהֹוָהאדניאהדונהי אֱלֹהֶיךָ׃ 25 וְנָתַתָּה בַּכָּסֶף וְצַרְתָּ הַכֶּסֶף בְּיָדְךָ
וְהָלַכְתָּ אֶל־הַמָּקוֹם אֲשֶׁר יִבְחַר יְהֹוָהאדניאהדונהי אֱלֹהֶיךָ בּוֹ׃
26 וְנָתַתָּה הַכֶּסֶף בְּכֹל לכב אֲשֶׁר־תְּאַוֶּה נַפְשְׁךָ בַּבָּקָר וּבַצֹּאן
וּבַיַּיִן מיכ, י״פ האא וּבַשֵּׁכָר י״פ ב״ן וּבְכֹל לכב אֲשֶׁר תִּשְׁאָלְךָ נַפְשֶׁךָ
וְאָכַלְתָּ שָּׁם לִפְנֵי חכמה, בינה יְהֹוָהאדניאהדונהי אֱלֹהֶיךָ וְשָׂמַחְתָּ
אַתָּה וּבֵיתֶךָ׃ 27 וְהַלֵּוִי אֲשֶׁר־בִּשְׁעָרֶיךָ לֹא תַעַזְבֶנּוּ כִּי אֵין
לוֹ חֵלֶק וְנַחֲלָה עִמָּךְ׃ 28 מִקְצֵה | **שָׁלֹשׁ** שָׁנִים תּוֹצִיא אֶת־
כָּל ילי ־מַעְשַׂר תְּבוּאָתְךָ בַּשָּׁנָה הַהִוא וְהִנַּחְתָּ בִּשְׁעָרֶיךָ׃
29 וּבָא הַלֵּוִי כִּי אֵין־לוֹ חֵלֶק וְנַחֲלָה עִמָּךְ וְהַגֵּר וְהַיָּתוֹם
וְהָאַלְמָנָה אֲשֶׁר בִּשְׁעָרֶיךָ וְאָכְלוּ וְשָׂבֵעוּ לְמַעַן יְבָרֶכְךָ
יְהֹוָהאדניאהדונהי אֱלֹהֶיךָ בְּכָל לכב ־מַעֲשֵׂה יָדְךָ אֲשֶׁר תַּעֲשֶׂה׃

שָׁלֹשׁ - Every three years, part of the tithing would go to the poor. Tithing to the poor should go to people who are both spiritually and physically poor. Not only should we give tithing to the place where we receive our spiritual nurturing and nourishment but we should see to it that the money goes to people who are truly needy in all respects.

Sixth Reading - Joseph - Yesod

15 1 מִקֵּץ מנק שֶֽׁבַע־שָׁנִים תַּעֲשֶׂה שְׁמִטָּה׃ 2 וְזֶה דְּבַר ראה
הַשְּׁמִטָּה שָׁמוֹט כָּל ילי ־בַּעַל מַשֵּׁה מהש יָדוֹ אֲשֶׁר יַשֶּׁה
בְּרֵעֵהוּ לֹא־יִגֹּשׂ אֶת־רֵעֵהוּ וְאֶת־אָחִיו כִּי־קָרָא שְׁמִטָּה
לַיהֹוָ‍אדני‍ה יאהדונהי׃ 3 אֶת־הַנָּכְרִי תִּגֹּשׂ וַאֲשֶׁר יִהְיֶה ייי לְךָ אֶת־
אָחִיךָ תַּשְׁמֵט יָדֶךָ׃ 4 אֶפֶס כִּי לֹא יִהְיֶה ייי ־בְּךָ אֶבְיוֹן
כִּי־בָרֵךְ יְבָרֶכְךָ יְהֹוָ‍אדני‍ה יאהדונהי בָּאָרֶץ אֲשֶׁר יְהֹוָ‍אדני‍ה יאהדונהי
אֱלֹהֶיךָ נֹתֵן ושר, אבג יתץ, אהבת חנם ־לְךָ נַחֲלָה לְרִשְׁתָּהּ׃ 5 רַק
אִם יוהך ־שָׁמוֹעַ תִּשְׁמַע בְּקוֹל יְהֹוָ‍אדני‍ה יאהדונהי אֱלֹהֶיךָ לִשְׁמֹר
לַעֲשׂוֹת אֶת־כָּל ילי ־הַמִּצְוָה הַזֹּאת אֲשֶׁר אָנֹכִי איע מְצַוְּךָ
הַיּוֹם נגד, מזבח, זן׃ 6 כִּי־יְהֹוָ‍אדני‍ה יאהדונהי אֱלֹהֶיךָ ילה בֵּרַכְךָ כַּאֲשֶׁר
דִּבֶּר ראה ־לָךְ וְהַעֲבַטְתָּ גּוֹיִם רַבִּים וְאַתָּה לֹא תַעֲבֹט
וּמָשַׁלְתָּ בְּגוֹיִם רַבִּים וּבְךָ לֹא יִמְשֹׁלוּ׃ 7 כִּי־יִהְיֶה ייי בְךָ
אֶבְיוֹן מֵאַחַד אהבה, דאגה אַחֶיךָ בְּאַחַד אהבה, דאגה שְׁעָרֶיךָ

שְׁמִטָּה - *Shemittah*: In the seventh year, the land would rest. It would have time to nurture itself and gain strength. With today's hormones and genetic engineering, what used to take a year to grow can take a day, but shortening or removing this growth process also removes the Light. Reading about *shemittah* helps us re-inject energy into what we eat so that we will be sustained both physically and spiritually.

אֶבְיוֹן - When someone asks us for help or when we're thinking about something we should be giving, we should never consider our cost. We

בְּאַרְצְךָ אֲשֶׁר־יְהֹוָ‍אדני יאהדונהי אֱלֹהֶיךָ נֹתֵן ושר, אבג יתץ, אהבת חנם
לָךְ לֹא תְאַמֵּץ אֶת־לְבָבְךָ וְלֹא תִקְפֹּץ אֶת־יָדְךָ מֵאָחִיךָ
הָאֶבְיוֹן: 8 כִּי־פָתֹחַ תִּפְתַּח אֶת־יָדְךָ לוֹ וְהַעֲבֵט תַּעֲבִיטֶנּוּ
דֵּי מַחְסֹרוֹ אֲשֶׁר יֶחְסַר לוֹ: 9 הִשָּׁמֶר לְךָ פֶּן־יִהְיֶה ייי דָבָר ראה
עִם־לְבָבְךָ בְלִיַּעַל לֵאמֹר קָרְבָה שְׁנַת־הַשֶּׁבַע שְׁנַת
הַשְּׁמִטָּה וְרָעָה רהע עֵינְךָ בְּאָחִיךָ הָאֶבְיוֹן וְלֹא תִתֵּן ב"פ כהת
לוֹ וְקָרָא עָלֶיךָ אֶל־יְהֹוָ‍אדני יאהדונהי וְהָיָה יהוה, יהה בְךָ חֵטְא:
10 נָתוֹן תִּתֵּן ב"פ כהת לוֹ וְלֹא־יֵרַע לְבָבְךָ בְּתִתְּךָ לוֹ כִּי בִּגְלַל ׀
הַדָּבָר ראה הַזֶּה והו יְבָרֶכְךָ יְהֹוָ‍אדני יאהדונהי אֱלֹהֶיךָ בְּכָל לכב
־מַעֲשֶׂךָ וּבְכֹל לכב מִשְׁלַח יָדֶךָ: 11 כִּי לֹא־יֶחְדַּל אֶבְיוֹן
מִקֶּרֶב הָאָרֶץ אלף למד הה יוד מם עַל־כֵּן אָנֹכִי איע מְצַוְּךָ לֵאמֹר
פָּתֹחַ תִּפְתַּח אֶת־יָדְךָ לְאָחִיךָ לַעֲנִיֶּךָ וּלְאֶבְיֹנְךָ בְּאַרְצֶךָ:
12 כִּי־יִמָּכֵר לְךָ אָחִיךָ הָעִבְרִי אוֹ הָעִבְרִיָּה וַעֲבָדְךָ פוי שֵׁשׁ
שָׁנִים וּבַשָּׁנָה הַשְּׁבִיעִת תְּשַׁלְּחֶנּוּ חָפְשִׁי מֵעִמָּךְ: 13 וְכִי־
תְשַׁלְּחֶנּוּ חָפְשִׁי מֵעִמָּךְ לֹא תְשַׁלְּחֶנּוּ רֵיקָם: 14 הַעֲנֵיק תַּעֲנִיק

should never give with strings attached; that is not giving. We must trust that when we give, we will also have. Doubt only ensures that what we give does not come back to us.

יִמָּכֵר - This section speaks about slavery. Today, spiritual slavery is running rampant. People are enslaved by their work, their anger, their desires. Through this reading, we can gain freedom from slavery.

לוֹ מִצֹּאנְךָ וּמִגָּרְנְךָ וּמִיִּקְבֶךָ אֲשֶׁר בֵּרַכְךָ יְהֹוָה יאהדונהי
אֱלֹהֶיךָ תִּתֶּן ב״פ כהת ־לוֹ׃ 15 וְזָכַרְתָּ כִּי עֶבֶד הָיִיתָ בְּאֶרֶץ
מִצְרַיִם מצר וַיִּפְדְּךָ יְהֹוָה יאהדונהי אֱלֹהֶיךָ עַל־כֵּן אָנֹכִי איע מְצַוְּךָ
אֶת־הַדָּבָר ראה הַזֶּה והו הַיּוֹם נגד, מזבח, זן׃ 16 וְהָיָה יהוה, יהה כִּי־יֹאמַר
אֵלֶיךָ לֹא אֵצֵא מֵעִמָּךְ כִּי אֲהֵבְךָ וְאֶת־בֵּיתֶךָ כִּי־טוֹב והו
לוֹ עִמָּךְ׃ 17 וְלָקַחְתָּ אֶת־הַמַּרְצֵעַ וְנָתַתָּה בְאָזְנוֹ וּבַדֶּלֶת
וְהָיָה יהוה, יהה לְךָ עֶבֶד עוֹלָם וְאַף לַאֲמָתְךָ תַּעֲשֶׂה־כֵּן׃
18 לֹא־יִקְשֶׁה בְעֵינֶךָ בְּשַׁלֵּחֲךָ אֹתוֹ חָפְשִׁי מֵעִמָּךְ כִּי מִשְׁנֶה
שְׂכַר י״פ בין שָׂכִיר עֲבָדְךָ פוי שֵׁשׁ שָׁנִים וּבֵרַכְךָ יְהֹוָה יאהדונהי
אֱלֹהֶיךָ בְּכֹל לכב אֲשֶׁר תַּעֲשֶׂה׃

Seventh Reading - David - Malchut

19 כָּל ילי ־הַבְּכוֹר אֲשֶׁר יִוָּלֵד בִּבְקָרְךָ וּבְצֹאנְךָ הַזָּכָר
תַּקְדִּישׁ לַיהֹוָה יאהדונהי אֱלֹהֶיךָ לֹא תַעֲבֹד בִּבְכֹר שׁוֹרֶךָ
וְלֹא תָגֹז בְּכוֹר צֹאנֶךָ׃ 20 לִפְנֵי חכמה, בינה יְהֹוָה יאהדונהי אֱלֹהֶיךָ
תֹאכְלֶנּוּ שָׁנָה בְשָׁנָה בַּמָּקוֹם אֲשֶׁר־יִבְחַר יְהֹוָה יאהדונהי
אַתָּה וּבֵיתֶךָ׃ 21 וְכִי־יִהְיֶה ייי בוֹ מוּם אלהים, אהיה - אדני פִּסֵּחַ אוֹ

הַבְּכוֹר - First-borns are imbued with the energy of death. But along with this, first-borns also contain the Light of all of the children to come. Because first-born animals also possess this aspect of death, they must be treated with greater respect and dignity because they have this added energy.

עִוֵּר כֹּל ילי מוּם אלהים, אהיה + אדני רָע לֹא תִזְבָּחֶנּוּ לַיהוָהאדניאהדונהי
אֱלֹהֶיךָ׃ 22 בִּשְׁעָרֶיךָ תֹּאכְלֶנּוּ הַטָּמֵא וְהַטָּהוֹר י״פ אכא יַחְדָּו
כַּצְּבִי וְכָאַיָּל׃ 23 רַק אֶת־דָּמוֹ לֹא תֹאכֵל עַל־הָאָרֶץ אלף
למד הה יוד מם תִּשְׁפְּכֶנּוּ כַּמָּיִם׃ 16 1 שָׁמוֹר אֶת־חֹדֶשׁ הָאָבִיב
וְעָשִׂיתָ **פֶּסַח** לַיהוָהאדניאהדונהי אֱלֹהֶיךָ כִּי בְּחֹדֶשׁ הָאָבִיב
הוֹצִיאֲךָ יְהוָהאדניאהדונהי אֱלֹהֶיךָ מִמִּצְרַיִם מצר לָיְלָה מלה׃
2 וְזָבַחְתָּ פֶּסַח לַיהוָהאדניאהדונהי אֱלֹהֶיךָ צֹאן וּבָקָר בַּמָּקוֹם
אֲשֶׁר־יִבְחַר יְהוָהאדניאהדונהי לְשַׁכֵּן שְׁמוֹ שָׁם׃ 3 לֹא־תֹאכַל
עָלָיו חָמֵץ שִׁבְעַת יָמִים נלך תֹּאכַל־עָלָיו מַצּוֹת לֶחֶם ג״פ יהו״ה
עֹנִי יוד יוד הא יוד הא ואו יוד הא ואו הא כִּי בְחִפָּזוֹן יָצָאתָ מֵאֶרֶץ מִצְרַיִם מצר
לְמַעַן תִּזְכֹּר אֶת־יוֹם נגד, מזבח, זן צֵאתְךָ מֵאֶרֶץ מִצְרַיִם מצר כֹּל ילי
יְמֵי חַיֶּיךָ׃ 4 וְלֹא־יֵרָאֶה ר״ו, גבורה לְךָ שְׂאֹר בְּכָל לכב ־גְּבֻלְךָ
שִׁבְעַת יָמִים נלך וְלֹא־יָלִין מִן־הַבָּשָׂר אֲשֶׁר תִּזְבַּח בָּעֶרֶב
בַּיּוֹם נגד, מזבח, זן הָרִאשׁוֹן לַבֹּקֶר׃ 5 לֹא תוּכַל לִזְבֹּחַ אֶת־
הַפָּסַח בְּאַחַד אהבה, דאגה שְׁעָרֶיךָ אֲשֶׁר־יְהוָהאדניאהדונהי אֱלֹהֶיךָ
נֹתֵן ושר, אבג יתץ, אהבת חנם לָךְ׃ 6 כִּי אִם יוהך ־אֶל־הַמָּקוֹם אֲשֶׁר־

פֶּסַח - Passover: Just as the ancient Israelites used the cosmic window in *Nisan*, the month of Aries, to break free from their slavery to Pharaoh, we can use this window every year to release ourselves from slavery to our desire to receive for the self alone. Each time we read about Passover, we gain support to do just that.

יִבְחַר יְהֹוָאדניאהדונהי אֱלֹהֶיךָ ילה לְשַׁכֵּן שְׁמוֹ שָׁם תִּזְבַּח אֶת־
הַפֶּסַח בָּעָרֶב כְּבוֹא הַשֶּׁמֶשׁ מוֹעֵד צֵאתְךָ מִמִּצְרָיִם מצר׃
7 וּבִשַּׁלְתָּ וְאָכַלְתָּ בַּמָּקוֹם אֲשֶׁר יִבְחַר יְהֹוָאדניאהדונהי אֱלֹהֶיךָ
בּוֹ וּפָנִיתָ בַבֹּקֶר וְהָלַכְתָּ לְאֹהָלֶיךָ׃ 8 שֵׁשֶׁת יָמִים נלך תֹּאכַל
מַצּוֹת וּבַיּוֹם נגד, מזבח, זן הַשְּׁבִיעִי עֲצֶרֶת לַיהֹוָאדניאהדונהי אֱלֹהֶיךָ
לֹא תַעֲשֶׂה מְלָאכָה׃ 9 שִׁבְעָה שָׁבֻעֹת תִּסְפָּר־לָךְ מֵהָחֵל
חֶרְמֵשׁ בַּקָּמָה תָּחֵל לִסְפֹּר שִׁבְעָה שָׁבֻעוֹת׃ 10 וְעָשִׂיתָ
חַג שָׁבֻעוֹת לַיהֹוָאדניאהדונהי אֱלֹהֶיךָ מִסַּת נִדְבַת יָדְךָ
אֲשֶׁר תִּתֵּן ב״פ כהת כַּאֲשֶׁר יְבָרֶכְךָ יְהֹוָאדניאהדונהי אֱלֹהֶיךָ׃
11 וְשָׂמַחְתָּ לִפְנֵי חכמה, בינה | יְהֹוָאדניאהדונהי אֱלֹהֶיךָ אַתָּה וּבִנְךָ
וּבִתֶּךָ וְעַבְדֶּךָ פוי וַאֲמָתֶךָ וְהַלֵּוִי אֲשֶׁר בִּשְׁעָרֶיךָ וְהַגֵּר
וְהַיָּתוֹם וְהָאַלְמָנָה אֲשֶׁר בְּקִרְבֶּךָ בַּמָּקוֹם אֲשֶׁר יִבְחַר
יְהֹוָאדניאהדונהי אֱלֹהֶיךָ לְשַׁכֵּן שְׁמוֹ שָׁם׃ 12 וְזָכַרְתָּ כִּי־עֶבֶד
הָיִיתָ בְּמִצְרָיִם מצר וְשָׁמַרְתָּ וְעָשִׂיתָ אֶת־הַחֻקִּים הָאֵלֶּה׃

שָׁבֻעֹת - Shavuot: This celebration not only concludes the seven weeks of counting the Omer that follow Passover but also offers us the same energy of immortality that the Israelites experienced when Moses revealed the Ten Utterances on Mount Sinai. At that moment in history, the blind were able to see, the deaf were able to hear, and there was no death of any sort. While we try to connect with this energy each day of our lives, it is more readily available throughout the cosmos during the holiday of Shavuot.

Maftir

13 חַג הַסֻּכֹּת תַּעֲשֶׂה לְךָ שִׁבְעַת יָמִים נלך בְּאָסְפְּךָ מִגָּרְנְךָ
וּמִיִּקְבֶךָ׃ 14 וְשָׂמַחְתָּ בְּחַגֶּךָ אַתָּה וּבִנְךָ וּבִתֶּךָ וְעַבְדְּךָ פוי
וַאֲמָתֶךָ וְהַלֵּוִי וְהַגֵּר וְהַיָּתוֹם וְהָאַלְמָנָה אֲשֶׁר בִּשְׁעָרֶיךָ׃
15 שִׁבְעַת יָמִים נלך תָּחֹג לַיהֹוָאדנָי יאהדונהי אֱלֹהֶיךָ בַּמָּקוֹם
אֲשֶׁר־יִבְחַר יְהֹוָאדנָי יאהדונהי כִּי יְבָרֶכְךָ יְהֹוָאדנָי יאהדונהי אֱלֹהֶיךָ
בְּכֹל לכב תְּבוּאָתְךָ וּבְכֹל לכב מַעֲשֵׂה יָדֶיךָ וְהָיִיתָ אַךְ שָׂמֵחַ׃
16 שָׁלוֹשׁ פְּעָמִים | בַּשָּׁנָה יֵרָאֶה ר״ע, גבורה כָל ילי ־זְכוּרְךָ אֶת־
פְּנֵי חכמה, בינה | יְהֹוָאדנָי יאהדונהי אֱלֹהֶיךָ בַּמָּקוֹם אֲשֶׁר יִבְחָר בְּחַג
הַמַּצּוֹת וּבְחַג הַשָּׁבֻעוֹת וּבְחַג הַסֻּכּוֹת וְלֹא יֵרָאֶה ר״ע, גבורה
אֶת־פְּנֵי חכמה, בינה יְהֹוָאדנָי יאהדונהי רֵיקָם׃ 17 אִישׁ כְּמַתְּנַת יָדוֹ
כְּבִרְכַּת יְהֹוָאדנָי יאהדונהי אֱלֹהֶיךָ אֲשֶׁר נָתַן־לָךְ׃

הַסֻּכֹּת - Sukkot: "And you shall be happy." The final letters of this phrase make the word *chet tav chaf,* which is the name of the angel of sustenance. Herein lies a precious secret: The happier we are, the more this angel is present in our lives. We may be doing all of the right actions for sustenance, but if we're not happy, we are blocking this angel from giving us the sustenance that we've rightly earned.

Haftarah of Re'eh

The haftarah of Re'eh says that when one is thirsty, one should drink water. The commentaries explain that this refers to the Torah: In order to learn, one must thirst for wisdom. The first step in studying is to desire to study.

Isaiah 54 ישעיהו פרק 54

11 עֲנִיָּה סֹעֲרָה לֹא נֻחָמָה הִנֵּה אָנֹכִי איע מַרְבִּיץ בַּפּוּךְ אֲבָנָיִךְ
וִיסַדְתִּיךְ בַּסַּפִּירִים: 12 וְשַׂמְתִּי כַּדְכֹד שִׁמְשֹׁתַיִךְ וּשְׁעָרַיִךְ
לְאַבְנֵי אֶקְדָּח וְכָל ילי -גְּבוּלֵךְ לְאַבְנֵי־חֵפֶץ: 13 וְכָל ילי -בָּנַיִךְ
לִמּוּדֵי יְהֹוָהאדני יאהדונהי וְרַב שְׁלוֹם בָּנָיִךְ: 14 בִּצְדָקָה א אל אלה
אלהי אלהים תִּכּוֹנָנִי רַחֲקִי מֵעֹשֶׁק כִּי־לֹא תִירָאִי וּמִמְּחִתָּה
כִּי לֹא־תִקְרַב אֵלָיִךְ: 15 הֵן גּוֹר יָגוּר אֶפֶס מֵאוֹתִי מִי ילי
-גָר אִתָּךְ עָלַיִךְ יִפּוֹל: 16 הן (הִנֵּה) אָנֹכִי איע בָּרָאתִי חָרָשׁ
נֹפֵחַ בְּאֵשׁ פֶּחָם וּמוֹצִיא כְלִי לְמַעֲשֵׂהוּ וְאָנֹכִי איע בָּרָאתִי
מַשְׁחִית לְחַבֵּל: 17 כָּל ילי -כְּלִי יוּצַר עָלַיִךְ לֹא יִצְלָח וְכָל ילי
-לָשׁוֹן תָּקוּם־אִתָּךְ לַמִּשְׁפָּט תַּרְשִׁיעִי זֹאת נַחֲלַת עַבְדֵי
יְהֹוָהאדני יאהדונהי וְצִדְקָתָם מֵאִתִּי נְאֻם־יְהֹוָהאדני יאהדונהי: 55 1 הוֹי
כָּל ילי -צָמֵא לְכוּ לַמַּיִם וַאֲשֶׁר אֵין־לוֹ כָּסֶף לְכוּ שִׁבְרוּ
וֶאֱכֹלוּ וּלְכוּ שִׁבְרוּ בְּלוֹא־כֶסֶף וּבְלוֹא מְחִיר יַיִן מיכ, י"פ האא
וְחָלָב: 2 לָמָּה יוד הא ואו הא תִשְׁקְלוּ־כֶסֶף בְּלוֹא־לֶחֶם ג"פ יהו"ה
וִיגִיעֲכֶם בְּלוֹא לְשָׂבְעָה שִׁמְעוּ שָׁמוֹעַ אֵלַי וְאִכְלוּ־טוֹב והו

וְתִתְעַנַּג בַּדֶּשֶׁן נַפְשְׁכֶם׃ 3 הַטּוּ אָזְנְכֶם וּלְכוּ אֵלַי שִׁמְעוּ
וּתְחִי נַפְשְׁכֶם וְאֶכְרְתָה לָכֶם בְּרִית עוֹלָם חַסְדֵי דָוִד
הַנֶּאֱמָנִים׃ 4 הֵן עֵד לְאוּמִּים נְתַתִּיו נָגִיד וּמְצַוֵּה לְאֻמִּים׃
5 הֵן גּוֹי לֹא־תֵדַע תִּקְרָא וְגוֹי לֹא־יְדָעוּךָ אֵלֶיךָ יָרוּצוּ לְמַעַן
יְהֹוָה אדני יאהדונהי אֱלֹהֶיךָ וְלִקְדוֹשׁ יִשְׂרָאֵל כִּי פֵאֲרָךְ׃

Lesson of Shoftim

"Be simple with your Creator"

Reading this week's portion, we might think that spiritual work is very easy: *"Be simple with your Creator."* If you are simple, then everything will be fine. It seems very straightforward. So why do we feel that our spiritual work is the most difficult thing we have to do in this world?

Kabbalah teaches that all the judgments that were brought upon us are based on two verses: First, "The Creator has commanded us...what is good for us is to live all our life like this day." Second, "You are Israel [the Zohar explains that "Israel" implies all people connected to the Light and aware of the spiritual system], and you should do what is good for you."

From these verses, we learn that everything was created solely for humankind, for us. To understand this, imagine a building contractor who takes it upon himself to build a palace for the king. Imagine further that the builder comes and asks the king for a loan. If it were a loan for the builder's personal use, he'd have to be careful how much he asked for. But if the builder is asking for a loan to construct the palace, he can ask for much more. The money is not for him but for the palace, which belongs to the king.

If following the spiritual laws were for the good of the Creator or for the good of others, Moses could not have asked the nation of Israel to follow the spiritual laws of the Torah. It would have been too difficult for them to do it essentially for someone else's benefit. But if we see ourselves in the role of the king, then the "loan" that the builder—Moses—is asking from us is never too big since all of it is for *our* benefit.

Even if we become righteous, what could we possibly give the Creator that He doesn't already have? All that the Creator asks from us is that we live in goodness and happiness by staying connected to the Light. According to "love your neighbor as yourself," treating others with human dignity and seeing the Creator in everyone and everything.

This is why it is so important for us to hear the reading of the Torah on Shabbat. Without the connection to the Torah and the Light, we cannot do our personal work. There are just too many negative forces in the world that don't want us to be happy and fulfilled. We need to "charge our batteries" every week so that the Light can shine in our lives.

Without a connection to Shabbat and the Zohar, it is impossible for "doing what is good for you" to actually take place. We need to understand that each of us has the Light of the Creator inside us. If this spark is diminished or lost because we did not connect to the Torah or the Zohar, it is impossible for us to feel happiness or fulfillment.

Now we can return to the verse in this week's portion: "Be simple with your Creator." What does it mean to be simple? In fact, the work of the Creator really is very simple once we understand that the whole purpose of the work is for our own good.

Regarding the month of Elul

We know that the portion of Shoftim is always read either on the Shabbat of the blessing of the new month of *Elul* or at some time during the month of *Elul*. And we know that the month of *Elul* enables us to go "back to the future" so that we can cleanse all our previous negative actions. The whole reason the month of *Elul* exists is to give us this opportunity. This power does not exist in any other month, not because *Elul* is the month before Rosh Hashanah but because the power of cleansing is inherent in the month of *Elul* itself. It is truly a unique and powerful time.

The secret behind the concept of "time" is very important. If we do not know the singular power that is revealed in each month and how to connect to it, it is very difficult to grow and to transform. Consider Hannukah: If at the time of Creation a window of time had not been inserted into the 25th day of the month of Kislev, the miracle of Hannukah could never have taken place. While it is true that had the people not been prepared to sacrifice their lives, nothing would have happened either, their willingness would not have been enough without this window.

What are the Days of Desire?

Consider this verse: "The days of *Elul* can remove the foreskin of the heart." Throughout the year, a covering is present on our hearts. In *Elul*, we have an opening in which we can remove this "foreskin"—but only if we prepare ourselves will this happen.

After the Golden Calf, God said to Moses, "What error did the people of Israel do? They are stubborn." The emphasis is on the stubbornness of the Israelites, not on the error. The error lies in their failure to change themselves, to remove the "foreskin" from their hearts. This is what Moses corrected in the month of *Elul*. During these great days, we have a once-a-year opportunity to fix and remove the "foreskin" of the heart, and then we will not be stubborn anymore.

Many people think that changing themselves takes years of hard work, and they give up even before they try. But with the power of this month, all that we need to do is prepare ourselves to take advantage of the energy that is available.

The Holy Zohar tells us that Bezalel did not require many years to build the Tabernacle with his hands. Everything was done through the power of thought and consciousness. Bezalel took the gold in his hand, and the gold became a menorah all by itself. The gold became walls and doors and tables; it even became the Ark. Bezalel didn't have to do it all on his own. We, too, do not need to do everything. We just have to prepare ourselves for the right times of the year. But without preparing ourselves, we cannot even think of receiving the Light. "If you build it, He will come"—but only if you build it!

What must we do to prepare ourselves for the month of *Elul*? We must purge the hatred that is inside us. As the Gemara teaches us, the Temple was destroyed because of hatred. And in every generation that the Temple is not rebuilt, it is as if it were destroyed in that generation. When we feel hatred, each and every one of us destroys the Holy Temple once again.

The Baal Shem Tov teaches that if only one person is completely cleansed of hatred, the Messiah will come and the Temple will be built. Unfortunately, we still don't have a person like that. Let's begin during this *Elul* by removing all the roots of hatred that are within us.

Synopsis of Shoftim

This is almost always the first portion we read in the month of *Elul*, a time when we look back on the year just past and see what we did during the year that we need to change. If anything went wrong, big or small, in the year it's because in the previous *Elul*, we didn't do our job, that is, we didn't do the process correctly.

First Reading - Abraham - Chesed

18 שֹׁפְטִים וְשֹׁטְרִים תִּתֶּן ב״פ כהת לְךָ בְּכָל לכב שְׁעָרֶיךָ אֲשֶׁר
יְהֹוָאדני יאהדונהי אֱלֹהֶיךָ נֹתֵן ושר, אבג יתץ, אהבת חנם לְךָ לִשְׁבָטֶיךָ
וְשָׁפְטוּ אֶת־הָעָם מִשְׁפַּט־צֶדֶק׃ 19 לֹא־תַטֶּה מִשְׁפָּט לֹא
תַכִּיר פָּנִים וְלֹא־תִקַּח שֹׁחַד כִּי הַשֹּׁחַד יְעַוֵּר עֵינֵי חֲכָמִים
וִיסַלֵּף דִּבְרֵי צַדִּיקִם׃ 20 צֶדֶק צֶדֶק תִּרְדֹּף לְמַעַן תִּחְיֶה
וְיָרַשְׁתָּ אֶת־הָאָרֶץ אלף למד הה יוד מם אֲשֶׁר־יְהֹוָאדני יאהדונהי אֱלֹהֶיךָ
נֹתֵן ושר, אבג יתץ, אהבת חנם לָךְ׃ 21 לֹא־תִטַּע לְךָ אֲשֵׁרָה כָּל ילי עֵץ
אֵצֶל מִזְבַּח זן, נגד יְהֹוָאדני יאהדונהי אֱלֹהֶיךָ אֲשֶׁר תַּעֲשֶׂה־לָּךְ׃
22 וְלֹא־תָקִים לְךָ מַצֵּבָה אֲשֶׁר שָׂנֵא יְהֹוָאדני יאהדונהי אֱלֹהֶיךָ׃
17 1 לֹא־תִזְבַּח לַיהֹוָאדני יאהדונהי אֱלֹהֶיךָ שׁוֹר ושר, אבג יתץ, אהבת חנם
וָשֶׂה אֲשֶׁר יִהְיֶה ייי בוֹ מוּם אלהים, אהיה - אדני כֹּל ילי דָּבָר ראה רָע
כִּי תוֹעֲבַת יְהֹוָאדני יאהדונהי אֱלֹהֶיךָ הוּא׃ 2 כִּי־יִמָּצֵא בְקִרְבְּךָ

שֹׁפְטִים - The portion starts with the Creator instructing Moses to appoint judges. These judges were agenda-free. Indeed, the second they had a personal agenda, they were relieved of their duties and replaced. Hidden agendas, just like judges who are unjust, can ruin even the most positive situations and prevent them from ever bearing fruit.

מוּם - This section discusses the kinds of sacrifices we're *not* supposed to offer, such as animals who are blemished. When we are coming close to the Creator, our sacrifices can't be blemished. We must make sacrifices purely because we want to be close to the Creator. The blemish of an ego-based desire cancels the energy of the sacrifice.

בְּאַחַד אהבה, דאגה שְׁעָרֶיךָ אֲשֶׁר־יְהֹוָה יאהדונהי אֱלֹהֶיךָ נֹתֵן ושר,
אבג יתץ, אהבת חנם לָךְ אִישׁ אוֹ־אִשָּׁה אֲשֶׁר יַעֲשֶׂה אֶת־הָרַע
בְּעֵינֵי יְהֹוָה־אֱלֹהֶיךָ יאהדונהי לַעֲבֹר בְּרִיתוֹ׃ 3 וַיֵּלֶךְ וַיַּעֲבֹד
אֱלֹהִים מום, ילה אֲחֵרִים וַיִּשְׁתַּחוּ לָהֶם וְלַשֶּׁמֶשׁ | אוֹ לַיָּרֵחַ
אוֹ לְכָל יה אדני ילי ־צְבָא הַשָּׁמַיִם כוזו, ר״פ טל אֲשֶׁר לֹא־צִוִּיתִי׃
4 וְהֻגַּד־לְךָ וְשָׁמָעְתָּ וְדָרַשְׁתָּ הֵיטֵב וְהִנֵּה אֱמֶת ר״פ ס״ג נָכוֹן
הַדָּבָר ראה נֶעֶשְׂתָה הַתּוֹעֵבָה הַזֹּאת בְּיִשְׂרָאֵל׃ 5 וְהוֹצֵאתָ
אֶת־הָאִישׁ הַהוּא אוֹ אֶת־הָאִשָּׁה הַהִוא אֲשֶׁר עָשׂוּ
אֶת־הַדָּבָר ראה הָרָע הַזֶּה והו אֶל־שְׁעָרֶיךָ אֶת־הָאִישׁ אוֹ
אֶת־הָאִשָּׁה וּסְקַלְתָּם בָּאֲבָנִים וָמֵתוּ׃ 6 עַל־פִּי | שְׁנַיִם
עֵדִים אוֹ שְׁלֹשָׁה עֵדִים יוּמַת הַמֵּת לֹא יוּמַת עַל־פִּי עֵד
אֶחָד אהבה, דאגה׃ 7 יַד הָעֵדִים תִּהְיֶה־בּוֹ בָרִאשֹׁנָה לַהֲמִיתוֹ
וְיַד כָּל ילי ־הָעָם בָּאַחֲרֹנָה וּבִעַרְתָּ הָרָע מִקִּרְבֶּךָ׃ 8 כִּי
יִפָּלֵא מִמְּךָ דָבָר ראה לַמִּשְׁפָּט בֵּין־דָּם | לְדָם בֵּין־דִּין

יִמָּצֵא - Idol worshipping is discussed. Modern-age idols include drugs, sex, and money. People use idols to avoid responsibility. We try to escape through sex, drugs, or other things of addictive nature. We need to take responsibility for our behavior and rid ourselves of these idols.

יִפָּלֵא - If there was no judge in the immediate area, people had to go to Jerusalem where there were 71 judges. Upon reaching a harmonious conclusion, they raised to the level of 72, which meant they reached the Lightforce. This harmony and the attainment of this level ensured that the

לְדִין וּבֵין נֶגַע לָנֶגַע דִּבְרֵי רִיבֹת בִּשְׁעָרֶיךָ וְקַמְתָּ וְעָלִיתָ
אֶל־הַמָּקוֹם אֲשֶׁר יִבְחַר יְהֹוָאדניאהדונהי אֱלֹהֶיךָ בּוֹ: 9 וּבָאתָ
אֶל־הַכֹּהֲנִים הַלְוִיִּם וְאֶל־הַשֹּׁפֵט אֲשֶׁר יִהְיֶה ייי בַּיָּמִים נלך
הָהֵם וְדָרַשְׁתָּ וְהִגִּידוּ לְךָ אֵת דְּבַר ראה הַמִּשְׁפָּט: 10 וְעָשִׂיתָ
עַל־פִּי הַדָּבָר ראה אֲשֶׁר יַגִּידוּ לְךָ מִן־הַמָּקוֹם הַהוּא אֲשֶׁר
יִבְחַר יְהֹוָאדניאהדונהי וְשָׁמַרְתָּ לַעֲשׂוֹת כְּכֹל ילי אֲשֶׁר יוֹרוּךָ:
11 עַל־פִּי הַתּוֹרָה אֲשֶׁר יוֹרוּךָ וְעַל־הַמִּשְׁפָּט אֲשֶׁר־יֹאמְרוּ
לְךָ תַּעֲשֶׂה לֹא תָסוּר מִן־הַדָּבָר ראה אֲשֶׁר־יַגִּידוּ לְךָ יָמִין
וּשְׂמֹאל: 12 וְהָאִישׁ אֲשֶׁר־יַעֲשֶׂה בְזָדוֹן לְבִלְתִּי שְׁמֹעַ אֶל־
הַכֹּהֵן מלה הָעֹמֵד לְשָׁרֶת שָׁם אֶת־יְהֹוָאדניאהדונהי אֱלֹהֶיךָ אוֹ
אֶל־הַשֹּׁפֵט וּמֵת הָאִישׁ הַהוּא וּבִעַרְתָּ הָרָע מִיִּשְׂרָאֵל:
13 וְכָל ילי ־הָעָם יִשְׁמְעוּ וְיִרָאוּ וְלֹא יְזִידוּן עוֹד:

Second Reading - Isaac - Gvurah

14 כִּי־תָבֹא אֶל־הָאָרֶץ אלף למד הה יוד מם אֲשֶׁר יְהֹוָאדניאהדונהי
אֱלֹהֶיךָ ילה נֹתֵן ושר, אבג יתץ, אהבת חנם לָךְ וִירִשְׁתָּהּ וְיָשַׁבְתָּה בָּהּ

judgment was valid. Even if a judgment seemed wrong for the situation at hand, it was certainly appropriate for past life debts. We want to achieve a consciousness in which, whatever judgment we get, we understand that it's the right one. If it's not right for the present moment, it's right for something we did in a past life. By resisting the situations we face in life, we inject new *tikkune* into our cassettes, requiring further judgment down the line.

וְאָמַרְתָּ אָשִׂימָה עָלַי מֶלֶךְ כְּכָל ילי ־הַגּוֹיִם אֲשֶׁר סְבִיבֹתָי׃
15 שׂוֹם תָּשִׂים עָלֶיךָ מֶלֶךְ אֲשֶׁר יִבְחַר יְהֹוָאדניאהדונהי אֱלֹהֶיךָ
בּוֹ מִקֶּרֶב אַחֶיךָ תָּשִׂים עָלֶיךָ מֶלֶךְ לֹא תוּכַל לָתֵת עָלֶיךָ
אִישׁ נָכְרִי אֲשֶׁר לֹא־אָחִיךָ הוּא׃ 16 רַק לֹא־יַרְבֶּה־לּוֹ
סוּסִים וְלֹא־יָשִׁיב אֶת־הָעָם מִצְרַיְמָה לְמַעַן הַרְבּוֹת
סוּס כוק, א אד אדנ אדני וַיהֹוָאדניאהדונהי אָמַר לָכֶם לֹא תֹסִפוּן לָשׁוּב
בַּדֶּרֶךְ הַזֶּה והו עוֹד׃ 17 וְלֹא יַרְבֶּה־לּוֹ נָשִׁים וְלֹא יָסוּר לְבָבוֹ
וְכֶסֶף וְזָהָב לֹא יַרְבֶּה־לּוֹ מְאֹד׃ 18 וְהָיָה יהוה, יהה כְשִׁבְתּוֹ
עַל כִּסֵּא מַמְלַכְתּוֹ וְכָתַב לוֹ אֶת־מִשְׁנֵה הַתּוֹרָה הַזֹּאת
עַל־סֵפֶר מִלִּפְנֵי חכמה, בינה הַכֹּהֲנִים הַלְוִיִּם׃ 19 וְהָיְתָה עִמּוֹ
וְקָרָא בוֹ כָּל ילי ־יְמֵי חַיָּיו לְמַעַן יִלְמַד לְיִרְאָה רי"ו, גבורה אֶת־
יְהֹוָאדניאהדונהי אֱלֹהָיו ילה לִשְׁמֹר אֶת־כָּל ילי ־דִּבְרֵי הַתּוֹרָה
הַזֹּאת וְאֶת־הַחֻקִּים הָאֵלֶּה לַעֲשֹׂתָם׃ 20 לְבִלְתִּי רוּם־לְבָבוֹ
מֵאֶחָיו וּלְבִלְתִּי סוּר מִן־הַמִּצְוָה יָמִין וּשְׂמֹאול לְמַעַן יַאֲרִיךְ
יָמִים נלך עַל־מַמְלַכְתּוֹ הוּא וּבָנָיו בְּקֶרֶב יִשְׂרָאֵל׃

מֶלֶךְ - The appointment of a king for Israel: All the kings in Israel carried a Torah with them, so if people showed them respect, they would know that it was for the word of the Creator, not for them personally. Kings had to lack all ego and selfishness. We don't have a king today, so what we can connect to is our personal king—our ability to remove chaos and bring the Messiah.

Third Reading - Jacob - Tiferet

18 1 לֹא־יִהְיֶה ייי לַכֹּהֲנִים הַלְוִיִּם כָּל ילי־שֵׁבֶט לֵוִי חֵלֶק
וְנַחֲלָה עִם־יִשְׂרָאֵל אִשֵּׁי יְהֹוָהאדניאהדונהי וְנַחֲלָתוֹ יֹאכֵלוּן:
2 וְנַחֲלָה לֹא־יִהְיֶה ייי־לּוֹ בְּקֶרֶב אֶחָיו יְהֹוָהאדניאהדונהי הוּא נַחֲלָתוֹ
כַּאֲשֶׁר דִּבֶּר ראה־לוֹ: 3 וְזֶה יִהְיֶה ייי מִשְׁפַּט הַכֹּהֲנִים מֵאֵת
הָעָם מֵאֵת זֹבְחֵי הַזֶּבַח אִם יוהך־שׁוֹר ושר, אבג יתץ, אהבת חנם אִם יוהך
־שֶׂה וְנָתַן אבג יתץ, ושר, אהבת חנם לַכֹּהֵן מלה הַזְּרֹעַ וְהַלְּחָיַיִם וְהַקֵּבָה:
4 רֵאשִׁית דְּגָנְךָ תִּירֹשְׁךָ וְיִצְהָרֶךָ וְרֵאשִׁית גֵּז צֹאנְךָ תִּתֶּן ב״פ
כהת־לּוֹ: 5 כִּי בוֹ בָּחַר יְהֹוָהאדניאהדונהי אֱלֹהֶיךָ מִכָּל ילי־שְׁבָטֶיךָ
לַעֲמֹד לְשָׁרֵת בְּשֵׁם־יְהֹוָהאדניאהדונהי הוּא וּבָנָיו כָּל ילי
־הַיָּמִים נלך:

לַכֹּהֲנִים הַלְוִיִּם - The *kohanim* and the Levites received no monetary or physical compensation, not even land. People who do the Light's work aren't supposed to take money for themselves. That's why Rav Ashlag and Rav Brandwein wouldn't take money for themselves. If they received any, they'd give it away. People spreading Kabbalah don't take for themselves, and Lightforce takes care of them. This is why so many people who study Kabbalah devote their lives to sharing rather than taking or even getting paid. They know that when they care for others and help empower them with the tools of Kabbalah, they will be taken care of.

מִשְׁפַּט הַכֹּהֲנִים - There were particular gifts given to the *kohanim.* People did not hesitate to give to the kohanim because they knew giving a gift to a *kohen* would bring them gifts in return. If we give for a spiritual purpose, we get more back. That's why it's important to know whether a gift of your money will be spent on the right thing. Giving to a *kohen* was more like getting for yourself instead.

Fourth Reading - Moses - Netzach

6 וְכִי־יָבֹא הַלֵּוִי מֵאַחַד שְׁעָרֶיךָ אהבה, דאגה מִכָּל ילי ־יִשְׂרָאֵל
אֲשֶׁר־הוּא גָּר שָׁם וּבָא בְּכָל לכב ־אַוַּת נַפְשׁוֹ אֶל־הַמָּקוֹם
אֲשֶׁר־יִבְחַר יְהֹוָ֣אדני אהדונהי׃ 7 וְשֵׁרֵת בְּשֵׁם יְהֹוָ֣אדני אהדונהי
אֱלֹהָיו ילה כְּכָל ילי ־אֶחָיו הַלְוִיִּם הָעֹמְדִים שָׁם לִפְנֵי חכמה,
בינה יְהֹוָ֣אדני אהדונהי׃ 8 חֵלֶק כְּחֵלֶק יֹאכֵלוּ לְבַד מִמְכָּרָיו
עַל־הָאָבוֹת׃ 9 כִּי אַתָּה בָּא אֶל־הָאָרֶץ אלף למד הה יוד מם אֲשֶׁר־
יְהֹוָ֣אדני אהדונהי אֱלֹהֶיךָ נֹתֵן ושר, אבג יתץ, אהבת חנם לָךְ לֹא־תִלְמַד
לַעֲשׂוֹת כְּתוֹעֲבֹת הַגּוֹיִם הָהֵם׃ 10 לֹא־יִמָּצֵא בְךָ מַעֲבִיר
בְּנוֹ־וּבִתּוֹ בָּאֵשׁ קֹסֵם קְסָמִים מְעוֹנֵן וּמְנַחֵשׁ וּמְכַשֵּׁף׃
11 וְחֹבֵר חָבֶר וְשֹׁאֵל אוֹב וְיִדְּעֹנִי וְדֹרֵשׁ אֶל־הַמֵּתִים׃ 12 כִּי־
תוֹעֲבַת יְהֹוָ֣אדני אהדונהי כָּל ילי ־עֹשֵׂה אֵלֶּה וּבִגְלַל הַתּוֹעֵבֹת
הָאֵלֶּה יְהֹוָ֣אדני אהדונהי אֱלֹהֶיךָ מוֹרִישׁ אוֹתָם מִפָּנֶיךָ׃ 13 תָּמִים
תִּהְיֶה עִם יְהֹוָ֣אדני אהדונהי אֱלֹהֶיךָ׃

קֹסֵם - Black magic is very dangerous because when practiced, the intention is to manipulate the future. It is just as dangerous to find out the past through magic because we can alter our *tikkune*, which will have to come back to us in a more negative way. But we can use dreams and astrology to understand the past and future. These tools help us understand that the future can be changed.

Fifth Reading - Aaron - Hod

14 כִּי | הַגּוֹיִם הָאֵלֶּה אֲשֶׁר אַתָּה יוֹרֵשׁ אוֹתָם אֶל־מְעֹנְנִים
וְאֶל־קֹסְמִים יִשְׁמָעוּ וְאַתָּה לֹא כֵן נָתַן לְךָ יְהֹוָאדניאהדונהי
אֱלֹהֶיךָ׃ 15 נָבִיא מִקִּרְבְּךָ מֵאַחֶיךָ כָּמֹנִי יָקִים לְךָ
יְהֹוָאדניאהדונהי אֱלֹהֶיךָ אֵלָיו תִּשְׁמָעוּן׃ 16 כְּכֹל ילי אֲשֶׁר־
שָׁאַלְתָּ מֵעִם יְהֹוָאדניאהדונהי אֱלֹהֶיךָ ילה בְּחֹרֵב בְּיוֹם נגד, מזבח,
זן הַקָּהָל לֵאמֹר לֹא אֹסֵף לִשְׁמֹעַ אֶת־קוֹל יְהֹוָאדניאהדונהי
אֱלֹהָי דמב, ילה וְאֶת־הָאֵשׁ הַגְּדֹלָה הַזֹּאת לֹא־אֶרְאֶה עוֹד
וְלֹא אָמוּת׃ 17 וַיֹּאמֶר יְהֹוָאדניאהדונהי אֵלָי הֵיטִיבוּ אֲשֶׁר
דִּבֵּרוּ׃ 18 נָבִיא אָקִים לָהֶם מִקֶּרֶב אֲחֵיהֶם כָּמוֹךָ וְנָתַתִּי
דְבָרַי בְּפִיו פוי וְדִבֶּר ראה אֲלֵיהֶם אֵת כָּל ילי ־אֲשֶׁר אֲצַוֶּנּוּ׃
19 וְהָיָה יהוה, יהה הָאִישׁ אֲשֶׁר לֹא־יִשְׁמַע אֶל־דְּבָרַי אֲשֶׁר
יְדַבֵּר בִּשְׁמִי אָנֹכִי איע אֶדְרֹשׁ מֵעִמּוֹ׃ 20 אַךְ הַנָּבִיא אֲשֶׁר
יָזִיד לְדַבֵּר ראה דָּבָר ראה בִּשְׁמִי אֵת אֲשֶׁר לֹא־צִוִּיתִיו

נָבִיא - We were given great prophets like Moses to take care of us. They are present in every generation. The Creator does not leave us on our own. The Zohar says that we don't have the same prophets we used to; today's prophets come in the form of children, and the blind. But more than that, everything is a message, and we have to be open to listen.

יָזִיד - False prophets are people who teach others when they haven't studied or prepared themselves to teach. When a person thinks he's ready to teach but isn't, he becomes a false prophet.

לְדַבֵּר ראה וַאֲשֶׁר יְדַבֵּר בְּשֵׁם אֱלֹהִים מום, ילה אֲחֵרִים וּמֵת
הַנָּבִיא הַהוּא׃ 21 וְכִי תֹאמַר בִּלְבָבֶךָ אֵיכָה נֵדַע אֶת־
הַדָּבָר ראה אֲשֶׁר לֹא־דִבְּרוֹ יְהוָה אדני אהדונהי׃ 22 אֲשֶׁר יְדַבֵּר
הַנָּבִיא בְּשֵׁם יְהוָה אדני אהדונהי וְלֹא־יִהְיֶה ייי הַדָּבָר ראה וְלֹא
יָבֹא הוּא הַדָּבָר ראה אֲשֶׁר לֹא־דִבְּרוֹ יְהוָה אדני אהדונהי בְּזָדוֹן
דִּבְּרוֹ הַנָּבִיא לֹא תָגוּר מִמֶּנּוּ׃ 19 1 כִּי־יַכְרִית יְהוָה אדני אהדונהי
אֱלֹהֶיךָ ילה אֶת־הַגּוֹיִם אֲשֶׁר יְהוָה אדני אהדונהי אֱלֹהֶיךָ נֹתֵן ושר,
אבג יתץ, אהבת וזינם לְךָ אֶת־אַרְצָם וִירִשְׁתָּם וְיָשַׁבְתָּ בְעָרֵיהֶם
וּבְבָתֵּיהֶם׃ 2 שָׁלוֹשׁ עָרִים תַּבְדִּיל לָךְ בְּתוֹךְ אַרְצְךָ אֲשֶׁר
יְהוָה אדני אהדונהי אֱלֹהֶיךָ נֹתֵן ושר, אבג יתץ, אהבת וזינם לְךָ לְרִשְׁתָּהּ׃
3 תָּכִין לְךָ הַדֶּרֶךְ ב"פ יב"ק וְשִׁלַּשְׁתָּ אֶת־גְּבוּל אַרְצְךָ אֲשֶׁר
יַנְחִילְךָ יְהוָה אדני אהדונהי אֱלֹהֶיךָ וְהָיָה יהוה, יהה לָנוּס שָׁמָּה יוד הא ואו
הא כָּל ילי ־רֹצֵחַ׃ 4 וְזֶה דְּבַר ראה הָרֹצֵחַ אֲשֶׁר־יָנוּס שָׁמָּה יוד
הא ואו הא וָחָי אֲשֶׁר יַכֶּה אֶת־רֵעֵהוּ בִּבְלִי־דַעַת וְהוּא לֹא־
שֹׂנֵא לוֹ מִתְּמֹל שִׁלְשֹׁם׃ 5 וַאֲשֶׁר יָבֹא אֶת־רֵעֵהוּ בַיַּעַר ערי,

יָנוּס - The cities of refuge that Moses designated for the Israelites: When someone killed a person without premeditation or by accident, he would be sent to one of these cities. But in reality, every person who was killed died because he had murdered someone either in this life or a previous one. There are no accidents. There are laws to this universe: Nothing just “happens.” One of Satan’s biggest tricks is letting us think that things happen by accident.

סוזחך, סנדלפון לַחְטֹב עֵצִים וְנִדְּחָה יָדוֹ בַגַּרְזֶן לִכְרֹת הָעֵץ וְנָשַׁל
הַבַּרְזֶל ר"ת - בלהה רחל זלפה לאה מִן־הָעֵץ וּמָצָא אֶת־רֵעֵהוּ וָמֵת
הוּא יָנוּס אֶל־אַחַת הֶעָרִים־הָאֵלֶּה וָחָי׃ 6 פֶּן־יִרְדֹּף גֹּאֵל א"ת
ב"ש - כתר הַדָּם אַחֲרֵי הָרֹצֵחַ כִּי־יֵחַם לְבָבוֹ וְהִשִּׂיגוֹ כִּי־יִרְבֶּה
הַדֶּרֶךְ וְהִכָּהוּ נָפֶשׁ וְלוֹ אֵין מִשְׁפַּט־מָוֶת כִּי לֹא שֹׂנֵא
הוּא לוֹ מִתְּמוֹל שִׁלְשׁוֹם׃ 7 עַל־כֵּן אָנֹכִי איע מְצַוְּךָ לֵאמֹר
שָׁלֹשׁ עָרִים תַּבְדִּיל לָךְ׃ 8 וְאִם יוהך יַרְחִיב יְהֹוָהאדנייאהדונהי
אֱלֹהֶיךָ ילה אֶת־גְּבֻלְךָ כַּאֲשֶׁר נִשְׁבַּע לַאֲבֹתֶיךָ וְנָתַן אבג יתץ,
ושר, אהבת חנם לְךָ אֶת־כָּל ילי ־הָאָרֶץ אלף למד הה יוד מם אֲשֶׁר דִּבֶּר ראה
לָתֵת לַאֲבֹתֶיךָ׃ 9 כִּי־תִשְׁמֹר אֶת־כָּל ילי ־הַמִּצְוָה הַזֹּאת
לַעֲשֹׂתָהּ אֲשֶׁר אָנֹכִי איע מְצַוְּךָ הַיּוֹם נגד, מזבח, זן לְאַהֲבָה אחד, דאגה
אֶת־יְהֹוָהאדנייאהדונהי אֱלֹהֶיךָ וְלָלֶכֶת בִּדְרָכָיו כָּל ילי ־הַיָּמִים נלך
וְיָסַפְתָּ לְךָ עוֹד שָׁלֹשׁ עָרִים עַל הַשָּׁלֹשׁ הָאֵלֶּה׃ 10 וְלֹא
יִשָּׁפֵךְ דָּם נָקִי אלף הי יוד הי בְּקֶרֶב אַרְצְךָ אֲשֶׁר יְהֹוָהאדנייאהדונהי
אֱלֹהֶיךָ נֹתֵן ושר, אבג יתץ, אהבת חנם לְךָ נַחֲלָה וְהָיָה יהוה, יהה עָלֶיךָ
דָּמִים׃ 11 וְכִי־יִהְיֶה ייי אִישׁ שֹׂנֵא לְרֵעֵהוּ וְאָרַב לוֹ וְקָם
עָלָיו וְהִכָּהוּ נֶפֶשׁ וָמֵת וְנָס יוד הא ואו הא - אדני אֶל־אַחַת הֶעָרִים

נֶפֶשׁ - Murder can be physical or it can be symbolic, as through evil tongue. Most of us will never kill someone by inflicting physical death, but we can assassinate in other ways. That makes us killers just the same.

הָאֵל לאה: 12 וְשָׁלְחוּ זִקְנֵי עִירוֹ וְלָקְחוּ אֹתוֹ מִשָּׁם וְנָתְנוּ אֹתוֹ
בְּיַד גֹּאֵל א"ת ב"ש - כתר הַדָּם וָמֵת: 13 לֹא־תָחוֹס עֵינְךָ עָלָיו
וּבִעַרְתָּ דַם־הַנָּקִי אלף הי יוד הי מִיִּשְׂרָאֵל וְטוֹב והו לָךְ:

Sixth Reading - Joseph - Yesod

14 לֹא תַסִּיג גְּבוּל רֵעֲךָ אֲשֶׁר גָּבְלוּ רִאשֹׁנִים בְּנַחֲלָתְךָ
אֲשֶׁר תִּנְחַל בָּאָרֶץ אֲשֶׁר יְהוָהאדניאהדונהי אֱלֹהֶיךָ נֹתֵן ושר, אבג יתץ,
אהבת חינם לְךָ לְרִשְׁתָּהּ: 15 לֹא־יָקוּם עֵד אֶחָד אהבה, דאגה בְּאִישׁ
לְכָל יה אדני ילי ־עָוֹן וּלְכָל יה אדני ילי ־חַטָּאת בְּכָל לכב ־חֵטְא
אֲשֶׁר יֶחֱטָא עַל־פִּי | שְׁנֵי עֵדִים אוֹ עַל־פִּי שְׁלֹשָׁה־עֵדִים
יָקוּם דָּבָר ראה: 16 כִּי־יָקוּם עֵד־חָמָס בְּאִישׁ לַעֲנוֹת בּוֹ
סָרָה: 17 וְעָמְדוּ שְׁנֵי־הָאֲנָשִׁים אֲשֶׁר־לָהֶם הָרִיב לִפְנֵי חכמה,
בינה יְהוָהאדניאהדונהי לִפְנֵי חכמה, בינה הַכֹּהֲנִים וְהַשֹּׁפְטִים אֲשֶׁר
יִהְיוּ בַּיָּמִים נלך הָהֵם: 18 וְדָרְשׁוּ הַשֹּׁפְטִים הֵיטֵב וְהִנֵּה

גְּבוּל - Preserving boundaries: You can bring the horse to the well, but you can't make it drink. There are limits to how much we can help others. We have to know those boundaries, and if people don't want to help themselves, sometimes there's nothing we can do about it. We just have to do as much as we possibly can, but we must also bear in mind that there are limits to what we can do.

עֵד - Conspiring witnesses: When someone bears false witness against another person, the punishment he wishes upon the innocent person rebounds onto him. Whatever we try to do to others comes back to us. The universe is a mirror that reflects everything back.

עֵד־שֶׁקֶר הָעֵד שֶׁקֶר עָנָה בְאָחִיו׃ 19 וַעֲשִׂיתֶם לוֹ כַּאֲשֶׁר
זָמַם לַעֲשׂוֹת לְאָחִיו וּבִעַרְתָּ הָרָע מִקִּרְבֶּךָ׃ 20 וְהַנִּשְׁאָרִים
יִשְׁמְעוּ וְיִרָאוּ וְלֹא־יֹסִפוּ לַעֲשׂוֹת עוֹד כַּדָּבָר ראה הָרָע
הַזֶּה והו בְּקִרְבֶּךָ׃ 21 וְלֹא תָחוֹס עֵינֶךָ נֶפֶשׁ בְּנֶפֶשׁ עַיִן יוד יוד הא
יוד הא ואו יוד הא ואו הא בְּעַיִן יוד יוד הא יוד הא ואו יוד הא ואו הא שֵׁן בְּשֵׁן יָד בְּיָד
רֶגֶל בְּרָגֶל׃ 20 1 כִּי־תֵצֵא **לַמִּלְחָמָה** עַל־אֹיְבֶךָ וְרָאִיתָ
סוּס כוק, א אד אדנ אדני וָרֶכֶב עַם רַב מִמְּךָ לֹא תִירָא מֵהֶם כִּי־
יְהֹוָהאדניאהדונהי אֱלֹהֶיךָ ילה עִמָּךְ הַמַּעַלְךָ מֵאֶרֶץ מִצְרָיִם מצר׃
2 וְהָיָה יהוה, יהה כְּקָרָבְכֶם אֶל־הַמִּלְחָמָה וְנִגַּשׁ הַכֹּהֵן מלה
וְדִבֶּר ראה אֶל־הָעָם׃ 3 וְאָמַר אֲלֵהֶם שְׁמַע יִשְׂרָאֵל אַתֶּם
קְרֵבִים הַיּוֹם נגד, מזבח, זן לַמִּלְחָמָה עַל־אֹיְבֵיכֶם אַל־יֵרַךְ
לְבַבְכֶם אַל־תִּירְאוּ וְאַל־תַּחְפְּזוּ וְאַל־תַּעַרְצוּ מִפְּנֵיהֶם׃
4 כִּי יְהֹוָהאדניאהדונהי אֱלֹהֵיכֶם ילה הַהֹלֵךְ עִמָּכֶם לְהִלָּחֵם לָכֶם
עִם־אֹיְבֵיכֶם לְהוֹשִׁיעַ אֶתְכֶם׃ 5 וְדִבְּרוּ הַשֹּׁטְרִים אֶל־
הָעָם לֵאמֹר מִי ילי ־הָאִישׁ אֲשֶׁר בָּנָה בַיִת ב"פ ראה ־חָדָשׁ י"ב
הוויות וְלֹא חֲנָכוֹ יֵלֵךְ וְיָשֹׁב לְבֵיתוֹ פֶּן־יָמוּת בַּמִּלְחָמָה וְאִישׁ
אַחֵר יַחְנְכֶנּוּ׃ 6 וּמִי ילי ־הָאִישׁ אֲשֶׁר־נָטַע כֶּרֶם וְלֹא חִלְּלוֹ

לַמִּלְחָמָה - Going out to war: The person unqualified to fight is the one who is afraid. We can't win the battle with Satan if we have fears.

יֵלֵךְ וְיָשֹׁב לְבֵיתוֹ פֶּן־יָמוּת בַּמִּלְחָמָה וְאִישׁ אַחֵר יְחַלְּלֶנּוּ׃
7 וּמִי ילי ־הָאִישׁ אֲשֶׁר־אֵרַשׂ אִשָּׁה וְלֹא לְקָחָהּ יֵלֵךְ וְיָשֹׁב
לְבֵיתוֹ פֶּן־יָמוּת בַּמִּלְחָמָה וְאִישׁ אַחֵר יִקָּחֶנָּה׃ 8 וְיָסְפוּ
הַשֹּׁטְרִים לְדַבֵּר ראה אֶל־הָעָם וְאָמְרוּ מִי ילי ־הָאִישׁ הַיָּרֵא
וְרַךְ הַלֵּבָב בוכו יֵלֵךְ וְיָשֹׁב לְבֵיתוֹ וְלֹא יִמַּס אֶת־לְבַב בוכו
אֶחָיו כִּלְבָבוֹ׃ 9 וְהָיָה יהוה, יהה כְּכַלֹּת הַשֹּׁטְרִים לְדַבֵּר ראה
אֶל־הָעָם וּפָקְדוּ שָׂרֵי צְבָאוֹת בְּרֹאשׁ הָעָם׃

Seventh Reading - David - Malchut

10 כִּי־תִקְרַב אֶל־עִיר ערי, סנדלפון לְהִלָּחֵם עָלֶיהָ וְקָרָאתָ אֵלֶיהָ
לְשָׁלוֹם׃ 11 וְהָיָה יהוה, יהה אִם יוהך ־שָׁלוֹם תַּעַנְךָ וּפָתְחָה
לָךְ וְהָיָה יהוה, יהה כָּל ילי ־הָעָם הַנִּמְצָא־בָהּ יִהְיוּ לְךָ לָמַס
וַעֲבָדוּךָ׃ 12 וְאִם יוהך ־לֹא תַשְׁלִים עִמָּךְ וְעָשְׂתָה עִמְּךָ
מִלְחָמָה וְצַרְתָּ עָלֶיהָ׃ 13 וּנְתָנָהּ יְהֹוָאדניאהדונהי אֱלֹהֶיךָ בְּיָדֶךָ
וְהִכִּיתָ אֶת־כָּל ילי ־זְכוּרָהּ לְפִי־חָרֶב׃ 14 רַק הַנָּשִׁים וְהַטַּף
וְהַבְּהֵמָה לכב וְכֹל ילי אֲשֶׁר יִהְיֶה ייי בָעִיר ערי, סנדלפון כָּל ילי
־שְׁלָלָהּ תָּבֹז לָךְ וְאָכַלְתָּ אֶת־שְׁלַל אֹיְבֶיךָ אֲשֶׁר נָתַן
יְהֹוָאדניאהדונהי אֱלֹהֶיךָ לָךְ׃ 15 כֵּן תַּעֲשֶׂה לְכָל יה אדני ילי ־הֶעָרִים

לְשָׁלוֹם - Peaceful overtures: This section helps connect us to the energy of global peace.

הָרְחֹקֹת מִמְּךָ מְאֹד אֲשֶׁר לֹא־מֵעָרֵי הַגֹּוִֽם־הָאֵלֶּה הֵנָּה׃
16 רַק מֵעָרֵי הָעַמִּים הָאֵלֶּה אֲשֶׁר יְהֹוָהאדני יאהדונהי אֱלֹהֶיךָ
נֹתֵן ושר, אבג יתץ, אהבת חנם לְךָ נַחֲלָה לֹא תְחַיֶּה כָּל ילי ־נְשָׁמָה׃
17 כִּי־הַחֲרֵם תַּחֲרִימֵם הַחִתִּי וְהָאֱמֹרִי הַכְּנַעֲנִי וְהַפְּרִזִּי הַחִוִּי
וְהַיְבוּסִי כַּאֲשֶׁר צִוְּךָ יְהֹוָהאדני יאהדונהי אֱלֹהֶיךָ׃ 18 לְמַעַן אֲשֶׁר
לֹא־יְלַמְּדוּ אֶתְכֶם לַעֲשׂוֹת כְּכֹל ילי תּוֹעֲבֹתָם אֲשֶׁר עָשׂוּ
לֵאלֹהֵיהֶם ילה וַחֲטָאתֶם לַיהֹוָהאדני יאהדונהי אֱלֹהֵיכֶם ילה׃ 19 כִּי־
תָצוּר אֶל־עִיר ערי, םןץףך, סנדלפון יָמִים נלך רַבִּים לְהִלָּחֵם עָלֶיהָ
לְתָפְשָׂהּ לֹא־תַשְׁחִית אֶת־עֵצָהּ לִנְדֹּחַ עָלָיו גַּרְזֶן כִּי מִמֶּנּוּ
תֹאכֵל וְאֹתוֹ לֹא תִכְרֹת כִּי הָאָדָם מ״ה, יוד הא ואו הא עֵץ הַשָּׂדֶה
לָבֹא מִפָּנֶיךָ בַּמָּצוֹר׃ 20 רַק עֵץ אֲשֶׁר־תֵּדַע כִּי־לֹא־עֵץ
מַאֲכָל הוּא אֹתוֹ תַשְׁחִית וְכָרָתָּ וּבָנִיתָ מָצוֹר אלף למד הה יוד מם
עַל־הָעִיר ערי, םןץףך, סנדלפון אֲשֶׁר־הִוא עֹשָׂה עִמְּךָ מִלְחָמָה עַד
רִדְתָּהּ׃ 21 1 כִּי־יִמָּצֵא חָלָל בָּאֲדָמָה אֲשֶׁר יְהֹוָהאדני יאהדונהי
אֱלֹהֶיךָ נֹתֵן ושר, אבג יתץ, אהבת חנם לְךָ לְרִשְׁתָּהּ נֹפֵל בַּשָּׂדֶה לֹא נוֹדַע
מִי ילי הִכָּהוּ׃ 2 וְיָצְאוּ זְקֵנֶיךָ וְשֹׁפְטֶיךָ וּמָדְדוּ אֶל־הֶעָרִים

לֹא־תַשְׁחִית - Fruit trees: We're not supposed to cut down fruit trees because they give life, and anything that gives life should not be harmed. Where there's life, there shouldn't be destruction.

אֲשֶׁר סְבִיבֹת הֶחָלָל׃ 3 וְהָיָה יהוה, יהה הָעִיר ערי, מוזחך, סנדלפון
הַקְּרֹבָה אֶל־הֶחָלָל וְלָקְחוּ זִקְנֵי הָעִיר ערי, מוזחך, סנדלפון הַהִוא
עֶגְלַת בָּקָר אֲשֶׁר לֹא־עֻבַּד בָּהּ אֲשֶׁר לֹא־מָשְׁכָה ה״פ אדני הי״
בְּעֹל׃ 4 וְהוֹרִדוּ זִקְנֵי הָעִיר ערי, מוזחך, סנדלפון הַהִוא אֶת־הָעֶגְלָה
אֶל־נַחַל אֵיתָן אֲשֶׁר לֹא־יֵעָבֵד בּוֹ וְלֹא יִזָּרֵעַ וְעָרְפוּ־שָׁם
אֶת־הָעֶגְלָה בַּנָּחַל׃ 5 וְנִגְּשׁוּ הַכֹּהֲנִים בְּנֵי לֵוִי כִּי בָם מב בָּחַר
יְהֹוָאדני יאהדונהי אֱלֹהֶיךָ ילה לְשָׁרְתוֹ וּלְבָרֵךְ בְּשֵׁם יְהֹוָאדני יאהדונהי
וְעַל־פִּיהֶם יִהְיֶה יי כָּל ילי ־רִיב וְכָל ילי ־נָגַע׃ 6 וְכֹל ילי זִקְנֵי
הָעִיר ערי, מוזחך, סנדלפון הַהִוא הַקְּרֹבִים אֶל־הֶחָלָל יִרְחֲצוּ אֶת־
יְדֵיהֶם עַל־הָעֶגְלָה הָעֲרוּפָה בַנָּחַל׃

Maftir

7 וְעָנוּ וְאָמְרוּ יָדֵינוּ לֹא שָׁפְכוּ (כתיב: שפכה) אֶת־הַדָּם הַזֶּה והו
וְעֵינֵינוּ לֹא רָאוּ׃ 8 כַּפֵּר לְעַמְּךָ יִשְׂרָאֵל אֲשֶׁר־פָּדִיתָ
יְהֹוָאדני יאהדונהי וְאַל־תִּתֵּן דָּם ב״פ כהת נָקִי אלף הי יוד הי בְּקֶרֶב עַמְּךָ
יִשְׂרָאֵל וְנִכַּפֵּר לָהֶם הַדָּם׃ 9 וְאַתָּה תְּבַעֵר הַדָּם הַנָּקִי אלף
הי יוד הי מִקִּרְבֶּךָ כִּי־תַעֲשֶׂה הַיָּשָׁר בְּעֵינֵי יְהֹוָאדני יאהדונהי׃

לֹא נוֹדַע - An unsolved murder: If a murder took place, the town closest to where the body was found was held responsible. This was a procedure to erase the negativity of a murder. We're not only individually responsible for our actions but collectively responsible as well.

Haftarah of Shoftim

This haftarah reminds us to awaken ourselves to see what's happening outside of our personal limited universe, not to just go on with our life, but to realize that if the world isn't getting better, it simply means that we have more to do.

Isaiah 51 ישעיהו פרק 51

12 אָנֹכִי איע אָנֹכִי איע הוּא מְנַחֶמְכֶם מִי ילי ־אַתְּ וַתִּירְאִי
מֵאֱנוֹשׁ יָמוּת וּמִבֶּן־אָדָם מ״ה, יוד הא ואו הא חָצִיר יִנָּתֵן׃ 13 וַתִּשְׁכַּח
יְהֹוָהאדניאהדונהי עֹשֶׂךָ נוֹטֶה שָׁמַיִם כוזו, י״פ טל וְיֹסֵד אָרֶץ וַתְּפַחֵד
תָּמִיד נתה, קס״א - קנ״א - קמ״ג כָּל ילי ־הַיּוֹם נגד, מזבח, זן מִפְּנֵי חכמה, בינה
חֲמַת הַמֵּצִיק כַּאֲשֶׁר כּוֹנֵן כוק, א אד אדנ אדני לְהַשְׁחִית וְאַיֵּה
חֲמַת הַמֵּצִיק׃ 14 מִהַר צֹעֶה לְהִפָּתֵחַ וְלֹא־יָמוּת לַשַּׁחַת
וְלֹא יֶחְסַר לַחְמוֹ׃ 15 וְאָנֹכִי איע יְהֹוָהאדניאהדונהי אֱלֹהֶיךָ רֹגַע
הַיָּם ילי וַיֶּהֱמוּ גַּלָּיו יְהֹוָהאדניאהדונהי צְבָאוֹת שְׁמוֹ׃ 16 וָאָשִׂם דְּבָרַי
בְּפִיךָ וּבְצֵל יָדִי כִּסִּיתִיךָ לִנְטֹעַ שָׁמַיִם כוזו, י״פ טל וְלִיסֹד אָרֶץ
וְלֵאמֹר לְצִיּוֹן יוסף עַמִּי־אָתָּה׃ 17 הִתְעוֹרְרִי הִתְעוֹרְרִי קוּמִי
יְרוּשָׁלִַם אֲשֶׁר שָׁתִית מִיַּד יְהֹוָהאדניאהדונהי אֶת־כּוֹס מום, אלהים,
אהיה - אדני חֲמָתוֹ אֶת־קֻבַּעַת כּוֹס מום, אלהים, אהיה - אדני הַתַּרְעֵלָה
שָׁתִית מָצִית׃ 18 אֵין־מְנַהֵל לָהּ מִכָּל ילי ־בָּנִים יָלָדָה וְאֵין
מַחֲזִיק בְּיָדָהּ מִכָּל ילי ־בָּנִים גִּדֵּלָה׃ 19 שְׁתַּיִם הֵנָּה קֹרְאֹתַיִךְ
מִי ילי יָנוּד לָךְ הַשֹּׁד וְהַשֶּׁבֶר וְהָרָעָב וְהַחֶרֶב מִי ילי אֲנַחֲמֵךְ׃

20 בָּנַיִךְ עֻלְּפוּ שָׁכְבוּ בְּרֹאשׁ כָּל ילי ־חוּצוֹת כְּתוֹא מִכְמָר
הַמְלֵאִים חֲמַת־יְהֹוָהאדני יאהדונהי גַּעֲרַת אֱלֹהָיִךְ׃ 21 לָכֵן שִׁמְעִי־
נָא זֹאת עֲנִיָּה וּשְׁכֻרַת וְלֹא מִיָּיִן מיכ, י״פ האא׃ 22 כֹּה היי ־אָמַר
אֲדֹנַיִךְ יְהֹוָהאדני יאהדונהי וֵאלֹהַיִךְ ילה יָרִיב עַמּוֹ הִנֵּה לָקַחְתִּי
מִיָּדֵךְ אֶת־כּוֹס מום, אלהים, אהיה ־ אדני הַתַּרְעֵלָה אֶת־קֻבַּעַת
כּוֹס מום, אלהים, אהיה ־ אדני חֲמָתִי לֹא־תוֹסִיפִי לִשְׁתּוֹתָהּ עוֹד׃
23 וְשַׂמְתִּיהָ בְּיַד־מוֹגַיִךְ אֲשֶׁר־אָמְרוּ לְנַפְשֵׁךְ שְׁחִי וְנַעֲבֹרָה
וַתָּשִׂימִי כָאָרֶץ גֵּוֵךְ וְכַחוּץ לַעֹבְרִים׃ 52 1 עוּרִי עוּרִי לִבְשִׁי
עֻזֵּךְ צִיּוֹן יוסף לִבְשִׁי | בִּגְדֵי והו תִפְאַרְתֵּךְ יְרוּשָׁלַ͏ִם עִיר ערי, בוזפ״ר,
סנדלפון הַקֹּדֶשׁ כִּי לֹא יוֹסִיף יָבֹא־בָךְ עוֹד עָרֵל וְטָמֵא׃
2 הִתְנַעֲרִי מֵעָפָר קוּמִי שְּׁבִי יְרוּשָׁלָ͏ִם התפתחו (הִתְפַּתְּחִי)
מוֹסְרֵי צַוָּארֵךְ שְׁבִיָּה ההה בַּת־צִיּוֹן יוסף׃ 3 כִּי־כֹה היי אָמַר
יְהֹוָהאדני יאהדונהי חִנָּם נִמְכַּרְתֶּם וְלֹא בְכֶסֶף תִּגָּאֵלוּ׃ 4 כִּי כֹה היי
אָמַר אֲדֹנָי יְהֹוִהאדני יאהדונהי מִצְרַיִם מצר יָרַד־עַמִּי בָרִאשֹׁנָה
לָגוּר שָׁם וְאַשּׁוּר בְּאֶפֶס עֲשָׁקוֹ׃ 5 וְעַתָּה מַה יוד הא ואו הא ־לִּי־
פֹה מילה נְאֻם־יְהֹוָהאדני יאהדונהי כִּי־לֻקַּח עַמִּי חִנָּם מֹשְׁלָו יְהֵילִילוּ
נְאֻם־יְהֹוָהאדני יאהדונהי וְתָמִיד נתה, קס״א ־ קנ״א ־ קמ״ג כָּל ילי ־הַיּוֹם נגד, מזבח,
זן שְׁמִי ילי מִנֹּאָץ׃ 6 לָכֵן יֵדַע עַמִּי שְׁמִי ילי לָכֵן בַּיּוֹם נגד, מזבח, זן
הַהוּא כִּי־אֲנִי אני ־הוּא הַמְדַבֵּר הִנֵּנִי׃ 7 מַה יוד הא ואו הא ־נָּאווּ

עַל־הֶהָרִים רַגְלֵי מְבַשֵּׂר מַשְׁמִיעַ שָׁלוֹם מְבַשֵּׂר טוֹב והו
מַשְׁמִיעַ יְשׁוּעָה אֹמֵר לְצִיּוֹן יוסף מָלַךְ אֱלֹהָיִךְ׃ 8 קוֹל צֹפַיִךְ
נָשְׂאוּ קוֹל יַחְדָּו יְרַנֵּנוּ כִּי עַיִן יוד יוד הא יוד הא ואו יוד הא ואו הא בְּעַיִן יוד יוד
הא יוד הא ואו יוד הא ואו הא יִרְאוּ בְּשׁוּב יְהֹוָהאדני יאהדונהי צִיּוֹן יוסף׃ 9 פִּצְחוּ
רַנְּנוּ יַחְדָּו חָרְבוֹת יְרוּשָׁלָםִ כִּי־נִחַם יְהֹוָהאדני יאהדונהי עַמּוֹ
גָּאַל א"ת ב"ש - כתר יְרוּשָׁלָםִ׃ 10 חָשַׂף יְהֹוָהאדני יאהדונהי אֶת־זְרוֹעַ
קָדְשׁוֹ לְעֵינֵי כָּל ילי ־הַגּוֹיִם וְרָאוּ כָּל ילי ־אַפְסֵי־אָרֶץ אֵת
יְשׁוּעַת אֱלֹהֵינוּ ילה׃ 11 סוּרוּ סוּרוּ צְאוּ מִשָּׁם טָמֵא אַל־
תִּגָּעוּ צְאוּ מִתּוֹכָהּ הִבָּרוּ נֹשְׂאֵי כְּלֵי יְהֹוָהאדני יאהדונהי׃ 12 כִּי
לֹא בְחִפָּזוֹן תֵצֵאוּ וּבִמְנוּסָה לֹא תֵלֵכוּן כִּי־הֹלֵךְ לִפְנֵיכֶם
יְהֹוָהאדני יאהדונהי וּמְאַסִּפְכֶם אֱלֹהֵי דמב, ילה יִשְׂרָאֵל׃

Lesson of Ki-Tetze

The War

We know that every word in the Torah is the Creator's word and is intended for each and every one of us at all times. The Zohar warns us against seeing the Torah as a mere anthology of interesting stories. Each letter, each dot, every crown upon every letter—all were written specifically for us living right now in the 21st century.

This week's portion begins: "When you go out to wage war on your enemies..." The beginning of the portion is very surprising, speaking as it does about what happens when a person goes to war and sees a beautiful woman among the enemy and falls in love with her. In Israel today, soldiers stand ready for battle against their enemies on a daily basis, but they are not faced with anything like what the Torah describes here! So what does this have to do with us?

To merit mention in the Torah, every word and every letter must apply to everyone universally. But what war are we waging when we go to work in the morning, return home in the evening, and watch a little television before going to sleep? Who is at war and with whom?

The kabbalists teach us that the war mentioned in this portion is our constant battle with the Negative Side, Satan, the Evil Inclination—call it what you want. The Torah is not referring to a physical war but to the spiritual battle in which we find ourselves every day.

Our first problem is that we do not even realize that a war is going on. How many of us, even those engaged in spiritual studies, truly feel that we are fighting a battle, day in and day out, with the Other Side? If we knew we were at war, we might at least fight. But we don't even acknowledge that a battle is taking place. We need to rid ourselves of this blindness. And we must also learn the purpose of the war, which is the replacement of darkness with Light. In our daily lives, we experience darkness resulting from our previous incarnations and darkness that intensifies during our current incarnation. Only through the Light of the Creator can we ever hope to eliminate this darkness.

If an army general were asked what it takes to prepare for a war, he would need to know what kind of war it would be: land, air, or sea, or all of these at once? Then he would ask about the enemy: how many soldiers they had, how many planes, how many ships. A great deal of information is required to adequately prepare for war. And after all of the information is gathered and the plan is prepared, the soldiers must then be trained. Until all these things are accomplished, the war can't be carried out effectively.

No army can expect to win a war in the physical realm without proper planning and preparation. This is even more true in the spiritual dimension. We are fighting an enemy who has continued to threaten us for almost 6000 years. This enemy knows all our tricks. If we don't even know that we are at war, the enemy has already won the battle.

The greatest weapon in our Opponent's arsenal is his ability to erode our will to fight. But if we are ready and eager to fight, the Light of the Creator will always be stronger than the darkness. In a pitch-black room, even the light from the tiniest match destroys the darkness. And that's only with a small matchstick! Imagine how much more powerful the Light of the Creator can be. But if our Opponent can convince us that we do not need the Light, then he automatically wins the war.

We must know that things can improve—that we don't have to endure problems every moment of our lives, that this world can really be a better place than the one we read about every day in the news. We must believe that there is this possibility—and that we can make it a reality. Without this desire, we don't stand a chance in the spiritual war.

More on war

Once we've realized that we are at war, we must begin to work for victory. We are obligated not only to make the future better but also to fix the past. Specifically, in the month of *Elul*, we must do internal cleansing. Without this cleansing, we stand no chance on Rosh Hashanah to change and to ensure a positive year.

The Maggid of Duvna told this story: Once, there was a man who never spent a day in school. He could not find work because he knew no trade. So he became a thief. All year, he would steal here and there, just to stay alive.

One day, he said to himself, "Why do I have to steal a little bit every day? I should just go out, once and for all and steal a lot."

He found a large and bustling store with profits that were more than adequate. He watched the store for a long time, noting that every day at closing time, a young clerk would leave with the day's revenue and deposit it at a local bank.

The thief knew that at closing time the streets were full of people, so there would be no way to snatch the envelope in broad daylight. He almost gave up on his plan until he came across an expensive custom-clothing store that was on the young clerk's way to the bank. When the thief realized this, he came up with a plan.

A few minutes before closing, the thief entered the expensive store and presented himself to the owner. "I am a servant in the home of a very rich man, and my employer has asked me to buy him a fabulous suit. The price is of no consequence, but the quality must be outstanding and the fabric must be excellent. Do you carry this kind of suit?"

"You've come to the right place," answered the salesman quickly. "Tell your employer that when he comes, I can measure him for the suit of his dreams, and I have no doubts that he will leave satisfied."

"I don't doubt it myself," answered the thief, "but that is precisely the problem. He has no time to come here for his measurements. He is busy from morning until night and hardly has time even for his family. He has therefore sent me in his place so that I may bring him this special suit."

"And how will I know his size?" asked the salesman.

The thief answered, "I have an idea. Let's stand outside until I see someone of my employer's stature, and you can measure him instead. Then you'll be able to create the perfect suit."

The two men stood at the door until the thief pointed to a young man in the streets. He said, "That man could be my employer's twin! They're exactly the same size!" Of course, this was the young man who deposited funds for the store and who was the thief's original target.

The salesman approached the youth and asked him if he wanted to be measured for an expensive suit. The young man thought to himself: I don't have any money of my own, but at least I will be able to see how I would look if I was wealthy.

He was led by the salesman into the store where he tried on the suit and was delighted. He stared at himself in the mirror, before long completely forgetting about the money. At that moment, the thief grabbed the money and ran. "Stop! Thief!" shouted the young man, running after him.

The salesman called after him, "Excuse me! You can't leave the store wearing a suit you haven't purchased. Please take off the suit and then you can be on your way." Needless to say, by the time the young man changed back into his own clothes, the thief was long gone.

The moral is simple. We are entrusted with a "bank deposit," which is actually full of our positive actions. The Opponent distracts us by sending us into all kinds of stores that are not right for us, to try on suits that are also not right for us. In short, he encourages us to waste our time with things that are not ours. And we have nothing with which to defend ourselves, neither in our bodies nor in our souls.

In so many situations where we experience excitement or pleasure, how long does the excitement or pleasure last? Why is it that when we go out to have a good time, we must eventually come home again, only to seek another place to enjoy ourselves the next night or the next week? Why isn't one "good time" enough for us? The answer is that we are not experiencing the true fulfillment that remains with us our entire lives—and even across lifetimes. But we do have a system for catching the thief and taking back the Light that Satan stole from us. It's by making *teshuvah* (sincere repentance) and by going to those we've hurt and removing the veils we've created between them and us.

What a shame it would be to arrive at Rosh Hashanah still trapped in the negative garments that we have not bothered to remove. Then the Creator will say, "You cannot try to catch the thief with the suit you are wearing!" But if we want to remove the suit on Rosh Hashanah, the Creator will tell us that it's too late. We have to take the opportunity that has been given to us in the month of *Elul*. We need to prepare ourselves for Rosh Hashanah so that it won't be too late. As it is written: "Whoever does not prepare for Shabbat does not eat on Shabbat."

Amalek

How is *Amalek* connected to the month of *Elul*? We know that the word *Amalek* has the same numerical value as *safek* (doubt). In other words, *Amalek* is the experience of not knowing, of uncertainty.

There is a brief story about uncertainty: A wise teacher once visited a seminary and saw two students studying. He told one of the students that he would grow to be a learned and renowned scholar because that was the student's sole desire. The other student asked the teacher why he did not see the same future for him. The teacher explained that the first student wanted *only* to be a learned scholar. The second student wanted to be a scholar, too, but he also wanted other things. The danger of *Amalek* lies in the difference between "also" and "only." May we merit, with the help of the Light, to be 100 percent committed to our spiritual work.

Synopsis of Ki-Tetze

Ki tetze la milchamah literally means "When you go out to war." We must be aware of the fact that we are in a constant battle with the Other Side. The first step to winning this war is knowing that a war is going on.

First Reading - Abraham - Chesed

10 כִּי־תֵצֵא לַמִּלְחָמָה עַל־אֹיְבֶיךָ וּנְתָנוֹ יְהֹוָהאדניאהדונהי
אֱלֹהֶיךָ בְּיָדֶךָ וְשָׁבִיתָ שִׁבְיוֹ׃ 11 וְרָאִיתָ בַּשִּׁבְיָה אֵשֶׁת
יְפַת־תֹּאַר וְחָשַׁקְתָּ בָהּ וְלָקַחְתָּ לְךָ לְאִשָּׁה׃ 12 וַהֲבֵאתָהּ
אֶל־תּוֹךְ בֵּיתֶךָ וְגִלְּחָה אֶת־רֹאשָׁהּ וְעָשְׂתָה אֶת־צִפָּרְנֶיהָ׃
13 וְהֵסִירָה אֶת־שִׂמְלַת שִׁבְיָהּ מֵעָלֶיהָ וְיָשְׁבָה בְּבֵיתֶךָ
וּבָכְתָה אֶת־אָבִיהָ וְאֶת־אִמָּהּ יֶרַח יָמִים נלך וְאַחַר כֵּן תָּבוֹא
אֵלֶיהָ וּבְעַלְתָּהּ וְהָיְתָה לְךָ לְאִשָּׁה׃ 14 וְהָיָה יהוה, יהה אִם יוהך
־לֹא חָפַצְתָּ בָּהּ וְשִׁלַּחְתָּהּ לְנַפְשָׁהּ וּמָכֹר לֹא־תִמְכְּרֶנָּה
בַּכָּסֶף לֹא־תִתְעַמֵּר בָּהּ תַּחַת אֲשֶׁר עִנִּיתָהּ׃ 15 כִּי־תִהְיֶיןָ
לְאִישׁ שְׁתֵּי נָשִׁים הָאַחַת אֲהוּבָה וְהָאַחַת שְׂנוּאָה וְיָלְדוּ־
לוֹ בָנִים הָאֲהוּבָה וְהַשְּׂנוּאָה וְהָיָה יהוה, יהה הַבֵּן הַבְּכֹר
לַשְּׂנִיאָה׃ 16 וְהָיָה יהוה, יהה בְּיוֹם נגד, מזבח, זן הַנְחִילוֹ אֶת־בָּנָיו

יְפַת־תֹּאַר - "When you see a woman who looks nice…": The woman who looks nice here represents negativity. Even though negativity is our enemy, we still are inclined to admire it. Satan will make negativity look like a beautiful woman or anything else that we desire.

שְׁתֵּי נָשִׁים - This next verse discusses a man with two wives, one whom he loves and one whom he hates. In a relationship, we cannot separate the things we like about a person from the things we dislike. It's a package deal. We don't get angry at our hand when it touches a hot pot. Likewise, we must look at our partner as if he or she were a part of us.

אֵת אֲשֶׁר־יִהְיֶה לוֹ לֹא יוּכַל לְבַכֵּר אֶת־בֶּן־הָאֲהוּבָה
עַל־פְּנֵי חכמה, בינה בֶן־הַשְּׂנוּאָה הַבְּכֹר: 17 כִּי אֶת־הַבְּכֹר
בֶּן־הַשְּׂנוּאָה יַכִּיר לָתֶת לוֹ פִּי שְׁנַיִם בְּכֹל לכב אֲשֶׁר־יִמָּצֵא
לוֹ כִּי־הוּא רֵאשִׁית אֹנוֹ לוֹ מִשְׁפַּט הַבְּכֹרָה: 18 כִּי־יִהְיֶה
לְאִישׁ בֵּן סוֹרֵר וּמוֹרֶה אֵינֶנּוּ שֹׁמֵעַ בְּקוֹל אָבִיו וּבְקוֹל
אִמּוֹ וְיִסְּרוּ אֹתוֹ וְלֹא יִשְׁמַע אֲלֵיהֶם: 19 וְתָפְשׂוּ בוֹ אָבִיו
וְאִמּוֹ וְהוֹצִיאוּ אֹתוֹ אֶל־זִקְנֵי עִירוֹ וְאֶל־שַׁעַר מְקֹמוֹ:
20 וְאָמְרוּ אֶל־זִקְנֵי עִירוֹ בְּנֵנוּ זֶה סוֹרֵר וּמֹרֶה אֵינֶנּוּ שֹׁמֵעַ
בְּקֹלֵנוּ זוֹלֵל וְסֹבֵא: 21 וּרְגָמֻהוּ כָּל ילי ־אַנְשֵׁי עִירוֹ בָאֲבָנִים
וָמֵת וּבִעַרְתָּ הָרָע מִקִּרְבֶּךָ וְכָל ילי ־יִשְׂרָאֵל יִשְׁמְעוּ וְיִרָאוּ:

Second Reading - Isaac - Gvurah

22 וְכִי־יִהְיֶה בְאִישׁ חֵטְא מִשְׁפַּט־מָוֶת וְהוּמָת וְתָלִיתָ אֹתוֹ
עַל־עֵץ: 23 לֹא־תָלִין נִבְלָתוֹ עַל־הָעֵץ כִּי־קָבוֹר תִּקְבְּרֶנּוּ
בַּיּוֹם נגד, מזבח, זן הַהוּא כִּי־קִלְלַת אֱלֹהִים מום, ילה תָּלוּי וְלֹא

בֵּן סוֹרֵר - The rebellious son: Parents need to be tough but loving with their children. If children are left alone to do as they please, Bread of Shame will manifest in the children's rebelliousness.

וְתָלִיתָ - This section deals with a person who is hanged. It states that a criminal's body should not be left hanging overnight. Even if a person has committed the worst crimes, it is still incumbent upon us to treat him with human dignity.

תְטַמֵּא אֶת־אַדְמָתְךָ אֲשֶׁר יְהֹוָהאדניאהדונהי אֱלֹהֶיךָ נֹתֵן ושר, אבג
יתץ, אהבת חינם לְךָ נַחֲלָה׃ 22 1 לֹא־תִרְאֶה אֶת־שׁוֹר ושר, אבג יתץ,
אהבת חנם אָחִיךָ אוֹ אֶת־שֵׂיוֹ נִדָּחִים וְהִתְעַלַּמְתָּ מֵהֶם הָשֵׁב
תְּשִׁיבֵם לְאָחִיךָ׃ 2 וְאִם יוהך ־לֹא קָרוֹב אָחִיךָ אֵלֶיךָ וְלֹא
יְדַעְתּוֹ וַאֲסַפְתּוֹ אֶל־תּוֹךְ בֵּיתֶךָ וְהָיָה יהוה, יהה עִמְּךָ עַד דְּרֹשׁ
אָחִיךָ אֹתוֹ וַהֲשֵׁבֹתוֹ לוֹ׃ 3 וְכֵן תַּעֲשֶׂה לַחֲמֹרוֹ וְכֵן תַּעֲשֶׂה
לְשִׂמְלָתוֹ וְכֵן תַּעֲשֶׂה לְכָל יה אדני ילי ־אֲבֵדַת אָחִיךָ אֲשֶׁר־
תֹּאבַד מִמֶּנּוּ וּמְצָאתָהּ לֹא תוּכַל לְהִתְעַלֵּם׃ 4 לֹא־תִרְאֶה
אֶת־חֲמוֹר אָחִיךָ אוֹ שׁוֹרוֹ נֹפְלִים בַּדֶּרֶךְ וְהִתְעַלַּמְתָּ מֵהֶם
הָקֵם תָּקִים עִמּוֹ׃ 5 לֹא־יִהְיֶה ייי כְלִי־גֶבֶר עַל־אִשָּׁה וְלֹא־
יִלְבַּשׁ גֶּבֶר שִׂמְלַת אִשָּׁה כִּי תוֹעֲבַת יְהֹוָהאדניאהדונהי אֱלֹהֶיךָ

וְהִתְעַלַּמְתָּ - This section teaches us to have concern for other people's property. If we find a lost or misplaced object, we should take care of it as though it were our own. The Light will give us nothing if we treat others' possessions like nothing.

נֹפְלִים - In this next section, we learn that we must have concern even for the pain of animals. Moses chased the lamb and returned it to the herd. The Creator saw that a man who had such concern for animals would have concern for the Israelites.

גֶּבֶר - Men in women's clothing: There are times when it is best not to mix the energy of men and women. Women represent the Vessel and men represent the Light. During certain times of prayer, for example, these two energies should not be combined.

כָּל ילי ־עֹשֵׂה אֵלֶּה׃ 6 כִּי יִקָּרֵא קַן־צִפּוֹר | לְפָנֶיךָ בַּדֶּרֶךְ
בְּכָל לכב ־עֵץ | אוֹ עַל־הָאָרֶץ אלף למד הה יוד מם אֶפְרֹחִים אוֹ
בֵיצִים וְהָאֵם יוהך רֹבֶצֶת עַל־הָאֶפְרֹחִים אוֹ עַל־הַבֵּיצִים
לֹא־תִקַּח הָאֵם יוהך עַל־הַבָּנִים׃ 7 שַׁלֵּחַ תְּשַׁלַּח אֶת־הָאֵם יוהך
וְאֶת־הַבָּנִים תִּקַּח־לָךְ לְמַעַן יִיטַב לָךְ וְהַאֲרַכְתָּ יָמִים נלך׃

Third Reading - Jacob - Tiferet

8 כִּי תִבְנֶה בַּיִת ב״פ ראה חָדָשׁ וְעָשִׂיתָ מַעֲקֶה לְגַגֶּךָ
וְלֹא־תָשִׂים דָּמִים בְּבֵיתֶךָ כִּי־יִפֹּל הַנֹּפֵל מִמֶּנּוּ׃ 9 לֹא־
תִזְרַע כַּרְמְךָ כִּלְאָיִם פֶּן־תִּקְדַּשׁ הַמְלֵאָה הַזֶּרַע אֲשֶׁר
תִּזְרָע וּתְבוּאַת הַכָּרֶם׃ 10 לֹא־תַחֲרֹשׁ בְּשׁוֹר ושר, אבג יתץ,
אהבת חנם ־וּבַחֲמֹר יַחְדָּו׃ 11 לֹא תִלְבַּשׁ שַׁעַטְנֵז צֶמֶר מצר

קַן־צִפּוֹר - This next section is a very difficult part of the Torah to understand. Without the Zohar, it would be impossible. It speaks about a mother bird and her eggs: "Send away the mother and take the eggs." The Zohar explains that this is connected to longevity. The energy of this reading aids us in living longer.

מַעֲקֶה - Here, the Torah discusses the fact that a person needs to build a protective barrier around his roof so that people do not fall off. This is really about having concern for others. The more we care about others, the more the Light protects us.

יַחְדָּו - This part of the Torah discusses the kinds of things that should not be mixed together: the unhealthy mixing of food, for example, or animals

וּפִשְׁתִּים יַחְדָּו׃ 12 גְּדִלִים תַּעֲשֶׂה־לָּךְ עַל־אַרְבַּע כַּנְפוֹת
כְּסוּתְךָ אֲשֶׁר תְּכַסֶּה־בָּהּ׃ 13 כִּי־יִקַּח וזעם אִישׁ אִשָּׁה
וּבָא אֵלֶיהָ וּשְׂנֵאָהּ׃ 14 וְשָׂם לָהּ עֲלִילֹת דְּבָרִים וְהוֹצִא
עָלֶיהָ שֵׁם רָע וְאָמַר אֶת־הָאִשָּׁה הַזֹּאת לָקַחְתִּי וָאֶקְרַב
אֵלֶיהָ וְלֹא־מָצָאתִי לָהּ בְּתוּלִים׃ 15 וְלָקַח אֲבִי הַנַּעֲרָ
וְאִמָּהּ וְהוֹצִיאוּ אֶת־בְּתוּלֵי הַנַּעֲרָ אֶל־זִקְנֵי הָעִיר ערי, בוזוך,
סנדלפון הַשָּׁעְרָה׃ 16 וְאָמַר אֲבִי הַנַּעֲרָ אֶל־הַזְּקֵנִים אֶת־בִּתִּי
נָתַתִּי לָאִישׁ הַזֶּה והו לְאִשָּׁה וַיִּשְׂנָאֶהָ׃ 17 וְהִנֵּה־הוּא שָׂם
עֲלִילֹת דְּבָרִים לֵאמֹר לֹא־מָצָאתִי לְבִתְּךָ בְּתוּלִים וְאֵלֶּה
בְּתוּלֵי בִתִּי וּפָרְשׂוּ הַשִּׂמְלָה לִפְנֵי חכמה, בינה זִקְנֵי הָעִיר ערי,
בוזוך, סנדלפון׃ 18 וְלָקְחוּ זִקְנֵי הָעִיר ערי, בוזוך, סנדלפון ־הַהִוא אֶת־
הָאִישׁ וְיִסְּרוּ אֹתוֹ׃ 19 וְעָנְשׁוּ אֹתוֹ מֵאָה כֶסֶף וְנָתְנוּ לַאֲבִי
הַנַּעֲרָה כִּי הוֹצִיא שֵׁם רָע עַל בְּתוּלַת יִשְׂרָאֵל וְלוֹ־תִהְיֶה
לְאִשָּׁה לֹא־יוּכַל לְשַׁלְּחָהּ כָּל ילי ־יָמָיו׃ 20 וְאִם יוהך ־אֱמֶת ז"פ

that should not be housed together. Certain people also do not mix well, and we should not put these people into uncomfortable situations by asking them to associate with each other.

שֵׁם רָע - Here, the Torah speaks about *lashon hara* (evil speech) with reference to a married woman who has gone off with other men. The Zohar says that *lashon hara* is one of the most difficult negative actions to correct. This section gives us the power to resist participating in *lashon hara*.

ס"ג הָיָה ההה יהה הַדָּבָר ראה הַזֶּה והו לֹא־נִמְצְאוּ בְּתוּלִים לַנַּעֲרָ׃
21 וְהוֹצִיאוּ אֶת־הַנַּעֲרָ אֶל־פֶּתַח בֵּית ב"פ ראה ־אָבִיהָ וּסְקָלוּהָ
אַנְשֵׁי עִירָהּ בָּאֲבָנִים וָמֵתָה כִּי־עָשְׂתָה נְבָלָה בְּיִשְׂרָאֵל
לִזְנוֹת בֵּית ב"פ ראה אָבִיהָ וּבִעַרְתָּ הָרָע מִקִּרְבֶּךָ׃ 22 כִּי־יִמָּצֵא אִישׁ
שֹׁכֵב | עִם־אִשָּׁה בְעֻלַת־בַּעַל וּמֵתוּ גַּם־שְׁנֵיהֶם הָאִישׁ
הַשֹּׁכֵב עִם־הָאִשָּׁה וְהָאִשָּׁה וּבִעַרְתָּ הָרָע מִיִּשְׂרָאֵל׃ 23 כִּי
יִהְיֶה ייי נַעֲרָ בְתוּלָה מְאֹרָשָׂה לְאִישׁ וּמְצָאָהּ אִישׁ בָּעִיר ערי,
בוזוהך, סנדלפון וְשָׁכַב עִמָּהּ׃ 24 וְהוֹצֵאתֶם אֶת־שְׁנֵיהֶם אֶל־
שַׁעַר | הָעִיר ערי, בוזוהך, סנדלפון הַהִוא וּסְקַלְתֶּם אֹתָם בָּאֲבָנִים
וָמֵתוּ אֶת־הַנַּעֲרָ עַל־דְּבַר ראה אֲשֶׁר לֹא־צָעֲקָה בָעִיר ערי,
בוזוהך, סנדלפון וְאֶת־הָאִישׁ עַל־דְּבַר ראה אֲשֶׁר־עִנָּה אֶת־אֵשֶׁת
רֵעֵהוּ וּבִעַרְתָּ הָרָע מִקִּרְבֶּךָ׃ 25 וְאִם יוהך ־בַּשָּׂדֶה יִמְצָא
הָאִישׁ אֶת־הַנַּעֲרָ הַמְאֹרָשָׂה וְהֶחֱזִיק־בָּהּ הָאִישׁ וְשָׁכַב

בְּתוּלִים - The Torah discusses a married woman who may have committed adultery. But this section is not limited to the specific sin of adultery. Sometimes, one act can destroy everything we have built, giving up so much for so little.

שֹׁכֵב - This next section discusses rape. The Zohar explains that this is really about the sin between Cain and Abel. Every negative action stems from that sin. Correcting this first sin is one of our most important tasks.

עִמָּהּ וּמֵת הָאִישׁ אֲשֶׁר־שָׁכַב עִמָּהּ לְבַדּוֹ׃ 26 וְלַנַּעֲרָ לֹא־
תַעֲשֶׂה דָבָר ראה אֵין לַנַּעֲרָ חֵטְא מָוֶת כִּי כַּאֲשֶׁר יָקוּם אִישׁ
עַל־רֵעֵהוּ וּרְצָחוֹ נֶפֶשׁ כֵּן הַדָּבָר ראה הַזֶּה והו׃ 27 כִּי בַשָּׂדֶה
מְצָאָהּ צָעֲקָה הַנַּעֲרָ הַמְאֹרָשָׂה וְאֵין מוֹשִׁיעַ לָהּ׃ 28 כִּי־
יִמְצָא אִישׁ נַעֲרָ בְתוּלָה אֲשֶׁר לֹא־אֹרָשָׂה וּתְפָשָׂהּ וְשָׁכַב
עִמָּהּ וְנִמְצָאוּ׃ 29 וְנָתַן אבג יתץ, ושר, אהבת חנם הָאִישׁ הַשֹּׁכֵב עִמָּהּ
לַאֲבִי הַנַּעֲרָ חֲמִשִּׁים כָּסֶף וְלוֹ־תִהְיֶה לְאִשָּׁה תַּחַת אֲשֶׁר
עִנָּהּ לֹא־יוּכַל שַׁלְּחָהּ כָּל ילי ־יָמָיו׃ 23 1 לֹא־יִקַּח חעם אִישׁ
אֶת־אֵשֶׁת אָבִיו וְלֹא יְגַלֶּה כְּנַף אלף הה יוד הה, אדני - אלהים אָבִיו׃
2 לֹא־יָבֹא פְצוּעַ־דַּכָּא וּכְרוּת שָׁפְכָה בִּקְהַל יְהֹוָ֯אדני֯אהדונהי׃
3 לֹא־יָבֹא מַמְזֵר בִּקְהַל יְהֹוָ֯אדני֯אהדונהי גַּם דּוֹר עֲשִׂירִי לֹא־
יָבֹא לוֹ בִּקְהַל יְהֹוָ֯אדני֯אהדונהי׃ 4 לֹא־יָבֹא עַמּוֹנִי וּמוֹאָבִי
בִּקְהַל יְהֹוָ֯אדני֯אהדונהי גַּם דּוֹר עֲשִׂירִי לֹא־יָבֹא לָהֶם בִּקְהַל
יְהֹוָ֯אדני֯אהדונהי עַד־עוֹלָם׃ 5 עַל־דְּבַר ראה אֲשֶׁר לֹא־קִדְּמוּ
אֶתְכֶם בַּלֶּחֶם ג"פ יהו"ה וּבַמַּיִם בַּדֶּרֶךְ בְּצֵאתְכֶם מִמִּצְרָיִם מצר
וַאֲשֶׁר שָׂכַר י"פ ב"ן עָלֶיךָ אֶת־בִּלְעָם עלם בֶּן־בְּעוֹר מִפְּתוֹר

לֹא־יִקַּח - Forbidden and restricted marriages: The Ari explains that soulmates are usually two people who live far from each other, thus making soulmate marriages very difficult to achieve. This section protects us from relationships that might cause us pain and that would be difficult to get out of.

אֲרַם נַהֲרַיִם לְקַלְלֶךָּ׃ 6 וְלֹא־אָבָה יְהֹוָאדניאהדונהי אֱלֹהֶיךָ ילה
לִשְׁמֹעַ אֶל־בִּלְעָם עלם וַיַּהֲפֹךְ יְהֹוָאדניאהדונהי אֱלֹהֶיךָ לְּךָ אֶת־
הַקְּלָלָה לִבְרָכָה כִּי אֲהֵבְךָ יְהֹוָאדניאהדונהי אֱלֹהֶיךָ׃ 7 לֹא־
תִדְרֹשׁ שְׁלֹמָם וְטֹבָתָם כָּל ילי ־יָמֶיךָ לְעוֹלָם׃

Fourth Reading - Moses - Netzach

8 לֹא־תְתַעֵב אֲדֹמִי כִּי אָחִיךָ הוּא לֹא־תְתַעֵב מִצְרִי מצפצ, אלף
למד הי יוד מם כִּי־גֵר הָיִיתָ בְאַרְצוֹ׃ 9 בָּנִים אֲשֶׁר־יִוָּלְדוּ לָהֶם דּוֹר
שְׁלִישִׁי יָבֹא לָהֶם בִּקְהַל יְהֹוָאדניאהדונהי׃ 10 כִּי־תֵצֵא מַחֲנֶה
עַל־אֹיְבֶיךָ וְנִשְׁמַרְתָּ מִכֹּל ילי דָּבָר ראה רָע׃ 11 כִּי־יִהְיֶה ייי בְךָ
אִישׁ אֲשֶׁר לֹא־יִהְיֶה ייי טָהוֹר י״פ אכא מִקְּרֵה־לָיְלָה מלה וְיָצָא
אֶל־מִחוּץ לַמַּחֲנֶה לֹא יָבֹא אֶל־תּוֹךְ הַמַּחֲנֶה׃ 12 וְהָיָה יהוה,
יהה לִפְנוֹת־עֶרֶב יִרְחַץ בַּמָּיִם וּכְבֹא הַשֶּׁמֶשׁ יָבֹא אֶל־תּוֹךְ
הַמַּחֲנֶה׃ 13 וְיָד תִּהְיֶה לְךָ מִחוּץ לַמַּחֲנֶה וְיָצָאתָ שָּׁמָּה יוד הא ואו
הא חוּץ׃ 14 וְיָתֵד תִּהְיֶה לְךָ עַל־אֲזֵנֶךָ וְהָיָה יהוה, יהה בְּשִׁבְתְּךָ חוּץ
וְחָפַרְתָּה בָהּ וְשַׁבְתָּ וְכִסִּיתָ אֶת־צֵאָתֶךָ׃ 15 כִּי יְהֹוָאדניאהדונהי
אֱלֹהֶיךָ מִתְהַלֵּךְ | בְּקֶרֶב מַחֲנֶךָ לְהַצִּילְךָ וְלָתֵת אֹיְבֶיךָ
לְפָנֶיךָ וְהָיָה יהוה, יהה מַחֲנֶיךָ קָדוֹשׁ וְלֹא־יִרְאֶה רי״ו, גבורה בְךָ

כִּי־תֵצֵא - This next section discusses the condition in which we keep our physical environment. We should never contribute to polluting our surroundings and thus not appreciating what the Light has given us.

עֶרְוַת דָּבָר ראה וְשָׁב מֵאַחֲרֶיךָ׃ 16 לֹא־תַסְגִּיר עֶבֶד אֶל־
אֲדֹנָיו אֲשֶׁר־יִנָּצֵל אֵלֶיךָ מֵעִם אֲדֹנָיו׃ 17 עִמְּךָ יֵשֵׁב בְּקִרְבְּךָ
בַּמָּקוֹם אֲשֶׁר־יִבְחַר בְּאַחַד אהבה, דאגה שְׁעָרֶיךָ בַּטּוֹב והו לוֹ
לֹא תּוֹנֶנּוּ׃ 18 לֹא־תִהְיֶה קְדֵשָׁה מִבְּנוֹת יִשְׂרָאֵל וְלֹא־
יִהְיֶה ייי קָדֵשׁ מִבְּנֵי יִשְׂרָאֵל׃ 19 לֹא־תָבִיא אֶתְנַן זוֹנָה וּמְחִיר
כֶּלֶב בֵּית ב"פ ראה יְהֹוָהאדניאהדונהי אֱלֹהֶיךָ לְכָל יה אדני ילי ־נֶדֶר כִּי
תוֹעֲבַת יְהֹוָהאדניאהדונהי אֱלֹהֶיךָ גַּם־שְׁנֵיהֶם׃ 20 לֹא־תַשִּׁיךְ
לְאָחִיךָ נֶשֶׁךְ כֶּסֶף נֶשֶׁךְ אֹכֶל נֶשֶׁךְ כָּל ילי ־דָּבָר ראה אֲשֶׁר
יִשָּׁךְ׃ 21 לַנָּכְרִי תַשִּׁיךְ וּלְאָחִיךָ לֹא תַשִּׁיךְ לְמַעַן יְבָרֶכְךָ
יְהֹוָהאדניאהדונהי אֱלֹהֶיךָ בְּכֹל לכב מִשְׁלַח יָדֶךָ עַל־הָאָרֶץ אלף למד

לֹא־תַסְגִּיר - Here, the Torah states that one should not return an escaped slave. This refers to our responsibility for teaching people Kabbalah. Everyone is a slave to Satan unless they begin the path of enlightenment. It is imperative that as many people as possible learn Kabbalah so that we can be freed from the bondage of Satan.

קְדֵשָׁה - Sexual purity: Sex is considered 1/60th of all the blessings, which is why Satan uses it to manipulate us. We must choose our partners not just so that they can satisfy our needs. Our goal in the sexual act is to be unselfish beings. If this is not the case, Satan becomes involved and interferes in the couple's connection.

לֹא־תַשִּׁיךְ - The Torah explains that there is a prohibition against charging interest. However, this does not refer only to loans and money. If we do someone a favor and expect a favor in return, our expectation erases the positivity created by our sharing.

הה יוד מם אֲשֶׁר־אַתָּה בָא־שָׁמָּה יוד הא ואו הא לְרִשְׁתָּהּ׃ 22 כִּי־תִדֹּר
נֶדֶר לַיהוָהאדניאהדונהי אֱלֹהֶיךָ לֹא תְאַחֵר לְשַׁלְּמוֹ כִּי־דָרֹשׁ
יִדְרְשֶׁנּוּ יְהוָהאדניאהדונהי אֱלֹהֶיךָ ילה מֵעִמָּךְ וְהָיָה יהוה, יהה בְךָ
חֵטְא׃ 23 וְכִי תֶחְדַּל לִנְדֹּר לֹא־יִהְיֶה ייי בְךָ חֵטְא׃ 24 מוֹצָא
שְׂפָתֶיךָ תִּשְׁמֹר וְעָשִׂיתָ כַּאֲשֶׁר נָדַרְתָּ לַיהוָהאדניאהדונהי
אֱלֹהֶיךָ ילה נְדָבָה אֲשֶׁר דִּבַּרְתָּ בְּפִיךָ׃

Fifth Reading - Aaron - Hod

25 כִּי תָבֹא בְּכֶרֶם רֵעֶךָ וְאָכַלְתָּ עֲנָבִים כְּנַפְשְׁךָ שָׂבְעֶךָ
וְאֶל־כֶּלְיְךָ לֹא תִתֵּן ב״פ כהת׃ 26 כִּי תָבֹא בְּקָמַת רֵעֶךָ וְקָטַפְתָּ
מְלִילֹת בְּיָדֶךָ וְחֶרְמֵשׁ לֹא תָנִיף עַל קָמַת רֵעֶךָ׃ 24 1 כִּי־
יִקַּח חעם אִישׁ אִשָּׁה וּבְעָלָהּ וְהָיָה יהוה, יהה אִם יוהך ־לֹא תִמְצָא־
חֵן מוזי בְעֵינָיו כִּי־מָצָא בָהּ עֶרְוַת דָּבָר ראה וְכָתַב לָהּ סֵפֶר
כְּרִיתֻת וְנָתַן אבג יתץ, ושר, אהבת חנם בְּיָדָהּ וְשִׁלְּחָהּ מִבֵּיתוֹ׃

נֶדֶר - When we make a promise, especially if it is work for the Lightforce, we should fulfill it as soon as possible. If we make a promise and do not keep it, we're just creating an opening for Satan.

וְאָכַלְתָּ - This section tells us that a worker should be granted the right to eat. We must treat those in our employ as equals, not as inferiors.

כְּרִיתֻת - This section tells us that there can be a *mitzvah* in divorce. For example, if one partner's soulmate is ready and waiting, then the present marriage must end. The only other option would be death: The spouse of the

2 וְיָצְאָה מִבֵּיתוֹ וְהָלְכָה וְהָיְתָה לְאִישׁ־אַחֵר: 3 וּשְׂנֵאָהּ
הָאִישׁ הָאַחֲרוֹן וְכָתַב לָהּ סֵפֶר כְּרִיתֻת וְנָתַן אבג יתץ, ושר,
אהבת חנם בְּיָדָהּ וְשִׁלְּחָהּ מִבֵּיתוֹ אוֹ כִי יָמוּת הָאִישׁ הָאַחֲרוֹן
אֲשֶׁר־לְקָחָהּ לוֹ לְאִשָּׁה: 4 לֹא־יוּכַל בַּעְלָהּ הָרִאשׁוֹן
אֲשֶׁר־שִׁלְּחָהּ לָשׁוּב לְקַחְתָּהּ לִהְיוֹת לוֹ לְאִשָּׁה אַחֲרֵי
אֲשֶׁר הֻטַּמָּאָה כִּי־תוֹעֵבָה הִוא לִפְנֵי חכמה, בינה יְהֹוָהאדניאהדונהי
וְלֹא תַחֲטִיא אֶת־הָאָרֶץ אלף למד הה יוד מם אֲשֶׁר יְהֹוָהאדניאהדונהי
אֱלֹהֶיךָ נֹתֵן ושר, אבג יתץ, אהבת חינם לְךָ נַחֲלָה:

Sixth Reading - Joseph - Yesod

5 כִּי־יִקַּח ועם אִישׁ אִשָּׁה חֲדָשָׁה לֹא יֵצֵא בַּצָּבָא וְלֹא־
יַעֲבֹר עָלָיו לְכָל יה אדני ילי ־דָּבָר ראה נָקִי אלף הי יוד הי יִהְיֶה ייי
לְבֵיתוֹ שָׁנָה אֶחָת וְשִׂמַּח אֶת־אִשְׁתּוֹ אֲשֶׁר־לָקָח: 6 לֹא־
יַחֲבֹל רֵחַיִם וָרָכֶב כִּי־נֶפֶשׁ הוּא חֹבֵל: 7 כִּי־יִמָּצֵא אִישׁ

person whose soulmate is waiting would need to leave this world if divorce was not an option. This is why divorce can be a positive step.

חֲדָשָׁה - This next section considers the significance of the first year of marriage. The first year is the foundation of the future relationship. If things go terribly wrong, the marriage can never last. While there will always be problems, we must ask at the end of the first year whether the union is positive or negative and we must be prepared to move on in the direction that the answer indicates.

גֹּנֵב נֶפֶשׁ מֵאֶחָיו מִבְּנֵי יִשְׂרָאֵל וְהִתְעַמֶּר־בּוֹ וּמְכָרוֹ וּמֵת
הַגַּנָּב הַהוּא וּבִעַרְתָּ הָרָע מִקִּרְבֶּךָ׃ 8 הִשָּׁמֶר בְּנֶגַע־
הַצָּרַעַת לִשְׁמֹר מְאֹד וְלַעֲשׂוֹת כְּכֹל ילי אֲשֶׁר־יוֹרוּ אֶתְכֶם
הַכֹּהֲנִים הַלְוִיִּם כַּאֲשֶׁר צִוִּיתִם תִּשְׁמְרוּ לַעֲשׂוֹת׃ 9 זָכוֹר אֵת
אֲשֶׁר־עָשָׂה יְהֹוָה יאהדונהי אֱלֹהֶיךָ לְמִרְיָם בַּדָּרֶךְ בְּצֵאתְכֶם
מִמִּצְרָיִם מצר׃ 10 כִּי־תַשֶּׁה בְרֵעֲךָ מַשַּׁאת מְאוּמָה לֹא־
תָבֹא אֶל־בֵּיתוֹ לַעֲבֹט עֲבֹטוֹ׃ 11 בַּחוּץ תַּעֲמֹד וְהָאִישׁ
אֲשֶׁר אַתָּה נֹשֶׁה בוֹ יוֹצִיא אֵלֶיךָ אֶת־הַעֲבוֹט הַחוּצָה׃
12 וְאִם יוהך ־אִישׁ עָנִי יוד יוד הא יוד הא ואו יוד הא ואו הא ואו הא הוּא לֹא תִשְׁכַּב
בַּעֲבֹטוֹ׃ 13 הָשֵׁב תָּשִׁיב לוֹ אֶת־הַעֲבוֹט כְּבוֹא הַשֶּׁמֶשׁ

גֹּנֵב נֶפֶשׁ - Here, the Torah speaks about kidnapping. Whenever a person is totally controlled in a relationship, a kind of kidnapping takes place. This applies even to parents and children.

הַצָּרַעַת - The Torah makes us aware that any skin condition is the result of *lashon hara*, or "evil speech." From this section, we gain protection from the trap of speaking *lashon hara*. Moreover, if we are suffering from a skin condition, this section can help heal it.

תַשֶּׁה - Here we find a discussion about the importance of treating our debtors with dignity. If we are in a better financial position than another person, we need to be humble. The reality could be that the person who lent the money may have come into this world solely for that purpose, meaning in effect that the lender is the one who needs the debtor. This is how the lender should look at it.

וְשָׁכַב בְּשַׂלְמָתוֹ וּבֵרֲכֶךָּ וּלְךָ תִּהְיֶה צְדָקָה א אל אלה אלהי אלהים
לִפְנֵי וחכמה, בינה יְהֹוָאדהנויאהדונהי אֱלֹהֶיךָ׃

Seventh Reading - David - Malchut

14 לֹא־תַעֲשֹׁק שְׂכִיר עָנִי יוד יוד הא יוד הא ואו יוד הא ואו הא וְאֶבְיוֹן
מֵאַחֶיךָ אוֹ מִגֵּרְךָ אֲשֶׁר בְּאַרְצְךָ בִּשְׁעָרֶיךָ׃ 15 בְּיוֹמוֹ
תִתֵּן ב״פ כהת שְׂכָרוֹ וְלֹא־תָבוֹא עָלָיו הַשֶּׁמֶשׁ כִּי עָנִי יוד יוד הא
יוד הא ואו יוד הא ואו הא הוּא וְאֵלָיו הוּא נֹשֵׂא אֶת־נַפְשׁוֹ וְלֹא־יִקְרָא
עָלֶיךָ אֶל־יְהֹוָאדהנויאהדונהי וְהָיָה יהוה, יהה בְךָ חֵטְא׃ 16 לֹא־יוּמְתוּ
אָבוֹת עַל־בָּנִים וּבָנִים לֹא־יוּמְתוּ עַל־אָבוֹת אִישׁ
בְּחֶטְאוֹ יוּמָתוּ׃ 17 לֹא תַטֶּה מִשְׁפַּט גֵּר יָתוֹם וְלֹא תַחֲבֹל
בֶּגֶד אַלְמָנָה׃ 18 וְזָכַרְתָּ כִּי עֶבֶד הָיִיתָ בְּמִצְרַיִם מצר וַיִּפְדְּךָ
יְהֹוָאדהנויאהדונהי אֱלֹהֶיךָ מִשָּׁם עַל־כֵּן אָנֹכִי איע מְצַוְּךָ לַעֲשׂוֹת

תַעֲשֹׁק - This section discusses the timely payment of workers and concerns the time interval between thought and action. If we owe someone, we should pay quickly and without hesitation. If we intend to perform a spiritual action, we should do it and not wait. Never leave for tomorrow what can be done today.

אָבוֹת - We should not allow our parents' cause-and-effect process to influence us. Someone can come from the worst family and be the best person, and the opposite can also be true. Don't let your parents' choices dictate your own.

תַטֶּה - This section deals with compassion for orphans and widows. We need to feel the pain of people who are not on a spiritual path. Anyone who is devoid of spirituality is an orphan.

אֶת־הַדָּבָר ראה הַזֶּה והו: 19 כִּי תִקְצֹר קְצִירְךָ בְשָׂדֶךָ וְשָׁכַחְתָּ
עֹמֶר בַּשָּׂדֶה לֹא תָשׁוּב לְקַחְתּוֹ לַגֵּר לַיָּתוֹם וְלָאַלְמָנָה
יִהְיֶה ייי לְמַעַן יְבָרֶכְךָ יְהֹוָאדהנה יאהדונהי אֱלֹהֶיךָ בְּכֹל לכב מַעֲשֵׂה
יָדֶיךָ: 20 כִּי תַחְבֹּט זֵיתְךָ לֹא תְפַאֵר אַחֲרֶיךָ לַגֵּר לַיָּתוֹם
וְלָאַלְמָנָה יִהְיֶה ייי: 21 כִּי תִבְצֹר כַּרְמְךָ לֹא תְעוֹלֵל אַחֲרֶיךָ
לַגֵּר לַיָּתוֹם וְלָאַלְמָנָה יִהְיֶה ייי: 22 וְזָכַרְתָּ כִּי־עֶבֶד הָיִיתָ
בְּאֶרֶץ מִצְרָיִם מצר עַל־כֵּן אָנֹכִי איע מְצַוְּךָ לַעֲשׂוֹת אֶת־
הַדָּבָר ראה הַזֶּה והו: 25 1 כִּי־יִהְיֶה ייי רִיב בֵּין אֲנָשִׁים וְנִגְּשׁוּ
אֶל־הַמִּשְׁפָּט וּשְׁפָטוּם וְהִצְדִּיקוּ אֶת־הַצַּדִּיק וְהִרְשִׁיעוּ
אֶת־הָרָשָׁע: 2 וְהָיָה יהוה, יהה אִם יוהך ־בִּן הַכּוֹת הָרָשָׁע וְהִפִּילוֹ
הַשֹּׁפֵט וְהִכָּהוּ לְפָנָיו כְּדֵי רִשְׁעָתוֹ בְּמִסְפָּר: 3 אַרְבָּעִים
יַכֶּנּוּ לֹא יֹסִיף פֶּן־יֹסִיף לְהַכֹּתוֹ עַל־אֵלֶּה מַכָּה היי רַבָּה
וְנִקְלָה אָחִיךָ לְעֵינֶיךָ: 4 לֹא־תַחְסֹם שׁוֹר ושר, אבג יתץ, אהבת חנם

קְצִירְךָ - Gifts for the poor: When we give a gift to the poor, we must be certain whom the gift is really going to and how it will be used. If we are not certain who is truly poor, either physically or spiritually, then we should support organizations that are qualified to distribute to those truly in need.

וְהִכָּהוּ - Believe it or not, there were floggings in the Temple. Unfortunately, we do not have the Temple, but we still have the lashes. Whenever we suffer minor pains—stubbing our toe, not having money in our pocket—these are the little wake-up calls that the Light is sending us. We should respond to these and make a change so that it will not take a major flogging to wake us up.

בְּדִישׁוֹ׃ 5 כִּי־יֵשְׁבוּ אַחִים יַחְדָּו וּמֵת אַחַד אהבה, דאגה מֵהֶם
וּבֵן אֵין־לוֹ לֹא־תִהְיֶה אֵשֶׁת־הַמֵּת הַחוּצָה לְאִישׁ זָר
יְבָמָהּ יָבֹא עָלֶיהָ וּלְקָחָהּ לוֹ לְאִשָּׁה וְיִבְּמָהּ׃ 6 וְהָיָה יהוה,
יהה הַבְּכוֹר אֲשֶׁר תֵּלֵד יָקוּם עַל־שֵׁם אָחִיו הַמֵּת וְלֹא־
יִמָּחֶה שְׁמוֹ מִיִּשְׂרָאֵל׃ 7 וְאִם ייהך לֹא יַחְפֹּץ הָאִישׁ לָקַחַת
אֶת־יְבִמְתּוֹ וְעָלְתָה יְבִמְתּוֹ הַשַּׁעְרָה אֶל־הַזְּקֵנִים וְאָמְרָה
מֵאֵן יְבָמִי לְהָקִים לְאָחִיו שֵׁם בְּיִשְׂרָאֵל לֹא אָבָה יַבְּמִי׃
8 וְקָרְאוּ־לוֹ זִקְנֵי־עִירוֹ וְדִבְּרוּ אֵלָיו וְעָמַד וְאָמַר לֹא חָפַצְתִּי
לְקַחְתָּהּ׃ 9 וְנִגְּשָׁה יְבִמְתּוֹ אֵלָיו לְעֵינֵי הַזְּקֵנִים וְחָלְצָה נַעֲלוֹ
מֵעַל עלם רַגְלוֹ וְיָרְקָה בְּפָנָיו וְעָנְתָה וְאָמְרָה כָּכָה היי יֵעָשֶׂה
לָאִישׁ אֲשֶׁר לֹא־יִבְנֶה אֶת־בֵּית ב"פ ראה אָחִיו׃ 10 וְנִקְרָא שְׁמוֹ
בְּיִשְׂרָאֵל בֵּית ב"פ ראה חֲלוּץ הַנָּעַל׃ 11 כִּי־יִנָּצוּ אֲנָשִׁים יַחְדָּו

יְבָמָהּ - The Torah includes a whole story here of a man who dies with no children. The Ari explains that this is actually describing a soul leaving this world and coming back. We don't always know why things happen. Often, the answers become clear in the future, but first we must understand that there is a bigger picture in which the answer can be found.

יִנָּצוּ - This section discusses the damage that we do when we embarrass someone. Whenever we cause pain in any form, we will soon enough feel the pain ourselves. Yet often we do not think twice about humiliating or causing pain or embarrassment to others. For many people, acting this way seems almost natural. It is our responsibility to set our own boundaries, but within reason. For example, if a person has an issue with alcohol, he should not go to a bar and say, "I won't drink." This is just asking Satan to test us. We should keep away from anything that Satan can use to tempt us.

אִישׁ וְאָחִיו וְקָרְבָה אֵשֶׁת הָאֶחָד אהבה, דאגה לְהַצִּיל אֶת־אִישָׁהּ
מִיַּד מַכֵּהוּ וְשָׁלְחָה יָדָהּ וְהֶחֱזִיקָה בִּמְבֻשָׁיו: 12 וְקַצֹּתָה אֶת־
כַּפָּהּ לֹא תָחוֹס עֵינֶךָ: 13 לֹא־יִהְיֶה ייי לְךָ בְּכִיסְךָ אֶבֶן וָאָבֶן
גְּדוֹלָה וּקְטַנָּה: 14 לֹא־יִהְיֶה ייי לְךָ בְּבֵיתְךָ אֵיפָה וְאֵיפָה
גְּדוֹלָה וּקְטַנָּה: 15 אֶבֶן שְׁלֵמָה יוד הא ואו הא וָצֶדֶק יִהְיֶה ייי ־לָּךְ
אֵיפָה שְׁלֵמָה יוד הא ואו הא וָצֶדֶק יִהְיֶה ייי ־לָּךְ לְמַעַן יַאֲרִיכוּ
יָמֶיךָ עַל הָאֲדָמָה אֲשֶׁר־יְהֹוָהאדניאהדונהי אֱלֹהֶיךָ נֹתֵן ושר, אבג יתץ,
אהבת חנם לָךְ: 16 כִּי תוֹעֲבַת יְהֹוָהאדניאהדונהי אֱלֹהֶיךָ כָּל ילי ־עֹשֵׂה
אֵלֶּה כֹּל ילי עֹשֵׂה עָוֶל:

Maftir

17 זָכוֹר אֵת אֲשֶׁר־עָשָׂה לְךָ עֲמָלֵק בַּדֶּרֶךְ בְּצֵאתְכֶם
מִמִּצְרָיִם מצר: 18 אֲשֶׁר קָרְךָ בַּדֶּרֶךְ וַיְזַנֵּב בְּךָ כָּל ילי
־הַנֶּחֱשָׁלִים אַחֲרֶיךָ וְאַתָּה עָיֵף וְיָגֵעַ וְלֹא יָרֵא אֱלֹהִים מום,
ילה: 19 וְהָיָה יהוה, יהה בְּהָנִיחַ יְהֹוָהאדניאהדונהי אֱלֹהֶיךָ | לְךָ מִכָּל ילי
־אֹיְבֶיךָ מִסָּבִיב בָּאָרֶץ אֲשֶׁר יְהֹוָהאדניאהדונהי ־אֱלֹהֶיךָ נֹתֵן ושר,
אבג יתץ, אהבת חנם לְךָ נַחֲלָה לְרִשְׁתָּהּ תִּמְחֶה אֶת־זֵכֶר עֲמָלֵק
מִתַּחַת הַשָּׁמָיִם כוזו, ייפ טל לֹא תִּשְׁכָּח:

עֲמָלֵק - The final section before the haftarah is about *Amalek*. This is to show us the power of doubt. If we have doubt, we cannot move forward or achieve anything. This section helps to create certainty and remove doubt.

Haftarah of Ki-Tetze

No matter where we are in our lives either physically or spiritually, we can still do good. What we should understand is that there is always this opportunity and that we should take advantage of it.

Isaiah 54 ישעיהו פרק 54

1 רָנִּי עֲקָרָה לֹא יָלָדָה פִּצְחִי רִנָּה וְצַהֲלִי לֹא־חָלָה להח
כִּי־רַבִּים בְּנֵי־שׁוֹמֵמָה מִבְּנֵי בְעוּלָה אָמַר יְהֹוָהאדניאהדונהי:
2 הַרְחִיבִי | מְקוֹם אָהֳלֵךְ וִירִיעוֹת מִשְׁכְּנוֹתַיִךְ יַטּוּ אַל־
תַּחְשֹׂכִי הַאֲרִיכִי מֵיתָרַיִךְ וִיתֵדֹתַיִךְ חַזֵּקִי: 3 כִּי־יָמִין
וּשְׂמֹאול תִּפְרֹצִי וְזַרְעֵךְ גּוֹיִם יִירָשׁ וְעָרִים נְשַׁמּוֹת יוֹשִׁיבוּ:
4 אַל־תִּירְאִי כִּי־לֹא תֵבוֹשִׁי וְאַל־תִּכָּלְמִי כִּי לֹא תַחְפִּירִי כִּי
בֹשֶׁת עֲלוּמַיִךְ תִּשְׁכָּחִי וְחֶרְפַּת אַלְמְנוּתַיִךְ לֹא תִזְכְּרִי־עוֹד:
5 כִּי בֹעֲלַיִךְ עֹשַׂיִךְ יְהֹוָהאדניאהדונהי צְבָאוֹת שְׁמוֹ וְגֹאֲלֵךְ קְדוֹשׁ
יִשְׂרָאֵל אֱלֹהֵי דמב, ילה כָל ילי ־הָאָרֶץ אלף למד הה יוד מם יִקָּרֵא:
6 כִּי־כְאִשָּׁה עֲזוּבָה וַעֲצוּבַת רוּחַ קְרָאָךְ יְהֹוָהאדניאהדונהי
וְאֵשֶׁת נְעוּרִים כִּי תִמָּאֵס אָמַר אֱלֹהָיִךְ: 7 בְּרֶגַע קָטֹן
עֲזַבְתִּיךְ וּבְרַחֲמִים מצפצ גְּדֹלִים אֲקַבְּצֵךְ: 8 בְּשֶׁצֶף קֶצֶף
הִסְתַּרְתִּי פָנַי חכמה, בינה רֶגַע מִמֵּךְ וּבְחֶסֶד יוד הי ויו הי, י יה יהו יהוה
עוֹלָם רִחַמְתִּיךְ אָמַר גֹּאֲלֵךְ יְהֹוָהאדניאהדונהי: 9 כִּי־מֵי ילי נֹחַ זֹאת
לִי אֲשֶׁר נִשְׁבַּעְתִּי מֵעֲבֹר מֵי ילי ־נֹחַ עוֹד עַל־הָאָרֶץ אלף למד

הה יוד מם כֵּן נִשְׁבַּעְתִּי מִקְּצֹף עָלַיִךְ וּמִגְּעָר־בָּךְ׃ 10 כִּי הֶהָרִים
יָמוּשׁוּ וְהַגְּבָעוֹת תְּמוּטֶינָה וְחַסְדִּי מֵאִתֵּךְ לֹא־יָמוּשׁ וּבְרִית
שְׁלוֹמִי לֹא תָמוּט אָמַר מְרַחֲמֵךְ יְהוָהאדנייאהדונהי׃

Lesson of Ki-Tavo

Why are there curses and blessings?

In this week's portion, we read about the curses and the blessings that the Creator gave the people of Israel through Moses. On the mountain of Gerizim, blessings were given, and curses were given on Mount Ebal. Now we must ask ourselves: How can we connect to the blessings and not to the curses? The power lies in this portion, but we must take action to connect with it.

We should also ask ourselves: Why do we need curses? If we didn't have curses, who would appreciate blessings? Curses help us differentiate between those who are connected to the Light and those who are not.

There is a story about the Ari, Rav Isaac Luria, that can help us understand this. One Saturday morning in the synagogue of the Ari, the time came for reading the Torah. The Ari told the announcer to call Aaron Ben Amram, the *kohen*, to perform the reading. The announcer looked at the Ari in total astonishment and said that there was no *kohen* by that name in the synagogue.

So the Ari said to him again a bit more insistently, "Please call Aaron Ben Amram, the *kohen*!" The announcer didn't have a choice, so he called out, "Aaron Ben Amram, the *kohen*, please stand!" Suddenly, a man who was totally of the Light walked into the synagogue and went up to the Torah. It was Aaron the High Priest, the Chariot of *Hod*.

When it was time for the portion of Levi, the Ari said to call Moshe Ben Amram, the Levi. The announcer didn't argue this time and immediately called, "Moshe Ben Amram, the Levi!" And from outside the synagogue came Moses who went up to the Torah. Third came Abraham the Patriarch, fourth was Isaac the Patriarch, fifth was Jacob the Patriarch, sixth was Joseph the Righteous, and seventh was King David.

I read this story a long time ago in the *Kitvei Ha'Ari*, the Ari's Writings. At first, I didn't think much about it, but then, I asked myself: The Ari obviously had the merit to see the seven Chariots going up to the Torah on Shabbat, but what about the rest of the people in the synagogue? Why did they merit being present when the seven Chariots went up to the Torah? We will not judge them or say that they didn't deserve it, but still, they were regular people like the rest of us who go to the synagogue on Saturday morning. There must be a secret as to why they merited all of this and how we can also merit these kinds of miracles.

I asked myself what those people thought to themselves as they went to the synagogue of the Ari. They must have thought: What a merit I have! I'm going to pray with the holy Ari! Everyone who went to the synagogue appreciated that they were praying in the same place as the Ari.

I realized that when we appreciate what we have, we receive much more, even more than we deserve. But on the other hand, when we do not appreciate what we have, we not only lose those things, but also the things we do truly deserve.

This is the secret of blessings and curses: nothing is unobtainable, and conversely, anything can be lost. It all depends on our sense and expression of appreciation.

Regarding the month of Elul

It is written: "It is better for a person to change something small and be consistent about it than to take on something more difficult for a shorter time with the intention of completing the task later." Many times, we commit to doing something even though it's clear to us that we won't be able to complete it. We must learn to commit to what we can accomplish and to be persistent. This concept is explained by the following allegory:

What is the difference between a rich man riding on a train and a poor man riding on a train? The rich man rides in first class comfortably and with a lot of space while the poor man crowds into third class and is not very comfortable.

Once, a poor beggar wanted to go to another city, which was three train stops away. He had enough money to travel there in third class, but the man wanted to go first class, telling himself that he deserved a rest after the hard work of begging. So he bought a ticket for only two stations. He planned to get off in the second station and collect more charity to complete the journey.

He spread himself out comfortably in first class and enjoyed himself like a very rich person. When the train stopped at the second station, the ticket master came to him and reminded him to get off the train. The poor man got up, took his bag, and was about to get off the train and start collecting charity when he realized that the stop was in the middle of the desert. There was no one there who could help him get to where he wanted to go—and he had no way of returning home either.

The moral of the story is that it is better for us to make a small "third class" commitment and get to where we want to go than to make a commitment that is too large, where we may have the desire but can't complete the work. We must take into account the possibility that the next stop is in the desert. Who knows if we will even want to go on? And if we do, who knows if we'll have the strength to do so?

More regarding the month of Elul

This is the month of *Elul*, which is an acronym for the phrase "*Ani ledodi vedodi li* – I am to my beloved as my beloved is to me." As the Rav explains, it is not that the Creator has more desire to help us get closer to Him in the month of *Elul* than in other months; rather, in the month of *Elul*, there is a power that can awaken our desire, as in the verse: "I am to my beloved...." Our desire should be "I am to my beloved," and then "as my beloved is to me" will follow by itself. Every month contains "as my beloved is to me," but only the month of *Elul* contains "I am to my beloved."

There is a story about Rav Elimelech and Rav Zusha, the holy brothers, that can teach us something about the month of *Elul*. Whenever they were traveling, their father would appear to them as Friday night approached to tell them where to spend the Shabbat.

One Friday evening, their father came to them in a certain city and told Rav Elimelech to go to the spiritual leader of the city and Rav Zusha to the shoemaker. Both accepted what their father said to them and expected a good Shabbat, especially Rav Zusha who knew that this was probably not a regular shoemaker but a hidden righteous person.

Rav Zusha arrived at the shoemaker's house, but the shoemaker's wife did not like the idea that he would spend Shabbat there. Rav Zusha begged until she relented. But then the shoemaker said to him, "I just want you to know that my Shabbat goes very fast because I work very hard all week and on Shabbat I want to rest." In fact, Friday night Kabbalat Shabbat took only ten minutes. Before Rav Zusha could understand what was happening, the shoemaker had said Kiddush, washed his hands, and said *Birkat Hamazon*. Then he got up and said he was going to sleep.

Rav Zusha could not understand how his father could "ruin" his Shabbat by sending him to this person. But he told himself that there was probably Light here that would be revealed. That night, Rav Zusha didn't sleep, thinking that maybe Elijah the Prophet would come to teach the shoemaker. But no one came. The next day, there were prayers for half an hour, Kiddush was said, and the shoemaker went to take a nap. At the time of third meal, Rav Zusha decided to try one more time to understand why he came there for Shabbat, but he couldn't find the shoemaker.

Rav Zusha went to the shoemaker's little boy and asked him where his father was. The boy answered that his father was on the roof. Rav Zusha understood that he was about to find out something. He went on the roof where he discovered a big table with 36 chairs (for the 36 righteous people). The shoemaker was sitting at the head of the table because he was the leader of the 36 righteous people. We know that the power of the third meal comes from the fact that it's the only meal that all 36 righteous people eat together. After the meal, the shoemaker said to Rav Zusha, "Be careful not to tell anybody what you saw."

Rav Zusha couldn't sleep all night because of all the Light he received during the third meal. When Rav Elimelech saw him the next morning and saw his face shining, he asked him what happened on Shabbat. Rav Zusha answered that nothing special had happened. Rav Elimelech asked again but received the same answer. This went on for two days until Rav Elimelech reminded his brother of their vow to honestly and completely tell each other whatever happened to them, no matter what it was. So Rav Zusha told his brother about everything he saw.

The next day, the governor's watch was stolen. The governor came to Rav Zusha and Rav Elimelech and accused them of stealing it because they had slept in the same hotel as the governor, awakened early to pray at dawn, and disappeared. Hence, they must have stolen the watch. The governor had them tied to horses and dragged them around the whole village. When the punishment was over, Rav Zusha saw that the governor was really the shoemaker who told him that both brothers had to be punished because Rav Zusha had told Rav Elimelech the secret of the 36.

There is an important lesson in this story. Rav Zusha knew what was going to happen to him if he revealed the shoemaker's secret to his brother, but he didn't want anything to come between the two of them. In every relationship, there should not be any separation. If there is separation, then it's not a real relationship. Rav Zusha didn't care about what would happen to him: The only thing that was important to him was his brother. He felt that Rav Elimelech was part of him, part of his body. He did for his brother more than he would do for himself.

In the month of *Elul*, we must work to have that kind of relationship at least with our families. In this way, our love for our brothers, sisters, fathers, mothers, sons, daughters, husbands, and wives will be, with the Lightforce's will, like the relationship between Rav Zusha and Rav Elimelech, the holy brothers. As the Rav, my father and my teacher, says of Rav Brandwein: If anyone had tried to shoot his teacher, he would have blocked the bullet with his own body. If we are not ready to give others everything and to feel that other people are really part of us, then there is separation. Let us bless all the people of the world, whom we will feel as one body and one heart in this month, so we will be well prepared for Rosh Hashanah.

Synopsis of Ki-Tavo

The number of verses in this portion is equivalent to the numerical value of the words "his slaves." When we come into this physical world, we are all slaves to something. This section helps us to remove the shackles of our own slavery.

First Reading - Abraham - Chesed

26 1 וְהָיָה יהוה, יהה כִּי־תָבוֹא אֶל־הָאָרֶץ אלף למד הה יוד מם
אֲשֶׁר יְהוָהאדניאהדונהי אֱלֹהֶיךָ נֹתֵן ושר, אבג יתץ, אהבת חנם לְךָ נַחֲלָה
וִירִשְׁתָּהּ וְיָשַׁבְתָּ בָּהּ: 2 וְלָקַחְתָּ מֵרֵאשִׁית | כָּל ילי ־פְּרִי
הָאֲדָמָה אֲשֶׁר תָּבִיא מֵאַרְצְךָ אֲשֶׁר יְהוָהאדניאהדונהי אֱלֹהֶיךָ
נֹתֵן ושר, אבג יתץ, אהבת חנם לָךְ וְשַׂמְתָּ בַטֶּנֶא וְהָלַכְתָּ אֶל־הַמָּקוֹם
אֲשֶׁר יִבְחַר יְהוָהאדניאהדונהי אֱלֹהֶיךָ לְשַׁכֵּן שְׁמוֹ שָׁם: 3 וּבָאתָ
אֶל־הַכֹּהֵן מלה אֲשֶׁר יִהְיֶה ייי בַּיָּמִים נלך הָהֵם וְאָמַרְתָּ אֵלָיו
הִגַּדְתִּי הַיּוֹם נגד, מזבח, זן לַיהוָהאדניאהדונהי אֱלֹהֶיךָ כִּי־בָאתִי אֶל־
הָאָרֶץ אלף למד הה יוד מם אֲשֶׁר נִשְׁבַּע יְהוָהאדניאהדונהי לַאֲבֹתֵינוּ
לָתֶת לָנוּ: 4 וְלָקַח הַכֹּהֵן מלה הַטֶּנֶא מִיָּדֶךָ וְהִנִּיחוֹ לִפְנֵי חכמה,
בינה מִזְבַּח זן, נגד יְהוָהאדניאהדונהי אֱלֹהֶיךָ: 5 וְעָנִיתָ וְאָמַרְתָּ
לִפְנֵי חכמה, בינה | יְהוָהאדניאהדונהי אֱלֹהֶיךָ אֲרַמִּי אֹבֵד אָבִי וַיֵּרֶד ריי
מִצְרַיְמָה וַיָּגָר שָׁם בִּמְתֵי מְעָט וַיְהִי־שָׁם לְגוֹי גָּדוֹל להח,
מבה עָצוּם וָרָב: 6 וַיָּרֵעוּ אֹתָנוּ הַמִּצְרִים מצר וַיְעַנּוּנוּ וַיִּתְּנוּ
עָלֵינוּ עֲבֹדָה קָשָׁה: 7 וַנִּצְעַק אֶל־יְהוָהאדניאהדונהי אֱלֹהֵי דמב,

מֵרֵאשִׁית - This next section discusses the first fruit. Just as there is a spiritual significance to a first-born human and a first-born animal, there is a special energy in the first fruits. The bigger lesson concerns the significance of and order to every aspect of life. Even a fruit has importance.

יֹלֹה אֲבֹתֵינוּ וַיִּשְׁמַע יְהֹוָֹאֱדֹנִיֹּאהדונהי אֶת־קֹלֵנוּ וַיַּרְא אֶת־עָנְיֵנוּ

וְאֶת־עֲמָלֵנוּ וְאֶת־לַחֲצֵנוּ: 8 וַיּוֹצִאֵנוּ יְהֹוָֹאֱדֹנִיֹּאהדונהי מִמִּצְרַיִם מֹצר

בְּיָד חֲזָקָה וּבִזְרֹעַ נְטוּיָה וּבְמֹרָא גָּדֹל וּבְאֹתוֹת וּבְמֹפְתִים:

9 וַיְבִאֵנוּ אֶל־הַמָּקוֹם הַזֶּה והו וַיִּתֶּן־לָנוּ מום, אלהים, אהיה ▪ אדני אֶת־

הָאָרֶץ אלף למד הה יוד מם הַזֹּאת אֶרֶץ זָבַת חָלָב וּדְבָשׁ: 10 וְעַתָּה

הִנֵּה הֵבֵאתִי אֶת־רֵאשִׁית פְּרִי הָאֲדָמָה אֲשֶׁר־נָתַתָּה לִּי

יְהֹוָֹאֱדֹנִיֹּאהדונהי וְהִנַּחְתּוֹ חכמה, בינה לִפְנֵי יְהֹוָֹאֱדֹנִיֹּאהדונהי אֱלֹהֶיךָ

וְהִשְׁתַּחֲוִיתָ לִפְנֵי חכמה, בינה יְהֹוָֹאֱדֹנִיֹּאהדונהי אֱלֹהֶיךָ: 11 וְשָׂמַחְתָּ

בְכָל לכב ־הַטּוֹב והו אֲשֶׁר נָתַן־לְךָ יְהֹוָֹאֱדֹנִיֹּאהדונהי אֱלֹהֶיךָ

וּלְבֵיתֶךָ אַתָּה וְהַלֵּוִי וְהַגֵּר אֲשֶׁר בְּקִרְבֶּךָ:

Second Reading - Isaac - Gvurah

12 כִּי תְכַלֶּה לַעְשֵׂר אֶת־כָּל יֹלֹי ־מַעְשַׂר תְּבוּאָתְךָ בַּשָּׁנָה

הַשְּׁלִישִׁת שְׁנַת הַמַּעֲשֵׂר וְנָתַתָּה לַלֵּוִי לַגֵּר לַיָּתוֹם

וְלָאַלְמָנָה וְאָכְלוּ בִשְׁעָרֶיךָ וְשָׂבֵעוּ: 13 וְאָמַרְתָּ לִפְנֵי חכמה,

בינה יְהֹוָֹאֱדֹנִיֹּאהדונהי אֱלֹהֶיךָ בִּעַרְתִּי הַקֹּדֶשׁ מִן־הַבַּיִת ב״פ ראה וְגַם

נְתַתִּיו לַלֵּוִי וְלַגֵּר לַיָּתוֹם וְלָאַלְמָנָה כְּכָל יֹלֹי ־מִצְוָתְךָ אֲשֶׁר

צִוִּיתָנִי לֹא־עָבַרְתִּי מִמִּצְוֹתֶיךָ וְלֹא שָׁכָחְתִּי: 14 לֹא־אָכַלְתִּי

לַעְשֵׂר - This next section discusses tithing. When we tithe, we merit the blessing of the Creator, the same blessing we receive from reading this section.

בְּאֹנִי אני מִמֶּנּוּ וְלֹא־בִעַרְתִּי מִמֶּנּוּ בְּטָמֵא וְלֹא־נָתַתִּי מִמֶּנּוּ
לְמֵת שָׁמַעְתִּי בְּקוֹל יְהֹוָאדניאהדונהי אֱלֹהָי דמב, ילה עָשִׂיתִי כְּכֹל ילי
אֲשֶׁר צִוִּיתָנִי׃ 15 הַשְׁקִיפָה מִמְּעוֹן קָדְשְׁךָ מִן־הַשָּׁמַיִם כוזו, י"פ
טל וּבָרֵךְ אֶת־עַמְּךָ אֶת־יִשְׂרָאֵל וְאֵת הָאֲדָמָה אֲשֶׁר נָתַתָּה
לָנוּ כַּאֲשֶׁר נִשְׁבַּעְתָּ לַאֲבֹתֵינוּ אֶרֶץ זָבַת חָלָב וּדְבָשׁ׃

Third Reading - Jacob - Tiferet

16 הַיּוֹם נגד, מזבח, זן הַזֶּה והו יְהֹוָאדניאהדונהי אֱלֹהֶיךָ מְצַוְּךָ לַעֲשׂוֹת
אֶת־הַחֻקִּים הָאֵלֶּה וְאֶת־הַמִּשְׁפָּטִים וְשָׁמַרְתָּ וְעָשִׂיתָ אוֹתָם
בְּכָל לכב ־לְבָבְךָ וּבְכָל לכב ־נַפְשֶׁךָ׃ 17 אֶת־יְהֹוָאדניאהדונהי
הֶאֱמַרְתָּ הַיּוֹם נגד, מזבח, זן לִהְיוֹת לְךָ לֵאלֹהִים מום, ילה וְלָלֶכֶת
בִּדְרָכָיו וְלִשְׁמֹר חֻקָּיו וּמִצְוֺתָיו וּמִשְׁפָּטָיו וְלִשְׁמֹעַ בְּקֹלוֹ׃
18 וַיהֹוָאדניאהדונהי הֶאֱמִירְךָ הַיּוֹם נגד, מזבח, זן לִהְיוֹת לוֹ לְעַם עלם
סְגֻלָּה כַּאֲשֶׁר דִּבֶּר ראה ־לָךְ וְלִשְׁמֹר כָּל ילי ־מִצְוֺתָיו׃
19 וּלְתִתְּךָ עֶלְיוֹן עַל כָּל עמם, ילי ־הַגּוֹיִם אֲשֶׁר עָשָׂה לִתְהִלָּה
וּלְשֵׁם וּלְתִפְאֶרֶת וְלִהְיֹתְךָ עַם־קָדֹשׁ לַיהֹוָאדניאהדונהי אֱלֹהֶיךָ
כַּאֲשֶׁר דִּבֵּר ראה׃

לְבָבְךָ - The following section states: "Do everything with all your hearts," referring to both aspects of the heart: the desire to receive and the desire to share. Every gift from the Creator can be used for either good or evil. Every negative attribute can be used for good, and every positive attribute can be used to do evil. For example, a person can either use his anger against friends and relatives or can turn this same anger against evil.

Fourth Reading - Moses - Netzach

27 1 וַיְצַו מֹשֶׁה מהש וְזִקְנֵי יִשְׂרָאֵל אֶת-הָעָם לֵאמֹר **שָׁמֹר**
אֶת-כָּל ילי -הַמִּצְוָה אֲשֶׁר אָנֹכִי איע מְצַוֶּה אֶתְכֶם הַיּוֹם נגד,
מזבח, זן: 2 וְהָיָה יהוה, יהה בַּיּוֹם נגד, מזבח, זן אֲשֶׁר תַּעַבְרוּ אֶת-הַיַּרְדֵּן
אֶל-הָאָרֶץ אלף למד הה יוד מם אֲשֶׁר-יְהֹוָהאדניאהדונהי אֱלֹהֶיךָ נֹתֵן ושר,
אבג יתץ, אהבת חנם לָךְ וַהֲקֵמֹתָ לְךָ אֲבָנִים גְּדֹלוֹת וְשַׂדְתָּ אֹתָם
בַּשִּׂיד: 3 וְכָתַבְתָּ עֲלֵיהֶן אֶת-כָּל ילי -דִּבְרֵי הַתּוֹרָה הַזֹּאת
בְּעָבְרֶךָ לְמַעַן אֲשֶׁר תָּבֹא אֶל-הָאָרֶץ אלף למד הה יוד מם אֲשֶׁר-
יְהֹוָהאדניאהדונהי אֱלֹהֶיךָ | נֹתֵן ושר, אבג יתץ, אהבת חנם לָךְ אֶרֶץ זָבַת
חָלָב וּדְבַשׁ כַּאֲשֶׁר דִּבֶּר ראה יְהֹוָהאדניאהדונהי אֱלֹהֵי דמב, ילה
-אֲבֹתֶיךָ לָךְ: 4 וְהָיָה יהוה, יהה בְּעָבְרְכֶם אֶת-הַיַּרְדֵּן תָּקִימוּ
אֶת-הָאֲבָנִים הָאֵלֶּה אֲשֶׁר אָנֹכִי איע מְצַוֶּה אֶתְכֶם הַיּוֹם נגד,
מזבח, זן בְּהַר עֵיבָל וְשַׂדְתָּ אוֹתָם בַּשִּׂיד: 5 וּבָנִיתָ שָּׁם מִזְבֵּחַ
לַיהֹוָהאדניאהדונהי אֱלֹהֶיךָ מִזְבַּח זן, נגד אֲבָנִים לֹא-תָנִיף עֲלֵיהֶם
בַּרְזֶל ר״ת - בלהה רחל זלפה לאה: 6 אֲבָנִים שְׁלֵמוֹת תִּבְנֶה אֶת-
מִזְבַּח זן, נגד יְהֹוָהאדניאהדונהי אֱלֹהֶיךָ וְהַעֲלִיתָ עָלָיו עוֹלֹת ושר, אבג

שָׁמֹר - Here, the Torah refers to the renewed commitments for spiritual work that the people made when they entered the land of Israel. Each time we have a new experience in our lives—marriage, birth of a child, a new career—we need to recommit ourselves to our spiritual path because what was enough yesterday is not good enough for tomorrow.

יתץ, אהבת חנם לַיהֹוָאדני יאהדונהי אֱלֹהֶיךָ׃ 7 וְזָבַחְתָּ שְׁלָמִים וְאָכַלְתָּ
שָּׁם וְשָׂמַחְתָּ לִפְנֵי חכמה, בינה יְהֹוָאדני יאהדונהי אֱלֹהֶיךָ׃ 8 וְכָתַבְתָּ
עַל־הָאֲבָנִים אֶת־כָּל ילי ־דִּבְרֵי הַתּוֹרָה הַזֹּאת בַּאֵר קנ״א־ב״ן
הֵיטֵב׃ 9 וַיְדַבֵּר מֹשֶׁה מהש וְהַכֹּהֲנִים הַלְוִיִּם אֶל כָּל ילי
־יִשְׂרָאֵל לֵאמֹר הַסְכֵּת | וּשְׁמַע יִשְׂרָאֵל הַיּוֹם נגד, מזבח, זן
הַזֶּה והו נִהְיֵיתָ לְעָם עלם לַיהֹוָאדני יאהדונהי אֱלֹהֶיךָ׃ 10 וְשָׁמַעְתָּ
בְּקוֹל יְהֹוָאדני יאהדונהי אֱלֹהֶיךָ וְעָשִׂיתָ אֶת־מִצְוֺתָו וְאֶת־חֻקָּיו
אֲשֶׁר אָנֹכִי איע מְצַוְּךָ הַיּוֹם נגד, מזבח, זן׃

Fifth Reading - Aaron - Hod

11 וַיְצַו מֹשֶׁה מהש אֶת־הָעָם בַּיּוֹם נגד, מזבח, זן הַהוּא לֵאמֹר׃
12 אֵלֶּה יַעַמְדוּ לְבָרֵךְ אֶת־הָעָם עַל־הַר גְּרִזִים בְּעָבְרְכֶם
אֶת־הַיַּרְדֵּן שִׁמְעוֹן וְלֵוִי וִיהוּדָה וְיִשָּׂשכָר וְיוֹסֵף ציון וּבִנְיָמִן׃
13 וְאֵלֶּה יַעַמְדוּ עַל־הַקְּלָלָה בְּהַר עֵיבָל רְאוּבֵן גָּד וְאָשֵׁר

יהוה - In this verse, we have a code—a sequence of the Name of God, *yud hey vav hey* —that connects us to the month of Leo. The month of Leo contains the most negative day, the 9th of Av, which is also the birthday of the Messiah. Likewise, we have a choice to be part of destruction or rebuilding: We can contribute to the creation of chaos or to the end of it.

אֵלֶּה - In this section, the twelve tribes divide, with six on one side of the mountain and six on the other. The Levites bless the people, and while the people should have responded with blessings, here the Torah only lists curses. In truth, all curses are blessings. Most people look back at the hardest times in their lives and know that they are better because of them.

וּזְבוּלֻן דָּן וְנַפְתָּלִי׃ 14 וְעָנוּ הַלְוִיִּם וְאָמְרוּ אֶל־כָּל ילי ־אִישׁ
יִשְׂרָאֵל קוֹל רָם׃ 15 אָרוּר הָאִישׁ אֲשֶׁר יַעֲשֶׂה פֶסֶל וּמַסֵּכָה
תּוֹעֲבַת יְהֹוָהאדני יאהדונהי מַעֲשֵׂה יְדֵי חָרָשׁ וְשָׂם בַּסָּתֶר ב״פ מצר
וְעָנוּ כָל ילי ־הָעָם וְאָמְרוּ אָמֵן יאהדונהי, סאל, פאי׃ 16 אָרוּר מַקְלֶה
אָבִיו וְאִמּוֹ וְאָמַר כָּל ילי ־הָעָם אָמֵן יאהדונהי, סאל, פאי׃ 17 אָרוּר
מַסִּיג גְּבוּל רֵעֵהוּ וְאָמַר כָּל ילי ־הָעָם אָמֵן יאהדונהי, סאל, פאי׃
18 אָרוּר מַשְׁגֶּה עִוֵּר בַּדָּרֶךְ וְאָמַר כָּל ילי ־הָעָם אָמֵן יאהדונהי,
סאל, פאי׃ 19 אָרוּר מַטֶּה מִשְׁפַּט גֵּר־יָתוֹם וְאַלְמָנָה וְאָמַר
כָּל ילי ־הָעָם אָמֵן יאהדונהי, סאל, פאי׃ 20 אָרוּר שֹׁכֵב עִם־אֵשֶׁת
אָבִיו כִּי גִלָּה כְּנַף אלף הה יוד הה, אדני - אלהים אָבִיו וְאָמַר כָּל ילי ־
הָעָם אָמֵן יאהדונהי, סאל, פאי׃ 21 אָרוּר שֹׁכֵב עִם־כָּל ילי ־בְּהֵמָה לכב
וְאָמַר כָּל ילי ־הָעָם אָמֵן יאהדונהי, סאל, פאי׃ 22 אָרוּר שֹׁכֵב עִם־
אֲחֹתוֹ בַת־אָבִיו אוֹ בַת־אִמּוֹ וְאָמַר כָּל ילי ־הָעָם אָמֵן יאהדונהי,
סאל, פאי׃ 23 אָרוּר שֹׁכֵב עִם־חֹתַנְתּוֹ וְאָמַר כָּל ילי ־הָעָם
אָמֵן יאהדונהי, סאל, פאי׃ 24 אָרוּר מַכֵּה היי רֵעֵהוּ בַּסָּתֶר ב״פ מצר וְאָמַר
כָּל ילי ־הָעָם אָמֵן יאהדונהי, סאל, פאי׃ 25 אָרוּר לֹקֵחַ שֹׁחַד לְהַכּוֹת
נֶפֶשׁ דָּם נָקִי אלף הי יוד הי וְאָמַר כָּל ילי ־הָעָם אָמֵן יאהדונהי, סאל, פאי׃
26 אָרוּר אֲשֶׁר לֹא־יָקִים אֶת־דִּבְרֵי הַתּוֹרָה־הַזֹּאת לַעֲשׂוֹת
אוֹתָם וְאָמַר כָּל ילי ־הָעָם אָמֵן יאהדונהי, סאל, פאי׃ 28 1 וְהָיָה יהוה, יהה

אִם יוהך ־שָׁמוֹעַ תִּשְׁמַע בְּקוֹל יְהֹוָהאדניאהדונהי אֱלֹהֶיךָ לִשְׁמֹר
לַעֲשׂוֹת אֶת־כָּל ילי ־מִצְוֹתָיו אֲשֶׁר אָנֹכִי איע מְצַוְּךָ הַיּוֹם נגד,
מזבח, זן וּנְתָנְךָ יְהֹוָהאדניאהדונהי אֱלֹהֶיךָ ילה עֶלְיוֹן עַל כָּל עמם, ילי ־גּוֹיֵי
הָאָרֶץ אלף למד הה יוד מם: 2 וּבָאוּ עָלֶיךָ כָּל ילי ־הַבְּרָכוֹת הָאֵלֶּה
וְהִשִּׂיגֻךָ כִּי תִשְׁמַע בְּקוֹל יְהֹוָהאדניאהדונהי אֱלֹהֶיךָ: 3 בָּרוּךְ
אַתָּה בָּעִיר ערי, סנדלפון, סנזהר וּבָרוּךְ אַתָּה בַּשָּׂדֶה: 4 בָּרוּךְ פְּרִי־
בִטְנְךָ וּפְרִי אַדְמָתְךָ וּפְרִי בְהֶמְתֶּךָ שְׁגַר אֲלָפֶיךָ וְעַשְׁתְּרוֹת
צֹאנֶךָ: 5 בָּרוּךְ טַנְאֲךָ וּמִשְׁאַרְתֶּךָ: 6 בָּרוּךְ אַתָּה בְּבֹאֶךָ
וּבָרוּךְ אַתָּה בְּצֵאתֶךָ:

Sixth Reading - Joseph - Yesod

7 יִתֵּן יְהֹוָהאדניאהדונהי אֶת־אֹיְבֶיךָ הַקָּמִים עָלֶיךָ נִגָּפִים לְפָנֶיךָ
בְּדֶרֶךְ אֶחָד אהבה, דאגה יֵצְאוּ אֵלֶיךָ וּבְשִׁבְעָה דְרָכִים יָנוּסוּ
לְפָנֶיךָ: 8 יְצַו יְהֹוָהאדניאהדונהי אִתְּךָ אֶת־הַבְּרָכָה בַּאֲסָמֶיךָ
וּבְכֹל לכב מִשְׁלַח יָדֶךָ וּבֵרַכְךָ בָּאָרֶץ אֲשֶׁר־יְהֹוָהאדניאהדונהי
אֱלֹהֶיךָ נֹתֵן ושר, אבג יתץ, אהבת חנם לָךְ: 9 יְקִימְךָ יְהֹוָהאדניאהדונהי לוֹ
לְעַם עלם קָדוֹשׁ כַּאֲשֶׁר נִשְׁבַּע־לָךְ כִּי תִשְׁמֹר אֶת־מִצְוֹת

תִּשְׁמַע - Here, Moses begins with the prophecy that when someone is on a spiritual path, he will receive blessings and sustenance. This tells us the mere choice to follow a spiritual path activates the flow of blessings.

יְהֹוָאדָנָהי אהדונהי אֱלֹהֶיךָ וְהָלַכְתָּ בִּדְרָכָיו: 10 וְרָאוּ כָּל ילי ־עַמֵּי
הָאָרֶץ אלף למד הה יוד מם כִּי שֵׁם יְהֹוָאדָנָהי אהדונהי נִקְרָא עָלֶיךָ וְיָרְאוּ
מִמֶּךָּ: 11 וְהוֹתִרְךָ יְהֹוָאדָנָהי אהדונהי לְטוֹבָה אכא בִּפְרִי בִטְנְךָ
וּבִפְרִי בְהֶמְתְּךָ וּבִפְרִי אַדְמָתֶךָ עַל הָאֲדָמָה אֲשֶׁר נִשְׁבַּע
יְהֹוָאדָנָהי אהדונהי לַאֲבֹתֶיךָ לָתֶת לָךְ: 12 יִפְתַּח יְהֹוָאדָנָהי אהדונהי | לְךָ
אֶת־אוֹצָרוֹ הַטּוֹב והו אֶת־הַשָּׁמַיִם כוזו, י״פ טל לָתֵת מְטַר־אַרְצְךָ
בְּעִתּוֹ וּלְבָרֵךְ אֵת כָּל ילי ־מַעֲשֵׂה יָדֶךָ וְהִלְוִיתָ גּוֹיִם רַבִּים
וְאַתָּה לֹא תִלְוֶה: 13 וּנְתָנְךָ יְהֹוָאדָנָהי אהדונהי לְרֹאשׁ וְלֹא לְזָנָב
וְהָיִיתָ רַק לְמַעְלָה וְלֹא תִהְיֶה לְמָטָּה כִּי־תִשְׁמַע אֶל־
מִצְוֹת | יְהֹוָאדָנָהי אהדונהי אֱלֹהֶיךָ אֲשֶׁר אָנֹכִי איע מְצַוְּךָ הַיּוֹם נגד,
מזבח, זן לִשְׁמֹר וְלַעֲשׂוֹת: 14 וְלֹא תָסוּר מִכָּל ילי ־הַדְּבָרִים
אֲשֶׁר אָנֹכִי איע מְצַוֶּה אֶתְכֶם הַיּוֹם נגד, מזבח, זן יָמִין וּשְׂמֹאול
לָלֶכֶת אַחֲרֵי אֱלֹהִים מום, ילה אֲחֵרִים לְעָבְדָם: 15 וְהָיָה יהוה, יהה
אִם יוהך ־לֹא תִשְׁמַע בְּקוֹל יְהֹוָאדָנָהי אהדונהי אֱלֹהֶיךָ לִשְׁמֹר
לַעֲשׂוֹת אֶת־כָּל ילי ־מִצְוֹתָיו וְחֻקֹּתָיו אֲשֶׁר אָנֹכִי איע מְצַוְּךָ
הַיּוֹם נגד, מזבח, זן וּבָאוּ עָלֶיךָ כָּל ילי ־הַקְּלָלוֹת הָאֵלֶּה וְהִשִּׂיגוּךָ:

לֹא תִשְׁמַע - This next section describes the curses and destruction—the unimaginable terrible things—that will come to those who do not choose a spiritual path. If we follow only our selfish desires, we will one day suffer the chaos of our choices. Everything we touch will become negative.

16 אָרוּר אַתָּה בָּעִיר ערי, סנזזפך, סנדלפון וְאָרוּר אַתָּה בַּשָּׂדֶה׃
17 אָרוּר טַנְאֲךָ וּמִשְׁאַרְתֶּךָ׃ 18 אָרוּר פְּרִי־בִטְנְךָ וּפְרִי
אַדְמָתֶךָ שְׁגַר אֲלָפֶיךָ וְעַשְׁתְּרֹת צֹאנֶךָ׃ 19 אָרוּר אַתָּה
בְּבֹאֶךָ וְאָרוּר אַתָּה בְּצֵאתֶךָ׃ 20 יְשַׁלַּח יְהֹוָ֯אדני֯אהדונהי | בְּךָ
אֶת־הַמְּאֵרָה אֶת־הַמְּהוּמָה וְאֶת־הַמִּגְעֶרֶת בְּכָל לכב -
מִשְׁלַח יָדְךָ אֲשֶׁר תַּעֲשֶׂה עַד הִשָּׁמֶדְךָ וְעַד־אֲבָדְךָ מַהֵר
מִפְּנֵי חכמה, בינה רֹעַ מַעֲלָלֶיךָ אֲשֶׁר עֲזַבְתָּנִי׃ 21 יַדְבֵּק
יְהֹוָ֯אדני֯אהדונהי בְּךָ אֶת־הַדָּבֶר ראה עַד כַּלֹּתוֹ אֹתְךָ מֵעַל עלם
הָאֲדָמָה אֲשֶׁר־אַתָּה בָא־שָׁמָּה יוד הא ואו הא לְרִשְׁתָּהּ׃ 22 יַכְּכָה
יְהֹוָ֯אדני֯אהדונהי בַּשַּׁחֶפֶת וּבַקַּדַּחַת וּבַדַּלֶּקֶת וּבַחַרְחֻר וּבַחֶרֶב
וּבַשִּׁדָּפוֹן וּבַיֵּרָקוֹן וּרְדָפוּךָ עַד אָבְדֶךָ׃ 23 וְהָיוּ שָׁמֶיךָ אֲשֶׁר
עַל־רֹאשְׁךָ נְחֹשֶׁת וְהָאָרֶץ אלף למד הה יוד מם אֲשֶׁר־תַּחְתֶּיךָ
בַּרְזֶל ר״ת - בלהה רחל זלפה לאה׃ 24 יִתֵּן יְהֹוָ֯אדני֯אהדונהי אֶת־מְטַר
אַרְצְךָ אָבָק וְעָפָר מִן־הַשָּׁמַיִם כוזו, י״פ טל יֵרֵד עָלֶיךָ עַד
הִשָּׁמְדָךְ׃ 25 יִתֶּנְךָ יְהֹוָ֯אדני֯אהדונהי | נִגָּף לִפְנֵי חכמה, בינה אֹיְבֶיךָ
בְּדֶרֶךְ אֶחָד אהבה, דאגה תֵּצֵא אֵלָיו וּבְשִׁבְעָה דְרָכִים תָּנוּס

נֶגֶף - The Ari has provided us with a code—*nu gee fay*—to scan and meditate upon while reading this section. This code gives us protection from any kind of plague. A plague occurs when Satan is given the ability to strike at will. Once started, a plague makes no distinction between good and evil people—everyone is destroyed. *Nu gee fay* protects us from this.

לְפָנָיו וְהָיִיתָ לְזַעֲוָה לְכֹל יה אדני ילי מַמְלְכוֹת הָאָרֶץ אלף למד הה יוד
מם: 26 וְהָיְתָה נִבְלָתְךָ לְמַאֲכָל לְכָל יה אדני ילי ־עוֹף הַשָּׁמַיִם כוזו,
י"פ טל וּלְבֶהֱמַת הָאָרֶץ אלף למד הה יוד מם וְאֵין מַחֲרִיד: 27 יַכְּכָה
יְהֹוָאדנֵיאהדונהי בִּשְׁחִין מִצְרַיִם מצר וּבַטְּחֹרִים (כתיב: ובעפלים)
וּבַגָּרָב וּבֶחָרֶס אֲשֶׁר לֹא־תוּכַל לְהֵרָפֵא: 28 יַכְּכָה
יְהֹוָאדנֵיאהדונהי בְּשִׁגָּעוֹן וּבְעִוָּרוֹן וּבְתִמְהוֹן לֵבָב בוכו: 29 וְהָיִיתָ
מְמַשֵּׁשׁ בַּצָּהֳרַיִם כַּאֲשֶׁר יְמַשֵּׁשׁ הָעִוֵּר בָּאֲפֵלָה וְלֹא
תַצְלִיחַ אֶת־דְּרָכֶיךָ וְהָיִיתָ אַךְ עָשׁוּק וְגָזוּל כָּל ילי ־הַיָּמִים נלך
וְאֵין מוֹשִׁיעַ: 30 אִשָּׁה תְאָרֵשׂ וְאִישׁ אַחֵר יִשְׁכָּבֶנָּה (כתיב: ישגלנה)
בַּיִת ב"פ ראה תִּבְנֶה וְלֹא־תֵשֵׁב בּוֹ כֶּרֶם תִּטַּע וְלֹא תְחַלְּלֶנּוּ:
31 שׁוֹרְךָ טָבוּחַ לְעֵינֶיךָ וְלֹא תֹאכַל מִמֶּנּוּ חֲמֹרְךָ גָּזוּל
מִלְּפָנֶיךָ וְלֹא יָשׁוּב לָךְ צֹאנְךָ נְתֻנוֹת לְאֹיְבֶיךָ וְאֵין לְךָ
מוֹשִׁיעַ: 32 בָּנֶיךָ וּבְנֹתֶיךָ נְתֻנִים לְעַם עלם אַחֵר וְעֵינֶיךָ רֹאוֹת
וְכָלוֹת אֲלֵיהֶם כָּל ילי ־הַיּוֹם נגד, מזבח, זן וְאֵין לְאֵל יָדֶךָ: 33 פְּרִי
אַדְמָתְךָ וְכָל ילי ־יְגִיעֲךָ יֹאכַל עַם אֲשֶׁר לֹא־יָדָעְתָּ וְהָיִיתָ
רַק עָשׁוּק וְרָצוּץ כָּל ילי ־הַיָּמִים נלך: 34 וְהָיִיתָ מְשֻׁגָּע מִמַּרְאֵה

וּבַטְּחֹרִים, יִשְׁכָּבֶנָּה- There are two places in the Torah where the word that we read aloud differs from the word written in the text. This change acts like a vaccine against negative things that can happen, for the Zohar says here that negative things will happen if we do not change our ways.

עֵינֶיךָ אֲשֶׁר תִּרְאֶה׃ 35 יַכְּכָה יְהֹוָהאדניאהדונהי בִּשְׁחִין רָע עַל־
הַבִּרְכַּיִם וְעַל־הַשֹּׁקַיִם אֲשֶׁר לֹא־תוּכַל לְהֵרָפֵא מִכַּף
רַגְלְךָ וְעַד קָדְקֳדֶךָ׃ 36 יוֹלֵךְ יְהֹוָהאדניאהדונהי אֹתְךָ וְאֶת־מַלְכְּךָ
אֲשֶׁר תָּקִים עָלֶיךָ אֶל־גּוֹי אֲשֶׁר לֹא־יָדַעְתָּ אַתָּה וַאֲבֹתֶיךָ
וְעָבַדְתָּ שָׁם אֱלֹהִים מום, ילה אֲחֵרִים עֵץ וָאָבֶן׃ 37 וְהָיִיתָ
לְשַׁמָּה לְמָשָׁל וְלִשְׁנִינָה בְּכֹל לכב הָעַמִּים אֲשֶׁר־יְנַהֶגְךָ
יְהֹוָהאדניאהדונהי שָׁמָּה יוד הא ואו הא׃ 38 זֶרַע רַב תּוֹצִיא הַשָּׂדֶה
וּמְעַט תֶּאֱסֹף כִּי יַחְסְלֶנּוּ הָאַרְבֶּה יצחק׃ 39 כְּרָמִים תִּטַּע
וְעָבָדְתָּ וְיַיִן מיכ, י״פ האא לֹא־תִשְׁתֶּה וְלֹא תֶאֱגֹר כִּי תֹאכְלֶנּוּ
הַתֹּלָעַת׃ 40 זֵיתִים יִהְיוּ לְךָ בְּכָל לכב ־גְּבוּלֶךָ וְשֶׁמֶן לֹא תָסוּךְ
כִּי יִשַּׁל זֵיתֶךָ׃ 41 בָּנִים וּבָנוֹת תּוֹלִיד וְלֹא־יִהְיוּ לָךְ כִּי יֵלְכוּ
בַּשֶּׁבִי׃ 42 כָּל ילי ־עֵצְךָ וּפְרִי אַדְמָתֶךָ יְיָרֵשׁ הַצְּלָצַל׃ 43 הַגֵּר
אֲשֶׁר בְּקִרְבְּךָ יַעֲלֶה עָלֶיךָ מַעְלָה מָּעְלָה וְאַתָּה תֵרֵד
מַטָּה מָּטָּה׃ 44 הוּא יַלְוְךָ וְאַתָּה לֹא תַלְוֶנּוּ הוּא יִהְיֶה ייי
לְרֹאשׁ וְאַתָּה תִּהְיֶה לְזָנָב׃ 45 וּבָאוּ עָלֶיךָ כָּל ילי ־הַקְּלָלוֹת
הָאֵלֶּה וּרְדָפוּךָ וְהִשִּׂיגוּךָ עַד הִשָּׁמְדָךְ כִּי־לֹא שָׁמַעְתָּ

הַגֵּר - The Torah says that whoever is considered lowly becomes powerful and whoever is powerful will become nothing. We should never judge anyone by appearances. Someone may appear to have power in this world, while a seemingly powerless person may nevertheless be a greater soul.

בְּקוֹל יְהֹוָאדנָי יאהדונהי אֱלֹהֶיךָ לִשְׁמֹר מִצְוֹתָיו וְחֻקֹּתָיו אֲשֶׁר
צִוָּךְ: 46 וְהָיוּ בְךָ לְאוֹת וּלְמוֹפֵת וּבְזַרְעֲךָ עַד־עוֹלָם: 47 תַּחַת
אֲשֶׁר לֹא־עָבַדְתָּ אֶת־יְהֹוָאדנָי יאהדונהי אֱלֹהֶיךָ בְּשִׂמְחָה
וּבְטוּב והו לֵבָב בוכו מֵרֹב כֹּל ילי: 48 וְעָבַדְתָּ אֶת־אֹיְבֶיךָ אֲשֶׁר
יְשַׁלְּחֶנּוּ יְהֹוָאדנָי יאהדונהי בָּךְ בְּרָעָב וּבְצָמָא וּבְעֵירֹם וּבְחֹסֶר
כֹּל ילי וְנָתַן אבג יתץ, ושר, אהבת חנם עֹל בַּרְזֶל ר"ת - בלהה רחל זילפה לאה עַל־
צַוָּארֶךָ עַד הִשְׁמִידוֹ אֹתָךְ: 49 יִשָּׂא יְהֹוָאדנָי יאהדונהי עָלֶיךָ גּוֹי
מֵרָחֹק מִקְצֵה הָאָרֶץ אלף למד הה יוד מם כַּאֲשֶׁר יִדְאֶה הַנָּשֶׁר גּוֹי
אֲשֶׁר לֹא־תִשְׁמַע לְשֹׁנוֹ: 50 גּוֹי עַז פָּנִים אֲשֶׁר לֹא־יִשָּׂא
פָנִים לְזָקֵן וְנַעַר לֹא יָחֹן: 51 וְאָכַל פְּרִי בְהֶמְתְּךָ וּפְרִי־
אַדְמָתְךָ עַד הִשָּׁמְדָךְ אֲשֶׁר לֹא־יַשְׁאִיר לְךָ דָּגָן תִּירוֹשׁ
וְיִצְהָר שְׁגַר אֲלָפֶיךָ וְעַשְׁתְּרֹת צֹאנֶךָ עַד הַאֲבִידוֹ אֹתָךְ:
52 וְהֵצַר לְךָ בְּכָל לכב ־שְׁעָרֶיךָ עַד רֶדֶת חֹמֹתֶיךָ הַגְּבֹהֹת
וְהַבְּצֻרוֹת אֲשֶׁר אַתָּה בֹּטֵחַ בָּהֵן בְּכָל לכב ־אַרְצֶךָ וְהֵצַר לְךָ
בְּכָל לכב ־שְׁעָרֶיךָ בְּכָל לכב ־אַרְצְךָ אֲשֶׁר נָתַן יְהֹוָאדנָי יאהדונהי
אֱלֹהֶיךָ לָךְ: 53 וְאָכַלְתָּ פְרִי־בִטְנְךָ בְּשַׂר בָּנֶיךָ וּבְנֹתֶיךָ
אֲשֶׁר נָתַן־לְךָ יְהֹוָאדנָי יאהדונהי אֱלֹהֶיךָ בְּמָצוֹר וּבְמָצוֹק אֲשֶׁר־
יָצִיק לְךָ אֹיְבֶךָ: 54 הָאִישׁ הָרַךְ בְּךָ וְהֶעָנֹג ר"ת - עדן נהר גן מְאֹד
תֵּרַע עֵינוֹ בְאָחִיו וּבְאֵשֶׁת חֵיקוֹ וּבְיֶתֶר בָּנָיו אֲשֶׁר יוֹתִיר:

55 מִתֵּת | לְאַחַד אהבה, דאגה מֵהֶם מִבְּשַׂר בָּנָיו אֲשֶׁר יֹאכֵל
מִבְּלִי הִשְׁאִיר־לוֹ כֹּל יכ״י בְּמָצוֹר וּבְמָצוֹק אֲשֶׁר יָצִיק לְךָ
אֹיִבְךָ בְּכָל לככ ־שְׁעָרֶיךָ׃ 56 הָרַכָּה בְךָ וְהָעֲנֻגָּה אֲשֶׁר לֹא־
נִסְּתָה כַף־רַגְלָהּ הַצֵּג עַל־הָאָרֶץ אלף למד הה יוד מם מֵהִתְעַנֵּג
וּמֵרֹךְ תֵּרַע עֵינָהּ בְּאִישׁ חֵיקָהּ וּבִבְנָהּ וּבְבִתָּהּ׃ 57 וּבְשִׁלְיָתָהּ
הַיּוֹצֵת | מִבֵּין רַגְלֶיהָ וּבְבָנֶיהָ אֲשֶׁר תֵּלֵד כִּי־תֹאכְלֵם
בְחֹסֶר־כֹּל יכ״י בַּסָּתֶר ב״פ מצר בְּמָצוֹר וּבְמָצוֹק אֲשֶׁר יָצִיק לְךָ
אֹיִבְךָ בִּשְׁעָרֶיךָ׃ 58 אִם יוהך ־לֹא תִשְׁמֹר לַעֲשׂוֹת אֶת־כָּל יכ״י ־
דִּבְרֵי הַתּוֹרָה הַזֹּאת הַכְּתֻבִים בַּסֵּפֶר הַזֶּה והו לְיִרְאָה רי״ו,
גבורה אֶת־הַשֵּׁם הַנִּכְבָּד וְהַנּוֹרָא הַזֶּה והו אֵת יְהֹוָאדני יאהדונהי
אֱלֹהֶיךָ׃ 59 וְהִפְלָא יְהֹוָאדני יאהדונהי אֶת־מַכֹּתְךָ וְאֵת מַכּוֹת
זַרְעֶךָ מַכּוֹת גְּדֹלֹת וְנֶאֱמָנוֹת וָחֳלָיִם רָעִים וְנֶאֱמָנִים׃
60 וְהֵשִׁיב בְּךָ אֵת כָּל יכ״י ־מַדְוֵה מִצְרַיִם מצר אֲשֶׁר יָגֹרְתָּ
מִפְּנֵיהֶם וְדָבְקוּ בָּךְ׃ 61 גַּם כָּל יכ״י ־חֳלִי וְכָל יכ״י ־מַכָּה הי״ אֲשֶׁר
לֹא כָתוּב בְּסֵפֶר הַתּוֹרָה הַזֹּאת יַעְלֵם יְהֹוָאדני יאהדונהי עָלֶיךָ
עַד הִשָּׁמְדָךְ׃ 62 וְנִשְׁאַרְתֶּם בִּמְתֵי מְעָט תַּחַת אֲשֶׁר הֱיִיתֶם
כְּכוֹכְבֵי הַשָּׁמַיִם כוזו, י״פ טל לָרֹב כִּי־לֹא שָׁמַעְתָּ בְּקוֹל
יְהֹוָאדני יאהדונהי אֱלֹהֶיךָ׃ 63 וְהָיָה יהוה, יהה כַּאֲשֶׁר־שָׂשׂ יְהֹוָאדני יאהדונהי
עֲלֵיכֶם לְהֵיטִיב אֶתְכֶם וּלְהַרְבּוֹת אֶתְכֶם כֵּן יָשִׂישׂ

יְהֹוָה יאהדונהי עֲלֵיכֶם לְהַאֲבִיד אֶתְכֶם וּלְהַשְׁמִיד אֶתְכֶם
וְנִסַּחְתֶּם מֵעַל עלם הָאֲדָמָה אֲשֶׁר־אַתָּה בָא־שָׁמָּה יוד הא ואו הא
לְרִשְׁתָּהּ׃ 64 וֶהֱפִיצְךָ יְהֹוָה יאהדונהי בְּכָל לכב ־הָעַמִּים מִקְצֵה
הָאָרֶץ אלף למד הה יוד מם וְעַד־קְצֵה הָאָרֶץ אלף למד הה יוד מם וְעָבַדְתָּ
שָּׁם אֱלֹהִים מום, ילה אֲחֵרִים אֲשֶׁר לֹא־יָדַעְתָּ אַתָּה וַאֲבֹתֶיךָ
עֵץ וָאָבֶן׃ 65 וּבַגּוֹיִם הָהֵם לֹא תַרְגִּיעַ וְלֹא־יִהְיֶה ייי מָנוֹחַ
לְכַף־רַגְלֶךָ וְנָתַן אבג יתץ, ושר, אהבת חנם יְהֹוָה יאהדונהי לְךָ שָׁם לֵב
רַגָּז וְכִלְיוֹן עֵינַיִם וְדַאֲבוֹן נָפֶשׁ׃ 66 וְהָיוּ חַיֶּיךָ תְּלֻאִים לְךָ
מִנֶּגֶד זן, מזבח וּפָחַדְתָּ לַיְלָה מלה וְיוֹמָם וְלֹא תַאֲמִין בְּחַיֶּיךָ׃
67 בַּבֹּקֶר תֹּאמַר מִי ילי ־יִתֵּן עֶרֶב וּבָעֶרֶב תֹּאמַר מִי ילי ־יִתֵּן
בֹּקֶר מִפַּחַד לְבָבְךָ אֲשֶׁר תִּפְחָד וּמִמַּרְאֵה עֵינֶיךָ אֲשֶׁר
תִּרְאֶה׃ 68 וֶהֱשִׁיבְךָ יְהֹוָה יאהדונהי ׀ מִצְרַיִם מצר בָּאֳנִיּוֹת
בַּדֶּרֶךְ ב"פ יב"ק אֲשֶׁר אָמַרְתִּי לְךָ לֹא־תֹסִיף עוֹד לִרְאֹתָהּ
וְהִתְמַכַּרְתֶּם שָׁם לְאֹיְבֶיךָ לַעֲבָדִים וְלִשְׁפָחוֹת וְאֵין קֹנֶה׃
69 אֵלֶּה דִבְרֵי הַבְּרִית אֲשֶׁר־צִוָּה יְהֹוָה יאהדונהי אֶת־מֹשֶׁה מהש
לִכְרֹת אֶת־בְּנֵי יִשְׂרָאֵל בְּאֶרֶץ מוֹאָב מִלְּבַד הַבְּרִית
אֲשֶׁר־כָּרַת אִתָּם בְּחֹרֵב׃

Seventh Reading - David - Malchut

29 1 וַיִּקְרָא מֹשֶׁה מהש אֶל־כָּל ילי ־יִשְׂרָאֵל וַיֹּאמֶר אֲלֵהֶם
אַתֶּם רְאִיתֶם אֵת כָּל ילי ־אֲשֶׁר עָשָׂה יְהֹוָאדני אהדונהי לְעֵינֵיכֶם
בְּאֶרֶץ מִצְרַיִם מצר לְפַרְעֹה וּלְכָל יה אדני ילי ־עֲבָדָיו וּלְכָל יה
אדני ילי ־אַרְצוֹ: 2 הַמַּסּוֹת הַגְּדֹלֹת אֲשֶׁר רָאוּ עֵינֶיךָ הָאֹתֹת
וְהַמֹּפְתִים הַגְּדֹלִים הָהֵם: 3 וְלֹא־נָתַן יְהֹוָאדני אהדונהי לָכֶם
לֵב לָדַעַת וְעֵינַיִם לִרְאוֹת וְאָזְנַיִם לִשְׁמֹעַ עַד הַיּוֹם נגד,
מזבח, זן הַזֶּה והו: 4 וָאוֹלֵךְ אֶתְכֶם אַרְבָּעִים שָׁנָה בַּמִּדְבָּר
לֹא־בָלוּ שַׂלְמֹתֵיכֶם מֵעֲלֵיכֶם וְנַעַלְךָ לֹא־בָלְתָה מֵעַל עלם
רַגְלֶךָ: 5 לֶחֶם ג"פ יהו"ה לֹא אֲכַלְתֶּם וְיַיִן מיכ, י"פ האא וְשֵׁכָר י"פ ב"ן לֹא
שְׁתִיתֶם לְמַעַן תֵּדְעוּ כִּי אֲנִי אני יְהֹוָאדני אהדונהי אֱלֹהֵיכֶם ילה:

Maftir

6 וַתָּבֹאוּ אֶל־הַמָּקוֹם הַזֶּה והו וַיֵּצֵא סִיחֹן מֶלֶךְ־חֶשְׁבּוֹן וְעוֹג
מֶלֶךְ־הַבָּשָׁן לִקְרָאתֵנוּ לַמִּלְחָמָה וַנַּכֵּם: 7 וַנִּקַּח אֶת־אַרְצָם
וַנִּתְּנָהּ לְנַחֲלָה לָרְאוּבֵנִי וְלַגָּדִי והו וְלַחֲצִי שֵׁבֶט הַמְנַשִּׁי:
8 וּשְׁמַרְתֶּם אֶת־דִּבְרֵי הַבְּרִית הַזֹּאת וַעֲשִׂיתֶם אֹתָם לְמַעַן
תַּשְׂכִּילוּ אֵת כָּל ילי ־אֲשֶׁר תַּעֲשׂוּן:

וַיֹּאמֶר - This last section is Moses' final speech to the people. When righteous people leave this world, they complete a cycle. When Moses speaks, we are hearing "the completed Moses." This energy encapsulates his entire life.

Haftarah of Ki-Tavo

The haftarah discusses two timelines for the coming of Messiah. The choice is up to us: We can choose the way of pain and suffering or the way of mercy and blessing.

Isaiah 60 ישעיהו פרק 60

1 קוּמִי אוֹרִי כִּי בָא אוֹרֵךְ וּכְבוֹד יְהֹוָהאדני אהדונהי עָלַיִךְ זָרָח:
2 כִּי־הִנֵּה הַחֹשֶׁךְ ש"ך נצוצות יְכַסֶּה־אֶרֶץ וַעֲרָפֶל לְאֻמִּים וְעָלַיִךְ
יִזְרַח יְהֹוָהאדני אהדונהי וּכְבוֹדוֹ עָלַיִךְ יֵרָאֶה רי"ו, גבורה: 3 וְהָלְכוּ גוֹיִם
לְאוֹרֵךְ וּמְלָכִים לְנֹגַהּ זַרְחֵךְ: 4 שְׂאִי־סָבִיב עֵינַיִךְ קס"א, אלף הי יוד
הי וּרְאִי כֻּלָּם נִקְבְּצוּ בָאוּ־לָךְ בָּנַיִךְ מֵרָחוֹק שדי יָבֹאוּ וּבְנֹתַיִךְ
עַל־צַד תֵּאָמַנָה: 5 אָז תִּרְאִי וְנָהַרְתְּ וּפָחַד וְרָחַב לְבָבֵךְ
כִּי־יֵהָפֵךְ עָלַיִךְ הֲמוֹן יָם ילי וְחֵיל ומב גּוֹיִם יָבֹאוּ לָךְ: 6 שִׁפְעַת
גְּמַלִּים תְּכַסֵּךְ בִּכְרֵי מִדְיָן וְעֵיפָה כֻּלָּם מִשְּׁבָא יָבֹאוּ זָהָב
וּלְבוֹנָה אדון יוה"ך סג יִשָּׂאוּ וּתְהִלֹּת יְהֹוָהאדני אהדונהי יְבַשֵּׂרוּ: 7 כָּל ילי
־צֹאן קֵדָר יִקָּבְצוּ לָךְ אֵילֵי נְבָיוֹת יְשָׁרְתוּנֶךְ יַעֲלוּ עַל־
רָצוֹן מהש מִזְבְּחִי וּבֵית ב"פ ראה תִּפְאַרְתִּי אֲפָאֵר: 8 מִי ילי ־אֵלֶּה
כָּעָב תְּעוּפֶינָה וְכַיּוֹנִים אֶל־אֲרֻבֹּתֵיהֶם: 9 כִּי־לִי | אִיִּים
יְקַוּוּ וָאֳנִיּוֹת תַּרְשִׁישׁ בָּרִאשֹׁנָה לְהָבִיא בָנַיִךְ מֵרָחוֹק שדי
כַּסְפָּם וּזְהָבָם אִתָּם לְשֵׁם יְהֹוָהאדני אהדונהי אֱלֹהַיִךְ וְלִקְדוֹשׁ
יִשְׂרָאֵל כִּי פֵאֲרָךְ: 10 וּבָנוּ בְנֵי־נֵכָר חֹמֹתַיִךְ וּמַלְכֵיהֶם

יְשָׁרְתוּנֶךְ כִּי בְקִצְפִּי הִכִּיתִיךְ וּבִרְצוֹנִי רִחַמְתִּיךְ׃ 11 וּפִתְּחוּ
שְׁעָרַיִךְ תָּמִיד נתה, קס״א - קנ״א - קמ״ג יוֹמָם וָלַיְלָה מלה לֹא יִסָּגֵרוּ
לְהָבִיא אֵלַיִךְ חֵיל ומב גּוֹיִם וּמַלְכֵיהֶם נְהוּגִים׃ 12 כִּי־הַגּוֹי
וְהַמַּמְלָכָה אֲשֶׁר לֹא־יַעַבְדוּךְ יֹאבֵדוּ וְהַגּוֹיִם חָרֹב יֶחֱרָבוּ׃
13 כְּבוֹד הַלְּבָנוֹן אֵלַיִךְ יָבוֹא בְּרוֹשׁ תִּדְהָר וּתְאַשּׁוּר יַחְדָּו
לְפָאֵר מְקוֹם מִקְדָּשִׁי וּמְקוֹם רַגְלַי אֲכַבֵּד׃ 14 וְהָלְכוּ
אֵלַיִךְ שְׁחוֹחַ בְּנֵי מְעַנַּיִךְ וְהִשְׁתַּחֲווּ עַל־כַּפּוֹת רַגְלַיִךְ כָּל ילי
־מְנַאֲצָיִךְ וְקָרְאוּ לָךְ עִיר ערי, סחחר, סנדלפון יְהֹוָהאדניאהדונהי צִיּוֹן יוסף
קְדוֹשׁ יִשְׂרָאֵל׃ 15 תַּחַת הֱיוֹתֵךְ עֲזוּבָה וּשְׂנוּאָה וְאֵין עוֹבֵר
וְשַׂמְתִּיךְ לִגְאוֹן עוֹלָם מְשׂוֹשׂ דּוֹר וָדוֹר רי״ו, גבורה׃ 16 וְיָנַקְתְּ
חֲלֵב גּוֹיִם וְשֹׁד מְלָכִים תִּינָקִי וְיָדַעַתְּ כִּי אֲנִי אני יְהֹוָהאדניאהדונהי
מוֹשִׁיעֵךְ וְגֹאֲלֵךְ אֲבִיר הרח יַעֲקֹב יאהדונהי, אידהנויה׃ 17 תַּחַת
הַנְּחֹשֶׁת אָבִיא זָהָב וְתַחַת הַבַּרְזֶל ר״ת - בלהה רחל זלפה לאה אָבִיא
כֶסֶף וְתַחַת הָעֵצִים נְחֹשֶׁת וְתַחַת הָאֲבָנִים בַּרְזֶל ר״ת - בלהה
רחל זלפה לאה וְשַׂמְתִּי פְקֻדָּתֵךְ שָׁלוֹם וְנֹגְשַׂיִךְ צְדָקָה א אל אלה אלהי
אלהים׃ 18 לֹא־יִשָּׁמַע עוֹד חָמָס בְּאַרְצֵךְ שֹׁד וָשֶׁבֶר בִּגְבוּלָיִךְ
וְקָרָאת יְשׁוּעָה חוֹמֹתַיִךְ וּשְׁעָרַיִךְ תְּהִלָּה׃ 19 לֹא־יִהְיֶה ייי
־לָּךְ עוֹד הַשֶּׁמֶשׁ לְאוֹר רז, אין סוף יוֹמָם וּלְנֹגַהּ הַיָּרֵחַ לֹא־
יָאִיר לָךְ וְהָיָה יהוה, יהה ־לָךְ יְהֹוָהאדניאהדונהי לְאוֹר רז, אין סוף עוֹלָם

וֵאלֹהַיִךְ לְתִפְאַרְתֵּךְ׃ 20 לֹא־יָבוֹא עוֹד שִׁמְשֵׁךְ וִירֵחֵךְ
לֹא יֵאָסֵף כִּי יְהֹוָהאדניאהדונהי יִהְיֶה ייי ־לָּךְ לְאוֹר רז, אין סוף עוֹלָם
וְשָׁלְמוּ יְמֵי אֶבְלֵךְ׃ 21 וְעַמֵּךְ כֻּלָּם צַדִּיקִים לְעוֹלָם יִירְשׁוּ
אָרֶץ נֵצֶר מטעו (מַטָּעַי) מַעֲשֵׂה יָדַי לְהִתְפָּאֵר׃ 22 הַקָּטֹן
יִהְיֶה ייי לָאֶלֶף וְהַצָּעִיר לְגוֹי עָצוּם אֲנִי אני יְהֹוָהאדניאהדונהי בְּעִתָּהּ
אֲחִישֶׁנָּה׃

Lesson of Nitzavim

The Big Lamed

We know that we do not bless the new moon on the Shabbat before the month of *Tishrei (the month of Libra)*, which ushers in the new year, or Rosh Hashanah. As the commentators explain, this is because it is written "*The Covering of Our Holiday,*" that this particular Shabbat must be concealed from both the angels and the Negative Side. But the question remains: What happens to the Light that we normally receive on the Shabbat before a new month? Without the Light we receive from the blessing of the new month, it is difficult for us to have a month without chaos. Is it possible that we were simply not given that extra Light, especially since this is the month of *Tishrei*, which includes Rosh Hashanah, Yom Kippur (the Day of Atonement), and Sukkot?

We know that the month of *Tishrei* is controlled and was created by the letter *lamed*, and the portion of Nitzavim is always read on the Shabbat before Rosh Hashanah. It is read either alone or connected to the portion of Vayelech, depending on the calendar. In the portion of Nitzavim we have a big *lamed* to give us the Light that would otherwise be revealed in the blessing of the new month. In this way, we receive the Light without awakening the Negative Side through reciting the monthly blessing.

This is a great lesson. With such a good reason *not* to do the blessing of the month, we still need the Light to help us during the holidays and the Day of Atonement. As Rav Zusha said: "I wish I could love the most righteous person in the world as much as the Creator loves the most wicked." There are no limits to what the Creator does for us. He makes sure Satan is not awakened, and He also gives us the Light we need.

Many times, we make up "spiritual" reasons not to do certain things. But in the end, we will be asked: Where is the Light that was supposed to be revealed? The Creator has a thousand and one reasons to distance Himself from us — and His reasons are a million times better than ours — yet He finds a way to give us the Light we need. When we think there is a reason not to do something, we should ask ourselves: "What about the Light that needs to be revealed?"

Part of the reason we don't bless the new moon of *Tishrei* is related to our desire to not awaken Satan. This is another great lesson: Satan comes *only* if we awaken him. But after thousands of years, he surely knows when Rosh Hashanah is and that we won't do the blessing of the month. We wouldn't try the same trick on one person a thousand times, so why does it work on Satan?

The answer is that he has strength in our lives only when we make an opening for him to be there. It's not really a matter of tricking him. As my father and my teacher says: "Just tell him that he is not here. If we say this, he has to go. The only condition is that we must believe we have the power."

In contrast, the Light is always with us. We ourselves bring chaos into our lives, and if we didn't do this, our lives would contain only good. It is written that the inclination of a person is evil from a young age, but only because it is our nature to pursue the desire to receive for the self alone. But we mustn't forget that deep inside us, there is only Light. If we don't let any darkness in our lives, we won't have to look for the Light — we will see that it's already in us.

Once, I sat with my father and my teacher, the Rav, and my brother, Michael, before the Rishon Letzion, the great kabbalist Mordechai Eliyahu. One of the new students of the Centre was with us. Rav Mordechai Eliyahu asked the student some questions about some areas of spiritual principle that the student had never studied, and he answered as best as he could. He even surprised us with what he knew! But this same student (I hope he wont be hurt if he hears this story) didnt really show Rav Mordechai the respect that a wise person deserves to be shown. But the honorable Rav Mordechai said in the end, Maybe you think that from the outside you are wild and stupid and that you dont understand anything (Esau), but inside you are a pure Sephardic person (Jacob). A pure Sephardic person - sfaradi tahor is the title that is given to the great Sephardic sages like Rav Chaim Vital or his son Rav Shmuel, who both knew that pure Sephardic is a title of honor.

Regarding the 11 dots

In the verse "*Lanu Ul'vanenu*" there are 11 dots. There are only 10 places in the Torah where there are dots, and this week we have the merit to have 11 such dots. The number 11 removes nega, like the 11 types of incense used to retrieve the Light that was given to the *klippah*, and the Tabernacle also had 11 layers or coverings to protect it against the *klippah.* So meditating on the 11 dots in this verse provides us with all the Light that they bring back.

But there is more than this. Rav Avraham Azulai explains in the *The People of the Covenant of Abraham* that any dots above letters in the Torah connect us to one of the ten Days of Atonement. In this week's portion, the dots connect us to the *tenth day* of the Ten Days of Atonement, which is Yom Kippur — the only day of the year when anyone connected to religion in even the smallest way goes to the synagogue. We think that Yom Kippur happens once a year, but Rav Avraham Azulai, through his explanation of the dots, teaches us that the same Light that is revealed on Yom Kippur and Rosh Hashana and during the month of *Elul* can be revealed through the weekly Torah readings. By connecting to the 11 dots, we return to everyone we caused sorrow and pain, and we take their pain away. In other words, we reclaim the Light that was taken by the Negative Side.

That's what taking the Light out of the *klippah* means. The only way to reclaim this Light is either to heal the pain of someone we have hurt or to let go of feeling hurt ourselves. If we do this, we will be able to connect to the Light.

Only in the month of *Elul* do most people worry about what they did to others. Their main concern is to erase the damage that they have done. This, unfortunately, is not the same as truly caring -- but the purpose of this month is to get us to a state where we really do care. Rav Avraham Azulai teaches us that we need to do this all year round, *especially* during the month of *Elul*. Rosh Hashanah affects the whole year, but the changes we make must be real and not just because the calendar says we are in the month of *Elul* — or because we are afraid of what might happen on Yom Kippur.

The dots teach us even more than that. They guide us as to what our feelings should be towards other people. Because the dots are above the words "to us and to our sons," we learn that the love that exists between a father and a son cannot be explained in words. The same applies to the love a mother has for her newborn child. This love is so deep that it's impossible to describe in words. This is certainly not love based on "what am I getting out of this?" or "what's in it for me?"

This is what is called "simple love" — a love without rules or boundaries, a love that simply exists. This is the love we should have for others all year round, not just in the month of *Elul*. We should have simple love towards the people we are close to, and if possible, even towards people whom we don't even know. It is impossible for us to have "simple love" for just a month or for the 40 days between the beginning of *Elul* and Yom Kippur, because then it is not simple love. The change must be real and consistent — for every day and every moment of the whole year.

If we really achieve this connection to others through simple love, we can cleanse all the negativity from within ourselves. Then we will truly merit the verse: "You are all standing today before the Creator." There will be nothing between us and the Creator. It will be like a father standing with his son.

I hope this is clear because it's a great lesson: If a connection between two people needs to be "worked on," it means there is a problem with the connection. When we really connect with the Light, we won't even have to ask the Creator to be with us. He will simply be with us for all time.

Synopsis of Nitzavim

The portion of Nitzavim always falls just before Rosh Hashanah. *Nitzavim* means "we are standing before." We are now standing before Rosh Hashanah. This portion prepares us for dealing with the judgment that comes during and after the holiday. It helps if we enter the holiday and listen to the *shofar* with the right meditations.

First Reading - Abraham - Chesed

9 אַתֶּם נִצָּבִים הַיּוֹם נגד, מזבח, זן כֻּלְּכֶם לִפְנֵי וחכמה, בינה
יְהֹוָהאדניאהדונהי אֱלֹהֵיכֶם ילה רָאשֵׁיכֶם שִׁבְטֵיכֶם זִקְנֵיכֶם
וְשֹׁטְרֵיכֶם כֹּל ילי אִישׁ יִשְׂרָאֵל׃ 10 טַפְּכֶם נְשֵׁיכֶם וְגֵרְךָ
אֲשֶׁר בְּקֶרֶב מַחֲנֶיךָ מֵחֹטֵב עֵצֶיךָ עַד שֹׁאֵב מֵימֶיךָ׃
11 לְעָבְרְךָ בִּבְרִית יְהֹוָהאדניאהדונהי אֱלֹהֶיךָ וּבְאָלָתוֹ אֲשֶׁר
יְהֹוָהאדניאהדונהי אֱלֹהֶיךָ כֹּרֵת עִמְּךָ הַיּוֹם נגד, מזבח, זן׃

Second Reading - Isaac - Gvurah

12 לְמַעַן הָקִים־אֹתְךָ הַיּוֹם נגד, מזבח, זן | לוֹ לְעָם עלם וְהוּא
יִהְיֶה ייי ־לְּךָ לֵאלֹהִים מום, ילה כַּאֲשֶׁר דִּבֶּר ראה ־לָךְ וְכַאֲשֶׁר
נִשְׁבַּע לַאֲבֹתֶיךָ לְאַבְרָהָם לְיִצְחָק וּלְיַעֲקֹב יאהדונהי, אידהנויה׃
13 וְלֹא אִתְּכֶם לְבַדְּכֶם אָנֹכִי איע כֹּרֵת אֶת־הַבְּרִית הַזֹּאת

כֻּלְּכֶם - The first section: For whom are these laws of the universe created? They were created for everyone; No one should feel he or she is too good or too evil for a spiritual path. The laws are meant to be inclusive, but historically, religion has been used to exclude people. The purpose of Kabbalah is to bring everyone together.

כֹּל - The people were given the laws: This refers to *all* the people—those who were on the spiritual path and those who were not on the path, the people who were there and those who were not there, the people who are here and those who are not here. We must understand how the laws unite us rather than divide us.

וְאֶת־הָאָלָה הַזֹּאת׃ 14 כִּי אֶת־אֲשֶׁר יֶשְׁנוֹ פֹּה מילה עִמָּנוּ עֹמֵד
הַיּוֹם נגד, מזבח, זן לִפְנֵי חכמה, בינה יְהֹוָה אהדונהי אֱלֹהֵינוּ ילה וְאֵת אֲשֶׁר
אֵינֶנּוּ פֹּה מילה עִמָּנוּ הַיּוֹם נגד, מזבח, זן׃

Third Reading - Jacob - Tiferet

15 כִּי־אַתֶּם יְדַעְתֶּם אֵת אֲשֶׁר־יָשַׁבְנוּ בְּאֶרֶץ מִצְרָיִם מצר
וְאֵת אֲשֶׁר־עָבַרְנוּ בְּקֶרֶב הַגּוֹיִם אֲשֶׁר עֲבַרְתֶּם׃
16 וַתִּרְאוּ אֶת־שִׁקּוּצֵיהֶם וְאֵת גִּלֻּלֵיהֶם עֵץ וָאֶבֶן כֶּסֶף
וְזָהָב אֲשֶׁר עִמָּהֶם׃ 17 פֶּן־יֵשׁ בָּכֶם אִישׁ אוֹ־אִשָּׁה אוֹ
מִשְׁפָּחָה אוֹ־שֵׁבֶט אֲשֶׁר לְבָבוֹ פֹנֶה ע״ב ס״ג הַיּוֹם נגד, מזבח, זן
מֵעִם יְהֹוָה אהדונהי אֱלֹהֵינוּ ילה לָלֶכֶת לַעֲבֹד אֶת־אֱלֹהֵי דמב,
ילה הַגּוֹיִם הָהֵם פֶּן־יֵשׁ בָּכֶם שֹׁרֶשׁ פֹּרֶה רֹאשׁ וְלַעֲנָה׃
18 וְהָיָה יהוה, יהה בְּשָׁמְעוֹ אֶת־דִּבְרֵי הָאָלָה הַזֹּאת וְהִתְבָּרֵךְ
בִּלְבָבוֹ לֵאמֹר שָׁלוֹם יִהְיֶה ייי ־לִּי כִּי בִּשְׁרִרוּת לִבִּי אֵלֵךְ
לְמַעַן סְפוֹת הָרָוָה אֶת־הַצְּמֵאָה׃ 19 לֹא־יֹאבֶה יְהֹוָה אהדונהי
סְלֹחַ לוֹ כִּי אָז יֶעְשַׁן אַף־יְהֹוָה אהדונהי וְקִנְאָתוֹ בָּאִישׁ הַהוּא
וְרָבְצָה בּוֹ כָּל ילי ־הָאָלָה הַכְּתוּבָה בַּסֵּפֶר הַזֶּה והו וּמָחָה

פֶּן - Here is a warning against idol-worshipping. This does not refer only to graven images. Anytime we treat something as more important than our spiritual growth, that thing becomes our idol.

יְהֹוָהאדני יאהדונהי אֶת־שְׁמוֹ מִתַּחַת הַשָּׁמָיִם כוזו, י״פ טל: 20 וְהִבְדִּילוֹ
יְהֹוָהאדני יאהדונהי לְרָעָה רהע מִכֹּל ילי שִׁבְטֵי יִשְׂרָאֵל כְּכֹל ילי אָלוֹת
הַבְּרִית הַכְּתוּבָה בְּסֵפֶר הַתּוֹרָה הַזֶּה והו: 21 וְאָמַר הַדּוֹר
הָאַחֲרוֹן בְּנֵיכֶם אֲשֶׁר יָקוּמוּ מֵאַחֲרֵיכֶם וְהַנָּכְרִי אֲשֶׁר יָבֹא
מֵאֶרֶץ רְחוֹקָה וְרָאוּ אֶת־מַכּוֹת הָאָרֶץ אלף למד הה יוד מם הַהִוא
וְאֶת־תַּחֲלֻאֶיהָ אֲשֶׁר־חִלָּה להח יְהֹוָהאדני יאהדונהי בָּהּ: 22 גָּפְרִית
וָמֶלַח ג״פ יהו״ה שְׂרֵפָה כָל ילי ־אַרְצָהּ לֹא תִזָּרַע וְלֹא תַצְמִחַ
וְלֹא־יַעֲלֶה בָהּ כָּל ילי ־עֵשֶׂב כְּמַהְפֵּכַת סְדֹם וַעֲמֹרָה
אַדְמָה וּצְבוֹיִים (כתיב: וצביים) אֲשֶׁר הָפַךְ יְהֹוָהאדני יאהדונהי בְּאַפּוֹ
וּבַחֲמָתוֹ: 23 וְאָמְרוּ כָּל ילי ־הַגּוֹיִם עַל־מֶה יוד הא ואו הא עָשָׂה
יְהֹוָהאדני יאהדונהי כָּכָה היי לָאָרֶץ הַזֹּאת מֶה יוד הא ואו הא חֳרִי הָאַף
הַגָּדוֹל להח, מבה הַזֶּה והו: 24 וְאָמְרוּ עַל אֲשֶׁר עָזְבוּ אֶת־בְּרִית
יְהֹוָהאדני יאהדונהי אֱלֹהֵי דמב, ילה אֲבֹתָם אֲשֶׁר כָּרַת עִמָּם בְּהוֹצִיאוֹ
אֹתָם מֵאֶרֶץ מִצְרָיִם מצר: 25 וַיֵּלְכוּ וַיַּעַבְדוּ אֱלֹהִים מום, ילה
אֲחֵרִים וַיִּשְׁתַּחֲווּ לָהֶם אֱלֹהִים מום, ילה אֲשֶׁר לֹא־יְדָעוּם וְלֹא
חָלַק לָהֶם: 26 וַיִּחַר־אַף יְהֹוָהאדני יאהדונהי בָּאָרֶץ הַהִוא לְהָבִיא
עָלֶיהָ פהל אֶת־כָּל ילי ־הַקְּלָלָה הַכְּתוּבָה בַּסֵּפֶר הַזֶּה והו:
27 וַיִּתְּשֵׁם יְהֹוָהאדני יאהדונהי מֵעַל עלם אַדְמָתָם בְּאַף וּבְחֵמָה

וּבְקֶצֶף גָּדוֹל להח, מבה וַיַּשְׁלִכֵם אֶל־אֶרֶץ אַחֶרֶת כַּיּוֹם נגד,
מזבח, זן הַזֶּה והו: 28 הַנִּסְתָּרֹת לַיהוָהאדניאהדונהי אֱלֹהֵינוּ ילה וְהַנִּגְלֹת
לָנוּ וּלְבָנֵינוּ עַד־עוֹלָם לַעֲשׂוֹת אֶת־כָּל ילי ־דִּבְרֵי הַתּוֹרָה
הַזֹּאת:

Fourth Reading - Moses - Netzach
(when connected: Second Reading - Isaac - Gvurah)

30 1 וְהָיָה יהוה, יהה כִי־יָבֹאוּ עָלֶיךָ כָּל ילי ־הַדְּבָרִים הָאֵלֶּה

וַיַּשְׁלִכֵם - There is a big *lamed* here. Every month on the Shabbat before the new moon, we bless the new moon and bring its energy upon us. In the month of *Tishrei* at this crucial time before Rosh Hashanah, we do not want to draw Satan's attention to us, so we do not bless the moon. What happens to the energy that we normally get from this action? We get it from the big *lamed*. This is an important lesson because without awareness of it, we cannot get this energy. But the bigger lesson is that the Light always looks after us. If there is some reason we cannot do something, the Creator still enables us to get the Light.

לָנוּ וּלְבָנֵינוּ עַד - Eleven dots: There are ten places in the Torah where we encounter dots above words. These ten sets of dots connect us to the ten days of judgment between Rosh Hashanah and Yom Kippur. In this verse, we have eleven dots, this being the tenth set of dots appearing in the Torah. These dots connect us to Yom Kippur, the tenth day of judgment, which is also *Binah*, the highest level of energy we can get throughout the year. Through the power of these dots, we get the energy of Yom Kippur.

וְהָיָה - We read about the Final Redemption. One day, the final removal of chaos will take place; the only thing separating us from that day is time. Time is one of the most powerful tools that Satan uses against us. Our job is to remove time and shorten the process; this section helps us to remove time.

הַבְּרָכָה וְהַקְּלָלָה אֲשֶׁר נָתַתִּי לְפָנֶיךָ וַהֲשֵׁבֹתָ אֶל־לְבָבֶךָ
בְּכָל לכב ־הַגּוֹיִם אֲשֶׁר הִדִּיחֲךָ יְהֹוָהאדני אהדונהי אֱלֹהֶיךָ שָׁמָּה יוד
הא ואו הא: 2 וְשַׁבְתָּ עַד־יְהֹוָהאדני אהדונהי אֱלֹהֶיךָ ילה וְשָׁמַעְתָּ בְקֹלוֹ
כְּכֹל ילי אֲשֶׁר־אָנֹכִי איע מְצַוְּךָ הַיּוֹם נגד, מזבח, זן אַתָּה וּבָנֶיךָ
בְּכָל לכב ־לְבָבְךָ וּבְכָל לכב ־נַפְשֶׁךָ: 3 וְשָׁב יְהֹוָהאדני אהדונהי
אֱלֹהֶיךָ אֶת־שְׁבוּתְךָ וְרִחֲמֶךָ וְשָׁב וְקִבֶּצְךָ מִכָּל ילי ־הָעַמִּים
אֲשֶׁר הֱפִיצְךָ יְהֹוָהאדני אהדונהי אֱלֹהֶיךָ שָׁמָּה יוד הא ואו הא: 4 אִם יוהך
־יִהְיֶה יי נִדַּחֲךָ בִּקְצֵה הַשָּׁמָיִם כוזו, י"פ טל מִשָּׁם יְקַבֶּצְךָ
יְהֹוָהאדני אהדונהי אֱלֹהֶיךָ וּמִשָּׁם יִקָּחֶךָ: 5 וֶהֱבִיאֲךָ יְהֹוָהאדני אהדונהי
אֱלֹהֶיךָ אֶל־הָאָרֶץ אלף למד הה יוד מם אֲשֶׁר־יָרְשׁוּ אֲבֹתֶיךָ
וִירִשְׁתָּהּ וְהֵיטִבְךָ וְהִרְבְּךָ מֵאֲבֹתֶיךָ: 6 וּמָל יְהֹוָהאדני אהדונהי
אֱלֹהֶיךָ אֶת־לְבָבְךָ וְאֶת־לְבַב בוכו זַרְעֶךָ לְאַהֲבָה אחד, דאגה
אֶת־יְהֹוָהאדני אהדונהי אֱלֹהֶיךָ בְּכָל לכב ־לְבָבְךָ וּבְכָל לכב ־נַפְשְׁךָ
לְמַעַן חַיֶּיךָ:

וֶהֱבִיאֲךָ - The Creator will give all the curses to your enemies: If a person is destined to experience judgment but does not judge others, then the judgment that was intended for him will go somewhere else. We have the choice to decide whether judgment will fall upon us. If we judge others, we are choosing judgment to come to us.

Fifth Reading - Aaron - Hod

(when connected: Third Reading - Jacob - Tiferet)

7 וְנָתַן אבג יתץ, ושר, אהבת חנם יְהֹוָאֲדֹנָיאהדונהי אֱלֹהֶיךָ אֵת כָּל ילי
-הָאָלוֹת הָאֵלֶּה עַל־אֹיְבֶיךָ וְעַל־שֹׂנְאֶיךָ אֲשֶׁר רְדָפוּךָ׃
8 וְאַתָּה תָשׁוּב וְשָׁמַעְתָּ בְּקוֹל יְהֹוָאֲדֹנָיאהדונהי וְעָשִׂיתָ
אֶת־כָּל ילי -מִצְוֺתָיו אֲשֶׁר אָנֹכִי איע מְצַוְּךָ הַיּוֹם נגד, מזבח, זן׃
9 וְהוֹתִירְךָ יְהֹוָאֲדֹנָיאהדונהי אֱלֹהֶיךָ בְּכֹל לכב | מַעֲשֵׂה יָדֶךָ
בִּפְרִי בִטְנְךָ וּבִפְרִי בְהֶמְתְּךָ וּבִפְרִי אַדְמָתְךָ לְטֹבָה
כִּי | יָשׁוּב יְהֹוָאֲדֹנָיאהדונהי לָשׂוּשׂ עָלֶיךָ לְטוֹב והו כַּאֲשֶׁר־שָׂשׂ
עַל־אֲבֹתֶיךָ׃ 10 כִּי תִשְׁמַע בְּקוֹל יְהֹוָאֲדֹנָיאהדונהי אֱלֹהֶיךָ
לִשְׁמֹר מִצְוֺתָיו וְחֻקֹּתָיו הַכְּתוּבָה בְּסֵפֶר הַתּוֹרָה הַזֶּה והו כִּי
תָשׁוּב אֶל־יְהֹוָאֲדֹנָיאהדונהי אֱלֹהֶיךָ בְּכָל לכב -לְבָבְךָ וּבְכָל לכב
-נַפְשֶׁךָ׃

Sixth Reading - Joseph - Yesod

11 כִּי הַמִּצְוָה הַזֹּאת אֲשֶׁר אָנֹכִי איע מְצַוְּךָ הַיּוֹם נגד, מזבח, זן
לֹא־נִפְלֵאת הִוא מִמְּךָ וְלֹא רְחֹקָה הִוא׃ 12 לֹא בַשָּׁמַיִם כוזו,
י״פ טל הִוא לֵאמֹר מִי ילי יַעֲלֶה־לָּנוּ הַשָּׁמַיְמָה וְיִקָּחֶהָ לָּנוּ

הַמִּצְוָה - Today, the Torah is accessible. It is not in the heavens, but rather it is right in front of us, thanks to the work of Kabbalist Rav Ashlag. We need to appreciate those who came before us. Every generation benefits from the work of the spiritual giants of the previous generation.

וְיַשְׁמִעֵנוּ אֹתָהּ וְנַעֲשֶׂנָּה׃ 13 וְלֹא־מֵעֵבֶר לַיָּם ילי הִוא לֵאמֹר
מִי ילי יַעֲבָר־לָנוּ אֶל־עֵבֶר הַיָּם ילי וְיִקָּחֶהָ לָּנוּ וְיַשְׁמִעֵנוּ אֹתָהּ
וְנַעֲשֶׂנָּה׃ 14 כִּי־קָרוֹב אֵלֶיךָ הַדָּבָר ראה מְאֹד בְּפִיךָ וּבִלְבָבְךָ
לַעֲשֹׂתוֹ׃

Seventh Reading - David - Malchut
Maftir
(when connected: Fourth Reading - Moses - Netzach)

15 רְאֵה ראה נָתַתִּי לְפָנֶיךָ הַיּוֹם נגד, מזבח, זן אֶת־הַחַיִּים בינה וְאֶת־
הַטּוֹב והו וְאֶת־הַמָּוֶת וְאֶת־הָרָע׃ 16 אֲשֶׁר אָנֹכִי איע מְצַוְּךָ
הַיּוֹם נגד, מזבח, זן לְאַהֲבָה אחד, דאגה אֶת־יְהֹוָהאדניאהדונהי אֱלֹהֶיךָ ילה
לָלֶכֶת בִּדְרָכָיו וְלִשְׁמֹר מִצְוֹתָיו וְחֻקֹּתָיו וּמִשְׁפָּטָיו וְחָיִיתָ
וְרָבִיתָ וּבֵרַכְךָ יְהֹוָהאדניאהדונהי אֱלֹהֶיךָ בָּאָרֶץ אֲשֶׁר־אַתָּה
בָא־שָׁמָּה יוד הא ואו הא לְרִשְׁתָּהּ׃ 17 וְאִם יוהך יִפְנֶה לְבָבְךָ
וְלֹא תִשְׁמָע וְנִדַּחְתָּ וְהִשְׁתַּחֲוִיתָ לֵאלֹהִים מום, ילה אֲחֵרִים
וַעֲבַדְתָּם׃ 18 הִגַּדְתִּי לָכֶם הַיּוֹם נגד, מזבח, זן כִּי אָבֹד תֹּאבֵדוּן
לֹא־תַאֲרִיכֻן יָמִים נלך עַל־הָאֲדָמָה אֲשֶׁר אַתָּה עֹבֵר אֶת־
הַיַּרְדֵּן לָבוֹא שָׁמָּה יוד הא ואו הא לְרִשְׁתָּהּ׃ 19 הַעִדֹתִי בָכֶם
הַיּוֹם נגד, מזבח, זן אֶת־הַשָּׁמַיִם כוזו, י״פ טל וְאֶת־הָאָרֶץ אלף למד הה יוד מם

נָתַתִּי - The next section says: “You should choose life in order for you to live.” What does this mean? The answer is that those who are alive are not always living; Some people are spiritually dead. Life is not just a matter of breathing; It is a matter of what we do with our life.

הַחַיִּים בינה וְהַמָּוֶת נָתַתִּי לְפָנֶיךָ הַבְּרָכָה וְהַקְּלָלָה וּבָחַרְתָּ
בַּחַיִּים בינה לְמַעַן תִּחְיֶה אַתָּה וְזַרְעֶךָ׃ 20 לְאַהֲבָה אחד, דאגה
אֶת־יְהֹוָהאדניאהדונהי אֱלֹהֶיךָ לִשְׁמֹעַ בְּקֹלוֹ וּלְדָבְקָה־בוֹ כִּי
הוּא חַיֶּיךָ וְאֹרֶךְ יָמֶיךָ לָשֶׁבֶת עַל־הָאֲדָמָה אֲשֶׁר נִשְׁבַּע
יְהֹוָהאדניאהדונהי לַאֲבֹתֶיךָ לְאַבְרָהָם לְיִצְחָק וּלְיַעֲקֹב יאהדונהי,
אידהנויה לָתֵת לָהֶם׃

Haftarah of Nitzavim

In the haftarah for *Nitzavim*, Edom (Rome) is defeated. Edom represents our reactive behavior and everything that is negative. The head of Edom is the Angel of Death himself—the source of everything negative in this world. We have the potential to defeat Edom, getting the power to do so from this haftarah.

Isaiah 61 | ישעיהו פרק 61

10 שׂוֹשׂ אָשִׂישׂ בַּיהֹוָה יאהדונהי תָּגֵל נַפְשִׁי בֵּאלֹהַי דמב, ילה
כִּי הִלְבִּישַׁנִי בִּגְדֵי־ והו יֶשַׁע מְעִיל צְדָקָה א אל אלה אלהי אלהים
יְעָטָנִי כֶּחָתָן יְכַהֵן פְּאֵר וְכַכַּלָּה מלה תַּעְדֶּה כֵלֶיהָ׃ 11 כִּי
כָאָרֶץ תּוֹצִיא צִמְחָהּ וּכְגַנָּה זֵרוּעֶיהָ תַצְמִיחַ כֵּן ׀ אֲדֹנָי
יְהֹוִה יאהדונהי יַצְמִיחַ צְדָקָה א אל אלה אלהי אלהים וּתְהִלָּה נֶגֶד ין,
מזבח כָּל־ ילי הַגּוֹיִם׃ 62 1 לְמַעַן צִיּוֹן יוסף לֹא אֶחֱשֶׁה וּלְמַעַן
יְרוּשָׁלַםִ לֹא אֶשְׁקוֹט עַד־יֵצֵא כַנֹּגַהּ מוזי צִדְקָהּ וִישׁוּעָתָהּ
כְּלַפִּיד יִבְעָר׃ 2 וְרָאוּ גוֹיִם צִדְקֵךְ וְכָל־ ילי מְלָכִים כְּבוֹדֵךְ
וְקֹרָא לָךְ שֵׁם חָדָשׁ אֲשֶׁר פִּי יְהֹוָה יאהדונהי יִקֳּבֶנּוּ׃ 3 וְהָיִית
עֲטֶרֶת תִּפְאֶרֶת בְּיַד־יְהֹוָה יאהדונהי וּצְנוֹף (וּצְנִיף) מְלוּכָה
בְּכַף־אֱלֹהָיִךְ׃ 4 לֹא־יֵאָמֵר לָךְ עוֹד עֲזוּבָה וּלְאַרְצֵךְ
לֹא־יֵאָמֵר עוֹד שְׁמָמָה יוד הא ואו הא כִּי לָךְ יִקָּרֵא חֶפְצִי־בָהּ
וּלְאַרְצֵךְ בְּעוּלָה כִּי־חָפֵץ יְהֹוָה יאהדונהי בָּךְ וְאַרְצֵךְ תִּבָּעֵל׃
5 כִּי־יִבְעַל בָּחוּר בְּתוּלָה יִבְעָלוּךְ בָּנָיִךְ וּמְשׂוֹשׂ חָתָן
עַל־כַּלָּה יָשִׂישׂ עָלַיִךְ אֱלֹהָיִךְ׃ 6 עַל־חוֹמֹתַיִךְ יְרוּשָׁלַםִ

הִפְקַדְתִּי שֹׁמְרִים כָּל ילי ־הַיּוֹם נגד, מזבח, זן וְכָל ילי ־הַלַּיְלָה מלה
תָּמִיד נתה, קס"א ־ קנ"א ־ קמ"ג לֹא יֶחֱשׁוּ הַמַּזְכִּרִים אֶת־יְהֹוָה אדני יאהדונהי
אַל־דֳּמִי לָכֶם׃ 7 וְאַל־תִּתְּנוּ דֳמִי לוֹ עַד־יְכוֹנֵן וְעַד־יָשִׂים
אֶת־יְרוּשָׁלַם תְּהִלָּה בָּאָרֶץ׃ 8 נִשְׁבַּע יְהֹוָה אדני יאהדונהי בִּימִינוֹ
וּבִזְרוֹעַ עֻזּוֹ אִם יוהך ־אֶתֵּן אֶת־דְּגָנֵךְ עוֹד מַאֲכָל לְאֹיְבַיִךְ
וְאִם יוהך ־יִשְׁתּוּ בְנֵי־נֵכָר תִּירוֹשֵׁךְ אֲשֶׁר יָגַעַתְּ בּוֹ׃ 9 כִּי
מְאַסְפָיו יֹאכְלֻהוּ וְהִלְלוּ אֶת־יְהֹוָה אדני יאהדונהי וּמְקַבְּצָיו
יִשְׁתֻּהוּ בְּחַצְרוֹת קָדְשִׁי׃ 10 עִבְרוּ עִבְרוּ בַּשְּׁעָרִים כתר פַּנּוּ
דֶּרֶךְ הָעָם סֹלּוּ סֹלּוּ הַמְסִלָּה סַקְּלוּ מֵאֶבֶן הָרִימוּ נֵס יוד
הא ואו הא ־ אדני עַל־הָעַמִּים׃ 11 הִנֵּה יְהֹוָה אדני יאהדונהי הִשְׁמִיעַ אֶל־
קְצֵה הָאָרֶץ אלף למד הה יוד מם אִמְרוּ לְבַת־צִיּוֹן יוסף הִנֵּה יִשְׁעֵךְ
בָּא הִנֵּה שְׂכָרוֹ אִתּוֹ וּפְעֻלָּתוֹ לְפָנָיו׃ 12 וְקָרְאוּ לָהֶם עַם־
הַקֹּדֶשׁ גְּאוּלֵי יְהֹוָה אדני יאהדונהי וְלָךְ יִקָּרֵא דְרוּשָׁה עִיר ערי,
סנזפך, סנדלפון לֹא נֶעֱזָבָה׃ 63 1 מִי ילי ־זֶה | בָּא מֵאֱדוֹם חֲמוּץ
בְּגָדִים מִבָּצְרָה זֶה הָדוּר בִּלְבוּשׁוֹ צֹעֶה בְּרֹב כֹּחוֹ אֲנִי אני
מְדַבֵּר ראה בִּצְדָקָה א אל אלה אלהי אלהים רַב לְהוֹשִׁיעַ׃ 2 מַדּוּעַ
אָדֹם מ"ה, יוד הא ואו הא לִלְבוּשֶׁךָ וּבְגָדֶיךָ כְּדֹרֵךְ בְּגַת׃ 3 פּוּרָה |
דָּרַכְתִּי לְבַדִּי וּמֵעַמִּים אֵין־אִישׁ אִתִּי וְאֶדְרְכֵם בְּאַפִּי
וְאֶרְמְסֵם בַּחֲמָתִי וְיֵז נִצְחָם עַל־בְּגָדַי והו וְכָל ילי ־מַלְבּוּשַׁי

אֶגְאָלְתִּי: 4 כִּי יוֹם נגד, מזבח, זן נָקָם מנק בְּלִבִּי וּשְׁנַת גְּאוּלַי בָּאָה:
5 וְאַבִּיט וְאֵין עֹזֵר וְאֶשְׁתּוֹמֵם וְאֵין סוֹמֵךְ וַתּוֹשַׁע לִי זְרֹעִי
וַחֲמָתִי הִיא סְמָכָתְנִי: 6 וְאָבוּס עַמִּים בְּאַפִּי וַאֲשַׁכְּרֵם
בַּחֲמָתִי וְאוֹרִיד לָאָרֶץ נִצְחָם: 7 חַסְדֵי יְהֹוָה אדני יאהדונהי |
אַזְכִּיר תְּהִלֹּת יְהֹוָה אדני יאהדונהי כְּעַל כֹּל עמם, ילי אֲשֶׁר־גְּמָלָנוּ
יְהֹוָה אדני יאהדונהי וְרַב־טוּב והו לְבֵית ב"פ ראה יִשְׂרָאֵל אֲשֶׁר־גְּמָלָם
כְּרַחֲמָיו וּכְרֹב חֲסָדָיו: 8 וַיֹּאמֶר אַךְ־עַמִּי הֵמָּה יוד הא ואו הא
בָּנִים לֹא יְשַׁקֵּרוּ וַיְהִי לָהֶם לְמוֹשִׁיעַ: 9 בְּכָל לכב ־צָרָתָם |
לֹא (לוֹ) צָר וּמַלְאַךְ פָּנָיו הוֹשִׁיעָם בְּאַהֲבָתוֹ וּבְחֶמְלָתוֹ הוּא
גְּאָלָם וַיְנַטְּלֵם וַיְנַשְּׂאֵם כָּל ילי ־יְמֵי עוֹלָם:

Lesson of Vayelech

The portion of Vayelech is read in the weeks surrounding Rosh Hashanah, a time when we are focused on repentance and on wiping the slate clean of the previous year's negativity. But we should not undertake any of this just because it's a certain time of the year. We must also ask ourselves: "What is the real purpose of these weeks of repentance? And what is the purpose of our spiritual work in general?"

The answer to these questions — and the secret of all spirituality — is written in the *Shema Yisrael*: "*beshivtecha beveitecha oovelechtecha baderech*" (in English, "in your staying in your homes, and in your walking on the way").

Once people have attained a certain level of spirituality, they tend to think of certain times as "spiritual" and other times as "not spiritual." Shabbat, for example, is considered a spiritual time. It is these "spiritual" periods that the verse refers to as "in your walking on the way." But having "spiritual time" is not enough: In the deepest sense, every moment of our lives is spiritual. In other words, we must be also spiritual "staying in your homes."

Spirituality must become an inherent part of ourselves, regardless of whether today is Shabbat, another holiday or just another day in our lives. Spirituality cannot be sometimes yes and sometimes no. It must be innate. Of course, we are not expected to reach this level of understanding in one or two days — or even in a year or two years. It is intended to be our life's work. "Getting there" is our true purpose.

Once Rav Brandwein, our Rav's teacher, was walking in the street when a kibbutz member approached him. When the man began to hug Rav Brandwein and the Rav saw this expression of love, the Rav asked, "What are you doing? What is your connection to this rabbi?" It was well known, after all, that kibbutz members were usually hostile to religious people. The man from the kibbutz answered the Rav, "This man is not a rabbi! He is a kabbalist!" In other words, Rav Brandwein was not a person who lived in the Garden of Eden. Rav Brandwein had the Garden of Eden within him.

On a number of occasions, Rav Brandwein spent Shabbat in Haifa, which is a city well known for its anti-religious attitude. It is the only city in Israel with bus service on Shabbat. As Rav Brandwein walked through a street in Haifa, he saw the mayor of the city, Abba Chushi. Abba Chushi was known to be a chain smoker, but on this occasion he was not smoking. Abba Chushi greeted Rav Brandwein, "A month ago you and I met in Haifa. I was smoking on Shabbat. You said nothing, but I could see that it caused you pain. So I have stopped, because I knew it hurt you and yet you did not say a word."

What Abba Chushi felt from Rav Brandwein was the Light of "in your walking on the way" – the Light of the Creator that is always within us. Our work must get us to a point in which we do not have to make an effort to be spiritual, because it is our nature at every moment. Then the Garden of Eden will truly be within us.

Synopsis of Vayelech

This is the shortest portion in the Torah – only 30 verses. The universal laws dictate that less is more, so there's a lot of Light to be revealed in this portion. We must appreciate what we receive from it; the lesson that less is more.

First Reading - Abraham - Chesed

31 1 וַיֵּלֶךְ מֹשֶׁה מהש וַיְדַבֵּר אֶת־הַדְּבָרִים הָאֵלֶּה אֶל־כָּל ילי
־יִשְׂרָאֵל׃ 2 וַיֹּאמֶר אֲלֵהֶם בֶּן־מֵאָה וְעֶשְׂרִים שָׁנָה אָנֹכִי איע
הַיּוֹם נגד, מזבח, זן לֹא־אוּכַל עוֹד לָצֵאת וְלָבוֹא וַיהֹוָאדניאהדונהי
אָמַר אֵלַי לֹא תַעֲבֹר אֶת־הַיַּרְדֵּן הַזֶּה והו׃ 3 יְהֹוָאדניאהדונהי
אֱלֹהֶיךָ הוּא | עֹבֵר לְפָנֶיךָ הוּא־יַשְׁמִיד אֶת־הַגּוֹיִם הָאֵלֶּה
מִלְּפָנֶיךָ וִירִשְׁתָּם יְהוֹשֻׁעַ הוּא עֹבֵר לְפָנֶיךָ כַּאֲשֶׁר דִּבֶּר ראה
יְהֹוָאדניאהדונהי׃

Second Reading - Isaac - Gvurah

4 וְעָשָׂה יְהֹוָאדניאהדונהי לָהֶם כַּאֲשֶׁר עָשָׂה לְסִיחוֹן וּלְעוֹג
מַלְכֵי נלך הָאֱמֹרִי וּלְאַרְצָם אֲשֶׁר הִשְׁמִיד אֹתָם׃ 5 וּנְתָנָם
יְהֹוָאדניאהדונהי לִפְנֵיכֶם וַעֲשִׂיתֶם לָהֶם כְּכָל ילי ־הַמִּצְוָה אֲשֶׁר

לֹא־אוּכַל - Moses is now 120 years old. He can't travel back and forth between the physical and the Upper Worlds anymore. However, since he left this physical realm, he has not been limited to the Upper World. He came down in the time of Rav Shimon to help write the Zohar, and has come back in every subsequent generation. *Tzaddikim*, righteous people, like Moses take care of us and make sure that even if they're not here physically, they'll be here spiritually. People close to the Light keep helping us. They help wherever they are, whether in the physical dimension or in the Upper Worlds.

צִוִּיתִי אֶתְכֶם: 6 חִזְקוּ וְאִמְצוּ אַל־תִּירְאוּ וְאַל־תַּעַרְצוּ
מִפְּנֵיהֶם כִּי | יְהֹוָהאדניאהדונהי אֱלֹהֶיךָ הוּא הַהֹלֵךְ עִמָּךְ לֹא
יַרְפְּךָ וְלֹא יַעַזְבֶךָּ:

Third Reading - Jacob - Tiferet
(when connected: Fifth Reading - Aaron - Hod)

7 וַיִּקְרָא מֹשֶׁה מהש לִיהוֹשֻׁעַ וַיֹּאמֶר אֵלָיו לְעֵינֵי כָל ילי
־יִשְׂרָאֵל חֲזַק פהל וֶאֱמָץ כִּי אַתָּה תָּבוֹא אֶת־הָעָם הַזֶּה והו
אֶל־הָאָרֶץ אלף למד הה יוד מם אֲשֶׁר נִשְׁבַּע יְהֹוָהאדניאהדונהי לַאֲבֹתָם
לָתֵת לָהֶם וְאַתָּה תַּנְחִילֶנָּה אוֹתָם: 8 וַיהֹוָהאדניאהדונהי הוּא |
הַהֹלֵךְ לְפָנֶיךָ הוּא יִהְיֶה ייי עִמָּךְ לֹא יַרְפְּךָ וְלֹא יַעַזְבֶךָּ לֹא
תִירָא וְלֹא תֵחָת: 9 וַיִּכְתֹּב מֹשֶׁה מהש אֶת־הַתּוֹרָה הַזֹּאת
וַיִּתְּנָהּ אֶל־הַכֹּהֲנִים בְּנֵי לֵוִי הַנֹּשְׂאִים אֶת־אֲרוֹן בְּרִית
יְהֹוָהאדניאהדונהי וְאֶל־כָּל ילי ־זִקְנֵי יִשְׂרָאֵל:

חִזְקוּ וְאִמְצוּ - Moses tells the people not to be afraid, that the Creator will be with them always. When we think the Creator isn't with us, He's with us even more. The times we feel weak are the times we have to reach out to the Creator. It's easy to be with Creator when things are good. The real test is being certain of His presence in difficult times.

לִיהוֹשֻׁעַ - Moses gives Joshua some of his life. Each student gets part of the soul of their teacher. Not only do we have to appreciate what we're getting, we also have a responsibility to share what we receive.

Fourth Reading - Moses - Netzach

10 וַיְצַו מֹשֶׁה מהש אוֹתָם לֵאמֹר מִקֵּץ מנק | שֶׁבַע שָׁנִים בְּמֹעֵד
שְׁנַת הַשְּׁמִטָּה בְּחַג הַסֻּכּוֹת׃ 11 בְּבוֹא כָל ילי ־יִשְׂרָאֵל
לֵרָאוֹת אֶת־פְּנֵי חכמה, בינה יְהֹוָאדנייאהדונהי אֱלֹהֶיךָ בַּמָּקוֹם אֲשֶׁר
יִבְחָר תִּקְרָא אֶת־הַתּוֹרָה הַזֹּאת נֶגֶד זן, מזבח כָּל ילי ־יִשְׂרָאֵל
בְּאָזְנֵיהֶם׃ 12 הַקְהֵל אֶת־הָעָם הָאֲנָשִׁים וְהַנָּשִׁים וְהַטַּף
וְגֵרְךָ אֲשֶׁר בִּשְׁעָרֶיךָ לְמַעַן יִשְׁמְעוּ וּלְמַעַן יִלְמְדוּ וְיָרְאוּ
אֶת־יְהֹוָאדנייאהדונהי אֱלֹהֵיכֶם ילה וְשָׁמְרוּ לַעֲשׂוֹת אֶת־כָּל ילי
־דִּבְרֵי הַתּוֹרָה הַזֹּאת׃ 13 וּבְנֵיהֶם אֲשֶׁר לֹא־יָדְעוּ יִשְׁמְעוּ
וְלָמְדוּ לְיִרְאָה רי״ו, גבורה אֶת־יְהֹוָאדנייאהדונהי אֱלֹהֵיכֶם ילה כָּל ילי
־הַיָּמִים נלך אֲשֶׁר אַתֶּם חַיִּים בינה עַל־הָאֲדָמָה אֲשֶׁר אַתֶּם
עֹבְרִים אֶת־הַיַּרְדֵּן שָׁמָּה יוד הא ואו הא לְרִשְׁתָּהּ׃

Fifth Reading - Aaron - Hod
(when connected: Sixth Reading - Joseph - Yesod)

14 וַיֹּאמֶר יְהֹוָאדנייאהדונהי אֶל־מֹשֶׁה מהש הֵן קָרְבוּ יָמֶיךָ
לָמוּת קְרָא אֶת־יְהוֹשֻׁעַ וְהִתְיַצְּבוּ בְּאֹהֶל מוֹעֵד וַאֲצַוֶּנּוּ

תִּקְרָא - The book of *Devarim* was read by the king after the *Shemittah,* or sabbatical. We no longer have a king to do the reading, so on *Hoshana Rabba*, we read the whole book of *Devarim*. This helps to remove the judgments that come to us just before *Hoshana Rabba*. We gain the energy of protection before the judgments take effect.

וַיֵּלֶךְ מֹשֶׁה מהש וִיהוֹשֻׁעַ וַיִּתְיַצְּבוּ בְּאֹהֶל מוֹעֵד׃ 15 וַיֵּרָא
יְהֹוָאדנָי יאהדונהי בָּאֹהֶל בְּעַמּוּד עָנָן וַיַּעֲמֹד עַמּוּד הֶעָנָן עַל־
פֶּתַח הָאֹהֶל׃ 16 וַיֹּאמֶר יְהֹוָאדנָי יאהדונהי אֶל־מֹשֶׁה מהש הִנְּךָ **שֹׁכֵב**
עִם־אֲבֹתֶיךָ וְקָם הָעָם הַזֶּה והו וְזָנָה ׀ אַחֲרֵי ׀ אֱלֹהֵי דמב, ילה
נֵכַר־הָאָרֶץ אלף למד הה יוד מם אֲשֶׁר הוּא בָא־שָׁמָּה יוד הא ואו הא
בְּקִרְבּוֹ וַעֲזָבַנִי וְהֵפֵר אֶת־בְּרִיתִי אֲשֶׁר כָּרַתִּי אִתּוֹ׃ 17 וְחָרָה
אַפִּי בוֹ בַיּוֹם נגד, מזבח, זן ־הַהוּא וַעֲזַבְתִּים וְהִסְתַּרְתִּי פָנַי וחכמה,
בינה מֵהֶם וְהָיָה יהוה, יהה לֶאֱכֹל וּמְצָאֻהוּ רָעוֹת רַבּוֹת וְצָרוֹת
וְאָמַר בַּיּוֹם נגד, מזבח, זן הַהוּא הֲלֹא עַל כִּי־אֵין אֱלֹהַי דמב, ילה
בְּקִרְבִּי שדי מְצָאוּנִי הָרָעוֹת הָאֵלֶּה׃ 18 וְאָנֹכִי איע הַסְתֵּר ב"פ
מצר אַסְתִּיר פָּנַי וחכמה, בינה בַּיּוֹם נגד, מזבח, זן הַהוּא עַל כָּל עמם, ילי
־הָרָעָה רהע אֲשֶׁר עָשָׂה כִּי פָנָה ע"ב-ס"ג אֶל־אֱלֹהִים מום, ילה
אֲחֵרִים׃ 19 וְעַתָּה **כִּתְבוּ** לָכֶם אֶת־הַשִּׁירָה הַזֹּאת וְלַמְּדָהּ

שֹׁכֵב - Moses says that he's going to pass on and that the Israelites are going to forget him. Unfortunately, this "memory loss" is one of Satan's tools. We forget our lessons, we forget appreciation, we forget everything. We always have to remember and appreciate. If we can forget Moses, we surely have no problem to forget the little things.

כִּתְבוּ - The final *mitzvah*, spiritual principle, written in the Torah is to write a Torah scroll. In this verse, the whole energy of the Torah is given to us. There are 248 positive *mitzvot*, corresponding to the bone segments of our body. We receive the protective energy of the entire Torah when we

אֶת־בְּנֵי־יִשְׂרָאֵל שִׂימָהּ בְּפִיהֶם לְמַעַן תִּהְיֶה־לִּי הַשִּׁירָה
הַזֹּאת לְעֵד ב״פ כ״ן בִּבְנֵי יִשְׂרָאֵל׃

Sixth Reading - Joseph - Yesod
(when connected: Seventh Reading - David - Malchut)

20 כִּי־אֲבִיאֶנּוּ אֶל־הָאֲדָמָה | אֲשֶׁר־נִשְׁבַּעְתִּי לַאֲבֹתָיו זָבַת
חָלָב וּדְבַשׁ וְאָכַל וְשָׂבַע וְדָשֵׁן וּפָנָה ע״ב ס״ג אֶל־אֱלֹהִים מום,
ילה אֲחֵרִים וַעֲבָדוּם וְנִאֲצוּנִי וְהֵפֵר אֶת־בְּרִיתִי׃ 21 וְהָיָה יהוה,
יהה כִּי־תִמְצֶאןָ אֹתוֹ רָעוֹת רַבּוֹת וְצָרוֹת וְעָנְתָה הַשִּׁירָה
הַזֹּאת לְפָנָיו לְעֵד ב״פ כ״ן כִּי לֹא תִשָּׁכַח מִפִּי זַרְעוֹ כִּי
יָדַעְתִּי אֶת־יִצְרוֹ אֲשֶׁר הוּא עֹשֶׂה הַיּוֹם נגד, מזבח, זן בְּטֶרֶם
אֲבִיאֶנּוּ אֶל־הָאָרֶץ אלף למד הה יוד מם אֲשֶׁר נִשְׁבָּעְתִּי׃ 22 וַיִּכְתֹּב
מֹשֶׁה מהש אֶת־הַשִּׁירָה הַזֹּאת בַּיּוֹם נגד, מזבח, זן הַהוּא וַיְלַמְּדָהּ
אֶת־בְּנֵי יִשְׂרָאֵל׃ 23 וַיְצַו אֶת־יְהוֹשֻׁעַ בִּן־נוּן וַיֹּאמֶר חֲזַק פהל
וֶאֱמָץ כִּי אַתָּה תָּבִיא אֶת־בְּנֵי יִשְׂרָאֵל אֶל־הָאָרֶץ אלף למד
הה יוד מם אֲשֶׁר־נִשְׁבַּעְתִּי לָהֶם וְאָנֹכִי איע אֶהְיֶה עִמָּךְ׃ 24 וַיְהִי |
כְּכַלּוֹת מֹשֶׁה מהש לִכְתֹּב אֶת־דִּבְרֵי הַתּוֹרָה־הַזֹּאת עַל־
סֵפֶר עַד תֻּמָּם׃

read this verse.

כִּי לֹא תִשָּׁכַח מִפִּי זַרְעוֹ - The last letters of the Hebrew words *ki lo tishakach mipi zaro* spell the name "Yochai." This is a reference to Rav

Seventh Reading - David - Malchut

25 וַיְצַו מֹשֶׁה מהש אֶת־הַלְוִיִּם נֹשְׂאֵי אֲרוֹן בְּרִית־יְהֹוָה יאהדונהי
לֵאמֹר: 26 לָקֹחַ אֵת סֵפֶר הַתּוֹרָה הַזֶּה והו וְשַׂמְתֶּם אֹתוֹ
מִצַּד אֲרוֹן בְּרִית־יְהֹוָה יאהדונהי אֱלֹהֵיכֶם ילה וְהָיָה יהוה, יהה ־שָׁם
בְּךָ לְעֵד ב״פ ב״ן: 27 כִּי אָנֹכִי איע יָדַעְתִּי אֶת־מֶרְיְךָ וְאֶת־עָרְפְּךָ
הַקָּשֶׁה הֵן בְּעוֹדֶנִּי חַי עִמָּכֶם הַיּוֹם נגד, מזבח, זן מַמְרִים הֱיִתֶם
עִם־יְהֹוָה יאהדונהי וְאַף כִּי־אַחֲרֵי מוֹתִי: 28 הַקְהִילוּ אֵלַי אֶת־
כָּל ילי ־זִקְנֵי שִׁבְטֵיכֶם וְשֹׁטְרֵיכֶם וַאֲדַבְּרָה בְאָזְנֵיהֶם אֵת
הַדְּבָרִים הָאֵלֶּה וְאָעִידָה בָּם מב אֶת־הַשָּׁמַיִם כוזו, י״פ טל וְאֶת־
הָאָרֶץ אלף למד הה יוד מם:

Maftir

29 כִּי יָדַעְתִּי אַחֲרֵי מוֹתִי כִּי־הַשְׁחֵת תַּשְׁחִתוּן וְסַרְתֶּם
מִן־הַדֶּרֶךְ אֲשֶׁר צִוִּיתִי אֶתְכֶם וְקָרָאת אֶתְכֶם הָרָעָה רהע
בְּאַחֲרִית הַיָּמִים נלך כִּי־תַעֲשׂוּ אֶת־הָרַע בְּעֵינֵי יְהֹוָה יאהדונהי
לְהַכְעִיסוֹ בְּמַעֲשֵׂה יְדֵיכֶם: 30 וַיְדַבֵּר מֹשֶׁה מהש בְּאָזְנֵי כָּל ילי
־קְהַל יִשְׂרָאֵל אֶת־דִּבְרֵי הַשִּׁירָה הַזֹּאת עַד תֻּמָּם:

Shimon Bar Yochai—and a hint that he is going to come to reveal the secrets of the Torah through the Zohar.

הַתּוֹרָה - The Torah was written in the desert and put in the Ark to provide us with a physical connection to both the desert and to Moses. It's vital

Haftarah of Vayelech

This haftarah is always read before Rosh Hashanah and Yom Kippur. It is about teshuvah, or repentance, the ultimate return to the Creator.

Hosea 14 הושע פרק 14

2 שׁוּבָה הו״ש יִשְׂרָאֵל עַד יְהֹוָאדנייאהדונהי אֱלֹהֶיךָ כִּי כָשַׁלְתָּ
בַּעֲוֺנֶךָ׃ 3 קְחוּ עִמָּכֶם דְּבָרִים וְשׁוּבוּ אֶל־יְהֹוָאדנייאהדונהי
אִמְרוּ אֵלָיו כָּל ילי ־תִּשָּׂא עָוֺן וְקַח־טוֹב והו וּנְשַׁלְּמָה פָרִים
שְׂפָתֵינוּ׃ 4 אַשּׁוּר | לֹא יוֹשִׁיעֵנוּ עַל־סוּס כוק, א אד אדנ אדני לֹא
נִרְכַּב וְלֹא־נֹאמַר עוֹד אֱלֹהֵינוּ ילה לְמַעֲשֵׂה יָדֵינוּ אֲשֶׁר־בְּךָ
יְרֻחַם יָתוֹם׃ 5 אֶרְפָּא מְשׁוּבָתָם אֹהֲבֵם נְדָבָה כִּי שָׁב אַפִּי
מִמֶּנּוּ׃ 6 אֶהְיֶה כַטַּל כוזו, יוד הא ואו לְיִשְׂרָאֵל יִפְרַח כַּשּׁוֹשַׁנָּה וְיַךְ
שָׁרָשָׁיו כַּלְּבָנוֹן׃ 7 יֵלְכוּ יֹנְקוֹתָיו וִיהִי כַזַּיִת הוֹדוֹ וְרֵיחַ לוֹ
כַּלְּבָנוֹן׃ 8 יָשֻׁבוּ יֹשְׁבֵי בְצִלּוֹ יְחַיּוּ דָגָן וְיִפְרְחוּ כַגֶּפֶן זִכְרוֹ
כְּיֵין מיכ, י״פ האא לְבָנוֹן׃ 9 אֶפְרַיִם מַה יוד הא ואו הא ־לִּי עוֹד לָעֲצַבִּים
אֲנִי אני עָנִיתִי וַאֲשׁוּרֶנּוּ אֲנִי אני כִּבְרוֹשׁ רַעֲנָן מִמֶּנִּי פֶּרְיְךָ נִמְצָא׃
10 מִי ילי חָכָם וְיָבֵן אֵלֶּה נָבוֹן וְיֵדָעֵם כִּי־יְשָׁרִים דַּרְכֵי
יְהֹוָאדנייאהדונהי וְצַדִּקִים יֵלְכוּ בָם מב וּפֹשְׁעִים יִכָּשְׁלוּ בָם מב׃

Micah 7 מיכה פרק 7

18 מִי ילי ־אֵל כָּמוֹךָ נֹשֵׂא עָוֺן וְעֹבֵר עַל־פֶּשַׁע לִשְׁאֵרִית
נַחֲלָתוֹ לֹא־הֶחֱזִיק לָעַד ב״פ ב״ן אַפּוֹ כִּי־חָפֵץ חֶסֶד יוד הי ויו הי, י יה יהו

יהוה הוּא: 19 יָשׁוּב יְרַחֲמֵנוּ יִכְבֹּשׁ עֲוֺנֹתֵינוּ וְתַשְׁלִיךְ בִּמְצֻלוֹת
יָם ילי כָּל ילי ־חַטֹּאותָם: 20 תִּתֵּן ב״פ כהת אֱמֶת ז״פ ס״ג לְיַעֲקֹב יאהדונהי,
אידהנויה וְחֶסֶד יוד הי ויו הי, י יה יהו יהוה לְאַבְרָהָם אֲשֶׁר־נִשְׁבַּעְתָּ
לַאֲבֹתֵינוּ מִימֵי קֶדֶם:

to have something in the world from the time of Moses, something that emanates that power. We need that physical connection.

Lesson of Ha'azinu

"Listen to the Heavens"

We have a great lesson at the beginning of this week's portion. This is *Shabbat Shuva* - the Shabbat of Returning—the Shabbat between Rosh Hashanah and Yom Kippur when we read the haftarah of "Return, Israel, to Hashem your Creator." So there is a lesson here that will help us reach Yom Kippur with more powerful tools so that we can win the fight against chaos in the coming year.

Whether the year will be good or bad depends on what we did on Rosh Hashanah and how much Light we revealed. Even if we didn't reveal any Light on Rosh Hashanah, we have the possibility of revealing all the Light meant for us on Yom Kippur. It all depends on what kind of inner change we make on Yom Kippur – the change we did not make in the past year. If we remain the same person, why should this coming year be any different than the last one?

The portion begins with the words: "Listen to the heavens and I will speak." But shouldn't this have been written the other way around: First, "I will speak" and then"listen"? It is impossible to hear before someone speaks, so what is the Torah teaching us?

Here is a story that will make everything clear. Once, in a village, there was a man who used to hit his wife and curse her and treat her in a terrible way as if she were one of his possessions and not a human being. We know the saying: "Behind every great man is a great woman." (Even the Rav, my father and teacher, would never have even thought of opening The Centre without my mother suggesting the idea. Without her telling the Rav to open the doors to everyone, it would not have been possible for the wisdom of Kabbalah and the Zohar to be known and learned not only in The Centre but throughout the whole world.)

One day, a neighbor of this cruel man had an idea. He decided to go to the kabbalist of the town and ask him to devote his sermon to the topic of respect towards women. So he told the wise teacher about the terrible way his neighbor treated his wife. The sage agreed to discuss this topic on Shabbat and to somehow make it relevant to the week's portion. Every portion contains the message to "love your neighbor as yourself," so the kabbalist believed he could make the connection.

Shabbat came, and the kabbalist began his sermon. He talked about the portion and then came to the subject of loving your neighbor as yourself, in particular emphasizing love towards one's wife. He continued to discuss how every man must respect his wife and take care of all her needs.

After the prayers, the kabbalist wanted to check if the cruel man had heard and understood what the lesson had to teach him. But when the kabbalist approached the man and asked what he thought of the sermon, the man just said that he hoped that all those who mistreated their wives understood that they shouldn't behave that way! In short, not only did he not learn anything but he was sure the kabbalist was addressing someone else. The kabbalist was amazed that the person didn't understand that he was talking about him and not about other people. Realizing there was nothing more to say, he wished the man "Shabbat Shalom" and left.

After a few minutes, a visiting scholar who just happened to be in town that Shabbat approached the wise sage. After exchanging greetings, the scholar told the sage, "You know, I learned so much from your sermon." The kabbalist was surprised since his entire speech was for the benefit of the man who behaved so badly towards his wife. The scholar explained, "Two weeks ago, my wife didn't do something I had asked her to do, and I got very angry at her and asked her why she didn't do it. She felt very humiliated. I haven't said anything more about it, but I've learned from your sermon that she has a lot to do every day, so if she didn't do what I asked, it's not because she doesn't care, but because she is so busy. I learned never to ask her in anger but gently and with the understanding that she has many other responsibilities."

This same thing happens in our community. Many times, the Rav speaks to a certain person or with a certain group of people in mind, and more often than not, they say, "Yes, very good sermon; I hope people heard it." This has happened many times. The people who need to hear don't hear, while those who don't have a very big problem in that particular area do hear and learn.

We must know that the Creator can teach us and give to us only if we are ready to hear and receive. That's why it is written: *ha'azinu*, "listen." If we are ready to receive, then: *adabra*, "I will speak." If we are not prepared to receive and see what is wrong with us, we have no chance on Yom Kippur.

Why should the Creator tell us anything if we won't listen? We always say, "If the student is ready, the teacher will appear." The spiritual law is even more emphatic: If we prepare ourselves to learn, the teacher *must* appear.

Synopsis of Ha'azinu

This portion is actually scribed as two triangles. It connects us to the six worlds right above us—the upper six dimensions of the Tree of Life. The six points of the two triangles influence the seventh dimension—our physical world in which we receive Light from the Upper Worlds. This portion has 52 verses, and we know that 52 relates to the realm of *Malchut*. Fifty-two is twice the numerical value of the Tetragrammaton, which equals 26. The Tetragrammaton times two means that our world is a mirror. If we love, we see love; if we hate, we see hate; if we do positive actions, we recognize only positivity in others.

First Reading - Abraham - Chesed

32 1 הַאֲזִינוּ הַשָּׁמַיִם כוזו, י״פ טל וַאֲדַבֵּרָה וְתִשְׁמַע הָאָרֶץ אלף
למד הה יוד מם אִמְרֵי־פִי׃ 2 יַעֲרֹף כַּמָּטָר לִקְחִי תִּזַּל כַּטַּל כוזו, יוד הא
ואו אִמְרָתִי כִּשְׂעִירִם עֲלֵי־דֶשֶׁא וְכִרְבִיבִים עֲלֵי־עֵשֶׂב׃ 3 כִּי
שֵׁם יְהֹוָהאדניאהדונהי אֶקְרָא הָבוּ גֹדֶל לֵאלֹהֵינוּ ילה׃ 4 הַצּוּר אלף
למד הה יוד מם תָּמִים פָּעֳלוֹ כִּי כָל ילי ־דְּרָכָיו מִשְׁפָּט אֵל אֱמוּנָה
וְאֵין עָוֶל צַדִּיק וְיָשָׁר הוּא׃ 5 שִׁחֵת לוֹ לֹא בָּנָיו מוּמָם דּוֹר
עִקֵּשׁ וּפְתַלְתֹּל׃ 6 הַ לַיהֹוָהאדניאהדונהי תִּגְמְלוּ־זֹאת עַם נָבָל
וְלֹא חָכָם הֲלוֹא־הוּא אָבִיךָ קָּנֶךָ הוּא עָשְׂךָ וַיְכֹנְנֶךָ׃

Second Reading - Isaac - Gvurah

7 זְכֹר יְמוֹת עוֹלָם בִּינוּ שְׁנוֹת דֹּר־וָדֹר שְׁאַל אָבִיךָ וְיַגֵּדְךָ
זְקֵנֶיךָ וְיֹאמְרוּ לָךְ׃ 8 בְּהַנְחֵל עֶלְיוֹן גּוֹיִם בְּהַפְרִידוֹ בְּנֵי

הַאֲזִינוּ - The next section begins with the song of Moses. *Ha'azinu* means "to listen." We may hear but we don't listen. This portion helps us to hear more of the truth—not what we want to hear but what we need to hear. When it hurts to hear the truth, we close ourselves off from listening to it. This portion gives us the power to really listen.

הַ לַיהֹוָהאדניאהדונהי - In this section, we have the large letter *hey*. *Hey* appears twice in the Tetragrammaton and represents the Vessel. The large *hey* represents the expansion of the Vessel—the desire for more. We can have everything in our lives. We should always desire more and never settle for less.

אָדָם מ״ה, יוד הא ואו הא יַצֵּב גְּבֻלֹת עַמִּים לְמִסְפַּר בְּנֵי יִשְׂרָאֵל׃
9 כִּי חֵלֶק יְהֹוָהאדניאהדונהי עַמּוֹ יַעֲקֹב יאהדונהי, אידהנויה חֶבֶל נַחֲלָתוֹ׃
10 יִמְצָאֵהוּ בְּאֶרֶץ מִדְבָּר ראה וּבְתֹהוּ יְלֵל יְשִׁמֹן יְסֹבְבֶנְהוּ
יְבוֹנְנֵהוּ יִצְּרֶנְהוּ כְּאִישׁוֹן עֵינוֹ׃ 11 כְּנֶשֶׁר יָעִיר קִנּוֹ עַל־
גּוֹזָלָיו יְרַחֵף יִפְרֹשׂ כְּנָפָיו יִקָּחֵהוּ יִשָּׂאֵהוּ עַל־אֶבְרָתוֹ׃
12 יְהֹוָהאדניאהדונהי בָּדָד יַנְחֶנּוּ וְאֵין עִמּוֹ אֵל נֵכָר׃

Third Reading - Jacob - Tiferet

13 יַרְכִּבֵהוּ עַל־במותי (בָּמֳתֵי) אָרֶץ וַיֹּאכַל תְּנוּבֹת שָׂדָי
וַיֵּנִקֵהוּ דְבַשׁ מִסֶּלַע וְשֶׁמֶן מֵחַלְמִישׁ צוּר אלף למד הה יוד
מם׃ 14 חֶמְאַת בָּקָר וַחֲלֵב צֹאן עִם־חֵלֶב כָּרִים וְאֵילִים
בְּנֵי־בָשָׁן וְעַתּוּדִים עִם־חֵלֶב כִּלְיוֹת חִטָּה אכא וְדַם־עֵנָב
תִּשְׁתֶּה־חָמֶר׃ 15 וַיִּשְׁמַן יְשֻׁרוּן וַיִּבְעָט שָׁמַנְתָּ עָבִיתָ
כָּשִׂיתָ וַיִּטֹּשׁ אֱלוֹהַ עָשָׂהוּ וַיְנַבֵּל צוּר אלף למד הה יוד מם יְשֻׁעָתוֹ׃
16 יַקְנִאֻהוּ בְּזָרִים בְּתוֹעֵבֹת יַכְעִיסֻהוּ׃ 17 יִזְבְּחוּ לַשֵּׁדִים לֹא

זְכֹר - This section concerns the need to remember the generations of the past. What does this mean? We have to understand that we all have past lives, and that we come into this world with baggage. We can't have a future if we don't understand that we have a past.

וַיִּשְׁמַן - This section helps us understand that prosperity brings illusions. When we become prosperous, we start losing belief in the Creator. Therefore, the challenge is not to forget where abundance comes from.

אֱלֹהַּ אֱלֹהִים מום, ילה לֹא יְדָעוּם חֲדָשִׁים מִקָּרֹב בָּאוּ לֹא
שְׂעָרוּם אֲבֹתֵיכֶם׃ 18 צוּר אלף למד הה יוד מם יְלָדְךָ תֶּשִׁי וַתִּשְׁכַּח
אֵל מְחֹלְלֶךָ׃

Fourth Reading - Moses - Netzach

19 וַיַּרְא יְהוָֹהאדניאהדונהי וַיִּנְאָץ מִכַּעַס בָּנָיו וּבְנֹתָיו׃ 20 וַיֹּאמֶר
אַסְתִּירָה פָנַי חכמה, בינה מֵהֶם אֶרְאֶה מָה יוד הא ואו הא אַחֲרִיתָם
כִּי דוֹר תַּהְפֻּכֹת הֵמָּה יוד הא ואו הא בָּנִים לֹא־אֵמֻן יאהדונהי, סאל,
פאי בָּם מבה׃ 21 הֵם קִנְאוּנִי בְלֹא־אֵל כִּעֲסוּנִי בְּהַבְלֵיהֶם
וַאֲנִי אני אַקְנִיאֵם בְּלֹא־עָם בְּגוֹי נָבָל אַכְעִיסֵם׃ 22 כִּי־אֵשׁ
קָדְחָה בְאַפִּי וַתִּיקַד עַד־שְׁאוֹל תַּחְתִּית וַתֹּאכַל אֶרֶץ
וִיבֻלָהּ וַתְּלַהֵט מוֹסְדֵי הָרִים׃ 23 אַסְפֶּה עָלֵימוֹ רָעוֹת
חִצַּי אֲכַלֶּה־בָּם מבה׃ 24 מְזֵי רָעָב וּלְחֻמֵי רֶשֶׁף וְקֶטֶב מְרִירִי

תֶּשִׁי - In this section, we have a small letter *yud*. *Yud* is the smallest letter in the Hebrew alphabet, but in this section, it is even smaller than usual; It is in fact the smallest letter in the Torah. This reduced letter represents the lowering of one's ego. The more we reduce our ego, the more we connect to the Light of the Creator.

וַיִּנְאָץ - Here, the Torah speaks about the Creator's wrath. According to Kabbalah, The Creator does not get angry. The Creator knows no anger. This section actually refers to the laws of cause and effect. If we do negative things, negativity comes back to us. It is very difficult and painful for the to do something that might hurt us, but He does it so that we can grow and transform.

וְשֵׁן־בְּהֵמֹת אֲשַׁלַּח־בָּם מב עִם־חֲמַת זֹחֲלֵי עָפָר׃ 25 מִחוּץ
תְּשַׁכֶּל־חֶרֶב וּמֵחֲדָרִים אֵימָה גַּם־בָּחוּר גַּם־בְּתוּלָה יוֹנֵק
עִם־אִישׁ שֵׂיבָה׃ 26 אָמַרְתִּי אַפְאֵיהֶם אַשְׁבִּיתָה מֵאֱנוֹשׁ
זִכְרָם׃ 27 לוּלֵי כַּעַס אוֹיֵב אָגוּר פֶּן־יְנַכְּרוּ צָרֵימוֹ פֶּן־יֹאמְרוּ
יָדֵנוּ רָמָה וְלֹא יְהוָֹהאדניאהדונהי פָּעַל כָּל ילי ־זֹאת׃ 28 כִּי־גוֹי
אֹבַד עֵצוֹת הֵמָּה יוד הא ואו הא וְאֵין בָּהֶם תְּבוּנָה׃

Fifth Reading - Aaron - Hod

29 לוּ חָכְמוּ יַשְׂכִּילוּ זֹאת יָבִינוּ לְאַחֲרִיתָם׃ 30 אֵיכָה יִרְדֹּף
אֶחָד אהבה, דאגה אֶלֶף וּשְׁנַיִם יָנִיסוּ רְבָבָה אִם יוהך ־לֹא כִּי־
צוּרָם מְכָרָם וַיהוָֹהאדניאהדונהי הִסְגִּירָם׃ 31 כִּי לֹא כְצוּרֵנוּ
צוּרָם וְאֹיְבֵינוּ פְּלִילִים׃ 32 כִּי־מִגֶּפֶן סְדֹם גַּפְנָם וּמִשַּׁדְמֹת
עֲמֹרָה עֲנָבֵמוֹ עִנְּבֵי־רוֹשׁ אַשְׁכְּלֹת מְרֹרֹת לָמוֹ׃ 33 חֲמַת
תַּנִּינִם יֵינָם וְרֹאשׁ פְּתָנִים אַכְזָר׃ 34 הֲלֹא־הוּא כָּמֻס עִמָּדִי
חָתוּם בְּאוֹצְרֹתָי׃ 35 לִי נָקָם מנק וְשִׁלֵּם לְעֵת תָּמוּט רַגְלָם

אֹבַד עֵצוֹת - Here, it seems as though the Lightforce is saying that we are stupid. If only we really understood the magnitude of the Light! We convince ourselves of the most ridiculous things and come up with silly ideas so that we don't have to take responsibility for our behavior. Satan makes us feel incapable so that we cannot live up to our potential. As with the Golden Calf incident, we convince ourselves that the Lightforce has left us, all because we do not want to take responsibility for ourselves.

כִּי קָרוֹב יוֹם נגד, מזבח, זן אֵידָם וְחָשׁ עֲתִדֹת לָמוֹ׃ 36 כִּי־יָדִין
יְהֹוָהאדניאהדונהי עַמּוֹ וְעַל־עֲבָדָיו יִתְנֶחָם כִּי יִרְאֶה ריו, גבורה כִּי־
אָזְלַת יָד וְאֶפֶס עָצוּר וְעָזוּב׃ 37 וְאָמַר אֵי אֱלֹהֵימוֹ צוּר אלף
למד הה יוד מם חָסָיוּ בוֹ׃ 38 אֲשֶׁר חֵלֶב זְבָחֵימוֹ יֹאכֵלוּ יִשְׁתּוּ יֵין מיכ,
י"פ האא נְסִיכָם יָקוּמוּ וְיַעְזְרֻכֶם יְהִי עֲלֵיכֶם סִתְרָה׃ 39 רְאוּ ׀
עַתָּה כִּי אֲנִי אני אֲנִי אני הוּא וְאֵין אֱלֹהִים מום, ילה עִמָּדִי אֲנִי אני
אָמִית וַאֲחַיֶּה מָחַצְתִּי וַאֲנִי אני אֶרְפָּא וְאֵין מִיָּדִי מַצִּיל׃

Sixth Reading - Joseph - Yesod

40 כִּי־אֶשָּׂא אֶל־שָׁמַיִם כוזו, י"פ טל ילי יָדִי וְאָמַרְתִּי חַי אָנֹכִי איע
לְעֹלָם׃ 41 אִם יוהך שַׁנּוֹתִי בְּרַק חַרְבִּי ריי וְתֹאחֵז בְּמִשְׁפָּט
יָדִי אָשִׁיב נָקָם מנק לְצָרָי מצפצ, אלף למד הי יוד מם וְלִמְשַׂנְאַי אֲשַׁלֵּם׃
42 אַשְׁכִּיר חִצַּי מִדָּם וְחַרְבִּי ריי תֹּאכַל בָּשָׂר מִדַּם חָלָל
וְשִׁבְיָה ההה מֵרֹאשׁ פַּרְעוֹת אוֹיֵב׃ 43 הַרְנִינוּ גוֹיִם עַמּוֹ כִּי
דַם־עֲבָדָיו יִקּוֹם וְנָקָם מנק יָשִׁיב לְצָרָיו וְכִפֶּר אַדְמָתוֹ עַמּוֹ׃

חַי - This section tells us that we will live forever. Immortality is up to us. We have a choice: We can base our belief of immortality on ego, thinking that we are invincible and not considering the consequences of what we do. If we think this way, we will most certainly bring an end, not only to our existence, but also to health, happiness, and more. But if we understand that it is only with the help of the Light that we can have immortality, we really *can* transcend death and rise above every possible form of loss.

Seventh Reading - David - Malchut

44 וַיָּבֹא מֹשֶׁה מהש וַיְדַבֵּר אֶת־כָּל ילי ־דִּבְרֵי הַשִּׁירָה־הַזֹּאת
בְּאָזְנֵי הָעָם הוּא וְהוֹשֵׁעַ בִּן־נוּן׃ 45 וַיְכַל מֹשֶׁה מהש לְדַבֵּר ראה
אֶת־כָּל ילי ־הַדְּבָרִים הָאֵלֶּה אֶל־כָּל ילי ־יִשְׂרָאֵל׃ 46 וַיֹּאמֶר
אֲלֵהֶם שִׂימוּ לְבַבְכֶם לְכָל יה אדני ילי ־הַדְּבָרִים אֲשֶׁר
אָנֹכִי איע מֵעִיד בָּכֶם הַיּוֹם נגד, מזבח, זן אֲשֶׁר תְּצַוֻּם אֶת־בְּנֵיכֶם
לִשְׁמֹר **לַעֲשׂוֹת** אֶת־כָּל ילי ־דִּבְרֵי הַתּוֹרָה הַזֹּאת׃ 47 כִּי
לֹא־דָבָר ראה רֵק הוּא מִכֶּם כִּי־הוּא חַיֵּיכֶם וּבַדָּבָר ראה
הַזֶּה והו תַּאֲרִיכוּ יָמִים נלך עַל־הָאֲדָמָה אֲשֶׁר אַתֶּם עֹבְרִים
אֶת־הַיַּרְדֵּן שָׁמָּה יוד הא ואו הא לְרִשְׁתָּהּ׃

Maftir

48 וַיְדַבֵּר יְהֹוָהאדניאהדונהי אֶל־מֹשֶׁה מהש בְּעֶצֶם הַיּוֹם נגד, מזבח, זן
הַזֶּה והו לֵאמֹר׃ 49 עֲלֵה אֶל־הַר הָעֲבָרִים הַזֶּה והו הַר־נְבוֹ
אֲשֶׁר בְּאֶרֶץ מוֹאָב אֲשֶׁר עַל־פְּנֵי חכמה, בינה יְרֵחוֹ וּרְאֵה ראה
אֶת־אֶרֶץ כְּנַעַן אֲשֶׁר אֲנִי אני נֹתֵן ושר, אבג יתץ, אהבת חנם לִבְנֵי

לַעֲשׂוֹת - Moses says that the Torah is our life because without any spiritual teaching, life has no point. When we connect to the Torah, we discover our destiny and realize that each one of us has a special job, a particular Light that we came to this physical world to reveal. It is then that life begins to have true meaning.

יִשְׂרָאֵל לַאֲחֻזָּה׃ 50 **וּמֻת** בָּהָר אֲשֶׁר אַתָּה עֹלֶה שָׁמָּה יוד
הא ואו הא וְהֵאָסֵף אֶל־עַמֶּיךָ כַּאֲשֶׁר־מֵת אַהֲרֹן אָחִיךָ בְּהֹר
הָהָר וַיֵּאָסֶף אֶל־עַמָּיו׃ 51 עַל אֲשֶׁר מְעַלְתֶּם בִּי בְּתוֹךְ בְּנֵי
יִשְׂרָאֵל בְּמֵי ילי ־מְרִיבַת קָדֵשׁ מִדְבַּר ראה ־צִן עַל אֲשֶׁר לֹא־
קִדַּשְׁתֶּם אוֹתִי בְּתוֹךְ בְּנֵי יִשְׂרָאֵל׃ 52 כִּי מִנֶּגֶד זן, מזבח תִּרְאֶה
אֶת־הָאָרֶץ אלף למד הה יוד מם וְשָׁמָּה יוד הא ואו הא יוד הא ואו הא יוד הא ואו הא
לֹא תָבוֹא אֶל־הָאָרֶץ אלף למד הה יוד מם אֲשֶׁר־אֲנִי אני נֹתֵן ושר, אבג יתץ,
אהבת חינם לִבְנֵי יִשְׂרָאֵל׃

וּמֻת - In this next section, Moses explains that he is going to die because he struck the rock. We know that Moses did nothing wrong but that the people had not earned his presence as a leader in Israel. This idea shows us there is a Moses in every generation and that he needed to leave us in the desert because of our negativity. While reading this verse, we can ask to be strong enough so that the same thing won't happen again.

Haftarah of Ha'azinu

In this haftarah, we have the Song of David. The haftarah helps us to hear the song of our own soul, to listen to what our soul is trying to tell us. If we really listened to the song of our soul, we would not have questions, only answers.

שמואל ב פרק כב

1 וַיְדַבֵּר דָּוִד לַיהֹוָהאדניאהדונהי אֶת־דִּבְרֵי הַשִּׁירָה הַזֹּאת
בְּיוֹם נגד, מזבח, זן הִצִּיל יְהֹוָהאדניאהדונהי אֹתוֹ מִכַּף כָּל ילי ־אֹיְבָיו
וּמִכַּף שָׁאוּל: 2 וַיֹּאמַר יְהֹוָהאדניאהדונהי סַלְעִי וּמְצֻדָתִי וּמְפַלְטִי־
לִי: 3 אֱלֹהֵי דמב, ילה צוּרִי אֶחֱסֶה־בּוֹ מָגִנִּי וְקֶרֶן יִשְׁעִי מִשְׂגַּבִּי
וּמְנוּסִי מֹשִׁעִי מֵחָמָס תֹּשִׁעֵנִי: 4 מְהֻלָּל ללה, אדני אֶקְרָא
יְהֹוָהאדניאהדונהי וּמֵאֹיְבַי אִוָּשֵׁעַ: 5 כִּי אֲפָפֻנִי מִשְׁבְּרֵי־מָוֶת נַחֲלֵי
בְלִיַּעַל יְבַעֲתֻנִי: 6 חֶבְלֵי שְׁאוֹל סַבֻּנִי קִדְּמֻנִי מֹקְשֵׁי־מָוֶת:
7 בַּצַּר־לִי אֶקְרָא יְהֹוָהאדניאהדונהי וְאֶל־אֱלֹהַי דמב, ילה אֶקְרָא
וַיִּשְׁמַע מֵהֵיכָלוֹ קוֹלִי וְשַׁוְעָתִי בְּאָזְנָיו: 8 ותגעש (וַיִּתְגָּעַשׁ)
וַתִּרְעַשׁ הָאָרֶץ אלף למד הה יוד מם מוֹסְדוֹת הַשָּׁמַיִם כוזו, י"פ טל יִרְגָּזוּ
וַיִּתְגָּעֲשׁוּ כִּי־חָרָה לוֹ: 9 עָלָה עָשָׁן בְּאַפּוֹ וְאֵשׁ מִפִּיו פוי
תֹּאכֵל גֶּחָלִים בָּעֲרוּ מִמֶּנּוּ: 10 וַיֵּט שָׁמַיִם כוזו, י"פ טל וַיֵּרַד רי"י
וַעֲרָפֶל תַּחַת רַגְלָיו: 11 וַיִּרְכַּב עַל־כְּרוּב וַיָּעֹף וַיֵּרָא עַל־
כַּנְפֵי־רוּחַ: 12 וַיָּשֶׁת חֹשֶׁךְ סְבִיבֹתָיו סֻכּוֹת חַשְׁרַת־מַיִם ילי
עָבֵי שְׁחָקִים: 13 מִנֹּגַהּ נֶגְדּוֹ בָּעֲרוּ גַּחֲלֵי־אֵשׁ: 14 יַרְעֵם

מִן־שָׁמַיִם כוזו, י״פ טל יְהֹוָהאדני יאהדונהי וְעֶלְיוֹן יִתֵּן קוֹלוֹ: 15 וַיִּשְׁלַח
חִצִּים וַיְפִיצֵם בָּרָק ויהמם (וַיָּהֹם): 16 וַיֵּרָאוּ אֲפִקֵי יָם ילי יִגָּלוּ
מֹסְדוֹת תֵּבֵל ב״פ רי״ו, ב״פ גבורה בְּגַעֲרַת יְהֹוָהאדני יאהדונהי מִנִּשְׁמַת רוּחַ
אַפּוֹ: 17 יִשְׁלַח מִמָּרוֹם יִקָּחֵנִי יַמְשֵׁנִי מִמַּיִם רַבִּים: 18 יַצִּילֵנִי
מֵאֹיְבִי עָז מִשֹּׂנְאַי כִּי אָמְצוּ מִמֶּנִּי: 19 יְקַדְּמֻנִי בְּיוֹם נגד, מזבח,
זן אֵידִי וַיְהִי יְהֹוָהאדני יאהדונהי מִשְׁעָן לִי: 20 וַיֹּצֵא לַמֶּרְחָב אֹתִי
יְחַלְּצֵנִי כִּי־חָפֵץ בִּי: 21 יִגְמְלֵנִי יְהֹוָהאדני יאהדונהי כְּצִדְקָתִי כְּבֹר
יָדַי יָשִׁיב לִי: 22 כִּי שָׁמַרְתִּי דַּרְכֵי יְהֹוָהאדני יאהדונהי וְלֹא רָשַׁעְתִּי
מֵאֱלֹהָי דמב, ילה: 23 כִּי כָל ילי ־מִשְׁפָּטָו לְנֶגְדִּי וְחֻקֹּתָיו לֹא־
אָסוּר מִמֶּנָּה פוי: 24 וָאֶהְיֶה תָמִים לוֹ וָאֶשְׁתַּמְּרָה מֵעֲוֹנִי:
25 וַיָּשֶׁב יְהֹוָהאדני יאהדונהי לִי כְּצִדְקָתִי כְּבֹרִי לְנֶגֶד זן, מזבח עֵינָיו:
26 עִם־חָסִיד תִּתְחַסָּד עִם־גִּבּוֹר תָּמִים תִּתַּמָּם: 27 עִם־נָבָר
תִּתָּבָר וְעִם־עִקֵּשׁ תִּתַּפָּל: 28 וְאֶת־עַם עָנִי יוד יוד הא יוד הא ואו יוד
הא ואו הא תּוֹשִׁיעַ וְעֵינֶיךָ עַל־רָמִים תַּשְׁפִּיל: 29 כִּי־אַתָּה נֵירִי
יְהֹוָהאדני יאהדונהי וַיהֹוָהאדני יאהדונהי יַגִּיהַּ חָשְׁכִּי: 30 כִּי בְכָה היי אָרוּץ
גְּדוּד בֵּאלֹהַי דמב, ילה אֲדַלֶּג־שׁוּר ושר, אבג יתץ, אהבת חנם: 31 הָאֵל לאה
תָּמִים דַּרְכּוֹ אִמְרַת יְהֹוָהאדני יאהדונהי צְרוּפָה מָגֵן ר״ת – מיכאל גבריאל
נוריאל הוּא לְכֹל יה אדני ילי הַחֹסִים בּוֹ: 32 כִּי מִי ילי ־אֵל מִבַּלְעֲדֵי
יְהֹוָהאדני יאהדונהי וּמִי ילי צוּר אלף למד הה יוד מם מִבַּלְעֲדֵי אֱלֹהֵינוּ ילה:

33 הָאֵל לאה מָעוּזִּי חָיִל ומב וַיַּתֵּר תָּמִים דרכו (דַּרְכִּי): 34 מְשַׁוֶּה
רַגְלַי (כתיב: רגליו) כָּאַיָּלוֹת וְעַל בָּמֹתַי יַעֲמִדֵנִי: 35 מְלַמֵּד יָדַי
לַמִּלְחָמָה וְנִחַת קֶשֶׁת-נְחוּשָׁה זְרֹעֹתָי: 36 וַתִּתֶּן ב"פ כהת -לִי
מָגֵן ר"ת – מיכאל גבריאל נוריאל יִשְׁעֶךָ וַעֲנֹתְךָ תַּרְבֵּנִי: 37 תַּרְחִיב צַעֲדִי
תַּחְתֵּנִי וְלֹא מָעֲדוּ קַרְסֻלָּי: 38 אֶרְדְּפָה אֹיְבַי וָאַשְׁמִידֵם
וְלֹא אָשׁוּב עַד-כַּלּוֹתָם: 39 וָאֲכַלֵּם וָאֶמְחָצֵם וְלֹא יְקוּמוּן
וַיִּפְּלוּ תַּחַת רַגְלָי: 40 וַתַּזְרֵנִי חַיִל ומב לַמִּלְחָמָה תַּכְרִיעַ קָמַי
תַּחְתֵּנִי: 41 וְאֹיְבַי תַּתָּה לִּי עֹרֶף מְשַׂנְאַי וָאַצְמִיתֵם: 42 יִשְׁעוּ
וְאֵין מֹשִׁיעַ אֶל-יְהֹוָה‍אדני יאהדונהי וְלֹא עָנָם: 43 וְאֶשְׁחָקֵם כַּעֲפַר-
אָרֶץ כְּטִיט-חוּצוֹת אֲדִקֵּם אֶרְקָעֵם: 44 וַתְּפַלְּטֵנִי מֵרִיבֵי
עַמִּי תִּשְׁמְרֵנִי לְרֹאשׁ גּוֹיִם עַם לֹא-יָדַעְתִּי יַעַבְדֻנִי: 45 בְּנֵי
נֵכָר יִתְכַּחֲשׁוּ-לִי לִשְׁמוֹעַ אֹזֶן יִשָּׁמְעוּ לִי: 46 בְּנֵי נֵכָר יִבֹּלוּ
וְיַחְגְּרוּ מִמִּסְגְּרוֹתָם: 47 חַי-יְהֹוָה‍אדני יאהדונהי וּבָרוּךְ צוּרִי וְיָרֻם
אֱלֹהֵי דמב, ילה צוּר אלף למד הה יוד מם יִשְׁעִי: 48 הָאֵל לאה הַנֹּתֵן ושר, אבג
יתץ, אהבת חנם נְקָמֹת לִי וּמוֹרִיד עַמִּים תַּחְתֵּנִי: 49 וּמוֹצִיאִי מֵאֹיְבָי
וּמִקָּמַי תְּרוֹמְמֵנִי מֵאִישׁ חֲמָסִים תַּצִּילֵנִי: 50 עַל-כֵּן אוֹדְךָ
יְהֹוָה‍אדני יאהדונהי בַּגּוֹיִם וּלְשִׁמְךָ אֲזַמֵּר: 51 מִגְדּוֹל (כתיב: מגדיל) (להוח,
מבה) יְשׁוּעוֹת מַלְכּוֹ וְעֹשֶׂה-חֶסֶד יוד הי ויו הי, י יה יהו יהוה לִמְשִׁיחוֹ
לְדָוִד וּלְזַרְעוֹ עַד-עוֹלָם:

Lesson of Vezot-Habracha

The portion of Vezot Habracha is both the final portion of the book of Devarim and the final portion of the Torah itself. Vezot Habracha, therefore, is the manifestation of the entire Torah. It is always read at Simchat Torah, and immediately afterward, we read the portion of Beresheet, which is the Torah's opening portion. These two sections are always linked and are always read on this special holiday.

On the day of Simchat Torah, we receive surrounding Light (*Or Mekif)* for the entire year. How is it possible for us to receive an entire year's portion of Light in just one day? There is only one answer: *by letting go.* If we cling to our present spiritual condition, we prevent the Light from entering our lives, and we exclude ourselves from the transformation the Light will bring. Then, heaven forbid, we hear Satan whispering: "If you received everything on Simchat Torah, then where is it?" In this way, doubt is introduced in us, and any connection with the Light disappears.

Simchat Torah, like the Torah itself, is a gift. It's as if a treasure of Light has been put into a bank vault for us, and all we have to do is access the account. Even those who did not prepare themselves on Rosh Hashanah, Yom Kippur, and Sukkot can receive Light. Simchat Torah is like a wedding: a union is taking place between *Zeir Anpin* and *Malchut*, between the male and female aspects of the Light. The bride and groom and their families have taken pains in preparing the event, and all the guests can enjoy the party. Anyone who enters the room can enjoy the Light for free, provided only that he or she is *conscious* of being *one* with all those present. But everyone who receives must also be willing to share, to make others happy as well, just like wedding guests who bring a gift for the bride and groom.

Through our connection with the Light on Simchat Torah, we are able to cure cancer and other serious diseases. How is this possible? We know that illness can exist only as long as the body itself is alive. The moment a person dies, all disease in his body must "die" as well. This same principle applies to all the obstacles we encounter in life. If we could skip over the processes of the physical world and rise above the illusion of the time continuum, then we could experience the liberation of leaving the body and immediately put an end to all chaos in our lives.

Simchat Torah provides *exactly* that opportunity. On this holiday, we rise above the illusion of time. Simchat Torah is surrounding Light — a unification of past, present, and future — and an unmatched opportunity to rid our lives of all chaos.

The secret power of Simchat Torah lies in the link between the two portions of Vezot Habracha and Beresheet. The final letter of Vezot Habracha is the Hebrew letter *lamed* and the first letter of the portion of Beresheet is *bet*. Together, these two letters spell *lev*, or "heart." No matter how we talk, no matter how we walk, no matter who we are, it is what lies in our hearts that makes the difference. By opening our hearts to these two portions — the manifestation of the Torah and the seed of the Torah — we can bring Light into our lives in a way that's possible at no other moment in the entire year.

Synopsis of Vezot-Habracha

This is the only portion in the Torah not actually read on Shabbat. It is only read on Simchat Torah. Normally, the energy of the Torah can only be revealed on Shabbat. But once a year, during Simchat Torah, the energy of Shabbat can be accessed, which is why Simchat Torah is one of the most powerful holidays and why it connects us to happiness.

First Reading - Abraham - Chesed

33 1 וְזֹאת הַבְּרָכָה אֲשֶׁר בֵּרַךְ מֹשֶׁה מהש אִישׁ הָאֱלֹהִים מום,
ילה אֶת־בְּנֵי יִשְׂרָאֵל לִפְנֵי וחכמה, בינה מוֹתוֹ: 2 וַיֹּאמַר יְהֹוָאדניאהדונהי
מִסִּינַי נמם בָּא וְזָרַח מִשֵּׂעִיר לָמוֹ הוֹפִיעַ מֵהַר פָּארָן וְאָתָה
מֵרִבְבֹת קֹדֶשׁ מִימִינוֹ אֵשׁ דָּת (כתיב: אשדת) לָמוֹ: 3 אַף
חֹבֵב עַמִּים כָּל ילי ־קְדֹשָׁיו בְּיָדֶךָ וְהֵם תֻּכּוּ לְרַגְלֶךָ יִשָּׂא
מִדַּבְּרֹתֶיךָ: 4 תּוֹרָה צִוָּה־לָנוּ מֹשֶׁה מהש מוֹרָשָׁה קְהִלַּת
יַעֲקֹב יאהדונהי, אידהנויה: 5 וַיְהִי בִישֻׁרוּן מֶלֶךְ בְּהִתְאַסֵּף רָאשֵׁי
עָם יַחַד שִׁבְטֵי יִשְׂרָאֵל: 6 יְחִי רְאוּבֵן וְאַל־יָמֹת וִיהִי מְתָיו

וְזֹאת הַבְּרָכָה - In this portion, Moses blesses every tribe and every person. Why is it so important to have the blessings of Moses given in this portion? Because this is the section that refers to the day when Moses left the world. On the day a righteous person leaves this world, he is actually traversing two worlds at the same time. His soul is already halfway into the next world. By connecting with the blessings that Moses gave each tribe, we are not only tapping into the blessings of this world but also into the blessings of the next world. This provides us with an important form of energy. When we deal with the problems of this physical world, we have to solve them after they have already been manifested, which is much more difficult. But when we are connected to the Upper Worlds, we can solve problems before they become manifested.

רְאוּבֵן - Reuben's blessing is that he should live and not die. When Jacob and Leah conceived Reuben, Jacob believed that he was making love to Rachel and not to Leah. This is the reason that Reuben has such an unbalanced energy about him. Jacob directed his consciousness to Rachel, so unbalanced energy was imbued in Reuben. When Moses gave him a blessing, he restored balance and stability for the whole tribe.

מִסְפָּר׃ 7 וְזֹאת לִיהוּדָה וַיֹּאמַר שְׁמַע יְהֹוָאדהנּהי יאהדונהי קוֹל
יְהוּדָה וְאֶל־עַמּוֹ תְּבִיאֶנּוּ יָדָיו רָב לוֹ וְעֵזֶר מִצָּרָיו תִּהְיֶה׃

Second Reading - Isaac - Gvurah

8 וּלְלֵוִי אָמַר תֻּמֶּיךָ וְאוּרֶיךָ לְאִישׁ חֲסִידֶךָ אֲשֶׁר נִסִּיתוֹ
בְּמַסָּה תְּרִיבֵהוּ עַל־מֵי ילי מְרִיבָה׃ 9 הָאֹמֵר לְאָבִיו וּלְאִמּוֹ
לֹא רְאִיתִיו וְאֶת־אֶחָיו לֹא הִכִּיר וְאֶת־בָּנָיו (בנו) לֹא יָדָע
כִּי שָׁמְרוּ אִמְרָתֶךָ וּבְרִיתְךָ יִנְצֹרוּ׃ 10 יוֹרוּ מִשְׁפָּטֶיךָ
לְיַעֲקֹב יאהדונהי, אידהנויה וְתוֹרָתְךָ לְיִשְׂרָאֵל יָשִׂימוּ קְטוֹרָה בְּאַפֶּךָ
וְכָלִיל עַל־מִזְבְּחֶךָ׃ 11 בָּרֵךְ יְהֹוָאדהנּהי יאהדונהי חֵילוֹ וּפֹעַל יָדָיו
תִּרְצֶה מְחַץ מָתְנַיִם קָמָיו וּמְשַׂנְאָיו מִן־יְקוּמוּן׃ 12 לְבִנְיָמִן

לִיהוּדָה - This section tells us to listen to the voice of Judah (Yehuda). According to the Zohar, the Messiah and King David will come from the lineage of Judah, hence reference to the "voice of Judah." "Voice" means the study of Kabbalah. This is the reason that Rav Ashlag, who established The Kabbalah Centre, called it *Yeshivat Kol Yehuda.*

וּלְלֵוִי - The Levites were chosen for the priesthood because they had a great inclination toward judgment. The Creator transformed all of their judgment into a form that allowed them to manifest their job. No matter how much judgment we have, it can be transformed into great Light. In fact, the greater a person's negativity, the greater his potential to do good.

לְבִנְיָמִן - The *Beit HaMikdash* (the Holy Temple) was located on the tract of land designated for the tribe of Benjamin. Benjamin was not yet born when all the other tribes bowed down in front of Esau; therefore, he was purer then the rest of the tribes. Each of the other tribes became contaminated

אָמַר יְדִיד יְהֹוָאדֹנָהִי יאהדונהי יִשְׁכֹּן לָבֶטַח עָלָיו חֹפֵף עָלָיו כָּל יל״י
־הַיּוֹם נגד, מזבח, זן וּבֵין כְּתֵפָיו שָׁכֵן:

Third Reading - Jacob - Tiferet

13 וּלְיוֹסֵף ציון אָמַר מְבֹרֶכֶת יְהֹוָאדֹנָהִי יאהדונהי אַרְצוֹ מִמֶּגֶד
שָׁמַיִם כוזו, י״פ טל ילי מִטָּל כוזו, יוד הא ואו וּמִתְּהוֹם רֹבֶצֶת תָּחַת:
14 וּמִמֶּגֶד תְּבוּאֹת שָׁמֶשׁ וּמִמֶּגֶד גֶּרֶשׁ יְרָחִים: 15 וּמֵרֹאשׁ
הַרְרֵי־קֶדֶם וּמִמֶּגֶד גִּבְעוֹת עוֹלָם: 16 וּמִמֶּגֶד אֶרֶץ וּמְלֹאָהּ
וּרְצוֹן מהש שֹׁכְנִי סְנֶה תָּבוֹאתָה לְרֹאשׁ יוֹסֵף ציון וּלְקָדְקֹד
נְזִיר אֶחָיו: 17 בְּכוֹר שׁוֹרוֹ הָדָר לוֹ וְקַרְנֵי רְאֵם קַרְנָיו בָּהֶם
עַמִּים יְנַגַּח יַחְדָּו אַפְסֵי־אָרֶץ וְהֵם רִבְבוֹת אֶפְרַיִם וְהֵם
אַלְפֵי מְנַשֶּׁה:

with a little part of Esau when they bent down before him. Esau refers to the force of Satan within them, but Benjamin was free of Satan's presence. Sometimes when we do negative things, we let Satan in and lose positive opportunities in our lives, just as the tribes lost the opportunity to have the Holy Temple in their region. This section provides us protection so that even if we give in to negative things, we will not lose an opportunity for positive things in our future.

וּלְיוֹסֵף - Joseph overcame being seduced by the wife of Potifar. He then became a channel for helping us overcome evil eye and evil people. According to the Zohar, evil eye can cause a person to die before his time. It is a force of negativity so powerful that it overrides the law of cause and effect; in other words, a person can get evil eye even if he did nothing to bring it into his life. This section provides us with protection from evil eye.

Fourth Reading - Moses - Netzach

18 וְלִזְבוּלֻן אָמַר שְׂמַח זְבוּלֻן בְּצֵאתֶךָ וְיִשָּׂשכָר בְּאֹהָלֶיךָ׃
19 עַמִּים הַר־יִקְרָאוּ שָׁם יִזְבְּחוּ זִבְחֵי־צֶדֶק כִּי שֶׁפַע י״פ ילה
יַמִּים נלך יִינָקוּ וּשְׂפֻנֵי חכמה, בינה טְמוּנֵי חוֹל׃ 20 וּלְגָד אָמַר
בָּרוּךְ מַרְחִיב גָּד כְּלָבִיא שָׁכֵן וְטָרַף זְרוֹעַ אַף־קָדְקֹד׃
21 וַיַּרְא רֵאשִׁית לוֹ כִּי־שָׁם חֶלְקַת מְחֹקֵק סָפוּן וַיֵּתֵא רָאשֵׁי
עָם צִדְקַת יְהֹוָאֵדנָי אהדונהי עָשָׂה וּמִשְׁפָּטָיו עִם־יִשְׂרָאֵל׃

Fifth Reading - Aaron - Hod

22 וּלְדָן אָמַר דָּן גּוּר אַרְיֵה רי״ו, ג״פ עב יְזַנֵּק מִן־הַבָּשָׁן׃

וְלִזְבוּלֻן, וְיִשָּׂשכָר - These two had a pact that Issachar would work spiritually all day while Zebulun would work physically all day; then they would split the physical and spiritual profits. We have a choice in this world: We can be among those doing more spiritual work or we can offer our money or time to help them.

וּלְגָד - While we know that Gad sinned, it is not clear what he did. When the world was created, Gad ruled the month of Capricorn. After he sinned, the energy of Messiah, which was originally associated with the month of Capricorn, was transferred to Aquarius. When we make mistakes or commit negative actions, we must not let these actions remove our opportunities. Gad lost his opportunity, but we want to make sure that we are protected so that the Light gives us another chance. This section gives us this protection.

וּלְדָן - *Dan* means "judgment" and controls the month of Scorpio. The letters of the month of Scorpio are *daled* and *nun*. Normally, the month of Scorpio is a time of tremendous judgment, but the *Sefer Yetzirah* (*The Book of Formation*) says that it is also connected to Messiah. We have two choices: to be a part of the negativity, or to be spiritual and to overcome our judgmental nature.

23 וּלְנַפְתָּלִי אָמַר נַפְתָּלִי שְׂבַע רָצוֹן מהש וּמָלֵא בִּרְכַּת
יְהֹוָה אדני אהדונהי יָם ילי וְדָרוֹם יְרָשָׁה׃ 24 וּלְאָשֵׁר אָמַר בָּרוּךְ
מִבָּנִים אָשֵׁר יְהִי רְצוּי אֶחָיו וְטֹבֵל בַּשֶּׁמֶן רַגְלוֹ׃ 25 בַּרְזֶל ר״ת -
בלהה רחל זילפה לאה וּנְחֹשֶׁת מִנְעָלֶךָ וּכְיָמֶיךָ דָּבְאֶךָ׃ 26 אֵין כָּאֵל
יְשֻׁרוּן רֹכֵב שָׁמַיִם כוזו, י״פ טל בְּעֶזְרֶךָ וּבְגַאֲוָתוֹ שְׁחָקִים׃

וּלְנַפְתָּלִי - The portion says: "Naphtali is satisfied." When we appreciate everything we have, when we are not worrying about why we don't have this or that or the other, then we have a chance to be truly fulfilled. When we are busy being concerned with what we don't have, we start losing appreciation, and when we lose appreciation, we lose what we do have.

וּלְאָשֵׁר - The portion says: "He shall be pleasing to his brothers." This seemingly positive quality often has a negative outcome. Rav Brandwein told a story of a man who arrived at the gates of Heaven and wanted to go in. The gatekeeper told him that he couldn't enter. The man was baffled and said, "But I was a good person. Everyone loved me. If you call my friends, they will tell you that I lived my life and never bothered a soul. I don't even have an enemy in this world." So the gatekeeper told him, "Then you have a one-way ticket to Hell." The man replied, "I don't understand." The gatekeeper explained that we come into this world to create change, to make a difference. But when we do this, we make people uncomfortable, and they challenge us and are unhappy with us. When we are liked by everyone, it means we did nothing with the opportunity we received this lifetime.

Sixth Reading - Joseph - Yesod

27 מְעֹנָה אֱלֹהֵי דמב, ילה קֶדֶם וּמִתַּחַת זְרֹעֹת עוֹלָם וַיְגָרֶשׁ
מִפָּנֶיךָ אוֹיֵב וַיֹּאמֶר הַשְׁמֵד׃ 28 וַיִּשְׁכֹּן יִשְׂרָאֵל בֶּטַח בָּדָד
עֵין יוד יוד הא יוד הא ואו יוד הא ואו הא יַעֲקֹב יאהדונהי, אידהנויה אֶל־אֶרֶץ דָּגָן
וְתִירוֹשׁ אַף־שָׁמָיו יַעַרְפוּ טָל כוזו, יוד הא ואו׃ 29 אַשְׁרֶיךָ יִשְׂרָאֵל
מִי ילי כָמוֹךָ עַם נוֹשַׁע בַּיהוָה יאהדונהי מָגֵן ר״ת - מיכאל גבריאל נוריאל
עֶזְרֶךָ וַאֲשֶׁר־חֶרֶב גַּאֲוָתֶךָ וְיִכָּחֲשׁוּ אֹיְבֶיךָ לָךְ וְאַתָּה עַל־
בָּמוֹתֵימוֹ תִדְרֹךְ׃

Seventh Reading - David - Malchut

34 1 וַיַּעַל מֹשֶׁה מהש מֵעַרְבֹת מוֹאָב אֶל־הַר נְבוֹ רֹאשׁ
הַפִּסְגָּה אֲשֶׁר עַל־פְּנֵי חכמה, בינה יְרֵחוֹ וַיַּרְאֵהוּ יְהוָה יאהדונהי

מְעֹנָה - After he blesses all the tribes individually, Moses then blesses them collectively. When Moses blessed each one individually, the blessing was scattered. The only way that we can access the collective blessing is when the world is united. As long as there is fragmentation, we can draw only a certain amount of Light. Collectively, we can reach much higher levels and get much more.

וַיַּעַל - The death of Moses: The Zohar says that Moses never died. This means that a part of him left this world and a part of him didn't. The part of Moses that did not leave comes back in every generation to help us. This help manifests in the Light that is created by the physical dissemination of the study of Kabbalah. The kabbalists explain that the spark of Moses that returns in every generation was in Rav Shimon and in the Ari. This section helps us to connect to the Moses of our generation.

אֶת־כָּל ילי ־הָאָרֶץ אלף למד הה יוד מם אֶת־הַגִּלְעָד עַד־דָּן׃ 2 וְאֵת
כָּל ילי ־נַפְתָּלִי וְאֶת־אֶרֶץ אֶפְרַיִם וּמְנַשֶּׁה וְאֵת כָּל ילי ־אֶרֶץ
יְהוּדָה עַד הַיָּם ילי הָאַחֲרוֹן׃ 3 וְאֶת־הַנֶּגֶב וְאֶת־הַכִּכָּר
בִּקְעַת יְרֵחוֹ עִיר ערי, סוזפך, סנדלפון הַתְּמָרִים עַד־צֹעַר׃ 4 וַיֹּאמֶר
יְהֹוָאדנ֗י יאהדונהי אֵלָיו זֹאת הָאָרֶץ אלף למד הה יוד מם אֲשֶׁר נִשְׁבַּעְתִּי
לְאַבְרָהָם לְיִצְחָק וּלְיַעֲקֹב יאהדונהי, אידהנויה לֵאמֹר לְזַרְעֲךָ אֶתְּנֶנָּה
הֶרְאִיתִיךָ בְעֵינֶיךָ וְשָׁמָּה לֹא תַעֲבֹר׃ 5 וַיָּמָת שָׁם מֹשֶׁה מהש
עֶבֶד־יְהֹוָאדנ֗י יאהדונהי בְּאֶרֶץ מוֹאָב עַל־פִּי יְהֹוָאדנ֗י יאהדונהי׃
6 וַיִּקְבֹּר אֹתוֹ בַגַּי בְּאֶרֶץ מוֹאָב מוּל בֵּית ב״פ ראה פְּעוֹר וְלֹא־
יָדַע אִישׁ אֶת־קְבֻרָתוֹ עַד הַיּוֹם נגד, מזבח, זן הַזֶּה והו׃ 7 וּמֹשֶׁה מהש
בֶּן־מֵאָה וְעֶשְׂרִים שָׁנָה בְּמֹתוֹ לֹא־כָהֲתָה עֵינוֹ וְלֹא־נָס יוד הא
ואו הא - אדני לֵחֹה׃ 8 וַיִּבְכּוּ בְנֵי יִשְׂרָאֵל אֶת־מֹשֶׁה מהש בְּעַרְבֹת
מוֹאָב שְׁלֹשִׁים יוֹם נגד, מזבח, זן וַיִּתְּמוּ יְמֵי בְכִי אֵבֶל מֹשֶׁה מהש׃
9 וִיהוֹשֻׁעַ בִּן־נוּן מָלֵא רוּחַ חָכְמָה כִּי־סָמַךְ מֹשֶׁה מהש אֶת־
יָדָיו עָלָיו וַיִּשְׁמְעוּ אֵלָיו בְּנֵי־יִשְׂרָאֵל וַיַּעֲשׂוּ כַּאֲשֶׁר צִוָּה
יְהֹוָאדנ֗י יאהדונהי אֶת־מֹשֶׁה מהש׃ 10 וְלֹא־קָם נָבִיא עוֹד בְּיִשְׂרָאֵל
כְּמֹשֶׁה מהש אֲשֶׁר יְדָעוֹ יְהֹוָאדנ֗י יאהדונהי פָּנִים אֶל־פָּנִים׃
11 לְכָל יה אדני ־הָאֹתֹת וְהַמּוֹפְתִים אֲשֶׁר שְׁלָחוֹ יְהֹוָאדנ֗י יאהדונהי
לַעֲשׂוֹת בְּאֶרֶץ מִצְרָיִם מצר לְפַרְעֹה וּלְכָל יה אדני ־עֲבָדָיו

וּלְכָל יה אדני ־אַרְצוֹ׃ 12 וּלְכֹל יה אדני הַיָּד וזהו הַחֲזָקָה וּלְכֹל יה
אדני הַמּוֹרָא הַגָּדוֹל להחו, מבה אֲשֶׁר עָשָׂה מֹשֶׁה מהש לְעֵינֵי
כָּל ילי ־יִשְׂרָאֵל׃

חזק חזק ונתחזק

יִשְׂרָאֵל - The last letter of the Torah is *lamed* and the first letter is *bet*. Together, they spell "heart." If the Torah's teachings remain stuck in our head and do not penetrate the heart, then we've missed the purpose entirely.

Haftarah of Vezot-Habracha

After Moses, Joshua becomes the leader of Israel. This is a powerful and important lesson about the Creator. When Moses departed, the Creator had someone ready to replace him. No matter what happens, the Light is always there. The next step is always calculated and always in place for us. The Light never leaves us and is always making sure that our needs will be provided for.

Joshua 1 — יהושע פרק 1

1 וַיְהִי אַחֲרֵי מוֹת מֹשֶׁה מהש עֶבֶד יְהֹוָאֲדֹנָיאהדונהי וַיֹּאמֶר
יְהֹוָאֲדֹנָיאהדונהי אֶל־יְהוֹשֻׁעַ בִּן־נוּן מְשָׁרֵת מֹשֶׁה מהש לֵאמֹר׃
2 מֹשֶׁה מהש עַבְדִּי מֵת וְעַתָּה קוּם עֲבֹר אֶת־הַיַּרְדֵּן הַזֶּה והו
אַתָּה וְכָל ילי ־הָעָם הַזֶּה והו אֶל־הָאָרֶץ אלף למד הה יוד מם אֲשֶׁר
אָנֹכִי איע נֹתֵן ושר, אבג יתץ, אהבת חנם לָהֶם לִבְנֵי יִשְׂרָאֵל׃ 3 כָּל ילי
־מָקוֹם אֲשֶׁר תִּדְרֹךְ כַּף־רַגְלְכֶם בּוֹ לָכֶם נְתַתִּיו כַּאֲשֶׁר
דִּבַּרְתִּי אֶל־מֹשֶׁה מהש׃ 4 מֵהַמִּדְבָּר וְהַלְּבָנוֹן הַזֶּה והו
וְעַד־הַנָּהָר הַגָּדוֹל להח, מבה נְהַר־פְּרָת כֹּל ילי אֶרֶץ הַחִתִּים
וְעַד־הַיָּם ילי הַגָּדוֹל להח, מבה מְבוֹא הַשָּׁמֶשׁ יִהְיֶה ייי גְּבוּלְכֶם׃
5 לֹא־יִתְיַצֵּב אִישׁ לְפָנֶיךָ כֹּל ילי יְמֵי חַיֶּיךָ כַּאֲשֶׁר הָיִיתִי עִם־
מֹשֶׁה מהש אֶהְיֶה עִמָּךְ לֹא אַרְפְּךָ וְלֹא אֶעֶזְבֶךָּ׃ 6 חֲזַק פהל וֶאֱמָץ
כִּי אַתָּה תַּנְחִיל אֶת־הָעָם הַזֶּה והו אֶת־הָאָרֶץ אלף למד הה יוד מם
אֲשֶׁר־נִשְׁבַּעְתִּי לַאֲבוֹתָם לָתֵת לָהֶם׃ 7 רַק חֲזַק פהל וֶאֱמַץ
מְאֹד לִשְׁמֹר לַעֲשׂוֹת כְּכָל ילי ־הַתּוֹרָה אֲשֶׁר צִוְּךָ מֹשֶׁה מהש

עַבְדִּי אַל־תָּסוּר מִמֶּנּוּ יָמִין וּשְׂמֹאול לְמַעַן תַּשְׂכִּיל בְּכֹל לכב
אֲשֶׁר תֵּלֵךְ׃ 8 לֹא־יָמוּשׁ סֵפֶר הַתּוֹרָה הַזֶּה והו מִפִּיךָ וְהָגִיתָ
בּוֹ יוֹמָם וָלַיְלָה מלה לְמַעַן תִּשְׁמֹר לַעֲשׂוֹת כְּכָל יכי ־הַכָּתוּב
בּוֹ כִּי־אָז תַּצְלִיחַ אֶת־דְּרָכֶךָ וְאָז תַּשְׂכִּיל׃ 9 הֲלוֹא צִוִּיתִיךָ
חֲזַק פהל וֶאֱמָץ אַל־תַּעֲרֹץ וְאַל־תֵּחָת כִּי עִמְּךָ יְהֹוָהאדני יאהדונהי
אֱלֹהֶיךָ בְּכֹל לכב אֲשֶׁר תֵּלֵךְ׃

Haftarah for the Eve of Rosh Chodesh

On one level, this Haftarah concerns the eve of Rosh Chodesh. In a deeper sense, this Haftarah speaks of the love between David and Jonathan. Although he himself was heir to the throne, Jonathan knew that David might become king. Yet Jonathan loved David and felt no jealously. To truly feel love for another person, we must give up our own selfish desires. To have a successful relationship of any kind, we must be willing to sacrifice.

Samuel 1, 2 — שמואל א, פרק 2

18 וַיֹּאמֶר־לוֹ יְהוֹנָתָן מָחָר חֹדֶשׁ י"ב הוויות וְנִפְקַדְתָּ כִּי יִפָּקֵד
מוֹשָׁבֶךָ׃ 19 וְשִׁלַּשְׁתָּ תֵּרֵד מְאֹד וּבָאתָ אֶל־הַמָּקוֹם אֲשֶׁר־
נִסְתַּרְתָּ שָּׁם בְּיוֹם נגד, מזבח, זן הַמַּעֲשֶׂה וְיָשַׁבְתָּ אֵצֶל הָאֶבֶן
הָאָזֶל׃ 20 וַאֲנִי אני שְׁלֹשֶׁת הַחִצִּים צִדָּה אוֹרֶה רז, אין סוף לְשַׁלַּח־
לִי לְמַטָּרָה׃ 21 וְהִנֵּה אֶשְׁלַח אֶת־הַנַּעַר לֵךְ מְצָא אֶת־
הַחִצִּים אִם־אָמֹר אֹמַר לַנַּעַר הִנֵּה הַחִצִּים ׀ מִמְּךָ וָהֵנָּה
קָחֶנּוּ ׀ וָבֹאָה כִּי־שָׁלוֹם לְךָ וְאֵין דָּבָר ראה חַי־יְהוָהאדניאהדונהי׃
22 וְאִם־כֹּה הי אֹמַר לָעֶלֶם הִנֵּה הַחִצִּים מִמְּךָ וָהָלְאָה לֵךְ
כִּי שִׁלַּחֲךָ יְהוָהאדניאהדונהי׃ 23 וְהַדָּבָר ראה אֲשֶׁר דִּבַּרְנוּ ראה אֲנִי אני
וָאָתָּה הִנֵּה יְהוָהאדניאהדונהי בֵּינִי וּבֵינְךָ עַד־עוֹלָם׃ 24 וַיִּסָּתֵר
דָּוִד בַּשָּׂדֶה וַיְהִי הַחֹדֶשׁ י"ב הוויות וַיֵּשֶׁב הַמֶּלֶךְ אֶל־ (כתיב: על)
הַלֶּחֶם ג"פ יהוה לֶאֱכוֹל׃ 25 וַיֵּשֶׁב הַמֶּלֶךְ עַל־מוֹשָׁבוֹ כְּפַעַם מנק ׀
בְּפַעַם מנק אֶל־מוֹשַׁב הַקִּיר וַיָּקָם יְהוֹנָתָן וַיֵּשֶׁב אַבְנֵר מִצַּד
שָׁאוּל וַיִּפָּקֵד מְקוֹם דָּוִד׃ 26 וְלֹא־דִבֶּר ראה שָׁאוּל מְאוּמָה

בַּיּוֹם נגד, מזבח, זן הַהוּא כִּי אָמַר מִקְרֶה הוּא בִּלְתִּי טָהוֹר י"פ אכא:
הוּא כִּי־לֹא טָהוֹר י"פ אכא 27 וַיְהִי מִמָּחֳרַת הַחֹדֶשׁ י"ב הוויות הַשֵּׁנִי
וַיִּפָּקֵד מְקוֹם דָּוִד וַיֹּאמֶר שָׁאוּל אֶל־יְהוֹנָתָן בְּנוֹ מַדּוּעַ לֹא־
בָא בֶן־יִשַׁי גַּם־תְּמוֹל גַּם־הַיּוֹם נגד, מזבח, זן אֶל־הַלָּחֶם: 28 וַיַּעַן
יְהוֹנָתָן אֶת־שָׁאוּל נִשְׁאֹל נִשְׁאַל דָּוִד מֵעִמָּדִי עַד־בֵּית ב"פ ראה
לָחֶם: 29 וַיֹּאמֶר שַׁלְּחֵנִי נָא כִּי זֶבַח מִשְׁפָּחָה לָנוּ מום, אהיה+אדני
בָּעִיר ערי, מנצפך, סנדלפון וְהוּא צִוָּה־לִי אָחִי וְעַתָּה אִם־מָצָאתִי
חֵן מוחי בְּעֵינֶיךָ אִמָּלְטָה נָּא וְאֶרְאֶה ראה אֶת־אֶחָי עַל־כֵּן לֹא־
בָא אֶל־שֻׁלְחַן הַמֶּלֶךְ: 30 וַיִּחַר־אַף שָׁאוּל בִּיהוֹנָתָן וַיֹּאמֶר
לוֹ בֶּן־נַעֲוַת הַמַּרְדּוּת הֲלוֹא יָדַעְתִּי כִּי־בֹחֵר אַתָּה לְבֶן־
יִשַׁי לְבָשְׁתְּךָ וּלְבֹשֶׁת עֶרְוַת אִמֶּךָ: 31 כִּי כָל ילי ־הַיָּמִים נלך
אֲשֶׁר בֶּן־יִשַׁי חַי עַל־הָאֲדָמָה לֹא תִכּוֹן אַתָּה וּמַלְכוּתֶךָ
וְעַתָּה שְׁלַח וְקַח אֹתוֹ אֵלַי כִּי בֶן־מָוֶת הוּא: 32 וַיַּעַן יְהוֹנָתָן
אֶת־שָׁאוּל אָבִיו וַיֹּאמֶר אֵלָיו לָמָּה יוּמַת מֶה עָשָׂה: 33 וַיָּטֶל
שָׁאוּל אֶת־הַחֲנִית עָלָיו לְהַכֹּתוֹ וַיֵּדַע יְהוֹנָתָן כִּי־כָלָה הִיא
מֵעִם אָבִיו לְהָמִית אֶת־דָּוִד: 34 וַיָּקָם יְהוֹנָתָן מֵעִם הַשֻּׁלְחָן
בָּחֳרִי־אָף וְלֹא־אָכַל בְּיוֹם נגד, מזבח, זן ־הַחֹדֶשׁ י"ב הוויות הַשֵּׁנִי
לֶחֶם ג"פ יהוה כִּי נֶעְצַב אֶל־דָּוִד כִּי הִכְלִמוֹ אָבִיו: 35 וַיְהִי
בַבֹּקֶר וַיֵּצֵא יְהוֹנָתָן הַשָּׂדֶה לְמוֹעֵד דָּוִד וְנַעַר קָטֹן עִמּוֹ:

36 וַיֹּאמֶר לְנַעֲרוֹ רֻץ מְצָא נָא אֶת־הַחִצִּים אֲשֶׁר אָנֹכִי איע
מוֹרֶה הַנַּעַר רָץ וְהוּא־יָרָה הַחֵצִי לְהַעֲבִרוֹ׃ 37 וַיָּבֹא הַנַּעַר
עַד־מְקוֹם הַחֵצִי אֲשֶׁר יָרָה יְהוֹנָתָן וַיִּקְרָא יְהוֹנָתָן אַחֲרֵי
הַנַּעַר וַיֹּאמֶר הֲלוֹא הַחֵצִי מִמְּךָ וָהָלְאָה׃ 38 וַיִּקְרָא יְהוֹנָתָן
אַחֲרֵי הַנַּעַר מְהֵרָה חוּשָׁה אַל־תַּעֲמֹד וַיְלַקֵּט נַעַר יְהוֹנָתָן
אֶת־הַחִצִּים (כתיב: ־החצי) וַיָּבֹא אֶל־אֲדֹנָיו׃ 39 וְהַנַּעַר לֹא־יָדַע
מְאוּמָה אַךְ אהיה יְהוֹנָתָן וְדָוִד יָדְעוּ אֶת־הַדָּבָר ראה׃ 40 וַיִּתֵּן
יְהוֹנָתָן אֶת־כֵּלָיו אֶל־הַנַּעַר אֲשֶׁר־לוֹ וַיֹּאמֶר לוֹ לֵךְ הָבֵיא
הָעִיר עִרי, סנזפך, סנדלפון׃ 41 הַנַּעַר בָּא וְדָוִד קָם מֵאֵצֶל הַנֶּגֶב
וַיִּפֹּל לְאַפָּיו אַרְצָה וַיִּשְׁתַּחוּ שָׁלֹשׁ פְּעָמִים מנק וַיִּשְּׁקוּ | אִישׁ
אֶת־רֵעֵהוּ רהע וַיִּבְכּוּ אִישׁ אֶת־רֵעֵהוּ רהע עַד־דָּוִד הִגְדִּיל׃
42 וַיֹּאמֶר יְהוֹנָתָן לְדָוִד לֵךְ לְשָׁלוֹם אֲשֶׁר נִשְׁבַּעְנוּ שְׁנֵינוּ
אֲנַחְנוּ בְּשֵׁם יְהוָה אדני יאהדונהי לֵאמֹר יְהוָה אדני יאהדונהי יִהְיֶה ייי |
בֵּינִי וּבֵינֶךָ וּבֵין זַרְעִי וּבֵין זַרְעֲךָ עַד־עוֹלָם׃

Maftir of Shabbat Rosh Chodesh

Leviticus 28 — במדבר פרק 28

9 וּבְיוֹם נגד, מזבח, זן הַשַּׁבָּת שְׁנֵי־כְבָשִׂים בְּנֵי־שָׁנָה תְּמִימִם וּשְׁנֵי
עֶשְׂרֹנִים סֹלֶת מִנְחָה ב״פ בין בְּלוּלָה בַשֶּׁמֶן וְנִסְכּוֹ: 10 עֹלַת
שַׁבַּת בְּשַׁבַּתּוֹ עַל־עֹלַת הַתָּמִיד נתה וְנִסְכָּהּ: 11 וּבְרָאשֵׁי
חָדְשֵׁיכֶם י״ב הויות תַּקְרִיבוּ עֹלָה לַיהֹוָהאדניאהדונהי פָּרִים בְּנֵי־
בָקָר שְׁנַיִם וְאַיִל אֶחָד אהבה, דאגה כְּבָשִׂים בְּנֵי־שָׁנָה שִׁבְעָה
תְּמִימִם: 12 וּשְׁלֹשָׁה עֶשְׂרֹנִים סֹלֶת מִנְחָה ב״פ בין בְּלוּלָה
בַשֶּׁמֶן לַפָּר הָאֶחָד אהבה, דאגה וּשְׁנֵי עֶשְׂרֹנִים סֹלֶת מִנְחָה ב״פ בין
בְּלוּלָה בַשֶּׁמֶן לָאַיִל הָאֶחָד: אהבה, דאגה 13 וְעִשָּׂרֹן עִשָּׂרוֹן סֹלֶת
מִנְחָה ב״פ בין בְּלוּלָה בַשֶּׁמֶן לַכֶּבֶשׂ הָאֶחָד אהבה, דאגה עֹלָה רֵיחַ
נִיחֹחַ אִשֶּׁה לַיהֹוָהאדניאהדונהי: 14 וְנִסְכֵּיהֶם חֲצִי הַהִין יִהְיֶה ייי
לַפָּר וּשְׁלִישִׁת הַהִין לָאַיִל וּרְבִיעִת הַהִין לַכֶּבֶשׂ יָיִן מיכ, י״פ האא
זֹאת עֹלַת חֹדֶשׁ י״ב הויות בְּחָדְשׁוֹ לְחָדְשֵׁי י״ב הויות הַשָּׁנָה:
15 וּשְׂעִיר עִזִּים אֶחָד אהבה, דאגה לְחַטָּאת לַיהֹוָהאדניאהדונהי עַל־
עֹלַת הַתָּמִיד נתה יֵעָשֶׂה וְנִסְכּוֹ:

Haftarah of Rosh Chodesh

We often underestimate the power of Rosh Chodesh. Just as the fires of Hell are cooled on Shabbat, these very same fires are shut down on Rosh Chodesh as well. Through Rosh Chodesh, therefore, we can gain the power to deflect and avoid judgment.

Isaiah 10 | ישעיהו פרק 10

1 כֹּה היי אָמַר יְהֹוָאדהנויאהדונהי הַשָּׁמַיִם כוזו, י״פ טל כִּסְאִי וְהָאָרֶץ אלף
למד הה יוד מם הֲדֹם רַגְלָי אֵי־זֶה בַּיִת ב״פ ראה אֲשֶׁר תִּבְנוּ־לִי וְאֵי־
זֶה מָקוֹם מְנוּחָתִי׃ 2 וְאֶת־כָּל־אֵלֶּה יָדִי עָשָׂתָה וַיִּהְיוּ כָל ילי
־אֵלֶּה ייא״י מילוי דס״ג נְאֻם־יְהֹוָאדהנויאהדונהי וְאֶל־זֶה אַבִּיט אֶל־עָנִי
וּנְכֵה־רוּחַ וְחָרֵד עַל־דְּבָרִי׃ 3 שׁוֹחֵט הַשּׁוֹר ושר, אבג יתץ, אהבת
חנם מַכֵּה־אִישׁ זוֹבֵחַ הַשֶּׂה עֹרֵף כֶּלֶב מַעֲלֵה עלם מִנְחָה ב״פ
בין דַּם־חֲזִיר מַזְכִּיר לְבֹנָה מְבָרֵךְ אָוֶן גַּם־הֵמָּה בָּחֲרוּ
בְּדַרְכֵיהֶם ב״פ יב״ק וּבְשִׁקּוּצֵיהֶם נַפְשָׁם חָפֵצָה׃ 4 גַּם־אֲנִי אני
אֶבְחַר בְּתַעֲלֻלֵיהֶם וּמְגוּרֹתָם אָבִיא לָהֶם יַעַן קָרָאתִי
וְאֵין עוֹנֶה דִּבַּרְתִּי ראה וְלֹא שָׁמֵעוּ וַיַּעֲשׂוּ הָרַע בְּעֵינַי
וּבַאֲשֶׁר לֹא־חָפַצְתִּי בָּחָרוּ׃ 5 שִׁמְעוּ דְּבַר ראה ־יְהֹוָאדהנויאהדונהי
הַחֲרֵדִים אֶל־דְּבָרוֹ ראה אִמְרוּ אֲחֵיכֶם שֹׂנְאֵיכֶם מְנַדֵּיכֶם
לְמַעַן שְׁמִי יִכְבַּד יְהֹוָאדהנויאהדונהי וְנִרְאֶה בְשִׂמְחַתְכֶם וְהֵם
יֵבֹשׁוּ׃ 6 קוֹל שָׁאוֹן מֵעִיר ערי, סוזחר, סנדלפון קוֹל מֵהֵיכָל אדני קוֹל
יְהֹוָאדהנויאהדונהי מְשַׁלֵּם גְּמוּל לְאֹיְבָיו׃ 7 בְּטֶרֶם תָּחִיל יָלָדָה

בְּטֶרֶם יָבוֹא חֵבֶל לָהּ וְהִמְלִיטָה זָכָר׃ 8 מִי ילי ־שָׁמַע
כָּזֹאת מִי ילי רָאָה ראה כָּאֵלֶּה הֲיוּחַל אֶרֶץ בְּיוֹם נגד, מזבח, זן
אֶחָד אהבה, דאגה אִם יוהך ־יִוָּלֵד גּוֹי פַּעַם מנק אֶחָת כִּי־חָלָה להח
גַּם־יָלְדָה צִיּוֹן יוסף אֶת־בָּנֶיהָ׃ 9 הַאֲנִי אני אַשְׁבִּיר וְלֹא אוֹלִיד
יֹאמַר יְהֹוָה אהדונהי אִם יוהך ־אֲנִי אני הַמּוֹלִיד וְעָצַרְתִּי אָמַר
אֱלֹהָיִךְ ילה׃ 10 שִׂמְחוּ אֶת־יְרוּשָׁלִַם וְגִילוּ בָהּ כָּל ילי ־אֹהֲבֶיהָ
שִׂישׂוּ אִתָּהּ מָשׂוֹשׂ כָּל ילי ־הַמִּתְאַבְּלִים עָלֶיהָ פהל׃ 11 לְמַעַן
תִּינְקוּ וּשְׂבַעְתֶּם מִשֹּׁד תַּנְחֻמֶיהָ לְמַעַן תָּמֹצּוּ וְהִתְעַנַּגְתֶּם
מִזִּיז כְּבוֹדָהּ׃ 12 כִּי־כֹה היי | אָמַר יְהֹוָה אהדונהי הִנְנִי נֹטֶה־
אֵלֶיהָ כְּנָהָר שָׁלוֹם וּכְנַחַל שׁוֹטֵף כְּבוֹד גּוֹיִם וִינַקְתֶּם
עַל־צַד תִּנָּשֵׂאוּ וְעַל־בִּרְכַּיִם תְּשָׁעֳשָׁעוּ׃ 13 כְּאִישׁ אֲשֶׁר
אִמּוֹ תְּנַחֲמֶנּוּ כֵּן אָנֹכִי איע אֲנַחֶמְכֶם וּבִירוּשָׁלִַם תְּנֻחָמוּ׃
14 וּרְאִיתֶם וְשָׂשׂ לִבְּכֶם וְעַצְמוֹתֵיכֶם כַּדֶּשֶׁא תִפְרַחְנָה
וְנוֹדְעָה יַד־יְהֹוָה אהדונהי אֶת־עֲבָדָיו וְזָעַם אֶת־אֹיְבָיו׃ 15 כִּי־
הִנֵּה יְהֹוָה אהדונהי בָּאֵשׁ יָבוֹא וְכַסּוּפָה מַרְכְּבֹתָיו לְהָשִׁיב
בְּחֵמָה אַפּוֹ וְגַעֲרָתוֹ בְּלַהֲבֵי־אֵשׁ׃ 16 כִּי בָאֵשׁ יְהֹוָה אהדונהי
נִשְׁפָּט וּבְחַרְבּוֹ רי"ו, גבורה אֶת־כָּל ילי ־בָּשָׂר וְרַבּוּ חַלְלֵי
יְהֹוָה אהדונהי׃ 17 הַמִּתְקַדְּשִׁים וְהַמִּטַּהֲרִים אֶל־הַגַּנּוֹת אַחַר
אַחַת (כתיב: אחד) בַּתָּוֶךְ אֹכְלֵי בְּשַׂר הַחֲזִיר וְהַשֶּׁקֶץ וְהָעַכְבָּר
יַחְדָּו יָסֻפוּ נְאֻם־יְהֹוָה אהדונהי׃ 18 וְאָנֹכִי איע מַעֲשֵׂיהֶם

וּמַחְשְׁבֹתֵיהֶם בָּאָה לְקַבֵּץ אֶת־כָּל־הַגּוֹיִם ילי וְהַלְּשֹׁנוֹת
וּבָאוּ וְרָאוּ אֶת־כְּבוֹדִי׃ 19 וְשַׂמְתִּי בָהֶם אוֹת וְשִׁלַּחְתִּי
מֵהֶם | פְּלֵיטִים אֶל־הַגּוֹיִם תַּרְשִׁישׁ פּוּל וְלוּד מֹשְׁכֵי קֶשֶׁת
תֻּבַל ב״פ רי״ו, ב״פ גבורה וְיָוָן הָאִיִּים הָרְחֹקִים אֲשֶׁר לֹא־שָׁמְעוּ
אֶת־שִׁמְעִי וְלֹא־רָאוּ אֶת־כְּבוֹדִי וְהִגִּידוּ אֶת־כְּבוֹדִי בַּגּוֹיִם׃
20 וְהֵבִיאוּ אֶת־כָּל ילי ־אֲחֵיכֶם מִכָּל ילי ־הַגּוֹיִם | מִנְחָה ב״פ ב״ן |
לַיהֹוָהאדניאהדונהי בַּסּוּסִים כוק וּבָרֶכֶב וּבַצַּבִּים וּבַפְּרָדִים
וּבַכִּרְכָּרוֹת עַל הַר קָדְשִׁי יְרוּשָׁלִַם אָמַר יְהֹוָהאדניאהדונהי
כַּאֲשֶׁר יָבִיאוּ בְנֵי יִשְׂרָאֵל אֶת־הַמִּנְחָה ב״פ ב״ן בִּכְלִי טָהוֹר י״פ
אכא בֵּית ב״פ ראה יְהֹוָהאדניאהדונהי׃ 21 וְגַם־מֵהֶם אֶקַּח לַכֹּהֲנִים מלה
לַלְוִיִּם אָמַר יְהֹוָהאדניאהדונהי׃ 22 כִּי כַאֲשֶׁר הַשָּׁמַיִם כוזו, י״פ טל
הַחֲדָשִׁים י״ב הוויות וְהָאָרֶץ אלף למד הה יוד מם הַחֲדָשָׁה אֲשֶׁר אֲנִי אני
עֹשֶׂה עֹמְדִים לְפָנַי נְאֻם־יְהֹוָהאדניאהדונהי כֵּן יַעֲמֹד זַרְעֲכֶם
וְשִׁמְכֶם׃ 23 וְהָיָה יהה מִדֵּי־חֹדֶשׁ י״ב הוויות בְּחָדְשׁוֹ י״ב הוויות וּמִדֵּי
שַׁבָּת בְּשַׁבַּתּוֹ יָבוֹא כָל־בָּשָׂר לְהִשְׁתַּחֲוֹת לְפָנַי אָמַר
יְהֹוָהאדניאהדונהי׃ 24 וְיָצְאוּ וְרָאוּ בְּפִגְרֵי הָאֲנָשִׁים הַפֹּשְׁעִים
בִּי כִּי תוֹלַעְתָּם לֹא תָמוּת וְאִשָּׁם לֹא תִכְבֶּה וְהָיוּ דֵרָאוֹן
לְכָל יה אדני ־בָּשָׂר׃ 23 וְהָיָה יהה מִדֵּי־חֹדֶשׁ י״ב הוויות בְּחָדְשׁוֹ י״ב הוויות
וּמִדֵּי שַׁבָּת בְּשַׁבַּתּוֹ יָבוֹא כָל־בָּשָׂר לְהִשְׁתַּחֲוֹת לְפָנַי אָמַר
יְהֹוָהאדניאהדונהי׃

Portion of Devarim

1,1 These are the words which Moses spoke unto all Israel beyond the Jordan; in the wilderness, in the Arabah, over against Suph, between Paran and Tophel, and Laban, and Hazeroth, and Di-zahab. 1,2 It is eleven days journey from Horeb unto Kadesh-barnea by the way of mount Seir. 1,3 And it came to pass in the fortieth year, in the eleventh month, on the first day of the month, that Moses spoke unto the children of Israel, according unto all that the LORD had given him in commandment unto them; 1,4 after he had smitten Sihon the king of the Amorites, who dwelt in Heshbon, and Og the king of Bashan, who dwelt in Ashtaroth, at Edrei; 1,5 beyond the Jordan, in the land of Moab, took Moses upon him to expound this law, saying: 1,6 The LORD our God spoke unto us in Horeb, saying: 'Ye have dwelt long enough in this mountain; 1,7 turn you, and take your journey, and go to the hill-country of the Amorites and unto all the places nigh thereunto, in the Arabah, in the hill-country, and in the Lowland, and in the South, and by the sea-shore; the land of the Canaanites, and Lebanon, as far as the great river, the river Euphrates. 1,8 Behold, I have set the land before you: go in and possess the land which the LORD swore unto your fathers, to Abraham, to Isaac, and to Jacob, to give unto them and to their seed after them.' 1,9 And I spoke unto you at that time, saying: 'I am not able to bear you myself alone; 1,10 the LORD your God hath multiplied you, and, behold, ye are this day as the stars of heaven for multitude.-- 1,11 The LORD, the God of your fathers, make you a thousand times so many more as ye are, and bless you, as He hath promised you!-- 1,12 How can I myself alone bear your cumbrance, and your burden, and your strife? 1,13 Get you, from each one of your tribes, wise men, and understanding, and full of knowledge, and I will make them heads over you.' 1,14 And ye answered me, and said: 'The thing which thou hast spoken is good for us to do.' 1,15 So I took the heads of your tribes, wise men, and full of knowledge, and made them heads over you, captains of thousands, and captains of hundreds, and captains of fifties, and captains of tens, and officers, tribe by tribe. 1,16 And I charged your judges at that time, saying: 'Hear the causes between your brethren, and judge righteously between a man and his brother, and the stranger that is with him. 1,17 Ye shall not respect persons in judgment; ye shall hear the small and the great alike; ye shall not be afraid of the face of any man; for the judgment is God's; and the cause that is too hard for you ye shall bring unto me, and I will hear it.' 1,18 And I commanded you at that time all the things which ye should do. 1,19 And we journeyed from Horeb, and went through all that great and dreadful wilderness which ye saw, by the way to the hill-country of the Amorites, as the LORD our God commanded us; and we came to Kadesh-barnea. 1,20 And I said unto you: 'Ye are come unto the hill-country of the Amorites, which the LORD our God giveth unto us. 1,21 Behold, the LORD thy God hath set the land before thee; go up, take possession, as the LORD, the God of thy fathers, hath spoken unto thee; fear not, neither be dismayed.' 1,22 And ye came near unto me every one of you, and said: 'Let us send men before us, that they may search the land for us, and bring us back word of the way by which we must go up, and the cities unto which we shall come.' 1,23 And the thing pleased me well; and I took twelve men of you, one man for every tribe; 1,24 and they turned and went up into the mountains, and came unto the valley of Eshcol, and spied it out. 1,25 And they took of the fruit of the land in their hands, and brought it down unto us, and brought us back word, and said: 'Good is the land which the LORD our God giveth unto us.' 1,26 Yet ye would not go up, but rebelled against the commandment of the LORD your God; 1,27 and ye murmured in your tents, and said: 'Because the LORD hated us, He hath brought us forth out of the land of Egypt, to deliver us into the hand of the Amorites, to destroy us. 1,28 Whither are we going up? our brethren have made our heart to melt, saying: The people is greater and taller than we; the cities are great and fortified up to heaven; and moreover we have seen the sons of the Anakim there.' 1,29 Then I said unto you: 'Dread not, neither be afraid of them. 1,30 The LORD your God who goeth before you, He shall fight for you, according to all that He did for you in Egypt before your eyes; 1,31 and in the wilderness, where thou hast seen how that the LORD thy God bore thee, as a man doth bear his son, in all the way that ye went, until ye came unto this place. 1,32 Yet in this thing ye do not believe the LORD your God, 1,33 Who went before you in the way, to seek you out a place to pitch your tents in: in fire by night, to show you by what way ye should go, and in the cloud by day.' 1,34 And the LORD heard the voice of your words, and was wroth, and swore, saying: 1,35 'Surely there shall not one of these men, even this evil generation, see the good land, which I swore to give unto your fathers, 1,36 save Caleb the son of Jephunneh,

he shall see it; and to him will I give the land that he hath
trodden upon, and to his children; because he hath wholly
followed the LORD.' 1,37 Also the LORD was angry with
me for your sakes, saying: Thou also shalt not go in thither;
1,38 Joshua the son of Nun, who standeth before thee, he
shall go in thither; encourage thou him, for he shall cause
Israel to inherit it. 1,39 Moreover your little ones, that ye
said should be a prey, and your children, that this day have
no knowledge of good or evil, they shall go in thither, and
unto them will I give it, and they shall possess it. 1,40 But
as for you, turn you, and take your journey into the
wilderness by the way to the Red Sea.' 1,41 Then ye
answered and said unto me: 'We have sinned against the
LORD, we will go up and fight, according to all that the
LORD our God commanded us.' And ye girded on every
man his weapons of war, and deemed it a light thing to go
up into the hill-country. 1,42 And the LORD said unto me:
'Say unto them: Go not up, neither fight; for I am not
among you; lest ye be smitten before your enemies.' 1,43
So I spoke unto you, and ye hearkened not; but ye rebelled
against the commandment of the LORD, and were
presumptuous, and went up into the hill-country. 1,44
And the Amorites, that dwell in that hill-country, came out
against you, and chased you, as bees do, and beat you
down in Seir, even unto Hormah. 1,45 And ye returned
and wept before the LORD; but the LORD hearkened not
to your voice, nor gave ear unto you. 1,46 So ye abode in
Kadesh many days, according unto the days that ye abode
there. 2,1 Then we turned, and took our journey into the
wilderness by the way to the Red Sea, as the LORD spoke
unto me; and we compassed mount Seir many days. {S}

2,2 And the LORD spoke unto me, saying: 2,3 'Ye have compassed this mountain long enough; turn you northward. 2,4 And command thou the people, saying: Ye are to pass through the border of your brethren the children of Esau, that dwell in Seir; and they will be afraid of you; take ye good heed unto yourselves therefore; 2,5 contend not with them; for I will not give you of their land, no, not so much as for the sole of the foot to tread on; because I have given mount Seir unto Esau for a possession. 2,6 Ye shall purchase food of them for money, that ye may eat; and ye shall also buy water of them for money, that ye may drink. 2,7 For the LORD thy God hath blessed thee in all the work of thy hand; He hath known thy walking through this great wilderness; these forty years the LORD thy God hath been with thee; thou hast lacked nothing.' 2,8 So we passed by from our brethren the children of Esau, that dwell in Seir, from the way of the Arabah, from Elath and from Ezion-geber. {S} And we turned and passed by the way of the wilderness of Moab. 2,9 And the LORD said unto me: 'Be not at enmity with Moab, neither contend with them in battle; for I will not give thee of his land for a possession; because I have given Ar unto the children of Lot for a possession.-- 2,10 The Emim dwelt therein aforetime, a people great, and many, and tall, as the Anakim; 2,11 these also are accounted Rephaim, as the Anakim; but the Moabites call them Emim. 2,12 And in Seir dwelt the Horites aforetime, but the children of Esau succeeded them; and they destroyed them from before them, and dwelt in their stead; as Israel did unto the land of his possession, which the LORD gave unto them.-- 2,13 Now rise up, and get you over the brook Zered.' And we

went over the brook Zered. 2,14 And the days in which we
came from Kadesh-barnea, until we were come over the
brook Zered, were thirty and eight years; until all the
generation, even the men of war, were consumed from the
midst of the camp, as the LORD swore unto them. 2,15
Moreover the hand of the LORD was against them, to
discomfit them from the midst of the camp, until they
were consumed. 2,16 So it came to pass, when all the
men of war were consumed and dead from among the
people, {S} 2,17 that the LORD spoke unto me saying:
2,18 'Thou art this day to pass over the border of Moab,
even Ar; 2,19 and when thou comest nigh over against the
children of Ammon, harass them not, nor contend with
them; for I will not give thee of the land of the children of
Ammon for a possession; because I have given it unto the
children of Lot for a possession.-- 2,20 That also is
accounted a land of Rephaim: Rephaim dwelt therein
aforetime; but the Ammonites call them Zamzummim,
2,21 a people great, and many, and tall, as the Anakim;
but the LORD destroyed them before them; and they
succeeded them, and dwelt in their stead; 2,22 as He did
for the children of Esau, that dwell in Seir, when He
destroyed the Horites from before them; and they
succeeded them, and dwelt in their stead even unto this
day; 2,23 and the Avvim, that dwelt in villages as far as
Gaza, the Caphtorim, that came forth out of Caphtor,
destroyed them, and dwelt in their stead.-- 2,24 Rise ye
up, take your journey, and pass over the valley of Arnon;
behold, I have given into thy hand Sihon the Amorite, king
of Heshbon, and his land; begin to possess it, and contend
with him in battle. 2,25 This day will I begin to put the

dread of thee and the fear of thee upon the peoples that are under the whole heaven, who, when they hear the report of thee, shall tremble, and be in anguish because of thee.' 2,26 And I sent messengers out of the wilderness of Kedemoth unto Sihon king of Heshbon with words of peace, saying: 2,27 'Let me pass through thy land; I will go along by the highway, I will neither turn unto the right hand nor to the left. 2,28 Thou shalt sell me food for money, that I may eat; and give me water for money, that I may drink; only let me pass through on my feet; 2,29 as the children of Esau that dwell in Seir, and the Moabites that dwell in Ar, did unto me; until I shall pass over the Jordan into the land which the LORD our God giveth us.' 2,30 But Sihon king of Heshbon would not let us pass by him; for the LORD thy God hardened his spirit, and made his heart obstinate, that He might deliver him into thy hand, as appeareth this day. {S} 2,31 And the LORD said unto me: 'Behold, I have begun to deliver up Sihon and his land before thee; begin to possess his land.' 2,32 Then Sihon came out against us, he and all his people, unto battle at Jahaz. 2,33 And the LORD our God delivered him up before us; and we smote him, and his sons, and all his people. 2,34 And we took all his cities at that time, and utterly destroyed every city, the men, and the women, and the little ones; we left none remaining; 2,35 only the cattle we took for a prey unto ourselves, with the spoil of the cities which we had taken. 2,36 From Aroer, which is on the edge of the valley of Arnon, and from the city that is in the valley, even unto Gilead, there was not a city too high for us: the LORD our God delivered up all before us. 2,37 Only to the land of the children of Ammon thou camest not

near; all the side of the river Jabbok, and the cities of the
hill-country, and wheresoever the LORD our God forbade
us. 3,1 Then we turned, and went up the way to Bashan;
and Og the king of Bashan came out against us, he and all
his people, unto battle at Edrei. 3,2 And the LORD said
unto me: 'Fear him not; for I have delivered him, and all
his people, and his land, into thy hand; and thou shalt do
unto him as thou didst unto Sihon king of the Amorites,
who dwelt at Heshbon.' 3,3 So the LORD our God delivered
into our hand Og also, the king of Bashan, and all his
people; and we smote him until none was left to him
remaining. 3,4 And we took all his cities at that time;
there was not a city which we took not from them;
threescore cities, all the region of Argob, the kingdom of
Og in Bashan. 3,5 All these were fortified cities, with high
walls, gates, and bars; beside the unwalled towns a great
many. 3,6 And we utterly destroyed them, as we did unto
Sihon king of Heshbon, utterly destroying every city, the
men, and the women, and the little ones. 3,7 But all the
cattle, and the spoil of the cities, we took for a prey unto
ourselves. 3,8 And we took the land at that time out of the
hand of the two kings of the Amorites that were beyond the
Jordan, from the valley of Arnon unto mount Hermon-- 3,9
which Hermon the Sidonians call Sirion, and the Amorites
call it Senir-- 3,10 all the cities of the plain, and all Gilead,
and all Bashan, unto Salcah and Edrei, cities of the
kingdom of Og in Bashan.-- 3,11 For only Og king of
Bashan remained of the remnant of the Rephaim; behold,
his bedstead was a bedstead of iron; is it not in Rabbah of
the children of Ammon? nine cubits was the length thereof,
and four cubits the breadth of it, after the cubit of a man.-

- 3,12 And this land we took in possession at that time; from Aroer, which is by the valley of Arnon, and half the hill-country of Gilead, and the cities thereof, gave I unto the Reubenites and to the Gadites; 3,13 and the rest of Gilead, and all Bashan, the kingdom of Og, gave I unto the half-tribe of Manasseh; all the region of Argob--all that Bashan is called the land of Rephaim. 3,14 Jair the son of Manasseh took all the region of Argob, unto the border of the Geshurites and the Maacathites, and called them, even Bashan, after his own name, Havvoth-jair, unto this day.-- 3,15 And I gave Gilead unto Machir. 3,16 And unto the Reubenites and unto the Gadites I gave from Gilead even unto the valley of Arnon, the middle of the valley for a border; even unto the river Jabbok, which is the border of the children of Ammon; 3,17 the Arabah also, the Jordan being the border thereof, from Chinnereth even unto the sea of the Arabah, the Salt Sea, under the slopes of Pisgah eastward. 3,18 And I commanded you at that time, saying: 'The LORD your God hath given you this land to possess it; ye shall pass over armed before your brethren the children of Israel, all the men of valour. 3,19 But your wives, and your little ones, and your cattle--I know that ye have much cattle--shall abide in your cities which I have given you; 3,20 until the LORD give rest unto your brethren, as unto you, and they also possess the land which the LORD your God giveth them beyond the Jordan; then shall ye return every man unto his possession, which I have given you. 3,21 And I commanded Joshua at that time, saying: 'Thine eyes have seen all that the LORD your God hath done unto these two kings; so shall the LORD do unto all the kingdoms whither thou goest over. 3,22 Ye shall not fear them; for the LORD your God, He it is that fighteth for you.' {S}

Portion of Va'etchanan

3,23 And I besought the LORD at that time, saying: 3,24 'O Lord GOD, Thou hast begun to show Thy servant Thy greatness, and Thy strong hand; for what god is there in heaven or on earth, that can do according to Thy works, and according to Thy mighty acts? 3,25 Let me go over, I pray Thee, and see the good land that is beyond the Jordan, that goodly hill-country, and Lebanon.' 3,26 But the LORD was wroth with me for your sakes, and hearkened not unto me; and the LORD said unto me: 'Let it suffice thee; speak no more unto Me of this matter. 3,27 Get thee up into the top of Pisgah, and lift up thine eyes westward, and northward, and southward, and eastward, and behold with thine eyes; for thou shalt not go over this Jordan. 3,28 But charge Joshua, and encourage him, and strengthen him; for he shall go over before this people, and he shall cause them to inherit the land which thou shalt see.' 3,29 So we abode in the valley over against Beth-peor. {P}

4,1 And now, O Israel, hearken unto the statutes and unto the ordinances, which I teach you, to do them; that ye may live, and go in and possess the land which the LORD, the God of your fathers, giveth you. 4,2 Ye shall not add unto the word which I command you, neither shall ye diminish from it, that ye may keep the commandments of the LORD your God which I command you. 4,3 Your eyes have seen what the LORD did in Baal-peor; for all the men that followed the Baal of Peor, the LORD thy God hath destroyed them from the midst of thee. 4,4 But ye that did cleave unto the LORD your God are alive every one of you this day. 4,5 Behold, I have taught you statutes and ordinances, even as the LORD my God commanded me, that ye should do so in the midst of the land whither ye go in to possess it. 4,6 Observe therefore and do them; for this is your wisdom and your understanding in the sight of the peoples, that, when they hear all these statutes, shall say: 'Surely this great nation is a wise and understanding people.' 4,7 For what great nation is there, that hath God so nigh unto them, as the LORD our God is whensoever we call upon Him? 4,8 And what great nation is there, that hath statutes and ordinances so righteous as all this law, which I set before you this day? 4,9 Only take heed to thyself, and keep thy soul diligently, lest thou forget the things which thine eyes saw, and lest they depart from thy heart all the days of thy life; but make them known unto thy children and thy children's children; 4,10 the day that thou stoodest before the LORD thy God in Horeb, when the LORD said unto me: 'Assemble Me the people, and I will make them hear My words that they may learn to fear Me all the days that they live upon the earth, and that they may teach their children.' 4,11 And ye came near and stood under the mountain; and the mountain burned with fire unto the heart of heaven, with darkness, cloud, and thick darkness. 4,12 And the LORD spoke unto you out of the midst of the fire; ye heard the voice of words, but ye saw no form; only a voice. 4,13 And He declared unto you His covenant, which He commanded you to perform, even the ten words; and He wrote them upon two tables of stone. 4,14 And the LORD commanded me at that time to teach you statutes and ordinances, that ye might do them in the land whither ye go over to possess it. 4,15 Take ye

therefore good heed unto yourselves--for ye saw no manner
of form on the day that the LORD spoke unto you in Horeb
out of the midst of the fire-- 4,16 lest ye deal corruptly,
and make you a graven image, even the form of any figure,
the likeness of male or female, 4,17 the likeness of any
beast that is on the earth, the likeness of any winged fowl
that flieth in the heaven, 4,18 the likeness of any thing
that creepeth on the ground, the likeness of any fish that
is in the water under the earth; 4,19 and lest thou lift up
thine eyes unto heaven, and when thou seest the sun and
the moon and the stars, even all the host of heaven, thou
be drawn away and worship them, and serve them, which
the LORD thy God hath allotted unto all the peoples under
the whole heaven. 4,20 But you hath the LORD taken
and brought forth out of the iron furnace, out of Egypt, to
be unto Him a people of inheritance, as ye are this day.
4,21 Now the LORD was angered with me for your sakes,
and swore that I should not go over the Jordan, and that I
should not go in unto that good land, which the LORD thy
God giveth thee for an inheritance; 4,22 but I must die
in this land, I must not go over the Jordan; but ye are to
go over, and possess that good land. 4,23 Take heed unto
yourselves, lest ye forget the covenant of the LORD your
God, which He made with you, and make you a graven
image, even the likeness of any thing which the LORD thy
God hath forbidden thee. 4,24 For the LORD thy God is a
devouring fire, a jealous God. {P}

4,25 When thou shalt beget children, and children's
children, and ye shall have been long in the land, and
shall deal corruptly, and make a graven image, even the

form of any thing, and shall do that which is evil in the sight of the LORD thy God, to provoke Him; 4,26 I call heaven and earth to witness against you this day, that ye shall soon utterly perish from off the land whereunto ye go over the Jordan to possess it; ye shall not prolong your days upon it, but shall utterly be destroyed. 4,27 And the LORD shall scatter you among the peoples, and ye shall be left few in number among the nations, whither the LORD shall lead you away. 4,28 And there ye shall serve gods, the work of men's hands, wood and stone, which neither see, nor hear, nor eat, nor smell. 4,29 But from thence ye will seek the LORD thy God; and thou shalt find Him, if thou search after Him with all thy heart and with all thy soul. 4,30 In thy distress, when all these things are come upon thee, in the end of days, thou wilt return to the LORD thy God, and hearken unto His voice; 4,31 for the LORD thy God is a merciful God; He will not fail thee, neither destroy thee, nor forget the covenant of thy fathers which He swore unto them. 4,32 For ask now of the days past, which were before thee, since the day that God created man upon the earth, and from the one end of heaven unto the other, whether there hath been any such thing as this great thing is, or hath been heard like it? 4,33 Did ever a people hear the voice of God speaking out of the midst of the fire, as thou hast heard, and live? 4,34 Or hath God assayed to go and take Him a nation from the midst of another nation, by trials, by signs, and by wonders, and by war, and by a mighty hand, and by an outstretched arm, and by great terrors, according to all that the LORD your God did for you in Egypt before thine eyes? 4,35 Unto thee it was shown, that thou mightiest know that the LORD, He is God; there is none else beside Him. 4,36 Out of heaven He made thee to hear His voice, that He might instruct thee; and upon earth He made thee to see His great fire; and thou didst hear His words out of the midst of the fire. 4,37 And because He loved thy fathers, and chose their seed after them, and brought thee out with His presence, with His great power, out of Egypt, 4,38 to drive out nations from before thee greater and mightier than thou, to bring thee in, to give thee their land for an inheritance, as it is this day; 4,39 know this day, and lay it to thy heart, that the LORD, He is God in heaven above and upon the earth beneath; there is none else. 4,40 And thou shalt keep His statutes, and His commandments, which I command thee this day, that it may go well with thee, and with thy children after thee, and that thou mayest prolong thy days upon the land, which the LORD thy God giveth thee, for ever. {P}

4,41 Then Moses separated three cities beyond the Jordan toward the sunrising; 4,42 that the manslayer might flee thither, that slayeth his neighbour unawares, and hated him not in time past; and that fleeing unto one of these cities he might live: 4,43 Bezer in the wilderness, in the table-land, for the Reubenites; and Ramoth in Gilead, for the Gadites; and Golan in Bashan, for the Manassites. 4,44 And this is the law which Moses set before the children of Israel; 4,45 these are the testimonies, and the statutes, and the ordinances, which Moses spoke unto the children of Israel, when they came forth out of Egypt; 4,46 beyond the Jordan, in the valley over against Beth-peor, in the land of Sihon king of the Amorites, who dwelt at Heshbon, whom Moses and the children of Israel smote, when they came forth out of Egypt; 4,47 and they took his land in possession, and the land of Og king of Bashan, the two kings of the Amorites, who were beyond the Jordan toward the sunrising; 4,48 from Aroer, which is on the edge of the valley of Arnon, even unto mount Sion-- the same is Hermon-- 4,49 and all the Arabah beyond the Jordan eastward, even unto the sea of the Arabah, under the slopes of Pisgah. {P}

5,1 And Moses called unto all Israel, and said unto them: Hear, O Israel, the statutes and the ordinances which I speak in your ears this day, that ye may learn them, and observe to do them. 5,2 The LORD our God made a covenant with us in Horeb. 5,3 The LORD made not this covenant with our fathers, but with us, even us, who are all of us here alive this day. 5,4 The LORD spoke with you face to face in the mount out of the midst of the fire-- 5,5 I stood between the LORD and you at that time, to declare unto you the word of the LORD; for ye were afraid because of the fire, and went not up into the mount--saying: {S} 5,6 I am the LORD thy God, who brought thee out of the land of Egypt, out of the house of bondage. Thou shalt have no other gods before Me. 5,7 Thou shalt not make unto thee a graven image, even any manner of likeness, of any thing that is in heaven above, or that is in the earth beneath, or that is in the water under the earth. 5,8 Thou shalt not bow down unto them, nor serve them; for I the LORD thy God am a jealous God, visiting the iniquity of the fathers upon the children, and upon the third and upon the fourth generation of them that hate Me, 5,9 and showing mercy unto the thousandth generation of them that love Me and keep My commandments. {S} 5,10 Thou shalt not take the name of the LORD thy God in vain; for the LORD will not hold him guiltless that taketh His name in vain. {S} 5,11 Observe the sabbath day, to keep it holy, as the LORD thy God commanded thee. 5,12 Six days shalt thou labour, and do all thy work; 5,13 but the seventh day is a sabbath unto the LORD thy God, in it thou shalt not do any manner of work, thou, nor thy son, nor thy daughter, nor thy man-servant, nor thy maid-servant, nor thine ox, nor thine ass, nor any of thy cattle, nor thy stranger that is within thy gates; that thy man-servant and thy maid-servant may rest as well as thou. 5,14 And thou shalt remember that thou was a servant in the land of Egypt, and the LORD thy God brought thee out thence by a mighty hand and by an outstretched arm; therefore the LORD thy God commanded thee to keep the sabbath day. {S} 5,15 Honour thy father and thy mother, as the LORD thy God commanded thee; that thy days may be long, and that it may go well with thee, upon the land which the LORD thy God giveth thee. {S} 5,16 Thou shalt not murder. {S} Neither shalt thou commit adultery. {S} Neither shalt thou steal. {S} Neither shalt thou bear false witness against thy neighbour. {S} 5,17 Neither shalt thou covet thy neighbour's wife; {S} neither shalt thou desire thy neighbour's house, his field, or his man-servant, or his maid-servant, his ox, or his ass, or any thing that is thy neighbour's. {S} 5,18 These words the LORD spoke unto all your assembly in the mount out of the midst of the fire, of the cloud, and of the thick darkness, with a great voice, and it went on no more. And He wrote them upon two tables of stone, and gave them unto me.

5,19 And it came to pass, when ye heard the voice out of the midst of the darkness, while the mountain did burn with fire, that ye came near unto me, even all the heads of your tribes, and your elders; 5,20 and ye said: 'Behold, the LORD our God hath shown us His glory and His greatness, and we have heard His voice out of the midst of the fire; we have seen this day that God doth speak with man, and he liveth. 5,21 Now therefore why should we die? for this great fire will consume us; if we hear the voice of the LORD our God any more, then we shall die. 5,22 For who is there of all flesh, that hath heard the voice of the living God speaking out of the midst of the fire, as we have, and lived? 5,23 Go thou near, and hear all that the LORD our God may say; and thou shalt speak unto us all that the LORD our God may speak unto thee; and we will hear it and do it.' 5,24 And the LORD heard the voice of your words, when ye spoke unto me; and the LORD said unto me: 'I have heard the voice of the words of this people, which they have spoken unto thee; they have well said all that they have spoken. 5,25 Oh that they had such a heart as this alway, to fear Me, and keep all My commandments, that it might be well with them, and with their children for ever! 5,26 Go say to them: Return ye to your tents. 5,27 But as for thee, stand thou here by Me, and I will speak unto thee all the commandment, and the statutes, and the ordinances, which thou shalt teach them, that they may do them in the land which I give them to possess it.' 5,28 Ye shall observe to do therefore as the LORD your God hath commanded you; ye shall not turn aside to the right hand or to the left. 5,29 Ye shall walk in all the way which the LORD your God hath commanded you, that ye may live,

and that it may be well with you, and that ye may prolong
your days in the land which ye shall possess. 6,1 Now this
is the commandment, the statutes, and the ordinances,
which the LORD your God commanded to teach you,
that ye might do them in the land whither ye go over to
possess it-- 6,2 that thou mightest fear the LORD thy God,
to keep all His statutes and His commandments, which I
command thee, thou, and thy son, and thy son's son, all
the days of thy life; and that thy days may be prolonged.
6,3 Hear therefore, O Israel, and observe to do it; that it
may be well with thee, and that ye may increase mightily,
as the LORD, the God of thy fathers, hath promised unto
thee--a land flowing with milk and honey. {P}

6,4 Hear, O Israel: the LORD our God, the LORD is one.
6,5 And thou shalt love the LORD thy God with all thy
heart, and with all thy soul, and with all thy might. 6,6
And these words, which I command thee this day, shall be
upon thy heart; 6,7 and thou shalt teach them diligently
unto thy children, and shalt talk of them when thou sittest
in thy house, and when thou walkest by the way, and when
thou liest down, and when thou risest up. 6,8 And thou
shalt bind them for a sign upon thy hand, and they shall
be for frontlets between thine eyes. 6,9 And thou shalt
write them upon the door-posts of thy house, and upon
thy gates. {S} 6,10 And it shall be, when the LORD thy
God shall bring thee into the land which He swore unto
thy fathers, to Abraham, to Isaac, and to Jacob, to give
thee--great and goodly cities, which thou didst not build,
6,11 and houses full of all good things, which thou didst
not fill, and cisterns hewn out, which thou the didst not

hew, vineyards and olive-trees, which thou didst not plant,
and thou shalt eat and be satisfied-- 6,12 then beware
lest thou forget the LORD, who brought thee forth out
of the land of Egypt, out of the house of bondage. 6,13
Thou shalt fear the LORD thy God; and Him shalt thou
serve, and by His name shalt thou swear. 6,14 Ye shall
not go after other gods, of the gods of the peoples that
are round about you; 6,15 for a jealous God, even the
LORD thy God, is in the midst of thee; lest the anger of
the LORD thy God be kindled against thee, and He destroy
thee from off the face of the earth. {S} 6,16 Ye shall not
try the LORD your God, as ye tried Him in Massah. 6,17
Ye shall diligently keep the commandments of the LORD
your God, and His testimonies, and His statutes, which He
hath commanded thee. 6,18 And thou shalt do that which
is right and good in the sight of the LORD; that it may be
well with thee, and that thou mayest go in and possess the
good land which the LORD swore unto thy fathers, 6,19
to thrust out all thine enemies from before thee, as the
LORD hath spoken. {S} 6,20 When thy son asketh thee
in time to come, saying: 'What mean the testimonies, and
the statutes, and the ordinances, which the LORD our God
hath commanded you? 6,21 then thou shalt say unto thy
son: 'We were Pharaoh's bondmen in Egypt; and the LORD
brought us out of Egypt with a mighty hand. 6,22 And the
LORD showed signs and wonders, great and sore, upon
Egypt, upon Pharaoh, and upon all his house, before our
eyes. 6,23 And He brought us out from thence, that He
might bring us in, to give us the land which He swore unto
our fathers. 6,24 And the LORD commanded us to do all
these statutes, to fear the LORD our God, for our good

always, that He might preserve us alive, as it is at this day.
6,25 And it shall be righteousness unto us, if we observe
to do all this commandment before the LORD our God, as
He hath commanded us.' {S} 7,1 When the LORD thy God
shall bring thee into the land whither thou goest to possess
it, and shall cast out many nations before thee, the Hittite,
and the Girgashite, and the Amorite, and the Canaanite,
and the Perizzite, and the Hivite, and the Jebusite, seven
nations greater and mightier than thou; 7,2 and when the
LORD thy God shall deliver them up before thee, and thou
shalt smite them; then thou shalt utterly destroy them; thou
shalt make no covenant with them, nor show mercy unto
them; 7,3 neither shalt thou make marriages with them: thy
daughter thou shalt not give unto his son, nor his daughter
shalt thou take unto thy son. 7,4 For he will turn away thy
son from following Me, that they may serve other gods; so
will the anger of the LORD be kindled against you, and He
will destroy thee quickly. 7,5 But thus shall ye deal with
them: ye shall break down their altars, and dash in pieces
their pillars, and hew down their Asherim, and burn their
graven images with fire. 7,6 For thou art a holy people unto
the LORD thy God: the LORD thy God hath chosen thee to
be His own treasure, out of all peoples that are upon the
face of the earth. 7,7 The LORD did not set His love upon
you, nor choose you, because ye were more in number than
any people--for ye were the fewest of all peoples-- 7,8 but
because the LORD loved you, and because He would keep
the oath which He swore unto your fathers, hath the LORD
brought you out with a mighty hand, and redeemed you out
of the house of bondage, from the hand of Pharaoh king
of Egypt. 7,9 Know therefore that the LORD thy God, He

is God; the faithful God, who keepeth covenant and mercy
with them that love Him and keep His commandments to
a thousand generations; 7,10 and repayeth them that hate
Him to their face, to destroy them; He will not be slack to
him that hateth Him, He will repay him to his face. 7,11
Thou shalt therefore keep the commandment, and the
statutes, and the ordinances, which I command thee this
day, to do them. {P}

Portion of Ekev

7,12 And it shall come to pass, because ye hearken to
these ordinances, and keep, and do them, that the LORD
thy God shall keep with thee the covenant and the mercy
which He swore unto thy fathers, 7,13 and He will love
thee, and bless thee, and multiply thee; He will also bless
the fruit of thy body and the fruit of thy land, thy corn and
thy wine and thine oil, the increase of thy kine and the
young of thy flock, in the land which He swore unto thy
fathers to give thee. 7,14 Thou shalt be blessed above all
peoples; there shall not be male or female barren among
you, or among your cattle. 7,15 And the LORD will take
away from thee all sickness; and He will put none of the
evil diseases of Egypt, which thou knowest, upon thee,
but will lay them upon all them that hate thee. 7,16 And
thou shalt consume all the peoples that the LORD thy
God shall deliver unto thee; thine eye shall not pity them;
neither shalt thou serve their gods; for that will be a snare
unto thee. {S} 7,17 If thou shalt say in thy heart: 'These
nations are more than I; how can I dispossess them?' 7,18
thou shalt not be afraid of them; thou shalt well remember
what the LORD thy God did unto Pharaoh, and unto all
Egypt: 7,19 the great trials which thine eyes saw, and the
signs, and the wonders, and the mighty hand, and the
outstretched arm, whereby the LORD thy God brought thee
out; so shall the LORD thy God do unto all the peoples of
whom thou art afraid. 7,20 Moreover the LORD thy God will
send the hornet among them, until they that are left, and
they that hide themselves, perish from before thee. 7,21
Thou shalt not be affrighted at them; for the LORD thy God

is in the midst of thee, a God great and awful. 7,22 And
the LORD thy God will cast out those nations before thee
by little and little; thou mayest not consume them quickly,
lest the beasts of the field increase upon thee. 7,23 But
the LORD thy God shall deliver them up before thee, and
shall discomfit them with a great discomfiture, until they
be destroyed. 7,24 And He shall deliver their kings into
thy hand, and thou shalt make their name to perish from
under heaven; there shall no man be able to stand against
thee, until thou have destroyed them. 7,25 The graven
images of their gods shall ye burn with fire; thou shalt not
covet the silver or the gold that is on them, nor take it unto
thee, lest thou be snared therein; for it is an abomination
to the LORD thy God. 7,26 And thou shalt not bring an
abomination into thy house, and be accursed like unto it;
thou shalt utterly detest it, and thou shalt utterly abhor it;
for it is a devoted thing. {P}

8,1 All the commandment which I command thee this day
shall ye observe to do, that ye may live, and multiply, and
go in and possess the land which the LORD swore unto
your fathers. 8,2 And thou shalt remember all the way
which the LORD thy God hath led thee these forty years in
the wilderness, that He might afflict thee, to prove thee, to
know what was in thy heart, whether thou wouldest keep
His commandments, or no. 8,3 And He afflicted thee, and
suffered thee to hunger, and fed thee with manna, which
thou knewest not, neither did thy fathers know; that He
might make thee know that man doth not live by bread
only, but by every thing that proceedeth out of the mouth
of the LORD doth man live. 8,4 Thy raiment waxed not

old upon thee, neither did thy foot swell, these forty years.
8,5 And thou shalt consider in thy heart, that, as a man
chasteneth his son, so the LORD thy God chasteneth thee.
8,6 And thou shalt keep the commandments of the LORD
thy God, to walk in His ways, and to fear Him. 8,7 For the
LORD thy God bringeth thee into a good land, a land of
brooks of water, of fountains and depths, springing forth in
valleys and hills; 8,8 a land of wheat and barley, and vines
and fig-trees and pomegranates; a land of olive-trees and
honey; 8,9 a land wherein thou shalt eat bread without
scarceness, thou shalt not lack any thing in it; a land
whose stones are iron, and out of whose hills thou mayest
dig brass. 8,10 And thou shalt eat and be satisfied, and
bless the LORD thy God for the good land which He hath
given thee. 8,11 Beware lest thou forget the LORD thy God,
in not keeping His commandments, and His ordinances,
and His statutes, which I command thee this day; 8,12
lest when thou hast eaten and art satisfied, and hast built
goodly houses, and dwelt therein; 8,13 and when thy
herds and thy flocks multiply, and thy silver and thy gold
is multiplied, and all that thou hast is multiplied; 8,14
then thy heart be lifted up, and thou forget the LORD thy
God, who brought thee forth out of the land of Egypt, out
of the house of bondage; 8,15 who led thee through the
great and dreadful wilderness, wherein were serpents, fiery
serpents, and scorpions, and thirsty ground where was no
water; who brought thee forth water out of the rock of flint;
8,16 who fed thee in the wilderness with manna, which
thy fathers knew not, that He might afflict thee, and that
He might prove thee, to do thee good at thy latter end;
8,17 and thou say in thy heart: 'My power and the might of

my hand hath gotten me this wealth.' 8,18 But thou shalt remember the LORD thy God, for it is He that giveth thee power to get wealth, that He may establish His covenant which He swore unto thy fathers, as it is this day. {P}

8,19 And it shall be, if thou shalt forget the LORD thy God, and walk after other gods, and serve them, and worship them, I forewarn you this day that ye shall surely perish. 8,20 As the nations that the LORD maketh to perish before you, so shall ye perish; because ye would not hearken unto the voice of the LORD your God. {P}

9,1 Hear, O Israel: thou art to pass over the Jordan this day, to go in to dispossess nations greater and mightier than thyself, cities great and fortified up to heaven, 9,2 a people great and tall, the sons of the Anakim, whom thou knowest, and of whom thou hast heard say: 'Who can stand before the sons of Anak?' 9,3 Know therefore this day, that the LORD thy God is He who goeth over before thee as a devouring fire; He will destroy them, and He will bring them down before thee; so shalt thou drive them out, and make them to perish quickly, as the LORD hath spoken unto thee. 9,4 Speak not thou in thy heart, after that the LORD thy God hath thrust them out from before thee, saying: 'For my righteousness the LORD hath brought me in to possess this land'; whereas for the wickedness of these nations the LORD doth drive them out from before thee. 9,5 Not for thy righteousness, or for the uprightness of thy heart, dost thou go in to possess their land; but for the wickedness of these nations the LORD thy God doth drive them out from before thee, and that He may establish the

word which the LORD swore unto thy fathers, to Abraham,
to Isaac, and to Jacob. 9,6 Know therefore that it is not for
thy righteousness that the LORD thy God giveth thee this
good land to possess it; for thou art a stiffnecked people.
9,7 Remember, forget thou not, how thou didst make
the LORD thy God wroth in the wilderness; from the day
that thou didst go forth out of the land of Egypt, until ye
came unto this place, ye have been rebellious against the
LORD. 9,8 Also in Horeb ye made the LORD wroth, and
the LORD was angered with you to have destroyed you. 9,9
When I was gone up into the mount to receive the tables
of stone, even the tables of the covenant which the LORD
made with you, then I abode in the mount forty days and
forty nights; I did neither eat bread nor drink water. 9,10
And the LORD delivered unto me the two tables of stone
written with the finger of God; and on them was written
according to all the words, which the LORD spoke with
you in the mount out of the midst of the fire in the day
of the assembly. 9,11 And it came to pass at the end of
forty days and forty nights, that the LORD gave me the two
tables of stone, even the tables of the covenant. 9,12 And
the LORD said unto me: 'Arise, get thee down quickly from
hence; for thy people that thou hast brought forth out of
Egypt have dealt corruptly; they are quickly turned aside
out of the way which I commanded them; they have made
them a molten image.' 9,13 Furthermore the LORD spoke
unto me, saying: 'I have seen this people, and, behold,
it is a stiffnecked people; 9,14 let Me alone, that I may
destroy them, and blot out their name from under heaven;
and I will make of thee a nation mightier and greater than
they.' 9,15 So I turned and came down from the mount,

and the mount burned with fire; and the two tables of the covenant were in my two hands. 9,16 And I looked, and, behold, ye had sinned against the LORD your God; ye had made you a molten calf; ye had turned aside quickly out of the way which the LORD had commanded you. 9,17 And I took hold of the two tables, and cast them out of my two hands, and broke them before your eyes. 9,18 And I fell down before the LORD, as at the first, forty days and forty nights; I did neither eat bread nor drink water; because of all your sin which ye sinned, in doing that which was evil in the sight of the LORD, to provoke Him. 9,19 For I was in dread of the anger and hot displeasure, wherewith the LORD was wroth against you to destroy you. But the LORD hearkened unto me that time also. 9,20 Moreover the LORD was very angry with Aaron to have destroyed him; and I prayed for Aaron also the same time. 9,21 And I took your sin, the calf which ye had made, and burnt it with fire, and beat it in pieces, grinding it very small, until it was as fine as dust; and I cast the dust thereof into the brook that descended out of the mount.-- 9,22 And at Taberah, and at Massah, and at Kibroth-hattaavah, ye made the LORD wroth. 9,23 And when the LORD sent you from Kadesh-barnea, saying: 'Go up and possess the land which I have given you'; then ye rebelled against the commandment of the LORD your God, and ye believed Him not, nor hearkened to His voice. 9,24 Ye have been rebellious against the LORD from the day that I knew you.-- 9,25 So I fell down before the LORD the forty days and forty nights that I fell down; because the LORD had said He would destroy you. 9,26 And I prayed unto the LORD, and said: 'O Lord GOD, destroy not Thy people and

Thine inheritance, that Thou hast redeemed through Thy greatness, that Thou hast brought forth out of Egypt with a mighty hand. 9,27 Remember Thy servants, Abraham, Isaac, and Jacob; look not unto the stubbornness of this people, nor to their wickedness, nor to their sin; 9,28 lest the land whence Thou broughtest us out say: Because the LORD was not able to bring them into the land which He promised unto them, and because He hated them, He hath brought them out to slay them in the wilderness. 9,29 Yet they are Thy people and Thine inheritance, that Thou didst bring out by Thy great power and by Thy outstretched arm.' {P}

10,1 At that time the LORD said unto me: 'Hew thee two tables of stone like unto the first, and come up unto Me into the mount; and make thee an ark of wood. 10,2 And I will write on the tables the words that were on the first tables which thou didst break, and thou shalt put them in the ark.' 10,3 So I made an ark of acacia-wood, and hewed two tables of stone like unto the first, and went up into the mount, having the two tables in my hand. 10,4 And He wrote on the tables according to the first writing, the ten words, which the LORD spoke unto you in the mount out of the midst of the fire in the day of the assembly; and the LORD gave them unto me. 10,5 And I turned and came down from the mount, and put the tables in the ark which I had made; and there they are, as the LORD commanded me.-- 10,6 And the children of Israel journeyed from Beeroth-benejaakan to Moserah; there Aaron died, and there he was buried; and Eleazar his son ministered in the priest's office in his stead. 10,7 From thence they journeyed unto Gudgod; and from Gudgod to Jotbah, a land of brooks of water.-- 10,8 At that time the LORD separated the tribe of Levi, to bear the ark of the covenant of the LORD, to stand before the LORD to minister unto Him, and to bless in His name, unto this day. 10,9 Wherefore Levi hath no portion nor inheritance with his brethren; the LORD is his inheritance, according as the LORD thy God spoke unto him.-- 10,10 Now I stayed in the mount, as at the first time, forty days and forty nights; and the LORD hearkened unto me that time also; the LORD would not destroy thee. 10,11 And the LORD said unto me: 'Arise, go before the people, causing them to set forward, that they may go in and possess the land, which I swore unto their fathers to give unto them.' {P}

10,12 And now, Israel, what doth the LORD thy God require of thee, but to fear the LORD thy God, to walk in all His ways, and to love Him, and to serve the LORD thy God with all thy heart and with all thy soul; 10,13 to keep for thy good the commandments of the LORD, and His statutes, which I command thee this day? 10,14 Behold, unto the LORD thy God belongeth the heaven, and the heaven of heavens, the earth, with all that therein is. 10,15 Only the LORD had a delight in thy fathers to love them, and He chose their seed after them, even you, above all peoples, as it is this day. 10,16 Circumcise therefore the foreskin of your heart, and be no more stiffnecked. 10,17 For the LORD your God, He is God of gods, and Lord of lords, the great God, the mighty, and the awful, who regardeth not persons, nor taketh reward. 10,18 He doth execute justice for the fatherless and widow, and loveth the stranger, in

giving him food and raiment. 10,19 Love ye therefore the
stranger; for ye were strangers in the land of Egypt. 10,20
Thou shalt fear the LORD thy God; Him shalt thou serve;
and to Him shalt thou cleave, and by His name shalt thou
swear. 10,21 He is thy glory, and He is thy God, that
hath done for thee these great and tremendous things,
which thine eyes have seen. 10,22 Thy fathers went down
into Egypt with threescore and ten persons; and now the
LORD thy God hath made thee as the stars of heaven
for multitude. 11,1 Therefore thou shalt love the LORD
thy God, and keep His charge, and His statutes, and His
ordinances, and His commandments, alway. 11,2 And
know ye this day; for I speak not with your children that
have not known, and that have not seen the chastisement
of the LORD your God, His greatness, His mighty hand,
and His outstretched arm, 11,3 and His signs, and His
works, which He did in the midst of Egypt unto Pharaoh
the king of Egypt, and unto all his land; 11,4 and what
He did unto the army of Egypt, unto their horses, and to
their chariots; how He made the water of the Red Sea
to overflow them as they pursued after you, and how the
LORD hath destroyed them unto this day; 11,5 and what
He did unto you in the wilderness, until ye came unto this
place; 11,6 and what He did unto Dathan and Abiram, the
sons of Eliab, the son of Reuben; how the earth opened
her mouth, and swallowed them up, and their households,
and their tents, and every living substance that followed
them, in the midst of all Israel; 11,7 but your eyes have
seen all the great work of the LORD which He did. 11,8
Therefore shall ye keep all the commandment which I
command thee this day, that ye may be strong, and go

in and possess the land, whither ye go over to possess it; 11,9 and that ye may prolong your days upon the land, which the LORD swore unto your fathers to give unto them and to their seed, a land flowing with milk and honey. {S} 11,10 For the land, whither thou goest in to possess it, is not as the land of Egypt, from whence ye came out, where thou didst sow thy seed, and didst water it with thy foot, as a garden of herbs; 11,11 but the land, whither ye go over to possess it, is a land of hills and valleys, and drinketh water as the rain of heaven cometh down; 11,12 a land which the LORD thy God careth for; the eyes of the LORD thy God are always upon it, from the beginning of the year even unto the end of the year. {S} 11,13 And it shall come to pass, if ye shall hearken diligently unto My commandments which I command you this day, to love the LORD your God, and to serve Him with all your heart and with all your soul, 11,14 that I will give the rain of your land in its season, the former rain and the latter rain, that thou mayest gather in thy corn, and thy wine, and thine oil. 11,15 And I will give grass in thy fields for thy cattle, and thou shalt eat and be satisfied. 11,16 Take heed to yourselves, lest your heart be deceived, and ye turn aside, and serve other gods, and worship them; 11,17 and the anger of the LORD be kindled against you, and He shut up the heaven, so that there shall be no rain, and the ground shall not yield her fruit; and ye perish quickly from off the good land which the LORD giveth you. 11,18 Therefore shall ye lay up these My words in your heart and in your soul; and ye shall bind them for a sign upon your hand, and they shall be for frontlets between your eyes. 11,19 And ye shall teach them your children, talking of them,

when thou sittest in thy house, and when thou walkest by
the way, and when thou liest down, and when thou risest
up. 11,20 And thou shalt write them upon the door-posts
of thy house, and upon thy gates; 11,21 that your days
may be multiplied, and the days of your children, upon the
land which the LORD swore unto your fathers to give them,
as the days of the heavens above the earth. {S} 11,22 For
if ye shall diligently keep all this commandment which
I command you, to do it, to love the LORD your God, to
walk in all His ways, and to cleave unto Him, 11,23 then
will the LORD drive out all these nations from before you,
and ye shall dispossess nations greater and mightier than
yourselves. 11,24 Every place whereon the sole of your
foot shall tread shall be yours: from the wilderness, and
Lebanon, from the river, the river Euphrates, even unto the
hinder sea shall be your border. 11,25 There shall no man
be able to stand against you: the LORD your God shall lay
the fear of you and the dread of you upon all the land that
ye shall tread upon, as He hath spoken unto you. {S}

Portion of Re'eh

11,26 Behold, I set before you this day a blessing and
a curse: 11,27 the blessing, if ye shall hearken unto the
commandments of the LORD your God, which I command
you this day; 11,28 and the curse, if ye shall not hearken
unto the commandments of the LORD your God, but turn
aside out of the way which I command you this day, to go
after other gods, which ye have not known. {S} 11,29 And
it shall come to pass, when the LORD thy God shall bring
thee into the land whither thou goest to possess it, that
thou shalt set the blessing upon mount Gerizim, and the
curse upon mount Ebal. 11,30 Are they not beyond the
Jordan, behind the way of the going down of the sun, in
the land of the Canaanites that dwell in the Arabah, over
against Gilgal, beside the terebinths of Moreh? 11,31 For
ye are to pass over the Jordan to go in to possess the land
which the LORD your God giveth you, and ye shall possess
it, and dwell therein. 11,32 And ye shall observe to do
all the statutes and the ordinances which I set before you
this day. 12,1 These are the statutes and the ordinances,
which ye shall observe to do in the land which the LORD,
the God of thy fathers, hath given thee to possess it, all
the days that ye live upon the earth. 12,2 Ye shall surely
destroy all the places, wherein the nations that ye are to
dispossess served their gods, upon the high mountains,
and upon the hills, and under every leafy tree. 12,3 And
ye shall break down their altars, and dash in pieces their
pillars, and burn their Asherim with fire; and ye shall hew
down the graven images of their gods; and ye shall destroy
their name out of that place. 12,4 Ye shall not do so unto

the LORD your God. 12,5 But unto the place which the LORD your God shall choose out of all your tribes to put His name there, even unto His habitation shall ye seek, and thither thou shalt come; 12,6 and thither ye shall bring your burnt-offerings, and your sacrifices, and your tithes, and the offering of your hand, and your vows, and your freewill-offerings, and the firstlings of your herd and of your flock; 12,7 and there ye shall eat before the LORD your God, and ye shall rejoice in all that ye put your hand unto, ye and your households, wherein the LORD thy God hath blessed thee. 12,8 Ye shall not do after all that we do here this day, every man whatsoever is right in his own eyes; 12,9 for ye are not as yet come to the rest and to the inheritance, which the LORD your God giveth thee. 12,10 But when ye go over the Jordan, and dwell in the land which the LORD your God causeth you to inherit, and He giveth you rest from all your enemies round about, so that ye dwell in safety; 12,11 then it shall come to pass that the place which the LORD your God shall choose to cause His name to dwell there, thither shall ye bring all that I command you: your burnt-offerings, and your sacrifices, your tithes, and the offering of your hand, and all your choice vows which ye vow unto the LORD. 12,12 And ye shall rejoice before the LORD your God, ye, and your sons, and your daughters, and your men-servants, and your maid-servants, and the Levite that is within your gates, forasmuch as he hath no portion nor inheritance with you. 12,13 Take heed to thyself that thou offer not thy burnt-offerings in every place that thou seest; 12,14 but in the place which the LORD shall choose in one of thy tribes, there thou shalt offer thy burnt-offerings, and there thou shalt do all that I command thee. 12,15 Notwithstanding thou mayest kill and eat flesh within all thy gates, after all the desire of thy soul, according to the blessing of the LORD thy God which He hath given thee; the unclean and the clean may eat thereof, as of the gazelle, and as of the hart. 12,16 Only ye shall not eat the blood; thou shalt pour it out upon the earth as water. 12,17 Thou mayest not eat within thy gates the tithe of thy corn, or of thy wine, or of thine oil, or the firstlings of thy herd or of thy flock, nor any of thy vows which thou vowest, nor thy freewill-offerings, nor the offering of thy hand; 12,18 but thou shalt eat them before the LORD thy God in the place which the LORD thy God shall choose, thou, and thy son, and thy daughter, and thy man-servant, and thy maid-servant, and the Levite that is within thy gates; and thou shalt rejoice before the LORD thy God in all that thou puttest thy hand unto. 12,19 Take heed to thyself that thou forsake not the Levite as long as thou livest upon thy land. {S} 12,20 When the LORD thy God shall enlarge thy border, as He hath promised thee, and thou shalt say: 'I will eat flesh', because thy soul desireth to eat flesh; thou mayest eat flesh, after all the desire of thy soul. 12,21 If the place which the LORD thy God shall choose to put His name there be too far from thee, then thou shalt kill of thy herd and of thy flock, which the LORD hath given thee, as I have commanded thee, and thou shalt eat within thy gates, after all the desire of thy soul. 12,22 Howbeit as the gazelle and as the hart is eaten, so thou shalt eat thereof; the unclean and the clean may eat thereof alike. 12,23 Only be stedfast in not eating the blood; for the blood is the life; and thou shalt not eat the life with the flesh. 12,24 Thou shalt not eat it;

thou shalt pour it out upon the earth as water. 12,25 Thou
shalt not eat it; that it may go well with thee, and with thy
children after thee, when thou shalt do that which is right
in the eyes of the LORD. 12,26 Only thy holy things which
thou hast, and thy vows, thou shalt take, and go unto the
place which the LORD shall choose; 12,27 and thou shalt
offer thy burnt-offerings, the flesh and the blood, upon the
altar of the LORD thy God; and the blood of thy sacrifices
shall be poured out against the altar of the LORD thy God,
and thou shalt eat the flesh. 12,28 Observe and hear all
these words which I command thee, that it may go well
with thee, and with thy children after thee for ever, when
thou doest that which is good and right in the eyes of the
LORD thy God. {S} 12,29 When the LORD thy God shall
cut off the nations from before thee, whither thou goest
in to dispossess them, and thou dispossessest them, and
dwellest in their land; 12,30 take heed to thyself that
thou be not ensnared to follow them, after that they are
destroyed from before thee; and that thou inquire not after
their gods, saying: 'How used these nations to serve their
gods? even so will I do likewise.' 12,31 Thou shalt not do
so unto the LORD thy God; for every abomination to the
LORD, which He hateth, have they done unto their gods;
for even their sons and their daughters do they burn in the
fire to their gods. 13,1 All this word which I command you,
that shall ye observe to do; thou shalt not add thereto, nor
diminish from it. {P}

13,2 If there arise in the midst of thee a prophet, or a
dreamer of dreams--and he give thee a sign or a wonder,
13,3 and the sign or the wonder come to pass, whereof

he spoke unto thee--saying: 'Let us go after other gods,
which thou hast not known, and let us serve them'; 13,4
thou shalt not hearken unto the words of that prophet,
or unto that dreamer of dreams; for the LORD your God
putteth you to proof, to know whether ye do love the
LORD your God with all your heart and with all your soul.
13,5 After the LORD your God shall ye walk, and Him
shall ye fear, and His commandments shall ye keep, and
unto His voice shall ye hearken, and Him shall ye serve,
and unto Him shall ye cleave. 13,6 And that prophet, or
that dreamer of dreams, shall be put to death; because
he hath spoken perversion against the LORD your God,
who brought you out of the land of Egypt, and redeemed
thee out of the house of bondage, to draw thee aside out
of the way which the LORD thy God commanded thee to
walk in. So shalt thou put away the evil from the midst
of thee. {S} 13,7 If thy brother, the son of thy mother,
or thy son, or thy daughter, or the wife of thy bosom, or
thy friend, that is as thine own soul, entice thee secretly,
saying: 'Let us go and serve other gods,' which thou hast
not known, thou, nor thy fathers; 13,8 of the gods of the
peoples that are round about you, nigh unto thee, or far
off from thee, from the one end of the earth even unto the
other end of the earth; 13,9 thou shalt not consent unto
him, nor hearken unto him; neither shall thine eye pity
him, neither shalt thou spare, neither shalt thou conceal
him; 13,10 but thou shalt surely kill him; thy hand shall
be first upon him to put him to death, and afterwards the
hand of all the people. 13,11 And thou shalt stone him
with stones, that he die; because he hath sought to draw
thee away from the LORD thy God, who brought thee out

of the land of Egypt, out of the house of bondage. 13,12
And all Israel shall hear, and fear, and shall do no more
any such wickedness as this is in the midst of thee. {S}
13,13 If thou shalt hear tell concerning one of thy cities,
which the LORD thy God giveth thee to dwell there, saying:
13,14 'Certain base fellows are gone out from the midst
of thee, and have drawn away the inhabitants of their city,
saying: Let us go and serve other gods, which ye have not
known'; 13,15 then shalt thou inquire, and make search,
and ask diligently; and, behold, if it be truth, and the thing
certain, that such abomination is wrought in the midst of
thee; 13,16 thou shalt surely smite the inhabitants of that
city with the edge of the sword, destroying it utterly, and
all that is therein and the cattle thereof, with the edge of
the sword. 13,17 And thou shalt gather all the spoil of it
into the midst of the broad place thereof, and shall burn
with fire the city, and all the spoil thereof every whit, unto
the LORD thy God; and it shall be a heap for ever; it shall
not be built again. 13,18 And there shall cleave nought
of the devoted thing to thy hand, that the LORD may turn
from the fierceness of His anger, and show thee mercy,
and have compassion upon thee, and multiply thee, as
He hath sworn unto thy fathers; 13,19 when thou shalt
hearken to the voice of the LORD thy God, to keep all His
commandments which I command thee this day, to do that
which is right in the eyes of the LORD thy God. {S} 14,1
Ye are the children of the LORD your God: ye shall not cut
yourselves, nor make any baldness between your eyes for
the dead. 14,2 For thou art a holy people unto the LORD
thy God, and the LORD hath chosen thee to be His own
treasure out of all peoples that are upon the face of the

earth. {S} 14,3 Thou shalt not eat any abominable thing. 14,4 These are the beasts which ye may eat: the ox, the sheep, and the goat, 14,5 the hart, and the gazelle, and the roebuck, and the wild goat, and the pygarg, and the antelope, and the mountain-sheep. 14,6 And every beast that parteth the hoof, and hath the hoof wholly cloven in two, and cheweth the cud, among the beasts, that ye may eat. 14,7 Nevertheless these ye shall not eat of them that only chew the cud, or of them that only have the hoof cloven: the camel, and the hare, and the rock-badger, because they chew the cud but part not the hoof, they are unclean unto you; 14,8 and the swine, because he parteth the hoof but cheweth not the cud, he is unclean unto you; of their flesh ye shall not eat, and their carcasses ye shall not touch. {S} 14,9 These ye may eat of all that are in the waters: whatsoever hath fins and scales may ye eat; 14,10 and whatsoever hath not fins and scales ye shall not eat; it is unclean unto you. {S} 14,11 Of all clean birds ye may eat. 14,12 But these are they of which ye shall not eat: the great vulture, and the bearded vulture, and the ospray; 14,13 and the glede, and the falcon, and the kite after its kinds; 14,14 and every raven after its kinds; 14,15 and the ostrich, and the night-hawk, and the sea-mew, and the hawk after its kinds; 14,16 the little owl, and the great owl, and the horned owl; 14,17 and the pelican, and the carrion-vulture, and the cormorant; 14,18 and the stork, and the heron after its kinds, and the hoopoe, and the bat. 14,19 And all winged swarming things are unclean unto you; they shall not be eaten. 14,20 Of all clean winged things ye may eat. 14,21 Ye shall not eat of any thing that dieth of itself; thou mayest give it unto the stranger that is within thy gates, that he may eat it; or thou mayest sell it unto a foreigner; for thou art a holy people unto the LORD thy God. Thou shalt not seethe a kid in its mother's milk. {P}

14,22 Thou shalt surely tithe all the increase of thy seed, that which is brought forth in the field year by year. 14,23 And thou shalt eat before the LORD thy God, in the place which He shall choose to cause His name to dwell there, the tithe of thy corn, of thy wine, and of thine oil, and the firstlings of thy herd and of thy flock; that thou mayest learn to fear the LORD thy God always. 14,24 And if the way be too long for thee, so that thou art not able to carry it, because the place is too far from thee, which the LORD thy God shall choose to set His name there, when the LORD thy God shall bless thee; 14,25 then shalt thou turn it into money, and bind up the money in thy hand, and shalt go unto the place which the LORD thy God shall choose. 14,26 And thou shalt bestow the money for whatsoever thy soul desireth, for oxen, or for sheep, or for wine, or for strong drink, or for whatsoever thy soul asketh of thee; and thou shalt eat there before the LORD thy God, and thou shalt rejoice, thou and thy household. 14,27 And the Levite that is within thy gates, thou shalt not forsake him; for he hath no portion nor inheritance with thee. {S} 14,28 At the end of every three years, even in the same year, thou shalt bring forth all the tithe of thine increase, and shall lay it up within thy gates. 14,29 And the Levite, because he hath no portion nor inheritance with thee, and the stranger, and the fatherless, and the widow, that are within thy gates, shall come, and shall eat and be satisfied; that the LORD thy God may bless thee in all the work of thy hand which thou doest. {S} 15,1 At the end of every seven years thou shalt make a release. 15,2 And this is the manner of the release: every creditor shall release that which he hath lent unto his neighbour; he shall not exact it of his neighbour and his brother; because the LORD'S release hath been proclaimed. 15,3 Of a foreigner thou mayest exact it; but whatsoever of thine is with thy brother thy hand shall release. 15,4 Howbeit there shall be no needy among you--for the LORD will surely bless thee in the land which the LORD thy God giveth thee for an inheritance to possess it-- 15,5 if only thou diligently hearken unto the voice of the LORD thy God, to observe to do all this commandment which I command thee this day. 15,6 For the LORD thy God will bless thee, as He promised thee; and thou shalt lend unto many nations, but thou shalt not borrow; and thou shalt rule over many nations, but they shall not rule over thee. {S} 15,7 If there be among you a needy man, one of thy brethren, within any of thy gates, in thy land which the LORD thy God giveth thee, thou shalt not harden thy heart, nor shut thy hand from thy needy brother; 15,8 but thou shalt surely open thy hand unto him, and shalt surely lend him sufficient for his need in that which he wanteth. 15,9 Beware that there be not a base thought in thy heart, saying: 'The seventh year, the year of release, is at hand'; and thine eye be evil against thy needy brother, and thou give him nought; and he cry unto the LORD against thee, and it be sin in thee. 15,10 Thou shalt surely give him, and thy heart shall not be grieved when thou givest unto him; because that for this thing the LORD thy God will bless thee in all thy work, and in all that thou puttest thy hand unto. 15,11 For the poor shall never cease out of the land; therefore I command thee, saying: 'Thou shalt surely open thy hand unto thy poor and needy brother, in thy land.' {S} 15,12 If thy brother, a Hebrew man, or a Hebrew woman, be sold unto thee, he shall serve thee six years; and in the seventh year thou shalt let him go free from thee. 15,13 And when thou lettest him go free from thee, thou shalt not let him go empty; 15,14 thou shalt furnish him liberally out of thy flock, and out of thy threshing-floor, and out of thy winepress; of that wherewith the LORD thy God hath blessed thee thou shalt give unto him. 15,15 And thou shalt remember that thou wast a bondman in the land of Egypt, and the LORD thy God redeemed thee; therefore I command thee this thing to-day. 15,16 And it shall be, if he say unto thee: 'I will not go out from thee'; because he loveth thee and thy house, because he fareth well with thee; 15,17 then thou shalt take an awl, and thrust it through his ear and into the door, and he shall be thy bondman for ever. And also unto thy bondwoman thou shalt do likewise. 15,18 It shall not seem hard unto thee, when thou lettest him go free from thee; for to the double of the hire of a hireling hath he served thee six years; and the LORD thy God will bless thee in all that thou doest. {P}

15,19 All the firstling males that are born of thy herd and of thy flock thou shalt sanctify unto the LORD thy God; thou shalt do no work with the firstling of thine ox, nor shear the firstling of thy flock. 15,20 Thou shalt eat it before the LORD thy God year by year in the place which the LORD shall choose, thou and thy household. 15,21 And if there be any blemish therein, lameness, or blindness, any ill blemish whatsoever, thou shalt not sacrifice it unto the LORD thy God. 15,22 Thou shalt eat it within thy gates; the unclean and the clean may eat it alike, as the gazelle, and as the hart. 15,23 Only thou shalt not eat the blood thereof; thou shalt pour it out upon the ground as water. {P}

16,1 Observe the month of Abib, and keep the passover unto the LORD thy God; for in the month of Abib the LORD thy God brought thee forth out of Egypt by night. 16,2 And thou shalt sacrifice the passover-offering unto the LORD thy God, of the flock and the herd, in the place which the LORD shall choose to cause His name to dwell there. 16,3 Thou shalt eat no leavened bread with it; seven days shalt thou eat unleavened bread therewith, even the bread of affliction; for in haste didst thou come forth out of the land of Egypt; that thou mayest remember the day when thou camest forth out of the land of Egypt all the days of thy life. 16,4 And there shall be no leaven seen with thee in all they borders seven days; neither shall any of the flesh, which thou sacrificest the first day at even, remain all night until the morning. 16,5 Thou mayest not sacrifice the passover-offering within any of thy gates, which the LORD thy God giveth thee; 16,6 but at the place which the LORD thy God shall choose to cause His name to dwell in, there thou shalt sacrifice the passover-offering at even, at the going down of the sun, at the season that thou camest forth out of Egypt. 16,7 And thou shalt roast and eat it in the place which the LORD thy God shall choose; and thou shalt turn in the morning, and go unto thy tents. 16,8 Six days thou shalt eat unleavened bread; and on the seventh day shall be a solemn assembly to the LORD thy God; thou shalt do no work therein. {S} 16,9 Seven weeks shalt thou number unto thee; from the time the sickle is first put to the standing corn shalt thou begin to number seven weeks. 16,10 And thou shalt keep the feast of weeks unto the LORD thy God after the measure of the freewill-offering of thy hand, which thou shalt give, according as the LORD thy God blesseth thee. 16,11 And thou shalt rejoice before the LORD thy God, thou, and thy son, and thy daughter, and thy man-servant, and thy maid-servant, and the Levite that is within they gates, and the stranger, and the fatherless, and the widow, that are in the midst of thee, in the place which the LORD thy God shall choose to cause His name to dwell there. 16,12 And thou shalt remember that thou wast a bondman in Egypt; and thou shalt observe and do these statutes. {P}

16,13 Thou shalt keep the feast of tabernacles seven days, after that thou hast gathered in from thy threshing-floor and from thy winepress. 16,14 And thou shalt rejoice in thy feast, thou, and thy son, and thy daughter, and thy man-servant, and thy maid-servant, and the Levite, and the stranger, and the fatherless, and the widow, that are within thy gates. 16,15 Seven days shalt thou keep a feast unto the LORD thy God in the place which the LORD shall choose; because the LORD thy God shall bless thee in all thine increase, and in all the work of thy hands, and thou shalt be altogether joyful. 16,16 Three times in a year shall all thy males appear before the LORD thy God in the place which He shall choose; on the feast of unleavened bread, and on the feast of weeks, and on the feast of tabernacles; and they shall not appear before the LORD empty; 16,17 every man shall give as he is able, according to the blessing of the LORD thy God which He hath given thee. {S}

Portion of Shoftim

16,18 Judges and officers shalt thou make thee in all thy gates, which the LORD thy God giveth thee, tribe by tribe; and they shall judge the people with righteous judgment. 16,19 Thou shalt not wrest judgment; thou shalt not respect persons; neither shalt thou take a gift; for a gift doth blind the eyes of the wise, and pervert the words of the righteous. 16,20 Justice, justice shalt thou follow, that thou mayest live, and inherit the land which the LORD thy God giveth thee. {S} 16,21 Thou shalt not plant thee an Asherah of any kind of tree beside the altar of the LORD thy God, which thou shalt make thee. 16,22 Neither shalt thou set thee up a pillar, which the LORD thy God hateth. {S} 17,1 Thou shalt not sacrifice unto the LORD thy God an ox, or a sheep, wherein is a blemish, even any evil thing; for that is an abomination unto the LORD thy God. {S} 17,2 If there be found in the midst of thee, within any of thy gates which the LORD thy God giveth thee, man or woman, that doeth that which is evil in the sight of the LORD thy God, in transgressing His covenant, 17,3 and hath gone and served other gods, and worshipped them, or the sun, or the moon, or any of the host of heaven, which I have commanded not; 17,4 and it be told thee, and thou

hear it, then shalt thou inquire diligently, and, behold, if
it be true, and the thing certain, that such abomination
is wrought in Israel; 17,5 then shalt thou bring forth that
man or that woman, who have done this evil thing, unto
thy gates, even the man or the woman; and thou shalt
stone them with stones, that they die. 17,6 At the mouth
of two witnesses, or three witnesses, shall he that is to die
be put to death; at the mouth of one witness he shall not
be put to death. 17,7 The hand of the witnesses shall be
first upon him to put him to death, and afterward the hand
of all the people. So thou shalt put away the evil from the
midst of thee. {P}

17,8 If there arise a matter too hard for thee in judgment,
between blood and blood, between plea and plea, and
between stroke and stroke, even matters of controversy
within thy gates; then shalt thou arise, and get thee up
unto the place which the LORD thy God shall choose.
17,9 And thou shall come unto the priests the Levites, and
unto the judge that shall be in those days; and thou shalt
inquire; and they shall declare unto thee the sentence of
judgment. 17,10 And thou shalt do according to the tenor
of the sentence, which they shall declare unto thee from
that place which the LORD shall choose; and thou shalt
observe to do according to all that they shall teach thee.
17,11 According to the law which they shall teach thee,
and according to the judgment which they shall tell thee,
thou shalt do; thou shalt not turn aside from the sentence
which they shall declare unto thee, to the right hand, nor
to the left. 17,12 And the man that doeth presumptuously,
in not hearkening unto the priest that standeth to minister

there before the LORD thy God, or unto the judge, even
that man shall die; and thou shalt exterminate the evil
from Israel. 17,13 And all the people shall hear, and fear,
and do no more presumptuously. {S} 17,14 When thou art
come unto the land which the LORD thy God giveth thee,
and shalt possess it, and shalt dwell therein; and shalt say:
'I will set a king over me, like all the nations that are round
about me'; 17,15 thou shalt in any wise set him king over
thee, whom the LORD thy God shall choose; one from among
thy brethren shalt thou set king over thee; thou mayest not
put a foreigner over thee, who is not thy brother. 17,16
Only he shall not multiply horses to himself, nor cause
the people to return to Egypt, to the end that he should
multiply horses; forasmuch as the LORD hath said unto
you: 'Ye shall henceforth return no more that way.' 17,17
Neither shall he multiply wives to himself, that his heart
turn not away; neither shall he greatly multiply to himself
silver and gold. 17,18 And it shall be, when he sitteth
upon the throne of his kingdom, that he shall write him a
copy of this law in a book, out of that which is before the
priests the Levites. 17,19 And it shall be with him, and he
shall read therein all the days of his life; that he may learn
to fear the LORD his God, to keep all the words of this law
and these statutes, to do them; 17,20 that his heart be
not lifted up above his brethren, and that he turn not aside
from the commandment, to the right hand, or to the left;
to the end that he may prolong his days in his kingdom, he
and his children, in the midst of Israel. {S} 18,1 The priests
the Levites, even all the tribe of Levi, shall have no portion
nor inheritance with Israel; they shall eat the offerings of
the LORD made by fire, and His inheritance. 18,2 And

they shall have no inheritance among their brethren; the LORD is their inheritance, as He hath spoken unto them. {S} 18,3 And this shall be the priests' due from the people, from them that offer a sacrifice, whether it be ox or sheep, that they shall give unto the priest the shoulder, and the two cheeks, and the maw. 18,4 The first-fruits of thy corn, of thy wine, and of thine oil, and the first of the fleece of thy sheep, shalt thou give him. 18,5 For the LORD thy God hath chosen him out of all thy tribes, to stand to minister in the name of the LORD, him and his sons for ever. {S} 18,6 And if a Levite come from any of thy gates out of all Israel, where he sojourneth, and come with all the desire of his soul unto the place which the LORD shall choose; 18,7 then he shall minister in the name of the LORD his God, as all his brethren the Levites do, who stand there before the LORD. 18,8 They shall have like portions to eat, beside that which is his due according to the fathers' houses. {S} 18,9 When thou art come into the land which the LORD thy God giveth thee, thou shalt not learn to do after the abominations of those nations. 18,10 There shall not be found among you any one that maketh his son or his daughter to pass through the fire, one that useth divination, a soothsayer, or an enchanter, or a sorcerer, 18,11 or a charmer, or one that consulteth a ghost or a familiar spirit, or a necromancer. 18,12 For whosoever doeth these things is an abomination unto the LORD; and because of these abominations the LORD thy God is driving them out from before thee. 18,13 Thou shalt be whole-hearted with the LORD thy God. 18,14 For these nations, that thou art to dispossess, hearken unto soothsayers, and unto diviners; but as for thee, the LORD thy God hath not suffered thee so to do. 18,15 A prophet will the LORD thy God raise up unto thee, from the midst of thee, of thy brethren, like unto me; unto him ye shall hearken; 18,16 according to all that thou didst desire of the LORD thy God in Horeb in the day of the assembly, saying: 'Let me not hear again the voice of the LORD my God, neither let me see this great fire any more, that I die not.' 18,17 And the LORD said unto me: 'They have well said that which they have spoken. 18,18 I will raise them up a prophet from among their brethren, like unto thee; and I will put My words in his mouth, and he shall speak unto them all that I shall command him. 18,19 And it shall come to pass, that whosoever will not hearken unto My words which he shall speak in My name, I will require it of him. 18,20 But the prophet, that shall speak a word presumptuously in My name, which I have not commanded him to speak, or that shall speak in the name of other gods, that same prophet shall die.' 18,21 And if thou say in thy heart: 'How shall we know the word which the LORD hath not spoken?' 18,22 When a prophet speaketh in the name of the LORD, if the thing follow not, nor come to pass, that is the thing which the LORD hath not spoken; the prophet hath spoken it presumptuously, thou shalt not be afraid of him. {S} 19,1 When the LORD thy God shall cut off the nations, whose land the LORD thy God giveth thee, and thou dost succeed them, and dwell in their cities, and in their houses; 19,2 thou shalt separate three cities for thee in the midst of thy land, which the LORD thy GOD giveth thee to possess it. 19,3 Thou shalt prepare thee the way, and divide the borders of thy land, which the LORD thy God causeth thee to inherit, into three parts, that every manslayer may flee thither. 19,4 And this

is the case of the manslayer, that shall flee thither and
live: whoso killeth his neighbour unawares, and hated him
not in time past; 19,5 as when a man goeth into the forest
with his neighbour to hew wood, and his hand fetcheth
a stroke with the axe to cut down the tree, and the head
slippeth from the helve, and lighteth upon his neighbour,
that he die; he shall flee unto one of these cities and live;
19,6 lest the avenger of blood pursue the manslayer, while
his heart is hot, and overtake him, because the way is long,
and smite him mortally; whereas he was not deserving of
death, inasmuch as he hated him not in time past. 19,7
Wherefore I command thee, saying: 'Thou shalt separate
three cities for thee.' 19,8 And if the LORD thy God
enlarge thy border, as He hath sworn unto thy fathers, and
give thee all the land which He promised to give unto thy
fathers-- 19,9 if thou shalt keep all this commandment to
do it, which I command thee this day, to love the LORD
thy God, and to walk ever in His ways--then shalt thou add
three cities more for thee, beside these three; 19,10 that
innocent blood be not shed in the midst of thy land, which
the LORD thy God giveth thee for an inheritance, and so
blood be upon thee. {P}

19,11 But if any man hate his neighbour, and lie in wait
for him, and rise up against him, and smite him mortally
that he die; and he flee into one of these cities; 19,12
then the elders of his city shall send and fetch him thence,
and deliver him into the hand of the avenger of blood, that
he may die. 19,13 Thine eye shall not pity him, but thou
shalt put away the blood of the innocent from Israel, that
it may go well with thee. {S} 19,14 Thou shalt not remove

thy neighbour's landmark, which they of old time have
set, in thine inheritance which thou shalt inherit, in the
land that the LORD thy God giveth thee to possess it. {S}
19,15 One witness shall not rise up against a man for any
iniquity, or for any sin, in any sin that he sinneth; at the
mouth of two witnesses, or at the mouth of three witnesses,
shall a matter be establishment 19,16 If an unrighteous
witness rise up against any man to bear perverted witness
against him; 19,17 then both the men, between whom the
controversy is, shall stand before the LORD, before the
priests and the judges that shall be in those days. 19,18
And the judges shall inquire diligently; and, behold, if
the witness be a false witness, and hath testified falsely
against his brother; 19,19 then shall ye do unto him, as
he had purposed to do unto his brother; so shalt thou put
away the evil from the midst of thee. 19,20 And those that
remain shall hear, and fear, and shall henceforth commit
no more any such evil in the midst of thee. 19,21 And thine
eye shall not pity: life for life, eye for eye, tooth for tooth,
hand for hand, foot for foot. {S} 20,1 When thou goest
forth to battle against thine enemies, and seest horses,
and chariots, and a people more than thou, thou shalt
not be afraid of them; for the LORD thy God is with thee,
who brought thee up out of the land of Egypt. 20,2 And it
shall be, when ye draw nigh unto the battle, that the priest
shall approach and speak unto the people, 20,3 and shall
say unto them: 'Hear, O Israel, ye draw nigh this day unto
battle against your enemies; let not your heart faint; fear
not, nor be alarmed, neither be ye affrighted at them; 20,4
for the LORD your God is He that goeth with you, to fight
for you against your enemies, to save you.' 20,5 And the

officers shall speak unto the people, saying: 'What man is
there that hath built a new house, and hath not dedicated
it? let him go and return to his house, lest he die in the
battle, and another man dedicate it. 20,6 And what man
is there that hath planted a vineyard, and hath not used
the fruit thereof? let him go and return unto his house, lest
he die in the battle, and another man use the fruit thereof.
20,7 And what man is there that hath betrothed a wife,
and hath not taken her? let him go and return unto his
house, lest he die in the battle, and another man take her.'
20,8 And the officers shall speak further unto the people,
and they shall say: 'What man is there that is fearful and
faint-hearted? let him go and return unto his house, lest
his brethren's heart melt as his heart.' 20,9 And it shall
be, when the officers have made an end of speaking unto
the people, that captains of hosts shall be appointed at
the head of the people. {S} 20,10 When thou drawest nigh
unto a city to fight against it, then proclaim peace unto
it. 20,11 And it shall be, if it make thee answer of peace,
and open unto thee, then it shall be, that all the people
that are found therein shall become tributary unto thee,
and shall serve thee. 20,12 And if it will make no peace
with thee, but will make war against thee, then thou shalt
besiege it. 20,13 And when the LORD thy God delivereth
it into thy hand, thou shalt smite every male thereof with
the edge of the sword; 20,14 but the women, and the little
ones, and the cattle, and all that is in the city, even all the
spoil thereof, shalt thou take for a prey unto thyself; and
thou shalt eat the spoil of thine enemies, which the LORD
thy God hath given thee. 20,15 Thus shalt thou do unto all
the cities which are very far off from thee, which are not

of the cities of these nations. 20,16 Howbeit of the cities of these peoples, that the LORD thy God giveth thee for an inheritance, thou shalt save alive nothing that breatheth, 20,17 but thou shalt utterly destroy them: the Hittite, and the Amorite, the Canaanite, and the Perizzite, the Hivite, and the Jebusite; as the LORD thy God hath commanded thee; 20,18 that they teach you not to do after all their abominations, which they have done unto their gods, and so ye sin against the LORD your God. {S} 20,19 When thou shalt besiege a city a long time, in making war against it to take it, thou shalt not destroy the trees thereof by wielding an axe against them; for thou mayest eat of them, but thou shalt not cut them down; for is the tree of the field man, that it should be besieged of thee? 20,20 Only the trees of which thou knowest that they are not trees for food, them thou mayest destroy and cut down, that thou mayest build bulwarks against the city that maketh war with thee, until it fall. {P}

21,1 If one be found slain in the land which the LORD thy God giveth thee to possess it, lying in the field, and it be not known who hath smitten him; 21,2 then thy elders and thy judges shall come forth, and they shall measure unto the cities which are round about him that is slain. 21,3 And it shall be, that the city which is nearest unto the slain man, even the elders of that city shall take a heifer of the herd, which hath not been wrought with, and which hath not drawn in the yoke. 21,4 And the elders of that city shall bring down the heifer unto a rough valley, which may neither be plowed nor sown, and shall break the heifer's neck there in the valley. 21,5 And the priests

the sons of Levi shall come near--for them the LORD thy
God hath chosen to minister unto Him, and to bless in the
name of the LORD; and according to their word shall every
controversy and every stroke be. 21,6 And all the elders of
that city, who are nearest unto the slain man, shall wash
their hands over the heifer whose neck was broken in the
valley. 21,7 And they shall speak and say: 'Our hands
have not shed this blood, neither have our eyes seen it.
21,8 Forgive, O LORD, Thy people Israel, whom Thou hast
redeemed, and suffer not innocent blood to remain in the
midst of Thy people Israel.' And the blood shall be forgiven
them. 21,9 So shalt thou put away the innocent blood
from the midst of thee, when thou shalt do that which is
right in the eyes of the LORD. {S}

Portion of Ki Tetze

21,10 When thou goest forth to battle against thine
enemies, and the LORD thy God delivereth them into
thy hands, and thou carriest them away captive, 21,11
and seest among the captives a woman of goodly form,
and thou hast a desire unto her, and wouldest take her to
thee to wife; 21,12 then thou shalt bring her home to thy
house; and she shall shave her head, and pare her nails;
21,13 and she shall put the raiment of her captivity from
off her, and shall remain in thy house, and bewail her
father and her mother a full month; and after that thou
mayest go in unto her, and be her husband, and she shall
be thy wife. 21,14 And it shall be, if thou have no delight
in her, then thou shalt let her go whither she will; but thou
shalt not sell her at all for money, thou shalt not deal with
her as a slave, because thou hast humbled her. {S} 21,15
If a man have two wives, the one beloved, and the other
hated, and they have borne him children, both the beloved
and the hated; and if the first-born son be hers that was
hated; 21,16 then it shall be, in the day that he causeth
his sons to inherit that which he hath, that he may not
make the son of the beloved the first-born before the son
of the hated, who is the first-born; 21,17 but he shall
acknowledge the first-born, the son of the hated, by giving
him a double portion of all that he hath; for he is the first-
fruits of his strength, the right of the first-born is his. {S}
21,18 If a man have a stubborn and rebellious son, that
will not hearken to the voice of his father, or the voice of
his mother, and though they chasten him, will not hearken
unto them; 21,19 then shall his father and his mother

lay hold on him, and bring him out unto the elders of his city, and unto the gate of his place; 21,20 and they shall say unto the elders of his city: 'This our son is stubborn and rebellious, he doth not hearken to our voice; he is a glutton, and a drunkard.' 21,21 And all the men of his city shall stone him with stones, that he die; so shalt thou put away the evil from the midst of thee; and all Israel shall hear, and fear. {S} 21,22 And if a man have committed a sin worthy of death, and he be put to death, and thou hang him on a tree; 21,23 his body shall not remain all night upon the tree, but thou shalt surely bury him the same day; for he that is hanged is a reproach unto God; that thou defile not thy land which the LORD thy God giveth thee for an inheritance. {S} 22,1 Thou shalt not see thy brother's ox or his sheep driven away, and hide thyself from them; thou shalt surely bring them back unto thy brother. 22,2 And if thy brother be not nigh unto thee, and thou know him not, then thou shalt bring it home to thy house, and it shall be with thee until thy brother require it, and thou shalt restore it to him. 22,3 And so shalt thou do with his ass; and so shalt thou do with his garment; and so shalt thou do with every lost thing of thy brother's, which he hath lost, and thou hast found; thou mayest not hide thyself. {S} 22,4 Thou shalt not see thy brother's ass or his ox fallen down by the way, and hide thyself from them; thou shalt surely help him to lift them up again. {S} 22,5 A woman shall not wear that which pertaineth unto a man, neither shall a man put on a woman's garment; for whosoever doeth these things is an abomination unto the LORD thy God. {P}

22,6 If a bird's nest chance to be before thee in the way,

in any tree or on the ground, with young ones or eggs, and the dam sitting upon the young, or upon the eggs, thou shalt not take the dam with the young; 22,7 thou shalt in any wise let the dam go, but the young thou mayest take unto thyself; that it may be well with thee, and that thou mayest prolong thy days. {S} 22,8 When thou buildest a new house, then thou shalt make a parapet for thy roof, that thou bring not blood upon thy house, if any man fall from thence. 22,9 Thou shalt not sow thy vineyard with two kinds of seed; lest the fulness of the seed which thou hast sown be forfeited together with the increase of the vineyard. {S} 22,10 Thou shalt not plow with an ox and an ass together. 22,11 Thou shalt not wear a mingled stuff, wool and linen together. {S} 22,12 Thou shalt make thee twisted cords upon the four corners of thy covering, wherewith thou coverest thyself. {S} 22,13 If any man take a wife, and go in unto her, and hate her, 22,14 and lay wanton charges against her, and bring up an evil name upon her, and say: 'I took this woman, and when I came nigh to her, I found not in her the tokens of virginity'; 22,15 then shall the father of the damsel, and her mother, take and bring forth the tokens of the damsel's virginity unto the elders of the city in the gate. 22,16 And the damsel's father shall say unto the elders: 'I gave my daughter unto this man to wife, and he hateth her; 22,17 and, lo, he hath laid wanton charges, saying: I found not in thy daughter the tokens of virginity; and yet these are the tokens of my daughter's virginity.' And they shall spread the garment before the elders of the city. 22,18 And the elders of that city shall take the man and chastise him. 22,19 And they shall fine him a hundred shekels of

silver, and give them unto the father of the damsel,
because he hath brought up an evil name upon a virgin of
Israel; and she shall be his wife; he may not put her away
all his days. {S} 22,20 But if this thing be true, that the
tokens of virginity were not found in the damsel; 22,21
then they shall bring out the damsel to the door of her
father's house, and the men of her city shall stone her with
stones that she die; because she hath wrought a wanton
deed in Israel, to play the harlot in her father's house; so
shalt thou put away the evil from the midst of thee. {S}
22,22 If a man be found lying with a woman married to a
husband, then they shall both of them die, the man that
lay with the woman, and the woman; so shalt thou put
away the evil from Israel. {S} 22,23 If there be a damsel
that is a virgin betrothed unto a man, and a man find her
in the city, and lie with her; 22,24 then ye shall bring
them both out unto the gate of that city, and ye shall stone
them with stones that they die: the damsel, because she
cried not, being in the city; and the man, because he hath
humbled his neighbour's wife; so thou shalt put away the
evil from the midst of thee. {S} 22,25 But if the man find
the damsel that is betrothed in the field, and the man take
hold of her, and lie with her; then the man only that lay
with her shall die. 22,26 But unto the damsel thou shalt
do nothing; there is in the damsel no sin worthy of death;
for as when a man riseth against his neighbour, and slayeth
him, even so is this matter. 22,27 For he found her in the
field; the betrothed damsel cried, and there was none to
save her. {S} 22,28 If a man find a damsel that is a virgin,
that is not betrothed, and lay hold on her, and lie with her,
and they be found; 22,29 then the man that lay with her

shall give unto the damsel's father fifty shekels of silver, and she shall be his wife, because he hath humbled her; he may not put her away all his days. {S} 23,1 A man shall not take his father's wife, and shall not uncover his father's skirt. {S} 23,2 He that is crushed or maimed in his privy parts shall not enter into the assembly of the LORD. {S} 23,3 A bastard shall not enter into the assembly of the LORD; even to the tenth generation shall none of his enter into the assembly of the LORD. {S} 23,4 An Ammonite or a Moabite shall not enter into the assembly of the LORD; even to the tenth generation shall none of them enter into the assembly of the LORD for ever; 23,5 because they met you not with bread and with water in the way, when ye came forth out of Egypt; and because they hired against thee Balaam the son of Beor from Pethor of Aram-naharaim, to curse thee. 23,6 Nevertheless the LORD thy God would not hearken unto Balaam; but the LORD thy God turned the curse into a blessing unto thee, because the LORD thy God loved thee. 23,7 Thou shalt not seek their peace nor their prosperity all thy days for ever. {S} 23,8 Thou shalt not abhor an Edomite, for he is thy brother; thou shalt not abhor an Egyptian, because thou wast a stranger in his land. 23,9 The children of the third generation that are born unto them may enter into the assembly of the LORD. {S} 23,10 When thou goest forth in camp against thine enemies, then thou shalt keep thee from every evil thing. 23,11 If there be among you any man, that is not clean by reason of that which chanceth him by night, then shall he go abroad out of the camp, he shall not come within the camp. 23,12 But it shall be, when evening cometh on, he shall bathe himself in water;

and when the sun is down, he may come within the camp. 23,13 Thou shalt have a place also without the camp, whither thou shalt go forth abroad. 23,14 And thou shalt have a paddle among thy weapons; and it shall be, when thou sittest down abroad, thou shalt dig therewith, and shalt turn back and cover that which cometh from thee. 23,15 For the LORD thy God walketh in the midst of thy camp, to deliver thee, and to give up thine enemies before thee; therefore shall thy camp be holy; that He see no unseemly thing in thee, and turn away from thee. {S} 23,16 Thou shalt not deliver unto his master a bondman that is escaped from his master unto thee; 23,17 he shall dwell with thee, in the midst of thee, in the place which he shall choose within one of thy gates, where it liketh him best; thou shalt not wrong him. {S} 23,18 There shall be no harlot of the daughters of Israel, neither shall there be a sodomite of the sons of Israel. 23,19 Thou shalt not bring the hire of a harlot, or the price of a dog, into the house of the LORD thy God for any vow; for even both these are an abomination unto the LORD thy God. {S} 23,20 Thou shalt not lend upon interest to thy brother: interest of money, interest of victuals, interest of any thing that is lent upon interest. 23,21 Unto a foreigner thou mayest lend upon interest; but unto thy brother thou shalt not lend upon interest; that the LORD thy God may bless thee in all that thou puttest thy hand unto, in the land whither thou goest in to possess it. {S} 23,22 When thou shalt vow a vow unto the LORD thy God, thou shalt not be slack to pay it; for the LORD thy God will surely require it of thee; and it will be sin in thee. 23,23 But if thou shalt forbear to vow, it shall be no sin in thee. 23,24 That which is gone out of thy lips thou shalt observe and do; according as thou hast vowed freely unto the LORD thy God, even that which thou hast promised with thy mouth. {S} 23,25 When thou comest into thy neighbour's vineyard, then thou mayest eat grapes until thou have enough at thine own pleasure; but thou shalt not put any in thy vessel. {S} 23,26 When thou comest into thy neighbour's standing corn, then thou mayest pluck ears with thy hand; but thou shalt not move a sickle unto thy neighbour's standing corn. {S} 24,1 When a man taketh a wife, and marrieth her, then it cometh to pass, if she find no favour in his eyes, because he hath found some unseemly thing in her, that he writeth her a bill of divorcement, and giveth it in her hand, and sendeth her out of his house, 24,2 and she departeth out of his house, and goeth and becometh another man's wife, 24,3 and the latter husband hateth her, and writeth her a bill of divorcement, and giveth it in her hand, and sendeth her out of his house; or if the latter husband die, who took her to be his wife; 24,4 her former husband, who sent her away, may not take her again to be his wife, after that she is defiled; for that is abomination before the LORD; and thou shalt not cause the land to sin, which the LORD thy God giveth thee for an inheritance. {S} 24,5 When a man taketh a new wife, he shall not go out in the host, neither shall he be charged with any business; he shall be free for his house one year, and shall cheer his wife whom he hath taken. 24,6 No man shall take the mill or the upper millstone to pledge; for he taketh a man's life to pledge. {S} 24,7 If a man be found stealing any of his brethren of the children of Israel, and he deal with him as a slave, and sell him; then that thief shall die; so shalt thou put away

the evil from the midst of thee. {S} 24,8 Take heed in the
plague of leprosy, that thou observe diligently, and do
according to all that the priests the Levites shall teach
you, as I commanded them, so ye shall observe to do. 24,9
Remember what the LORD thy God did unto Miriam, by
the way as ye came forth out of Egypt. {S} 24,10 When
thou dost lend thy neighbour any manner of loan, thou
shalt not go into his house to fetch his pledge. 24,11 Thou
shalt stand without, and the man to whom thou dost lend
shall bring forth the pledge without unto thee. 24,12 And
if he be a poor man, thou shalt not sleep with his pledge;
24,13 thou shalt surely restore to him the pledge when the
sun goeth down, that he may sleep in his garment, and
bless thee; and it shall be righteousness unto thee before
the LORD thy God. {S} 24,14 Thou shalt not oppress a
hired servant that is poor and needy, whether he be of thy
brethren, or of thy strangers that are in thy land within thy
gates. 24,15 In the same day thou shalt give him his hire,
neither shall the sun go down upon it; for he is poor, and
setteth his heart upon it: lest he cry against thee unto the
LORD and it be sin in thee. {S} 24,16 The fathers shall not
be put to death for the children, neither shall the children
be put to death for the fathers; every man shall be put to
death for his own sin. {S} 24,17 Thou shalt not pervert the
justice due to the stranger, or to the fatherless; nor take
the widow's raiment to pledge. 24,18 But thou shalt
remember that thou wast a bondman in Egypt, and the
LORD thy God redeemed thee thence; therefore I command
thee to do this thing. {S} 24,19 When thou reapest thy
harvest in thy field, and hast forgot a sheaf in the field,
thou shalt not go back to fetch it; it shall be for the

stranger, for the fatherless, and for the widow; that the LORD thy God may bless thee in all the work of thy hands. {S} 24,20 When thou beatest thine olive-tree, thou shalt not go over the boughs again; it shall be for the stranger, for the fatherless, and for the widow. 24,21 When thou gatherest the grapes of thy vineyard, thou shalt not glean it after thee; it shall be for the stranger, for the fatherless, and for the widow. 24,22 And thou shalt remember that thou wast a bondman in the land of Egypt; therefore I command thee to do this thing. {S} 25,1 If there be a controversy between men, and they come unto judgment, and the judges judge them, by justifying the righteous, and condemning the wicked, 25,2 then it shall be, if the wicked man deserve to be beaten, that the judge shall cause him to lie down, and to be beaten before his face, according to the measure of his wickedness, by number. 25,3 Forty stripes he may give him, he shall not exceed; lest, if he should exceed, and beat him above these with many stripes, then thy brother should be dishonoured before thine eyes. 25,4 Thou shalt not muzzle the ox when he treadeth out the corn. {S} 25,5 If brethren dwell together, and one of them die, and have no child, the wife of the dead shall not be married abroad unto one not of his kin; her husband's brother shall go in unto her, and take her to him to wife, and perform the duty of a husband's brother unto her. 25,6 And it shall be, that the first-born that she beareth shall succeed in the name of his brother that is dead, that his name be not blotted out of Israel. 25,7 And if the man like not to take his brother's wife, then his brother's wife shall go up to the gate unto the elders, and say: 'My husband's brother refuseth to raise up

unto his brother a name in Israel; he will not perform the
duty of a husband's brother unto me.' 25,8 Then the elders
of his city shall call him, and speak unto him; and if he
stand, and say: 'I like not to take her'; 25,9 then shall his
brother's wife draw nigh unto him in the presence of the
elders, and loose his shoe from off his foot, and spit in his
face; and she shall answer and say: 'So shall it be done
unto the man that doth not build up his brother's house.'
25,10 And his name shall be called in Israel The house of
him that had his shoe loosed. {S} 25,11 When men strive
together one with another, and the wife of the one draweth
near to deliver her husband out of the hand of him that
smiteth him, and putteth forth her hand, and taketh him
by the secrets; 25,12 then thou shalt cut off her hand,
thine eye shall have no pity. {S} 25,13 Thou shalt not have
in thy bag diverse weights, a great and a small. 25,14
Thou shalt not have in thy house diverse measures, a great
and a small. 25,15 A perfect and just weight shalt thou
have; a perfect and just measure shalt thou have; that thy
days may be long upon the land which the LORD thy God
giveth thee. 25,16 For all that do such things, even all
that do unrighteously, are an abomination unto the LORD
thy God. {P}

25,17 Remember what Amalek did unto thee by the way
as ye came forth out of Egypt; 25,18 how he met thee by
the way, and smote the hindmost of thee, all that were
enfeebled in thy rear, when thou wast faint and weary; and
he feared not God. 25,19 Therefore it shall be, when the
LORD thy God hath given thee rest from all thine enemies
round about, in the land which the LORD thy God giveth

thee for an inheritance to possess it, that thou shalt blot out the remembrance of Amalek from under heaven; thou shalt not forget. {P}

Portion of Ki-Tavo

26,1 And it shall be, when thou art come in unto the land which the LORD thy God giveth thee for an inheritance, and dost possess it, and dwell therein; 26,2 that thou shalt take of the first of all the fruit of the ground, which thou shalt bring in from thy land that the LORD thy God giveth thee; and thou shalt put it in a basket and shalt go unto the place which the LORD thy God shall choose to cause His name to dwell there. 26,3 And thou shalt come unto the priest that shall be in those days, and say unto him: 'I profess this day unto the LORD thy God, that I am come unto the land which the LORD swore unto our fathers to give us.' 26,4 And the priest shall take the basket out of thy hand, and set it down before the altar of the LORD thy God. 26,5 And thou shalt speak and say before the LORD thy God: 'A wandering Aramean was my father, and he went down into Egypt, and sojourned there, few in number; and he became there a nation, great, mighty, and populous. 26,6 And the Egyptians dealt ill with us, and afflicted us, and laid upon us hard bondage. 26,7 And we cried unto the LORD, the God of our fathers, and the LORD heard our voice, and saw our affliction, and our toil, and our oppression. 26,8 And the LORD brought us forth out of Egypt with a mighty hand, and with an outstretched arm, and with great terribleness, and with signs, and with wonders. 26,9 And He hath brought us into this place, and hath given us this land, a land flowing with milk and honey. 26,10 And now, behold, I have brought the first of the fruit of the land, which Thou, O LORD, hast given me.' And thou shalt set it down before the LORD thy God, and

worship before the LORD thy God. 26,11 And thou shalt
rejoice in all the good which the LORD thy God hath given
unto thee, and unto thy house, thou, and the Levite, and
the stranger that is in the midst of thee. {S} 26,12 When
thou hast made an end of tithing all the tithe of thine
increase in the third year, which is the year of tithing,
and hast given it unto the Levite, to the stranger, to the
fatherless, and to the widow, that they may eat within
thy gates, and be satisfied, 26,13 then thou shalt say
before the LORD thy God: 'I have put away the hallowed
things out of my house, and also have given them unto
the Levite, and unto the stranger, to the fatherless, and
to the widow, according to all Thy commandment which
Thou hast commanded me; I have not transgressed any of
Thy commandments, neither have I forgotten them. 26,14
I have not eaten thereof in my mourning, neither have I
put away thereof, being unclean, nor given thereof for the
dead; I have hearkened to the voice of the LORD my God,
I have done according to all that Thou hast commanded
me. 26,15 Look forth from Thy holy habitation, from
heaven, and bless Thy people Israel, and the land which
Thou hast given us, as Thou didst swear unto our fathers,
a land flowing with milk and honey.' {S} 26,16 This day
the LORD thy God commandeth thee to do these statutes
and ordinances; thou shalt therefore observe and do them
with all thy heart, and with all thy soul. 26,17 Thou hast
avouched the LORD this day to be thy God, and that thou
wouldest walk in His ways, and keep His statutes, and His
commandments, and His ordinances, and hearken unto
His voice. 26,18 And the LORD hath avouched thee this
day to be His own treasure, as He hath promised thee, and

that thou shouldest keep all His commandments; 26,19 and to make thee high above all nations that He hath made, in praise, and in name, and in glory; and that thou mayest be a holy people unto the LORD thy God, as He hath spoken. {P}

27,1 And Moses and the elders of Israel commanded the people, saying: 'Keep all the commandment which I command you this day. 27,2 And it shall be on the day when ye shall pass over the Jordan unto the land which the LORD thy God giveth thee, that thou shalt set thee up great stones, and plaster them with plaster. 27,3 And thou shalt write upon them all the words of this law, when thou art passed over; that thou mayest go in unto the land which the LORD thy God giveth thee, a land flowing with milk and honey, as the LORD, the God of thy fathers, hath promised thee. 27,4 And it shall be when ye are passed over the Jordan, that ye shall set up these stones, which I command you this day, in mount Ebal, and thou shalt plaster them with plaster. 27,5 And there shalt thou build an altar unto the LORD thy God, an altar of stones; thou shalt lift up no iron tool upon them. 27,6 Thou shalt build the altar of the LORD thy God of unhewn stones; and thou shalt offer burnt-offerings thereon unto the LORD thy God. 27,7 And thou shalt sacrifice peace-offerings, and shalt eat there; and thou shalt rejoice before the LORD thy God. 27,8 And thou shalt write upon the stones all the words of this law very plainly.' {S} 27,9 And Moses and the priests the Levites spoke unto all Israel, saying: 'Keep silence, and hear, O Israel; this day thou art become a people unto the LORD thy God. 27,10 Thou shalt therefore hearken to the voice of the LORD thy God, and do His commandments and His statutes, which I command thee this day.' {S} 27,11 And Moses charged the people the same day, saying: 27,12 'These shall stand upon mount Gerizim to bless the people, when ye are passed over the Jordan: Simeon, and Levi, and Judah, and Issachar, and Joseph, and Benjamin; 27,13 and these shall stand upon mount Ebal for the curse: Reuben, Gad, and Asher, and Zebulun, Dan, and Naphtali. 27,14 And the Levites shall speak, and say unto all the men of Israel with a loud voice: {S} 27,15 Cursed be the man that maketh a graven or molten image, an abomination unto the LORD, the work of the hands of the craftsman, and setteth it up in secret. And all the people shall answer and say: Amen. {S} 27,16 Cursed be he that dishonoureth his father or his mother. And all the people shall say: Amen. {S} 27,17 Cursed be he that removeth his neighbour's landmark. And all the people shall say: Amen. {S} 27,18 Cursed be he that maketh the blind to go astray in the way. And all the people shall say: Amen. {S} 27,19 Cursed be he that perverteth the justice due to the stranger, fatherless, and widow. And all the people shall say: Amen. 27,20 Cursed be he that lieth with his father's wife; because he hath uncovered his father's skirt. And all the people shall say: Amen. {S} 27,21 Cursed be he that lieth with any manner of beast. And all the people shall say: Amen. {S} 27,22 Cursed be he that lieth with his sister, the daughter of his father, or the daughter of his mother. And all the people shall say: Amen. {S} 27,23 Cursed be he that lieth with his mother-in-law. And all the people shall say: Amen. {S} 27,24 Cursed be he that smiteth his neighbour in secret.

And all the people shall say: Amen. {S} 27,25 Cursed be
he that taketh a bribe to slay an innocent person. And all
the people shall say: Amen. {S} 27,26 Cursed be he that
confirmeth not the words of this law to do them. And all
the people shall say: Amen.' {P}

28,1 And it shall come to pass, if thou shalt hearken
diligently unto the voice of the LORD thy God, to observe
to do all His commandments which I command thee this
day, that the LORD thy God will set thee on high above all
the nations of the earth. 28,2 And all these blessings shall
come upon thee, and overtake thee, if thou shalt hearken
unto the voice of the LORD thy God. 28,3 Blessed shalt
thou be in the city, and blessed shalt thou be in the field.
28,4 Blessed shall be the fruit of thy body, and the fruit
of thy land, and the fruit of thy cattle, the increase of thy
kine, and the young of thy flock. 28,5 Blessed shall be thy
basket and thy kneading-trough. 28,6 Blessed shalt thou
be when thou comest in, and blessed shalt thou be when
thou goest out. 28,7 The LORD will cause thine enemies
that rise up against thee to be smitten before thee; they
shall come out against thee one way, and shall flee before
thee seven ways. 28,8 The LORD will command the
blessing with thee in thy barns, and in all that thou puttest
thy hand unto; and He will bless thee in the land which the
LORD thy God giveth thee. 28,9 The LORD will establish
thee for a holy people unto Himself, as He hath sworn unto
thee; if thou shalt keep the commandments of the LORD
thy God, and walk in His ways. 28,10 And all the peoples
of the earth shall see that the name of the LORD is called
upon thee; and they shall be afraid of thee. 28,11 And the

LORD will make thee over-abundant for good, in the fruit of thy body, and in the fruit of thy cattle, and in the fruit of thy land, in the land which the LORD swore unto thy fathers to give thee. 28,12 The LORD will open unto thee His good treasure the heaven to give the rain of thy land in its season, and to bless all the work of thy hand; and thou shalt lend unto many nations, but thou shalt not borrow. 28,13 And the LORD will make thee the head, and not the tail; and thou shalt be above only, and thou shalt not be beneath; if thou shalt hearken unto the commandments of the LORD thy God, which I command thee this day, to observe and to do them; 28,14 and shalt not turn aside from any of the words which I command you this day, to the right hand, or to the left, to go after other gods to serve them. {P}

28,15 But it shall come to pass, if thou wilt not hearken unto the voice of the LORD thy God, to observe to do all His commandments and His statutes which I command thee this day; that all these curses shall come upon thee, and overtake thee. 28,16 Cursed shalt thou be in the city, and cursed shalt thou be in the field. 28,17 Cursed shall be thy basket and thy kneading-trough. 28,18 Cursed shall be the fruit of thy body, and the fruit of thy land, the increase of thy kine, and the young of thy flock. 28,19 Cursed shalt thou be when thou comest in, and cursed shalt thou be when thou goest out. 28,20 The LORD will send upon thee cursing, discomfiture, and rebuke, in all that thou puttest thy hand unto to do, until thou be destroyed, and until thou perish quickly; because of the evil of thy doings, whereby thou hast forsaken Me. 28,21

The LORD will make the pestilence cleave unto thee, until He have consumed thee from off the land, whither thou goest in to possess it. 28,22 The LORD will smite thee with consumption, and with fever, and with inflammation, and with fiery heat, and with drought, and with blasting, and with mildew; and they shall pursue thee until thou perish. 28,23 And thy heaven that is over thy head shall be brass, and the earth that is under thee shall be iron. 28,24 The LORD will make the rain of thy land powder and dust; from heaven shall it come down upon thee, until thou be destroyed. 28,25 The LORD will cause thee to be smitten before thine enemies; thou shalt go out one way against them, and shalt flee seven ways before them; and thou shalt be a horror unto all the kingdoms of the earth. 28,26 And thy carcasses shall be food unto all fowls of the air, and unto the beasts of the earth, and there shall be none to frighten them away. 28,27 The LORD will smite thee with the boil of Egypt, and with the emerods, and with the scab, and with the itch, whereof thou canst not be healed. 28,28 The LORD will smite thee with madness, and with blindness, and with astonishment of heart. 28,29 And thou shalt grope at noonday, as the blind gropeth in darkness, and thou shalt not make thy ways prosperous; and thou shalt be only oppressed and robbed alway, and there shall be none to save thee. 28,30 Thou shalt betroth a wife, and another man shall lie with her; thou shalt build a house, and thou shalt not dwell therein; thou shalt plant a vineyard, and shalt not use the fruit thereof. 28,31 Thine ox shall be slain before thine eyes, and thou shalt not eat thereof; thine ass shall be violently taken away from before thy face, and shall not be restored to thee; thy sheep shall

be given unto thine enemies; and thou shalt have none to
save thee. 28,32 Thy sons and thy daughters shall be
given unto another people, and thine eyes shall look, and
fail with longing for them all the day; and there shall be
nought in the power of thy hand. 28,33 The fruit of thy
land, and all thy labours, shall a nation which thou knowest
not eat up; and thou shalt be only oppressed and crushed
away: 28,34 so that thou shalt be mad for the sight of
thine eyes which thou shalt see. 28,35 The LORD will
smite thee in the knees, and in the legs, with a sore boil,
whereof thou canst not be healed, from the sole of thy foot
unto the crown of thy head. 28,36 The LORD will bring
thee, and thy king whom thou shalt set over thee, unto a
nation that thou hast not known, thou nor thy fathers; and
there shalt thou serve other gods, wood and stone. 28,37
And thou shalt become an astonishment, a proverb, and a
byword, among all the peoples whither the LORD shall
lead thee away. 28,38 Thou shalt carry much seed out into
the field, and shalt gather little in; for the locust shall
consume it. 28,39 Thou shalt plant vineyards and dress
them, but thou shalt neither drink of the wine, nor gather
the grapes; for the worm shall eat them. 28,40 Thou shalt
have olive-trees throughout all thy borders, but thou shalt
not anoint thyself with the oil; for thine olives shall drop
off. 28,41 Thou shalt beget sons and daughters, but they
shall not be thine; for they shall go into captivity. 28,42
All thy trees and the fruit of thy land shall the locust
possess. 28,43 The stranger that is in the midst of thee
shall mount up above thee higher and higher; and thou
shalt come down lower and lower. 28,44 He shall lend to
thee, and thou shalt not lend to him; he shall be the head,

and thou shalt be the tail. 28,45 And all these curses shall come upon thee, and shall pursue thee, and overtake thee, till thou be destroyed; because thou didst not hearken unto the voice of the LORD thy God, to keep His commandments and His statutes which He commanded thee. 28,46 And they shall be upon thee for a sign and for a wonder, and upon thy seed for ever; 28,47 because thou didst not serve the LORD thy God with joyfulness, and with gladness of heart, by reason of the abundance of all things; 28,48 therefore shalt thou serve thine enemy whom the LORD shall send against thee, in hunger, and in thirst, and in nakedness, and in want of all things; and he shall put a yoke of iron upon thy neck, until he have destroyed thee. 28,49 The LORD will bring a nation against thee from far, from the end of the earth, as the vulture swoopeth down; a nation whose tongue thou shalt not understand; 28,50 a nation of fierce countenance, that shall not regard the person of the old, nor show favour to the young. 28,51 And he shall eat the fruit of thy cattle, and the fruit of thy ground, until thou be destroyed; that also shall not leave thee corn, wine, or oil, the increase of thy kine, or the young of thy flock, until he have caused thee to perish. 28,52 And he shall besiege thee in all thy gates, until thy high and fortified walls come down, wherein thou didst trust, throughout all thy land; and he shall besiege thee in all thy gates throughout all thy land, which the LORD thy God hath given thee. 28,53 And thou shalt eat the fruit of thine own body, the flesh of thy sons and of thy daughters whom the LORD thy God hath given thee; in the siege and in the straitness, wherewith thine enemies shall straiten thee. 28,54 The man that is tender among you, and very delicate, his eye shall be evil against his brother, and against the wife of his bosom, and against the remnant of his children whom he hath remaining; 28,55 so that he will not give to any of them of the flesh of his children whom he shall eat, because he hath nothing left him; in the siege and in the straitness, wherewith thine enemy shall straiten thee in all thy gates. 28,56 The tender and delicate woman among you, who would not adventure to set the sole of her foot upon the ground for delicateness and tenderness, her eye shall be evil against the husband of her bosom, and against her son, and against her daughter; 28,57 and against her afterbirth that cometh out from between her feet, and against her children whom she shall bear; for she shall eat them for want of all things secretly; in the siege and in the straitness, wherewith thine enemy shall straiten thee in thy gates. 28,58 If thou wilt not observe to do all the words of this law that are written in this book, that thou mayest fear this glorious and awful Name, the LORD thy God; 28,59 then the LORD will make thy plagues wonderful, and the plagues of thy seed, even great plagues, and of long continuance, and sore sicknesses, and of long continuance. 28,60 And He will bring back upon thee all the diseases of Egypt, which thou wast in dread of; and they shall cleave unto thee. 28,61 Also every sickness, and every plague, which is not written in the book of this law, them will the LORD bring upon thee, until thou be destroyed. 28,62 And ye shall be left few in number, whereas ye were as the stars of heaven for multitude; because thou didst not hearken unto the voice of the LORD thy God. 28,63 And it shall come to pass, that as the LORD rejoiced over you to do you good, and to multiply you; so the LORD will rejoice over you to cause you to perish, and to destroy you; and ye shall be plucked from off the land whither thou goest in to possess it. 28,64 And the LORD shall scatter thee among all peoples, from the one end of the earth even unto the other end of the earth; and there thou shalt serve other gods, which thou hast not known, thou nor thy fathers, even wood and stone. 28,65 And among these nations shalt thou have no repose, and there shall be no rest for the sole of thy foot; but the LORD shall give thee there a trembling heart, and failing of eyes, and languishing of soul. 28,66 And thy life shall hang in doubt before thee; and thou shalt fear night and day, and shalt have no assurance of thy life. 28,67 In the morning thou shalt say: 'Would it were even!' and at even thou shalt say: 'Would it were morning!' for the fear of thy heart which thou shalt fear, and for the sight of thine eyes which thou shalt see. 28,68 And the LORD shall bring thee back into Egypt in ships, by the way whereof I said unto thee: 'Thou shalt see it no more again'; and there ye shall sell yourselves unto your enemies for bondmen and for bondwoman, and no man shall buy you. {S} 28,69 These are the words of the covenant which the LORD commanded Moses to make with the children of Israel in the land of Moab, beside the covenant which He made with them in Horeb. {P}

29,1 And Moses called unto all Israel, and said unto them: Ye have seen all that the LORD did before your eyes in the land of Egypt unto Pharaoh, and unto all his servants, and unto all his land; 29,2 the great trials which thine eyes saw, the signs and those great wonders; 29,3 but the

LORD hath not given you a heart to know, and eyes to see,
and ears to hear, unto this day. 29,4 And I have led you
forty years in the wilderness; your clothes are not waxen
old upon you, and thy shoe is not waxen old upon thy foot.
29,5 Ye have not eaten bread, neither have ye drunk wine
or strong drink; that ye might know that I am the LORD
your God. 29,6 And when ye came unto this place, Sihon
the king of Heshbon, and Og the king of Bashan, came
out against us unto battle, and we smote them. 29,7 And
we took their land, and gave it for an inheritance unto the
Reubenites, and to the Gadites, and to the half-tribe of
the Manassites. 29,8 Observe therefore the words of this
covenant, and do them, that ye may make all that ye do to
prosper. {P}

Portion of Nitzavim

29,9 Ye are standing this day all of you before the LORD your God: your heads, your tribes, your elders, and your officers, even all the men of Israel, 29,10 your little ones, your wives, and thy stranger that is in the midst of thy camp, from the hewer of thy wood unto the drawer of thy water; 29,11 that thou shouldest enter into the covenant of the LORD thy God--and into His oath--which the LORD thy God maketh with thee this day; 29,12 that He may establish thee this day unto Himself for a people, and that He may be unto thee a God, as He spoke unto thee, and as He swore unto thy fathers, to Abraham, to Isaac, and to Jacob. 29,13 Neither with you only do I make this covenant and this oath; 29,14 but with him that standeth here with us this day before the LORD our God, and also with him that is not here with us this day-- 29,15 for ye know how we dwelt in the land of Egypt; and how we came through the midst of the nations through which ye passed; 29,16 and ye have seen their detestable things, and their idols, wood and stone, silver and gold, which were with them-- 29,17 lest there should be among you man, or woman, or family, or tribe, whose heart turneth away this day from the LORD our God, to go to serve the gods of those nations; lest there should be among you a root that beareth gall and wormwood; 29,18 and it come to pass, when he heareth the words of this curse, that he bless himself in his heart, saying: 'I shall have peace, though I walk in the stubbornness of my heart--that the watered be swept away with the dry'; 29,19 the LORD will not be willing to pardon him, but then the anger of the LORD and His jealousy shall be kindled against that man, and all the curse that is written in this book shall lie upon him, and the LORD shall blot out his name from under heaven; 29,20 and the LORD shall separate him unto evil out of all the tribes of Israel, according to all the curses of the covenant that is written in this book of the law. 29,21 And the generation to come, your children that shall rise up after you, and the foreigner that shall come from a far land, shall say, when they see the plagues of that land, and the sicknesses wherewith the LORD hath made it sick; 29,22 and that the whole land thereof is brimstone, and salt, and a burning, that it is not sown, nor beareth, nor any grass groweth therein, like the overthrow of Sodom and Gomorrah, Admah and Zeboiim, which the LORD overthrew in His anger, and in His wrath; 29,23 even all the nations shall say 'Wherefore hath the LORD done thus unto this land? what meaneth the heat of this great anger?' 29,24 then men shall say: 'Because they forsook the covenant of the LORD, the God of their fathers, which He made with them when He brought them forth out of the land of Egypt; 29,25 and went and served other gods, and worshipped them, gods that they knew not, and that He had not allotted unto them; 29,26 therefore the anger of the LORD was kindled against this land, to bring upon it all the curse that is written in this book; 29,27 and the LORD rooted them out of their land in anger, and in wrath, and in great indignation, and cast them into another land, as it is this day'.-- 29,28 The secret things belong unto the LORD our God; but the things that are revealed belong unto us and to our children for ever, that we may do all the words of this law. {S} 30,1 And it shall come to pass, when all these things are come upon thee, the blessing and the

curse, which I have set before thee, and thou shalt bethink
thyself among all the nations, whither the LORD thy God
hath driven thee, 30,2 and shalt return unto the LORD
thy God, and hearken to His voice according to all that
I command thee this day, thou and thy children, with all
thy heart, and with all thy soul; 30,3 that then the LORD
thy God will turn thy captivity, and have compassion upon
thee, and will return and gather thee from all the peoples,
whither the LORD thy God hath scattered thee. 30,4 If
any of thine that are dispersed be in the uttermost parts of
heaven, from thence will the LORD thy God gather thee,
and from thence will He fetch thee. 30,5 And the LORD
thy God will bring thee into the land which thy fathers
possessed, and thou shalt possess it; and He will do thee
good, and multiply thee above thy fathers. 30,6 And the
LORD thy God will circumcise thy heart, and the heart of
thy seed, to love the LORD thy God with all thy heart, and
with all thy soul, that thou mayest live. 30,7 And the LORD
thy God will put all these curses upon thine enemies, and
on them that hate thee, that persecuted thee. 30,8 And
thou shalt return and hearken to the voice of the LORD,
and do all His commandments which I command thee this
day. 30,9 And the LORD thy God will make thee over-
abundant in all the work of thy hand, in the fruit of thy
body, and in the fruit of thy cattle, and in the fruit of thy
land, for good; for the LORD will again rejoice over thee
for good, as He rejoiced over thy fathers; 30,10 if thou
shalt hearken to the voice of the LORD thy God, to keep
His commandments and His statutes which are written in
this book of the law; if thou turn unto the LORD thy God
with all thy heart, and with all thy soul. {S} 30,11 For this

commandment which I command thee this day, it is not
too hard for thee, neither is it far off. 30,12 It is not in
heaven, that thou shouldest say: 'Who shall go up for us to
heaven, and bring it unto us, and make us to hear it, that
we may do it?' 30,13 Neither is it beyond the sea, that
thou shouldest say: 'Who shall go over the sea for us, and
bring it unto us, and make us to hear it, that we may do it?'
30,14 But the word is very nigh unto thee, in thy mouth,
and in thy heart, that thou mayest do it. {S} 30,15 See,
I have set before thee this day life and good, and death
and evil, 30,16 in that I command thee this day to love
the LORD thy God, to walk in His ways, and to keep His
commandments and His statutes and His ordinances; then
thou shalt live and multiply, and the LORD thy God shall
bless thee in the land whither thou goest in to possess it.
30,17 But if thy heart turn away, and thou wilt not hear,
but shalt be drawn away, and worship other gods, and
serve them; 30,18 I declare unto you this day, that ye shall
surely perish; ye shall not prolong your days upon the land,
whither thou passest over the Jordan to go in to possess it.
30,19 I call heaven and earth to witness against you this
day, that I have set before thee life and death, the blessing
and the curse; therefore choose life, that thou mayest live,
thou and thy seed; 30,20 to love the LORD thy God, to
hearken to His voice, and to cleave unto Him; for that is
thy life, and the length of thy days; that thou mayest dwell
in the land which the LORD swore unto thy fathers, to
Abraham, to Isaac, and to Jacob, to give them. {P}

Portion of Vayakhel

31,1 And Moses went and spoke these words unto all
Israel. 31,2 And he said unto them: 'I am a hundred and
twenty years old this day; I can no more go out and come
in; and the LORD hath said unto me: Thou shalt not go
over this Jordan. 31,3 The LORD thy God, He will go over
before thee; He will destroy these nations from before
thee, and thou shalt dispossess them; and Joshua, he
shall go over before thee, as the LORD hath spoken. 31,4
And the LORD will do unto them as He did to Sihon and to
Og, the kings of the Amorites, and unto their land; whom
He destroyed. 31,5 And the LORD will deliver them up
before you, and ye shall do unto them according unto all
the commandment which I have commanded you. 31,6
Be strong and of good courage, fear not, nor be affrighted
at them; for the LORD thy God, He it is that doth go with
thee; He will not fail thee, nor forsake thee.' {S} 31,7 And
Moses called unto Joshua, and said unto him in the sight
of all Israel: 'Be strong and of good courage; for thou shalt
go with this people into the land which the LORD hath
sworn unto their fathers to give them; and thou shalt cause
them to inherit it. 31,8 And the LORD, He it is that doth
go before thee; He will be with thee, He will not fail thee,
neither forsake thee; fear not, neither be dismayed.' 31,9
And Moses wrote this law, and delivered it unto the priests
the sons of Levi, that bore the ark of the covenant of the
LORD, and unto all the elders of Israel. 31,10 And Moses
commanded them, saying: 'At the end of every seven
years, in the set time of the year of release, in the feast
of tabernacles, 31,11 when all Israel is come to appear

before the LORD thy God in the place which He shall choose, thou shalt read this law before all Israel in their hearing. 31,12 Assemble the people, the men and the women and the little ones, and thy stranger that is within thy gates, that they may hear, and that they may learn, and fear the LORD your God, and observe to do all the words of this law; 31,13 and that their children, who have not known, may hear, and learn to fear the LORD your God, as long as ye live in the land whither ye go over the Jordan to possess it.' {P}

31,14 And the LORD said unto Moses: 'Behold, thy days approach that thou must die; call Joshua, and present yourselves in the tent of meeting, that I may give him a charge.' And Moses and Joshua went, and presented themselves in the tent of meeting. 31,15 And the LORD appeared in the Tent in a pillar of cloud; and the pillar of cloud stood over the door of the Tent. 31,16 And the LORD said unto Moses: 'Behold, thou art about to sleep with thy fathers; and this people will rise up, and go astray after the foreign gods of the land, whither they go to be among them, and will forsake Me, and break My covenant which I have made with them. 31,17 Then My anger shall be kindled against them in that day, and I will forsake them, and I will hide My face from them, and they shall be devoured, and many evils and troubles shall come upon them; so that they will say in that day: Are not these evils come upon us because our God is not among us? 31,18 And I will surely hide My face in that day for all the evil which they shall have wrought, in that they are turned unto other gods. 31,19 Now therefore write ye this song for

you, and teach thou it the children of Israel; put it in their
mouths, that this song may be a witness for Me against
the children of Israel. 31,20 For when I shall have brought
them into the land which I swore unto their fathers, flowing
with milk and honey; and they shall have eaten their fill,
and waxen fat; and turned unto other gods, and served
them, and despised Me, and broken My covenant; 31,21
then it shall come to pass, when many evils and troubles
are come upon them, that this song shall testify before
them as a witness; for it shall not be forgotten out of the
mouths of their seed; for I know their imagination how
they do even now, before I have brought them into the land
which I swore.' 31,22 So Moses wrote this song the same
day, and taught it the children of Israel. 31,23 And he
gave Joshua the son of Nun a charge, and said: 'Be strong
and of good courage; for thou shalt bring the children of
Israel into the land which I swore unto them; and I will be
with thee.' 31,24 And it came to pass, when Moses had
made an end of writing the words of this law in a book,
until they were finished, 31,25 that Moses commanded
the Levites, that bore the ark of the covenant of the LORD,
saying: 31,26 'Take this book of the law, and put it by
the side of the ark of the covenant of the LORD your God,
that it may be there for a witness against thee. 31,27 For I
know thy rebellion, and thy stiff neck; behold, while I am
yet alive with you this day, ye have been rebellious against
the LORD; and how much more after my death? 31,28
Assemble unto me all the elders of your tribes, and your
officers, that I may speak these words in their ears, and
call heaven and earth to witness against them. 31,29 For I
know that after my death ye will in any wise deal corruptly,

and turn aside from the way which I have commanded you; and evil will befall you in the end of days; because ye will do that which is evil in the sight of the LORD, to provoke Him through the work of your hands.' 31,30 And Moses spoke in the ears of all the assembly of Israel the words of this song, until they were finished: {P}

Portion of Ha'azinu

32,1 Give ear, ye heavens, and I will speak; and let the earth hear the words of my mouth. 32,2 My doctrine shall drop as the rain, my speech shall distil as the dew; as the small rain upon the tender grass, and as the showers upon the herb. 32,3 For I will proclaim the name of the LORD; ascribe ye greatness unto our God. 32,4 The Rock, His work is perfect; for all His ways are justice; a God of faithfulness and without iniquity, just and right is He. 32,5 Is corruption His? No; His children's is the blemish; a generation crooked and perverse. 32,6 Do ye thus requite the LORD, O foolish people and unwise? is not He thy father that hath gotten thee? hath He not made thee, and established thee? 32,7 Remember the days of old, consider the years of many generations; ask thy father, and he will declare unto thee, thine elders, and they will tell thee. 32,8 When the Most High gave to the nations their inheritance, when He separated the children of men, He set the borders of the peoples according to the number of the children of Israel. 32,9 For the portion of the LORD is His people, Jacob the lot of His inheritance. 32,10 He found him in a desert land, and in the waste, a howling

wilderness; He compassed him about, He cared for him, He
kept him as the apple of His eye. 32,11 As an eagle that
stirreth up her nest, hovereth over her young, spreadeth
abroad her wings, taketh them, beareth them on her
pinions-- 32,12 The LORD alone did lead him, and there
was no strange god with Him. 32,13 He made him ride on
the high places of the earth, and he did eat the fruitage
of the field; and He made him to suck honey out of the
crag, and oil out of the flinty rock; 32,14 Curd of kine, and
milk of sheep, with fat of lambs, and rams of the breed of
Bashan, and he-goats, with the kidney-fat of wheat; and
of the blood of the grape thou drankest foaming wine.
32,15 But Jeshurun waxed fat, and kicked--thou didst
wax fat, thou didst grow thick, thou didst become gross-
-and he forsook God who made him, and contemned the
Rock of his salvation. 32,16 They roused Him to jealousy
with strange gods, with abominations did they provoke
Him. 32,17 They sacrificed unto demons, no-gods, gods
that they knew not, new gods that came up of late, which
your fathers dreaded not. 32,18 Of the Rock that begot
thee thou wast unmindful, and didst forget God that bore
thee. 32,19 And the LORD saw, and spurned, because of
the provoking of His sons and His daughters. 32,20 And
He said: 'I will hide My face from them, I will see what
their end shall be; for they are a very froward generation,
children in whom is no faithfulness. 32,21 They have
roused Me to jealousy with a no-god; they have provoked
Me with their vanities; and I will rouse them to jealousy
with a no-people; I will provoke them with a vile nation.
32,22 For a fire is kindled in My nostril, and burneth unto
the depths of the nether-world, and devoureth the earth

with her produce, and setteth ablaze the foundations of
the mountains. 32,23 I will heap evils upon them; I will
spend Mine arrows upon them; 32,24 The wasting of
hunger, and the devouring of the fiery bolt, and bitter
destruction; and the teeth of beasts will I send upon them,
with the venom of crawling things of the dust. 32,25
Without shall the sword bereave, and in the chambers
terror; slaying both young man and virgin, the suckling
with the man of gray hairs. 32,26 I thought I would make
an end of them, I would make their memory cease from
among men; 32,27 Were it not that I dreaded the enemy's
provocation, lest their adversaries should misdeem, lest
they should say: Our hand is exalted, and not the LORD
hath wrought all this.' 32,28 For they are a nation void of
counsel, and there is no understanding in them. 32,29 If
they were wise, they would understand this, they would
discern their latter end. 32,30 How should one chase a
thousand, and two put ten thousand to flight, except their
Rock had given them over and the LORD had delivered
them up? 32,31 For their rock is not as our Rock, even our
enemies themselves being judges. 32,32 For their vine
is of the vine of Sodom, and of the fields of Gomorrah;
their grapes are grapes of gall, their clusters are bitter;
32,33 Their wine is the venom of serpents, and the cruel
poison of asps. 32,34 'Is not this laid up in store with Me,
sealed up in My treasuries? 32,35 Vengeance is Mine, and
recompense, against the time when their foot shall slip;
for the day of their calamity is at hand, and the things
that are to come upon them shall make haste. 32,36 For
the LORD will judge His people, and repent Himself for
His servants; when He seeth that their stay is gone, and

there is none remaining, shut up or left at large. 32,37
And it is said: Where are their gods, the rock in whom they
trusted; 32,38 Who did eat the fat of their sacrifices, and
drank the wine of their drink-offering? let him rise up and
help you, let him be your protection. 32,39 See now that
I, even I, am He, and there is no god with Me; I kill, and I
make alive; I have wounded, and I heal; and there is none
that can deliver out of My hand. 32,40 For I lift up My
hand to heaven, and say: As I live for ever, 32,41 If I whet
My glittering sword, and My hand take hold on judgment;
I will render vengeance to Mine adversaries, and will
recompense them that hate Me. 32,42 I will make Mine
arrows drunk with blood, and My sword shall devour flesh;
with the blood of the slain and the captives, from the
long-haired heads of the enemy.' 32,43 Sing aloud, O ye
nations, of His people; for He doth avenge the blood of His
servants, and doth render vengeance to His adversaries,
and doth make expiation for the land of His people. {P}

32,44 And Moses came and spoke all the words of this
song in the ears of the people, he, and Hoshea the son of
Nun. 32,45 And when Moses made an end of speaking all
these words to all Israel, 32,46 he said unto them: 'Set
your heart unto all the words wherewith I testify against
you this day; that ye may charge your children therewith to
observe to do all the words of this law. 32,47 For it is no
vain thing for you; because it is your life, and through this
thing ye shall prolong your days upon the land, whither ye
go over the Jordan to possess it.' {P}

32,48 And the LORD spoke unto Moses that selfsame day,

saying: 32,49 'Get thee up into this mountain of Abarim,
unto mount Nebo, which is in the land of Moab, that is
over against Jericho; and behold the land of Canaan,
which I give unto the children of Israel for a possession;
32,50 and die in the mount whither thou goest up, and
be gathered unto thy people; as Aaron thy brother died
in mount Hor, and was gathered unto his people. 32,51
Because ye trespassed against Me in the midst of the
children of Israel at the waters of Meribath-kadesh, in
the wilderness of Zin; because ye sanctified Me not in the
midst of the children of Israel. 32,52 For thou shalt see
the land afar off; but thou shalt not go thither into the land
which I give the children of Israel.' {P}

Portion of Vezot-Habracha

33,1 And this is the blessing wherewith Moses the man of
God blessed the children of Israel before his death. 33,2
And he said: The LORD came from Sinai, and rose from
Seir unto them; He shined forth from mount Paran, and He
came from the myriads holy, at His right hand was a fiery
law unto them. 33,3 Yea, He loveth the peoples, all His
holy ones--they are in Thy hand; and they sit down at Thy
feet, receiving of Thy words. 33,4 Moses commanded us
a law, an inheritance of the congregation of Jacob. 33,5
And there was a king in Jeshurun, when the heads of the
people were gathered, all the tribes of Israel together. 33,6
Let Reuben live, and not die in that his men become few.
{S} 33,7 And this for Judah, and he said: Hear, LORD,
the voice of Judah, and bring him in unto his people; his
hands shall contend for him, and Thou shalt be a help
against his adversaries. {P}

33,8 And of Levi he said: Thy Thummim and Thy Urim be
with Thy holy one, whom Thou didst prove at Massah, with
whom Thou didst strive at the waters of Meribah; 33,9
Who said of his father, and of his mother: 'I have not seen
him'; neither did he acknowledge his brethren, nor knew
he his own children; for they have observed Thy word, and
keep Thy covenant. 33,10 They shall teach Jacob Thine
ordinances, and Israel Thy law; they shall put incense
before Thee, and whole burnt-offering upon Thine altar.
33,11 Bless, LORD, his substance, and accept the work
of his hands; smite through the loins of them that rise up
against him, and of them that hate him, that they rise not

again. {S} 33,12 Of Benjamin he said: The beloved of the LORD shall dwell in safety by Him; He covereth him all the day, and He dwelleth between his shoulders. {S} 33,13 And of Joseph he said: Blessed of the LORD be his land; for the precious things of heaven, for the dew, and for the deep that coucheth beneath, 33,14 And for the precious things of the fruits of the sun, and for the precious things of the yield of the moons, 33,15 And for the tops of the ancient mountains, and for the precious things of the everlasting hills, 33,16 And for the precious things of the earth and the fulness thereof, and the good will of Him that dwelt in the bush; let the blessing come upon the head of Joseph, and upon the crown of the head of him that is prince among his brethren. 33,17 His firstling bullock, majesty is his; and his horns are the horns of the wild-ox; with them he shall gore the peoples all of them, even the ends of the earth; and they are the ten thousands of Ephraim, and they are the thousands of Manasseh. {S} 33,18 And of Zebulun he said: Rejoice, Zebulun, in thy going out, and, Issachar, in thy tents. 33,19 They shall call peoples unto the mountain; there shall they offer sacrifices of righteousness; for they shall suck the abundance of the seas, and the hidden treasures of the sand. {S} 33,20 And of Gad he said: Blessed be He that enlargeth Gad; he dwelleth as a lioness, and teareth the arm, yea, the crown of the head. 33,21 And he chose a first part for himself, for there a portion of a ruler was reserved; and there came the heads of the people, he executed the righteousness of the LORD, and His ordinances with Israel. {S} 33,22 And of Dan he said: Dan is a lion's whelp, that leapeth forth from Bashan. 33,23 And of Naphtali he said: O Naphtali, satisfied with favour, and full with the blessing of the LORD: possess thou the sea and the south. {S} 33,24 And of Asher he said: Blessed be Asher above sons; let him be the favoured of his brethren, and let him dip his foot in oil. 33,25 Iron and brass shall be thy bars; and as thy days, so shall thy strength be. 33,26 There is none like unto God, O Jeshurun, who rideth upon the heaven as thy help, and in His excellency on the skies. 33,27 The eternal God is a dwelling-place, and underneath are the everlasting arms; and He thrust out the enemy from before thee, and said: 'Destroy.' 33,28 And Israel dwelleth in safety, the fountain of Jacob alone, in a land of corn and wine; yea, his heavens drop down dew. 33,29 Happy art thou, O Israel, who is like unto thee? a people saved by the LORD, the shield of thy help, and that is the sword of thy excellency! And thine enemies shall dwindle away before thee; and thou shalt tread upon their high places. {S} 34,1 And Moses went up from the plains of Moab unto mount Nebo, to the top of Pisgah, that is over against Jericho. And the LORD showed him all the land, even Gilead as far as Dan; 34,2 and all Naphtali, and the land of Ephraim and Manasseh, and all the land of Judah as far as the hinder sea; 34,3 and the South, and the Plain, even the valley of Jericho the city of palm-trees, as far as Zoar. 34,4 And the LORD said unto him: 'This is the land which I swore unto Abraham, unto Isaac, and unto Jacob, saying: I will give it unto thy seed; I have caused thee to see it with thine eyes, but thou shalt not go over thither.' 34,5 So Moses the servant of the LORD died there in the land of Moab, according to the word of the LORD. 34,6 And he was buried in the valley in the land of Moab over against Beth-peor; and no man

knoweth of his sepulchre unto this day. 34,7 And Moses
was a hundred and twenty years old when he died: his eye
was not dim, nor his natural force abated. 34,8 And the
children of Israel wept for Moses in the plains of Moab
thirty days; so the days of weeping in the mourning for
Moses were ended. 34,9 And Joshua the son of Nun was
full of the spirit of wisdom; for Moses had laid his hands
upon him; and the children of Israel hearkened unto him,
and did as the LORD commanded Moses. 34,10 And there
hath not arisen a prophet since in Israel like unto Moses,
whom the LORD knew face to face; 34,11 in all the signs
and the wonders, which the LORD sent him to do in the
land of Egypt, to Pharaoh, and to all his servants, and to
all his land; 34,12 and in all the mighty hand, and in all
the great terror, which Moses wrought in the sight of all
Israel. {P}